THE MILITANT GOSPEL

ORBIS BOOKS
Maryknoll, New York 10545

THE MILITANT GOSPEL

A Critical Introduction to Political Theologies

ALFREDO FIERRO

TRANSLATED BY JOHN DRURY

Printed in the United States of America

Library of Congress Cataloging in Publication Data

Fierro Bardaji, Alfredo, 1936–
The militant gospel.

Translation of El evangelio beligerante.
Bibliography: p.
Includes index.
1. Christianity and politics. 2. Theology—20th century. 3. Communism and Christianity. I. Title.
BR115.P7F4713 261.7 77-1652
ISBN 0-88344-310-4
ISBN 0-88344-311-2 pbk.

CONTENTS

PROLOGUE ix
PREFACE TO THE ENGLISH EDITION xiii

PART ONE: SITUATION

1. FROM ANTHROPOCENTRISM TO POLITICS 3

1. Man as protagonist 3
2. Existential theology 7
3. A change in view 12
4. The political theologies 17
5. A theology concerned with praxis 19
6. A theology that is public and critical 23
7. Politics in a mediating role 28
8. Comment on terminology 33
9. Favorable and unfavorable reactions 36
10. The question of existence pursued 41

2. THE REJECTION OF CHRISTENDOM 48

1. Constantinianism and Christian institutions 48
2. The idea-set of the New Christendom movement 53
3. A theological ethics for politics 57
4. The medieval world as model 60
5. A theology of corporatism 62
6. The Jesus era 65
7. The fading of the New Christendom ideal 67
8. Further contrasts between old and new political theology 70

3. THE ERA OF DIALECTICAL THINKING 76

1. Cultural milieu and theology 76
2. The humus of Marxism 78
3. Contemporary history and the human sciences 80
4. The disappearance of man 83
5. The role of praxis in the process of knowing 88

6. The critical and subversive nature of knowledge 91
7. Dialectical totalities and the unity of science 94
8. The West and dialectical reasoning 98
9. Contemporary isomorphisms 102
10. References to Marxism in theology 110
11. Marxism accepted with restrictions 114
12. Marxism fully accepted 118
13. Grounding in the cultural situation 120

PART TWO: PROGRAM

4. LOOKING AT THE PAST: LIBERATIVE MEMORIES 129

1. Outlines of a program 129
2. Model events, sects, and prophetism 133
3. Exodus theology 140
4. Interpretation and happening 145
5. From an apolitical Jesus to a critical Jesus 152
6. The confrontation with power 158
7. A Zealot messianism? 160
8. History and evocation 165
9. Christological poetics 171
10. The question of grounding 175
11. Critical memory and dogma 178

5. LOOKING AT THE PRESENT: POLITICAL PRAXIS AND THEOLOGICAL REPRESENTATIONS 182

1. The present and praxis 182
2. The political realm and its alteration 185
3. Liberation 189
4. Revolution and protest 193
5. Violence 201
6. Transitory theologies 207
7. A religion of the oppressed 212
8. Christians and the building of socialism 216
9. The hermeneutic-political regrounding of Christian tradition 222
10. Salvation or liberation 224
11. Brotherhood and communion 227
12. Political charity 229
13. Conversion 233

14. Theological ideas 236
15. Theology and ideology 242
16. A specifically Christian element? 247
17. Rational analysis and Christian symbols 252

6. LOOKING TO THE FUTURE: UTOPIA AND THE ADVENT OF GOD 257

1. Eschatology and theology of the future 257
2. God as future 261
3. The current passion for eschatology 265
4. Christianity and utopian socialism 271
5. Utopia as the rationally possible 274
6. Christian hope and utopia 276
7. Eschatological criticism of utopia 278
8. Theoretical criticism of eschatology 282
9. The future and transcendence 288
10. The other face of reality 291
11. The resurrection of the dead 295
12. The dilemma of hope 298

PART THREE: THEORY

7. THEOLOGICAL SPECIFICATIONS 305

1. Pending alternatives 305
2. Ethics and theology 309
3. Theological language and theological discourse 315
4. Critique of the theology of revolution 318
5. Critique of liberation theology 323
6. From dogmatic methodology to fundamental validation 329
7. Restoration of the sacred? 339
8. The secular accepted 348
9. Theology as negative, critical, and symbolic 351
10. The requisites of political theology 360

8. THEOLOGY AND THE HYPOTHESIS OF HISTORICAL MATERIALISM 363

1. Hypotheses preliminary to theology 363
2. A historical-materialist theology 367
3. Faith after Marx 372
4. Socioeconomic correlates of belief 378

5. Different Gods 383
6. The parable of the kingdom and the silence of theology 388
7. De-alienating faith 392
8. Validation by praxis 395
9. Belief that sanctions the status quo versus belief that liberates people 401
10. Words and social change 403
11. The dialectics of structures 406
12. The presence of faith and the absence of God 410
13. Validation by the future 413
14. Emancipated humanity 414
15. Now and the end of history 420

BIBLIOGRAPHY 427

AUTHOR INDEX 455

PROLOGUE

The genesis and development of a particular investigation do have something to do with the final results that appear in book form. The gestation period contains incidents that would be of no interest to the reader, but it also contains deeper influences that do indeed have an impact on the final reading. Pointing out some of these influences may help to situate the book more precisely and assist the reader in understanding its structure.

This project was undertaken at the urging of other people. I was asked to write a book that would reflect the varying and divergent strands of present-day political theology. I have tried to carry out that task with impartiality and, insofar as I could, without gross oversights. Since one of the major aims was to present a summary and panorama of contemporary political interpretations of the gospel, I felt I should let others speak for themselves whenever I could. The numerous direct citations from other authors help to make clear the present state or situation of theology. My task in this connection was to take pre-existing materials and arrange them in accordance with some principle of systematic ordering.

The need to reconcile numerous citations with the expository and informational purpose of the book accounts for the approach used in providing bibliographical references. A complete, numbered bibliography is provided at the end of the book. In place of footnotes in the main text, each direct citation or summary paraphrase is followed by a parenthesis that refers the reader to the pertinent work in question, the proper page number in the editions that I used, and the volume number where that is pertinent. The first numeral in parenthesis refers to the item listed in the bibliography of this book. It is followed by a colon, then the volume number in Roman numerals where that is relevant, and one or more page numbers. If there is reference to more than one bibliographic item, the distinct items are separated by a semicolon. All page numbers refer to the first entry in the bibliography under a given Arabic numeral, though the original language version or other translations may be noted directly afterwards.

To offer a few examples, the first reference in chapter 1 (274:38) refers to page 38 of item 274 in the bibliography (Maldonado, Luis, *El menester de la predicación)*. The reference (315; 67) refers to items 315 and 67 in the bibliography; no pages are noted. A more complicated reference (92:I, 34; 187:235) would refer to Volume I, page 34, of item 92 in the bibliography and page 235 of item 187.

As the product of an assignment given to the author, then, the book is meant to serve as an introduction to the various political theologies of the present day. Its title highlights the fact that the gospel message, as interpreted in such politico-theological terms, takes on a definite air of social militance. This militance must be properly understood, however. The gospel message can never serve as a weapon to be pointed or brandished at others. Its cutting edge is a threat to believers themselves, if it is a threat to anyone; only in and through them does it acquire real social impact. The critical militance of the gospel message works on Christians, and through them it becomes history.

As a personal work of the author, this book shares something of the qualities to be found in two different kinds of theological studies that I have undertaken in the past. On the one hand it follows in the footsteps of other works where I have tried to develop a critical theology of the Christian faith by examining basic concepts and methodology (190; 188). Here I am attempting to develop one of the possibilities of the critical theology that I championed in those works. Thus this introduction to political theologies is not positivist or dogmatic in approach. It is meant to be a *critical* introduction that stands apart from these theologies in order to be able to form some judgment about them. In dealing with the political interpretation of the gospel message, this book presents a critical theory about the nature of theology as such and about the nature of faith as well.

Insofar as content material is concerned, this work is concerned with certain matters that I have already dealt with in some detail in another work (186): love and justice, revolution, power and violence, church and state. My earlier work, which was also concerned with political theology, attempted to explore thematically a few specific points. This present work attempts to provide methodical understanding and exploration in more general terms, and hence it cannot explore specific concrete themes in great depth. The two works are mutually complementary; neither renders the other out-of-date or superfluous.

In Part Three I make certain personal options, adopting a theoretical hypothesis in the concluding chapter. That will undoubtedly alienate some readers who had agreed with the preceding chapters. But the fact that those options would be debated and debatable did not justify leaving them out of the book. Indeed it made it all the more necessary to spell them out here so that they might be discussed further and hence clarified.

It is also possible that I may alienate some readers with my criticism of certain spokesmen of liberation theology in chapter 7. There they may come off in worse terms than my own sympathy for them and their cause would have wished. Perhaps my work would also merit the verdict of radical incomprehension that Hugo Assmann has passed on the theology and the Christians of the affluent world. He has felt it necessary to pass this severe sentence on them all, even on those most sympathetic to the Latin American movements. In his opinion the Christians of Latin America, once they realize that their historical experience is uniquely theirs, will find themselves "all alone on a journey that is theirs alone" (55:151). Here again the risk does not excuse me from making the attempt. I fully realize that I may have an inadequate grasp of a theology that arose in a situation very different from the European one. But I could not simply overlook it or refuse to subject it to critical analysis, and so I have assumed the risks and difficulties involved in forming a judgment from the outside.

To put it as simply and as plainly as possible, this book was written in Spain, not in Peru or some other Latin American country, and hence it could not help but stand aloof from Latin American liberation theology as well as German political theology. Though it has learned much from them, it could not help but stand at a critical distance from them. The same thing works both ways, of course, and so this book will also be relativized from other social contexts. The recently acquired conviction that there is no universal and perennial theology, that theology is framed in contingent terms, obliges us to indicate the place and date of our theological work.

This work, then, was written in Madrid, Spain, and finished in the month of June 1974.

PREFACE TO THE ENGLISH EDITION

In the two years that have passed since the appearance of the original Spanish edition, political theologies have continued to be productive and reproductive. For the most part this theological production has followed pathways already traced out, with perhaps some side explorations into the surrounding terrain. Such, for example, is Boff's theology of captivity, [1] which seems to me to be little more than a variation on the liberation theology presented by Gustavo Gutiérrez.

Other innovations or contributions have been more important and critical insofar as the substance of this book of mine is concerned. First and foremost is the fact that in the past two years people have been talking much more forthrightly and explicitly about a Christian Marxism. Both within and outside the movement of Christians favoring socialism, more and more people are professing to be both Christians and Marxists. This confronts them with the task of elaborating a theology in line with what they now profess.

In 1974 the hypothesis of a historico-materialistic theology was proposed timidly by an unprejudiced theologian here and there. By the end of 1976 that hypothesis had taken on flesh and bones and gained much plausibility, so much in fact that in some Christian groups it was no longer regarded as scandalous but as absolutely indispensable. My feeling is, however, that the points which I elaborated earlier in chapter 8 of this book are as valid today as they were then, that they definitely have not been rendered useless or superfluous by later contributions from others.

The most subversive reformulation of this book's basic theme, and of political theologies in general, has been provoked by Fernando Belo and his book, *Lecture matérialiste de l'évangile de Marc.*[2] Here we are no longer dealing with a Marxist theology at all; we are dealing with a non-theology based on both a Marxist critique and a Christian standpoint. Over against "theology" Belo sets a subversive messianic account or narrative such as that of Mark. He then analyzes that account under the grill of historical materialism, without proposing at all to undertake any theological construction. Someone might jump in at this point and say that the same sort of thing has already been done by Ernst Bloch, and even by Engels himself. But the novel and provocative feature here is that whereas the latter two figures did their critical analysis from the outside, Belo does it from the inside. His analysis is an essay in self-criticism. He is trying to come to grips with his own tradition, a tradition that he does not renounce.

We are now seeing a convergence between the theology based on historical materialism which I proposed in chapter 8 of this book and the growing trend toward critical theology that has been deeply inspired by the heterodox Marxism of the Frankfurt School of social research. This latter trend seems to be gaining ground among the younger generation of German and Dutch theologians. Leaders in this movement are Gremmels and Herrmann whose work,[3] I must confess, was unknown to me when my own book first came out. Since 1971 they have been talking about a materialistic theology in terms that are very close to my own, though their Frankfurt accent does differentiate us. The ultimate conclusion or discovery of this critical, materialistic theology is that theology, by virtue of its own inner logic, ought to be turning into a theory of Christianity if it is not doing so already.

That is the key we are in. It marks the non-theological investigation of Belo, the theoretical reflection of Christian Marxists and Christians favoring socialism, and the critical, materialistic "theology" which still retains the latter label. That is the key that marks my own current work of investigation.[4] The historico-materialistic theology that I alluded to in this book is now perforce making way for a critical theory of Christianity that is neither theological nor confessional.

Madrid, September 1976

Notes

1. Leonardo Boff, *Teologia do cativeiro e da libertacão* (Lisbon: Multinova, 1976).

2. Published by Les Editions du Cerf (Paris) in 1974. Others have followed in Belo's footsteps, undertaking a materialistic interpretation of the Bible and Christian tradition: Michel Clévenot, *Approches matérialistes de la Bible* (Paris: Cerf, 1976); and René Nouailhat, *Le spiritualisme chrétien dans sa constitution: Approche matérialiste des discours d'Augustin* (Paris: Desclée, 1976).The works by Belo and Clévenot will be published in English translation by Orbis Books.

3. C. Gremmels and W. Herrmann, *Vorurteil und Utopie: Zur Aufklärung der Theologie* (Stuttgart, 1971); C. Gremmels, *Der Gott der zweiten Schöpfung* (Stuttgart, 1971); W. Herrmann, *Die Angst der Theologen vor der Kirche* (Stuttgart, 1972).

4. See my studies: "Fe cristiana y mediación política," in A. Fierro and R. Mate, *Cristianos por el socialismo* (Estella: Verbo Divino, 1975); "La identidad cristiana: Modelos de planteamiento y de respuesta," in the anthology entitled *Identidad cristiana* (Estella: Verbo Divino, 1976); *Semántica del lenguaje religioso* (Madrid: Fundación Juan March, 1976).

PART ONE

SITUATION

1

From Anthropocentrism to Politics

1. MAN AS PROTAGONIST

Humanism and authentic personal existence polarized theology for several decades in the recent past, starting in the 1930s. This was particularly true around the middle of this century when theology dealt with *homo* and his existential characteristics either as an explicit theme or as a constant point of reference. Depending on the doctrinal thrust of a given approach, the existential and anthropocentric emphasis was more or less in evidence; and it should be remembered that the theological panorama in the second third of the twentieth century was quite varied. Yet when we contrast the theology of that period with the political theologies that arose around 1965, we can say that the theology of the earlier period did its work under the signpost of humanism and existential thinking.

In that earlier theology man took center stage as the main character on the theological scene. That does not mean, of course, that God was removed from the picture, for God remained the object of theology. But for the first time in the history of theology man—concrete man who had always been taken for granted by dogmatic theology as the intended recipient of Christ's gifts—stepped from the shadows into the light of midday and became the explicit concern of theological thinking. Theological doctrine underwent "the great anthropological shift" (274:38). Man was now viewed as God's interlocutor, as the necessary correlate of any and every dogmatic statement. Noteworthy is the emphasis that was placed on considerations about "God and man" (378), "the dialogue between man and God" (252), and "man before God" (22). Leading the way towards this new anthropological frontier for theology was Rudolf Bultmann, the theologian who attracted the most attention and debate with his flat statement: "If we are asked how it might be possible to talk about God, we must reply that such talk is possible only insofar as it is talk about us" (90:I,33).

When World War II ended, Christians, and Catholics in particular, deeply shared the hope of Western culture in the appearance of a different and better human being. There was an ever increasing number of dialogues, discussions, and debates about a "new humanism," and believers eagerly participated in them (12). In most cases this expectant hope did not reach the pitch that was evident in the thinking of Teilhard de Chardin, chiefly between 1945 and 1950, as he began to talk more insistently about the "ultra-humanity" that lay ahead of us (402). His was a hope writ large, but many others shared his basic confidence in the appearance of a "new man." In 1944 Chenu described the present moment of history as one that held rich promise for Christendom because "humanity was waiting expectantly for a new man" (139:102). And as late as 1961 Karl Rahner still considered the whole issue of "Christianity and the new man" to be important (344: V,157).

In referring to humanity, then, the theology of that period interpreted it in terms of humanism. Needless to say, it was not humanism in the Renaissance sense of the term; it was not centered around a cultivation of the humanities or devotion to the classics of antiquity. It was humanism in the more modern sense of the term, involving an emphatic valuation of man and an ethics based on absolute respect for the human person. Back in 1936 Maritain had written about "integral humanism" (284). In 1948 Sartre gave his provocative lecture in which he asserted that existentialism was a humanism (372), and it did much to induce theologians to compare their religious views with those of various lay humanisms.

That does not mean to say that theologians propounded or defended the existence of a specifically Christian humanism. With their pessimistic concept of human nature, Protestants tended to view the humanistic thrust as the work of man the sinner. Among Catholics some (292:97; 222), denied that Christianity was a humanism; others spoke about "Christian humanism" and attempted to view Christianity as the full and perfect humanism (345:35-53). But even among theologians who did not try to make Christianity into a brand of humanism or into the most perfect embodiment of humanism, there was a real concern to describe and define the Christian faith in relation to the prevailing humanisms of the day.

Christianity was presented in the light of contemporary humanisms and in conflict with them (174). Science merited the attention of theologians not so much as a method for verifying or attaining truth but rather as a humanist attitude (155). Atheism was viewed in the same perspective—as an atheistic humanism. In a brief and now classic work (249), Jean Lacroix saw in scientific, political, and moral humanism the deeper underlying sense of modern atheism. Another well known work by Henri de Lubac (265) attempted to portray the drama and the ultimate failure of any such atheistic humanism. Irreligious humanism was also viewed with high regard as a lay outlook imbued with ethical import (378:57-106). Even Protestant theologians, who had not been prone to take any deep interest in human and humanist values, now felt obliged to define their own position. The theme of "humanism and Christianity" pressed upon them too. In a relatively short space of time Bultmann published two consecutive volumes on the issue (90:II,133, and III,61).

Theologians had gradually become aware of the anthropocentric leanings of their thought and adopted it as a methodological exigency. Karl Rahner moved more and more decidedly toward a dogmatic approach guided by a transcendental anthropology (349:99). His pupil, Johannes Metz, attempted to trace this anthropocentric turn in theology back to Saint Thomas Aquinas (295). This anthropocentric focus meant that deeper exploration into the mystery of man would pave the way for the encounter with God. The search for meaning in human life would flow ultimately into the search for the divine presence. The ultimate depth in the unknown reaches of man himself could only be clarified in the mystery of God (184:7-8), if not actually identified with God. So it made sense to talk about "meeting God in man" (82). The existence of God would be demonstrated or made clear by way of anthropological approaches rather than cosmological ones. Man, not nature or the natural world, was the pathway to God.

So far I have been stressing the humanist note of this particular period of theology, but I might just as well have described the period in terms of personalism. It was a theology seriously concerned to extol the values of the person and to discover the personalizing dimension in every dogma. According to Mounier, its principal spokesman, personalism was "a sound and significant sign, a convenient overall designation for different doctrines" which were at one in affirming "the primacy of the human person over material necessities and collective mechanisms" (316:9).

Theology moved quickly to become personalist in that general sense: that is, in focusing on the spiritual side of man and on the transcendence of the individual vis-à-vis socioeconomic factors. Mounier himself helped this trend along by talking about Christian personalism. The expression "Christian humanism" never won many adherents, undoubtedly because of the lay origins of the new postwar humanism. By contrast the expression "Christian personalism" won wider acceptance, along with other variants of the same notion (e.g., "personal Christianity" or "personalist Christianity").

Personalist Christianity signified that faith was viewed as a personal bond between God and the believer (415:113 and 121). In a celebrated little book (317), Jean Mouroux elaborated on the personal or personalist structure of faith. Faith did not consist primarily in believing something but rather in believing in someone, in a "Thou." This stress on the personal element was reflected in Roger Aubert's monumental study of contemporary controversies concerning the act of faith. Among other things he recorded the shift from a community focus to an individualist focus as a characteristic of our century in the consideration of the matter of faith (60:670). The essential features of the Christian faith found flesh and substance in the relationship of person to person and of man to God. The latter relationship could take different forms: acceptance of God's grace, obedience to his word, or obscure certainty based on his testimony.

2. EXISTENTIAL THEOLOGY

Theology was tinged with vaguely existential overtones or decidedly existentialist ones. Two major Protestant theologians of that era, Rudolf Bultmann and Paul Tillich, incorporated existentialism into theology and attempted a hermeneutic of the Christian message based on categories taken from the philosophy of existence. Bultmann's program of demythologizing the New Tesament was in line with his existential interpretation (92:27-48). Tillich's method of correlation, the key to his systematic theology, was essentially an attempt to establish a relationship between the existential questions arising from the human situation and the answers offered by the articles of the Christian gospel (406:I,76). Theology was now more likely to be viewed as a theology of existence in which God, revelation, grace, and Christological realities bespoke some relationship to an authentic human way of existing (95). One strain of existentialism came to call itself a theological, religious, and Christian existentialism (105).

All the philosophers of existence were hailed and carried into the theological arena. Heidegger was summoned because his phenomenology of existence did not prejudge a potential decision for or against a life as believer, and also because it provided an ontology that was not hard to integrate into traditional Christian thinking. Jaspers was summoned because he was the only one of the lay philosophers to speak about transcendence (or the "encompassing") and faith in it—albeit a philosophical faith. Marcel was invoked because his work was Christian in its inspiration and because he elaborated a set of categories that could be of real help to theology: e.g., the notions of mystery, *homo viator,* and being versus having or possessing. Sartre was invoked because even though he would eventually conclude that man was a useless passion, he had said earlier that man was the being who has the project of being God (373:653 and 708). That seemed to leave open a crack for concern with such a project. In the search for philosophical and theological patrons, and for people who might be both at the same time, existential theology made Kierkegaard and Pascal the fashion. They were celebrated as precursors of the present-day experience of faith with all its paradox, uncertainty, and need for decision-making.

The existential face of this theology must be viewed and

interpreted in a broad sense. Besides the existentialist current in the strictest sense of the term, we should also include other related tendencies and currents of thought: e.g., the philosophy of values, the philosophy of intersubjectivity, and historical hermeneutics. The thinking of Dilthey about the sciences of the spirit *(Geisteswissenschaften)* and the understanding of history, along with his writings, favored the notion of theology as a hermeneutics, as a science designed to interpret the historicity of man along with the historical texts of Christianity (Bultmann, Fuchs, Ebeling). Max Scheler, and the whole theory of values in general, had been of great help to theological conceptualization (60:548). The separation made between the physical realm of things (the object of science) on the one hand and the human and historical realm of values (capable of being known in a different way) on the other hand favored the possibility of a knowledge connected with faith that could not be reduced to sense experience and rational logic.

On a different front the I-Thou philosophy elaborated mainly by Martin Buber, but also by Ebner and Marcel, provided categories that were suitable for contemplating God as the absolute, pure Thou, as the terminus of man's invocation who could never be turned into an "it," into an object of objectifying discourse (87:57-59). The biblical flavor of Buber's thinking, who was one of the greatest Jewish exegetes of our time, made it easier to find affinities between the philosophy of intersubjectivity and the major themes of the Bible. It was a propitious moment for biblical theology to bring to the forefront the notion of the "covenant" between God and his people.

The existential thrust could be detected elsewhere too, in places where there was no explicit reference to the philosophers of existence. It shone clearly in the very themes of theology. There was concern for such questions as the purpose of existence (315; 67), the meaning of death (348;

410:120), and the general issue of meaningfulness. That is also what favored the aforementioned concern with theology as a science or hermeneutics of theological signification. Attention was directed to the aspect of "decision" and hazarded option in the matter of faith, and theologians talked about the courage to believe (405; 169:90–100).

In general theologians sought to correlate faith with authentic human existence (92:I,34; 187:235). The anguish, anxiety, and vexation attributed to man were taken up and utilized by theologians—either as the starting point for apologetic or fundamental theology (68), as was the case with the *Dutch Catechism,* or as the opposite pole over against which Christian faith stood (412).

In the middle decades of this century few theologians were exempt from these humanist and existentialist strains, even among those who expressly repudiated the invasion of cultural and philosophical modes and fashions into theology. The work of Barth is the clearest and best example of that fact. Despite his own desire to oppose any such trend, his work is suffused with strains of humanism and existentialism. Barth attempted to elaborate a "pure" theology devoid of any involvement with the sensibility and idea-set of his own era. With more rigor and energy than anyone else he denounced the temptation to anthropocentrism and the accommodation of theology to the spirit of the times. But he continued to be a theologian of existence in spite of himself, and his work on dogmatics is filled with existential resonances—from his emphasis on God's word and covenant to his definition of man in terms of "co-humanity" (which comes quite close to Heidegger's notion of *Mitsein).* However little this coincidence may have pleased Barth himself (62:XI,299), his dogmatics reiterates the themes of existential philosophy and the philosophy of intersubjectivity: "The authentic 'I am,' that is, the 'I am' which possesses content, means in the last analysis that 'I am in an encounter' " (62:X,268). And though Barth sought to distance himself from any and all humanisms, he could still celebrate the "humanism of God" (63:82).

Insofar as radical theology was concerned, it could easily be regarded as the ultimate extreme to which the despoliation of dogma might go along existential lines. The well-known formula of Bonhoeffer, "being for others is the one and only experience of transcendence," could also be expressed in another version: i.e., that transcendence consists "in the nearest *Thou* at hand" (364:76). At the apex of his own critical theology, Bishop Robinson professed preoccupations of a personalist and existentialist cast and a sympathy with the I-Thou philosophy. His faith was bound up with the conviction that *Thou* is the ultimate reality of all things (363:22–31).

In short, then, the humanist and existentialist strain pervaded the work of a whole generation of theologians, the more famous and the not so famous, the most radically critical and those most suspicious of cultural fashions. By some it was openly professed; by others it was adopted unwittingly or reluctantly. Personalism, humanism, and the ideology of existence were dominant in theology during the second third of this century, just as the thought of Plato and the Stoics was dominant in patristic theology and that of Aristotle was dominant in scholastic philosophy.

One point should be noted here. The anthropocentrism, personalism, and humanism of that whole theology had to do with generic man (humanity) on the one hand and individual man ("I" or "I-Thou") on the other. No real consideration was given to historical, social, or economic determinations: e.g., social class, one's place in the production process and the power structure, and so forth. Concrete man evaporated somewhere between the species on the one hand and an imprecise individuality on the other. The man in that theology was an undetermined man without concrete circumstances. To talk of politics in such a context would have been akin to "firing a pistol at a concert," to use the image of Guichard (224:17).

3. A CHANGE IN VIEW

I have had to go into a somewhat lengthy description of the theology that held sway up to 1965 so that I might be better able to highlight the change in the theological climate that occurred around that date. Suddenly theologians stopped talking about humanism and existence. An entirely different idiom and set of themes appeared on the scene. The break or lack of continuity with the previous theology was notable indeed. Few breaks in the past history of theology could compare with it, in terms of the brusqueness of the change and the scope of the shift. It must also be noted that this discontinuity affected not only theology but also, and even more importantly, the practical implementation of Christianity. This fact demonstrates how profound the change really was. The subversion that took place in the realm of theology on this occasion, as was true at other decisive occasions, was due to a change in the doing and even being of Christians.

The crucial years were 1965 and 1966, when we moved into the last third of the twentieth century. In 1965 Vatican II, the beginning and the end of many things, came to a close for the Roman Catholic church. The ending of the Council quickly permitted people to distinguish not only between a "conciliar" and a "preconciliar" outlook but also between a "conciliar" and a "postconciliar" outlook. In the Catholic world a new kind of theology could now flourish, a theology that gleaned from the Council not so much its claims to legitimacy but rather its right to divest itself of the dead weight of the whole prior dogmatics.

More significant, however, was the international conference that the World Council of Churches held in Geneva in

July 1966. The theme of that conference, "Church and Society," broke ground for a truly different theology. With much more vigor than Vatican II ever displayed, even in its most forward-looking documents such as *Gaudium et Spes,* the Geneva Conference would define the new realm of theological reflection in terms of its relationship to society. Moreover, in Geneva Richard Shaull would talk about a "theology of revolution" (6). To find an event of comparable theologico-political import in the Catholic church, one must look ahead to 1968 and the Conference of the Latin American bishops in Medellín, which served as the springboard for the Latin American theology of liberation.

In the strictly theological realm a comparable shift was taking place, only it was even more profound. The whole scene changed within a couple of years. It was precisely there, among the avant-garde theologians, that the jargon of existential ideology began to be muted around 1965, giving way to a new theological idiom associated with a theory that faith was to be viewed as public, political praxis designed to transform society.

In 1965 Harvey Cox published *The Secular City* (126). It was the first theological work on modern secularity that tackled the issue primarily from the political side. Secular theology, which was on the rise during those years, had also found expression in existential (Robinson) and neopositivist (Van Buren) versions. With the work of Cox it took on a political tinge. Cox's basic question in *The Secular City* was how God operates through rapid social change. A theology of social change would now serve as the point of departure for ecclesiology, and thus political and civil reality was incorporated into theology itself. That reality was now linked up not only with ecclesiology but also with any talk about God. Whereas tribal man had spoken of God in mythological terms and village man had spoken of God in metaphysical terms, the man of the secular city and the technopolis could only speak about God in the idiom of politics.

Thus talking about God came down to being a political matter. Cox thereby formally certified the failure of existentialism, accusing it of immaturity and narcissism. He criticized the pastoral approach of preachers who had felt it was necessary to attract people to the dizzy heights of existentialism before communicating the gospel message to them. He turned his back just as resolutely on the whole personalist theology of intersubjectivity. Feeling that it had been a mistake for modern theology to focus on the I-Thou relationship, on the relationship between the single I and the singular you, Cox eulogized the anonymity of the big city and called for the elaboration of a theology that would deal with the relationship between the "I" and the plural "you." Cox's secular man would meet God not as a "Thou" but as a plural "you."

In 1964 Jürgen Moltmann had published his *Theology of Hope*. He too put the theology of existence to the test and found it to be fragile. His favorite opponent was any theology of subjectivity that abandoned concrete experience and the transformation of the world to a positivist science without values and reserved to theology Pascal's logic of the heart and the subject's private inner world—an inner world into which solitary man withdrew in order to escape depersonalization (312:61-94, 398-408). Even though his debate with that opponent often took on excessively culturalist overtones and came close to being a merely ideological debate, the final result was an ecclesiology of the Christian community as a community involved in the exodus. Through its hope in God's promise, the community in exodus enters into a polemical and liberative relationship with political society (312:419–27).

In these same years there appeared the first works of J.B. Metz on political theology (297–303). Even more directly than Cox and Moltmann, Metz attacked existential theology for taking its categories from the realm of private, apolitical life. He called for the "de-privatization" of theology and proposed an ecclesiology in which the church would be an institution exercising critical liberty vis-à-vis society. In his view eschatology had to be turned into political and critical theology in which the eschatological promises operate as a liberative imperative giving rise to social effects here and now in history.

A similar turn toward politics soon appeared in Latin America. Its particular situation was a general one of inequality within each country and dependence vis-à-vis the outside world. This fostered the rise of a new kind of theological reflection cut off from the earlier dogmatics and essentially focused on the process of liberation in connection with exploited peoples. This new theology was usually presented as a "theology of liberation." It was rooted in the social context of Latin American Christians and their public praxis and embodied a maturing critical awareness of their faith. As such it was fully autonomous and autochtonous, not merely a reflection of European theology. The latter, however, could not help but exercise influence and attraction on the theologians of liberation. Faced with the political theologies of the affluent nations, Latin American theologians adopted a complicated stance. On the one hand they identified themselves to some extent with those theologies, concretely joining them in the shift from the private to the public realm and dedicating themselves to a political interpretation of the gospel message. On the other hand they stood at a critical distance from those theologies, criticizing Metz and Moltmann for their tendency towards abstraction and culturalist analysis; this reaction sometimes took on overtones of rejecting the "theological colonization" to which they had been previously subjected. In varying forms and degrees that is the stance of the most well known authors such as Assmann, Gutiérrez, and Alves. They published their first major works on this theme in 1968 and 1969 (10:402–407), shortly after the appearance of the other new theologies and the Medellín Conference.

I must also mention here several encounters and meetings between Marxists and Christians that took place in 1964 and 1965. Explicit and implicit dialogue between theologians and Marxist theoreticians has exercised a decisive influence on the recent shift in theology. Indeed this is so true that the present-day theology of liberation and revolution can be regarded as the specific Christian reaction to the fresh impact of Marxism on the second half of this century. Since I propose here to be as precise and correct as possible in trying to pinpoint the moment of the theological leap from existentialism to politics, I must stress what I regard as some of the principal events. There was the series of conversations between French Christians and Marxists in Lyons and Paris in 1964 (21), the 1965 meeting in Salzburg between a distinguished group of theologians and Marxist theoreticians (23), and the appearance of Roger Garaudy's book, *From Anathema to Dialogue.* First published in 1965, it was subtitled; "A Marxist addresses himself to the Council" (201). Later editions contained further commentaries by Metz and Rahner (202). Meetings between Marxists and Christians have continued since 1965 (47), and there have been additional books that have tried to continue the dialogue or have been the result of collaborative effort (3; 14).

Historical materialism has been the overt or covert interlocutor of the most recent theology—that is to say, of the theologies mentioned here which, by virtue of their clear involvement in the realm of the *polis,* can be described as political theologies. In some authors, however, acceptance of the historical-materialist analysis of socioeconomic relationships has moved to the forefront and decisively shaped their theological position. That is the case with those theologians who accept the fact of class conflict and the consequent need to opt for some class. It is even more true of those theologians who go further and, as we shall see, accept the validity of the Marxist interpretation of the superstructure—including religion.

4. THE POLITICAL THEOLOGIES

Shaull and his theology of revolution, Cox and his view of theological language as a political problem, Moltmann and his theology of hope, Metz and his critical and political theology, the Latin American theologians of liberation, and Christian reflection based upon a full acceptance of Marx: these, in my opinion, are the names and approaches that cleared a new theological space as we moved into the last third of the twentieth century. It may seem unfair and rather conventional by now to cite those names and overlook others in talking about the pioneers of the new trend in theology; but I think it serves our purpose here to mention how people began to speak a new theological language and who these people were, without going into evaluational comments. My mention of these people does not necessarily mean that they were the ones who best grasped or understood the new theological space that was being opened up. It is quite possible that others after them understood the situation better, more in depth, and with greater critical and systematic intelligence. That is another question, however, and it is not what I am trying to accomplish here. At this point I simply want to point out where and when a new theology appeared, involving itself in political praxis and breaking with an earlier brand of theology. My account is not meant to be complete or exhaustive.

Needless to say, not all the theologians who were mentioned above, or who might be mentioned in addition to the above, say the same thing. The political theology of Metz does not coincide with Moltmann's theology of hope or Cox's secular theology. There is a question that must be asked before one tries to set forth a program that will integrate these different theologies, as I shall try to do in Part Two of this book. The question is whether it is even possible to arrange and organize these theologies into a single, homogeneous discourse. That particular question will be discussed and clarified in the chapters that follow.

First we shall discover a basic unity beneath the surface differences (chapters 4 to 6). Then we shall discover and focus on several more hidden differences underlying the earlier homogeneity that we had detected (chapter 7).

Right now I simply want to make it clear that when I link up various theologians as the creators of a new theological space, as I have just done, I am not trying to overlook or eliminate their differences on the surface level or at deeper levels. But right now I would also maintain that it is impossible to view them apart from one another, for all their differences, unless one wants to succumb to sterile abstraction. Catholic political theology is not the same as the Protestant theology of hope. The theology of revolution is not equivalent to any theology of liberation. Each has its own emphasis, its own distinctive originality, and its polemic focus; it may even be opposed to the other theologies. But that does not change the fact that chronologically they all belong to the same generation of Christians, that logically they can be coordinated in one and the same theological discourse, and that dialectically they are a response to one and the same historical situation. This threefold link—in contemporaneity, argumentative consistency, and historical function—means that the only way to concretely examine these different theologies is in terms of their contiguous relationship to one another.

From this standpoint it is quite possible that one may be led astray by their insistence on differences between them. For example, Gustavo Gutiérrez has repeatedly stressed the gap between his own theology of liberation, the theology of revolution or violence (230:316), and Metz's political theology (230:288–97). Such remarks may foster a false perspective concerning the specific points of agreement and disagreement between these theologies. To start out with an overall point of similarity between them, it is undeniable that all of them are much closer to each other and mutually interrelated than they are to any other theology of the past, even of the recent past. That fact is enough to justify treating them initially as a unit.

If we were to take each of these theologies as distinct and separate for purposes of analysis and discussion, we would be engaging in an arbitrary abstraction of no beneficial use. Such an approach would be in danger of abandoning the real-life framework and overall context of theological problems since 1965. Around that date a shift of major importance took place in theology. It was characterized negatively by a break with the earlier existential theology and with the whole confessional theology of the past that was excessively preoccupied with denominational orthodoxy. Precisely because the newly arisen theologies broke with the earlier denominational formulations of dogma, their ecumenism is grounded on bases wholly different from those of classical ecumenism. Confessional differences due to a myopic theological positivism (190:11–12) have been surmounted by shifting the weight of reflection outside the churches to society. The theologies that arose around 1965 are naturally ecumenical rather than artificially so. For the first time since the Reformation we see the rise of a basically interdenominational theology, and we can envision a real overcoming of the divisions between Christians.

There are three common features in these latest theologies. They agree in projecting a theology that is practical, public, and critical. It is this common denominator that justifies our attempt to view them as a unit, to see in them different tendencies and accents of a new theological discourse that is homogeneous in itself and different from any other.

5. A THEOLOGY CONCERNED WITH PRAXIS

An earlier theology that centered around theological representations (188) and a purely contemplative interpretation of man and the world has given way to a theology basically concerned with a praxis that will transform society. The shift to praxis coincided with a feeling of indifference toward traditional orthodox dogmas, the indifference itself resulting from a more or less open acceptance of the modern criticism of ideologies, and of Marxist criticism in particular. Acknowledging that traditional dogmatic theology, which was wholly based on a naive trust in the representational and objective value of ideas, came wholly under the devastating attack of this criticism, theologians are now trying to escape from it at all costs.

And so there has arisen the theological thesis that faith is not an ideology. This thesis, as we shall see (chapter 5), is quite ambiguous. But the basic thrust underlying its varied and even opposing senses is to avoid identifying the faith with any system of ideas. Rahner, for example, attempts to prove that Christianity is not an ideology—though he operates with a valuational and purely formal notion of ideology: "Ideology is here understood in a negative sense . . . as a false and erroneous system that must be rejected in any correct interpretation of reality" (344:VI,58). Such a notion clarifies nothing about the nature of the representations of faith. In *Octogesima Adveniens* Paul VI devotes several sections to noting the collapse of ideologies and celebrating the event as a new opportunity for the faith, though his own conception of Christian dogmatics is certainly ideological (185). With much greater correctness, and on the basis of suppositions that he tries to make non-ideological, Girardi engages in criticism of "ideologism," that is to say, of thinking detached or completely independent from action (209:300–3). So even when they are dogmatizing in ideological terms, Christians are now trying to persuade others or themselves that their faith does not constitute an ideology. That is clearly symptomatic of the devaluation of ideas and doctrines.

This devaluation of the doctrinal and representational element also finds expression in another formulation that is much in fashion. It stresses a shift from a theology primarily interested in orthodoxy to a theology primarily concerned with orthopraxis. This formulation adheres quite closely to the traditional one insofar as it does nothing more than assert that now is the time to place greater stress on acting and doing (381:10–11). It is also quite traditional when it simply regards orthopraxis as the touchstone of orthodoxy: "The orthodoxy of faith must be constantly verified in an operational praxis oriented toward the end of time, since the promised truth is a truth that must *be done*" (302:150; 380:93–103). This is nothing more than an attempt to recover a dimension that had been lost for theology and the faith (162). But the formulation is also quite capable of being framed in much less traditional versions that are not concerned one bit with orthodoxy. Raimundo Panikkar explicitly proposes a conception of faith as orthopraxis that leaves behind the old identification of faith with orthodoxy as a one-sided concept belonging to a stage that has now been passed (330–32). As for myself, in an earlier work I analyzed the factors both within and outside theology that make orthodoxy impossible today (188).

The problem of meaning and definition, that is, of the interpretation of the Christian texts and of the meaning of life, has quietly been forgotten. The hermeneutics and theology that predominated in the previous theological generation have slipped into history. They were not even missed at the 1966 Geneva Conference of the World Council of Churches (420:97).

The fact is that the older hermeneutic problem has been translated into one dealing with praxis. "The hermeneutics of the kingdom of God," writes Schillebeeckx, "is primarily to improve the world" (381:15). Metz notes that "hermeneutic behavior is itself a behavior related to praxis," and that the process of clarifying the horizon and the conditions of comprehension is connected with the task of modifying that horizon and those conditions in praxis (301:283). He is even more clear on the point when he says: "The fundamental hermeneutic problem of theology is not really the relationship between systematic theology and history, between dogma and history, but rather the relationship between theory and practice, between intelligent understanding of the faith and social praxis" (297:390). In this context theology is defined or redefined as "critical reflection in and on historical praxis," in a confrontation with the Lord's word accepted through faith (227:244).

The older question of relating God's word and human existence has faded from the attention of theologians, to be replaced by the question of relating faith and praxis. At the 1968 Uppsala Assembly of the World Council of Churches, Doctor Adler put it pointedly and well, demolishing the now classic and outmoded accusations of "horizontalism" directed against involved Christians: "More important and relevant than trying to stress a correspondence between the vertical dimension and the horizontal dimension, in my opinion, would be stressing a correspondence between what one says and what one does" (37:50–51).

There is a serious effort to establish consistency and harmony between what Christians do on the one hand and what they think, say, and believe on the other hand. Thus faith jumps to the realm of praxis. Theologal belief is no longer identified with a way of thinking but with a way of acting. It is not equivalent to a conception of the world, but rather to an action performed in and on the world. It is militant commitment and involvement rather than the gaze of a mere spectator. González Ruiz makes the point succinctly in one of his book titles, which usually announce and enunciate their basic themes: "To believe is to be committed" (218). A faith understood in those terms comes to constitute a social factor and a force in history (16).

The key to this shift of theology towards praxis can be found in Marx's eleventh thesis against Feuerbach: "Philosophers have done nothing more than *interpret* the world in different ways; but it is really a matter of *transforming* it." In contrast to a contemplative dogmatics that was content to interpret the universe, present-day theology has decided to be active and transforming in the practical realm. It means to be a theology with hands as well as eyes. This open acceptance of Marx's thesis cited above is the first trait shared by present-day theologies: They are oriented basically toward a praxis that will alter the world. Cox, therefore, is hardly original when he asserts that theologians have spent too much time interpreting the world, that the time has come for them to change it (129:572).

6. A THEOLOGY THAT IS PUBLIC AND CRITICAL

In the modern age religion has been characteristically conceived as a private affair. This conception has now been replaced by a stress on the public character of the gospel message. This is a second feature shared by all the theology of the present day. The praxis it has in mind is public and political.

In this connection it is worth pointing out that the existential theology of the mid-century was the logical culmination of a process in which Christianity was increasingly privatized. The process of "privatization" characterized modern times, and it was even more dominant in Protestant Christianity than in Catholic Christianity. Luther himself seems to have been chiefly responsible for withdrawing the gospel to the inner life of the individual and abandoning public functions to game rules that were not only autonomous but alien to any ethical element (79:152–81). Without any word of protest being heard, except perhaps from movements for a new cultural Christendom, movements that were usually Catholic, one could calmly assert that "religion is a private affair" (382:72). Marxists and even

Lenin himself had agreed on that point, using the same phrase to eliminate the problem of the relationship between faith and communist society.

In the bourgeois Western world, therefore, religious sentiments had been cloistered in the innermost depths of a person's private life. Gironella's book exploring the beliefs and feelings of one hundred Spaniards about God, *Cien españoles y Dios,* is filled with statements couched in terms of religious modesty and rooted in the notion that such beliefs are an intimate and private affair. A scientist had this reaction to such an inquiry into people's faith in God: "We are to strip naked. That is more or less what Gironella intends with his brutal questioning. And in public no less . . . " (212:436). A journalist felt that asking a person about his creed and his religious life could bespeak a rudeness in the questioner, especially when it was done in public and the questions were directed to someone who was not an intimate friend (212:610). Even Gironella himself shares that conception of such an inquiry because he talks about "crossing the threshold of another person's conscience" and about the reluctance of these interviewed to "strip naked before the eyes of the public" (212:14).

At its furthest limits this reduction of religiosity to the subjective realm might be phrased in Whitehead's terms: Religion is "what man does with his solitude." Such a definition is so in line with the modern conception of religion that Bochenski, a Dominican philosopher, calmly takes it for granted and asserts that religion is a subjective problem (80:36). Now suddenly a new thesis has appeared on the scene to challenge that four-hundred-year old tendency in Christianity and theology.

The new thesis stresses the public character of the gospel message. It is not simply alluding to the public profession of faith as a religious witness given before others. It also includes the militance of Christianity in the political arena, the irruption of "Christians into political life" (413); and this is the more important aspect. Today theology has come to see that the gospel message is a summons not only to individual human beings but also to social structures and institutions. Stress is now put on the "public character" of the Christian message vis-à-vis society, and on the need to redeem societal structures (217:444). It is a fact of the utmost importance that it is a collectivity, the Christian community, that bears witness to the gospel. This fact, along with the social scope of the proclaimed message encompassing not only individuals but also social units, serves as the foundation for the public character of Christianity.

On this front the great danger facing the new theology is that it might fall back into the hoary ideal of ancient Christendom with its now discredited political theology. But it is safeguarded from that danger by its configuration as a theology of exodus, liberation, and revolution. This configuration draws a sharp line between present-day political theologies and the older political theology involved in the project to fashion a cultural Christendom and to proclaim it as something already realized. The relationship of the newer theology to the idea of Christendom merits separate consideration (see chapter 2), but one point should be stressed here and now. The theology of the present day has a critical and polemical relationship not only with existing society but also with any and every sociopolitical ideal that presents something fixed and finished once and for all.

Theologians are currently stressing the critical, subversive, and revolutionary character of the faith. Faith polemically confronts and challenges any real or ideal order that would seek shelter in its own finished "establishment." In this viewpoint faith is seen as something that liberates people from the given situation and proposes various alternatives. Faith "radically dislocates the believer" (258:49). Without a doubt this is the most important and original feature of the most recent theology, and it is stressed time and again. We shall run across it repeatedly.

The appearance of the critical element in theology precisely as social criticism is in line with a general tendency in all areas of modern thought (see chapter 3). Its concrete shape and texture will be considered later on (see chapter 5) in terms of the categories through which it is elaborated: liberation, revolution, and rejection. It is this critical element, complementing and correcting the public dimension of the new theology, that marks it off as different from other theologies of the past which also had been open to society. As a first attempt to appreciate this difference, we might note the distinct social functions that sociology attributes to religion. Desroche, for example, makes a distinction between two functions of religion: the "function of bearing witness" and the function of "protesting." Under these two headings he attempts to group the diverse functional variables that sociologists have discovered in religion.

The first function is associated with the fact that every society expresses and bears witness to itself in its corresponding religion. On that front religious tradition operates as a factor helping to integrate and preserve society. The second function of religion indicated above is one that forces society to ask questions about itself, that thereby nourishes social rebelliousness and resistance to the process of integration (148:60–74). With this conceptualization of religion, or others of a similar sort, sociology and social theory point up the functional ambivalence of religion vis-à-vis society: On the one hand religion can function as a source of approval; on the other hand it can serve as a source of societal criticism. Marx himself referred to religious beliefs both as the opiate of the people and their form of protest.

The sociology of religion tends to emphasize the political service of religion, its function of helping to integrate society. As Pannenberg notes, the sociological outlook tends to regard religion as "the spiritual foundation for the unity of a people" (333:245). This is a point of view that is quite consistent with that of certain politicians like Machiavelli, who advised rulers to look out for "the maintenance of religion" as a means of keeping their domain and rule in peace (177:122).

Such an analysis of the social ambivalence of religious traditions can be incorporated into theology. Moltmann, for example, defines "political religions" as those that appear on the scene as a result of the "symbolic integration of a people." Such religions "help to bring out homogeneity and self-consistency in a people. In them the nation or people mystifies its own origins and glorifies its own history." According to Moltmann, the New Testament doctrine of the Trinity has the precise and specific role of fostering criticism of all such political religions (313:26,49).

Such is the ordering, integrating, and "nomic" function of religion that is generally stressed by sociologists. Over against that function other theologians set another function that is "transforming, critical and prophetical, apocalyptic or catastrophic" (in the root sense of the Greek word *kata-strofe*, which means "radical overturning" or "new beginning"). Insofar as it also has this function, religion operates as a factor fostering extreme mobility (45:149–50).

Viewed in terms of these social functions, the big difference between the most recent theology of a public and practical cast and other theological doctrines centered around the public and practical realm lies in the great stress that the newer theology places on the factor of criticism. In the past Christian theology had almost always been subservient to a Christianity that was regarded as a "political religion." It helped to provide the peoples and nations of the West with an integrative symbolization. To be sure, there is more than one feature that distinguishes present-day theology from theologies of the past, even from past theologies of an apocalyptic or "catastrophic" cast, and we shall consider these features in chapter 7. But it certainly can be said that one strikingly new feature in present-day theology is the predominance of the critical element, the determination to comprehend the process of Christian symbolization for the sake of altering society rather than consolidating its present form.

A theologian like Metz (297:394) has stressed that political theology defines the church as an institutionalization of this criticism of society. Other theologians have rebuked political theology for attempting any such ecclesiastical institutionalization. If a church were viewed in such terms, society would then accord it the "role" of being a critical institution and the church would be in danger of being limited to the role of "extra-parliamentary opposition" (273:3,13,17).

Assigning such a function of institutionalized criticism to the church is not a trait shared by all critical-public theology. The fact that theology fosters a critical awareness of society does not automatically mean that this awareness is to become institutionalized in the church and that the church, as such, is supposed to adopt a political option. The fact that theology is engaged in public criticism and is characterized by that fact does give rise to ecclesiological effects. But precisely because it obliges us to modify the concept and the reality of the church, there is ambiguity both in affirming and in denying that evangelical criticism is to be institutionalized in the church.

7. POLITICS IN A MEDIATING ROLE

As we have noted, the new theology is practical (or praxis-oriented), public, and critical. These three traits can be summed up by saying that in this theology politics plays the mediating role. Thus theological language is made possible and concrete in and through the mediation of political language.

The political realm is the broadest horizon within which human life unfolds and develops (309:233), the most all-embracing and decisive arena of praxis (396:69), the most overall fact conditioning man's fulfillment (229:19). Thus it represents "the highest level of apprehending human problems" (175:1058). In that sense the political realm is equivalent to the anthropological realm, or simply to the human realm taken in both its most all-encompassing and concrete sense.

The political realm has always constituted the encompassing and decisive horizon of the human. But people today have a much more lively awareness of it, realizing that they are not just the objects but also the active subjects of political history. In the concrete experience of modernity, and specifically in the modern experience of the political, people feel themselves to be ultimately responsible for their social and institutional creations. These creations are no longer attributed to nature or the gods. People recognize them as their own work, which they can do or undo.

This awareness of being the active subject of history is relatively recent (309:438), and to it is due the positive valuation of the political sphere in the present day. Also bound up with that awareness are the present-day political theologies, and it constitutes another point where there is a sharp break of continuity with past theologies. Only present-day theology can and does operate on the premise that people are conscious and critical subjects of history, the ultimate agents of political realities who can alter the conditions of their own existence. The theology of revolution is the ultimate consequence of that premise, revolution being nothing but the creation of human beings by and for themselves.

Such is the *kairos* of present-day theology: politics taken as the general horizon of human life and as the space where people realize themselves as the subjects of their own history and the agents of their own destiny. Theological discourse is truly up to the times and topical insofar as it does its work through the medium of the political. A political theology has appeared on the scene today simply because "a real-life theology has appeared, and reality is political at its most decisive level" (59:24).

The mediating role of the political element justifies one's talking about a "politicizing" of the faith (135:93). There is no reason to be afraid of that term, although it tends to figure prominently in the accusations made by opponents of the new political theology. Ruling out a depoliticized faith comes down to calling for a politicized one. There is no need to reject or deny the latter. One must simply explain what it means: that is, a faith that adopts the mediating role of the political element in order to realize itself precisely as faith. Or, to paraphrase Hugo Assmann, ultimate questions take on historical reality only in penultimate questions; without the latter, the former end up being irrelevant (54:223). The ultimate horizon of faith takes on flesh and blood in the penultimate horizon of the political.

When we compare this politically mediated theology with the earlier theological tradition we find lines of continuity and sharp breaks. On this front some stress "the continuity of theology with itself" (28). This continuity is highlighted in some forms of the theology of liberation, for example, which are dogmatic and re-sacralizing in the form in which they are presented (see chapter 7). But where the mediation of the political element is accepted in all its rigor, it is the discontinuity with the past that stands out in the new theology. Concretely, a theology that fully adopts a historical-materialistic analysis represents an almost complete break with the theology inherited from the past, their only connection being their common profession of the Christian faith.

Continuity or discontinuity also depends on exactly where one lays hold of the tangled skein of theological tradition. It is not difficult to discern a logical connection between the historical criticism of theology in the past century and the political criticism of theology at present. Focusing primarily on the demythologizing language of Bultmann, Moltmann and Sölle have not found it hard to make it clear that a critical theology leads quite logically to a theology of revolution. Historical criticism of tradition goes hand in hand with sociological criticism of institutions (309:217). "The radical consequence of criticizing myths is no longer simply existential interpretation but rather the revolutionary implanting of liberty" (309:230), for the very simple reason that any image of the world which purports to present war, hunger, and oppression as fated and inevitable is itself mythological (396:71). The "de-fatalizing" of society propounded by the new theology is in continuity with the demythologizing of beliefs. On the one hand Dorothee Sölle points out that "criticism as such is a political factor since in principle it brings before the bar of reason not only theses and dogmas but also institutions and power centers that are almost always bound up with the former" (396:24). On the other hand she calls attention to the fact that Bultmann's demythologizing proceeded simply to eliminate myth or cosmological images, whereas "a political theology can read the political intentions in cosmological images" (396:58).

A critical theology finds its logical completion in political criticism. Various theologians have pointed out that the historico-critical method developed in theology during the last century and the political hermeneutics of present-day theology have their common roots in the Enlightenment. Thus the political theologies of the present represent the last stage of the processes unleased in the church by the Enlightenment. Metz reminds people that for Kant enlightened human beings are ones who make public and critical use of their reason, so that the Enlightenment itself triggered the "deprivatizing" of reason (297:390). In his judgment the Enlightenment, viewed critically rather than chronologically, drew the dividing line between older theologies and the new political theology by virtue of its liberating distinction between the state and society (301:269–70). Rendtorff agrees with Metz in judging that the theology of revolution is indebted to the critical heritage of the Enlightenment though it has not always grasped the deeper intentions and motivations of that period (353:73–74).

Likewise, an anthropocentric theology finds concrete insertion into human life only insofar as it is a political theology. This is the profound link to be noted between the theology of the last third of the twentieth century and the anthropocentric or humanist theology of the second third of the century. The humanism of the earlier theology was idealist and abstract. It spoke of the human being in two equally abstract terms, in terms of humanity on the one hand and of the individual on the other. The new political theologies arose from an approach to persons in the concrete; only through the mediation of politics do persons appear as concrete, real-life figures. The political element in present-day theology represents concrete anthropocentrism.

So there is a logic leading from anthropocentrism to politics. The anthropological shift in contemporary theology has developed most recently as a shift of attention toward the political sphere. It is the latter that has given concrete orientation and shape to the earlier shift. It does not surprise us, then, to note the direction taken by a theologian such as Metz as his thinking proceeded. He began his work with a study of Christian anthropocentrism (295) and gradually moved on to a political theology. At one point he explicitly points out that his shift to the political element was due to the demands posed by his anthropological and existential formulation of the problem: "If we really want to get down to existence today, we cannot talk in a merely existential manner" (304:167).

Insofar as an existential theology of Bultmann's cast is concerned, Sölle seems to be correct when she notes that there is a bridge between such existential thinking and a political line of thought, that Bultmann's own starting point logically compels one to pass over from one to the other

(396:12–13). That is not just because all criticism is called to tackle the political sphere eventually, as was noted above. It is also because "only political theology leads us into the existential in all its reality," by making possible a language that touches the real-life existence of the individual (396:102). As she puts it, "We cannot conceive of any serious comprehension of existence, even of individual existence, without a social mediation" (396:53).

8. COMMENT ON TERMINOLOGY

So far in this book I have fluctuated in my use of terms. In order to characterize the most recent brands of theology, I have alluded to three traits which they share in common. These theologies are practical, public, and critical. I have also called them "political theologies," a term that is justified insofar as they all stress the mediating role of politics. Among these theologies I expressly alluded to these theologies as the theology of liberation and the theology of revolution.

In the last section, however, I spoke of "political theology" in the singular when I touched upon the thinking of Metz and Sölle. Here, then, I should like to explain briefly why I shall henceforth use that term in the singular to designate any theology that is politically mediated, public, critical, and praxis-oriented—including theologies of liberation and revolution.

In its narrowest sense the term "political theology" refers to the theology which has been outlined by J.B. Metz, and which shall be considered in due time. The papers brought together by Helmut Peukert in a volume that discusses the merits of "political theology" (4) represent judgments and evaluations of Metz's formulations. Taken in this specific and restricted sense, then, "political theology" is not identical with the theology of liberation or the theology of revolution; it stands over against them as the approach of a particular theologian. But other theologians (such as Sölle, for example) have used the term "political theology" also, though their thinking is quite independent of that of Metz; and thus they have broadened the accepted meaning of the term. Sölle herself is not wholly pleased with the term. She would prefer some other expression such as "political interpretation" or "political hermeneutics" of the gospel message (396:66–68). It is now customary, however, to speak about "political theology" because that term is simple and straightforward and stylistically more succinct than more precise terms might be.

From here on I shall use the term "political theology" because of its grammatical and stylistic simplicity. It just would not do to keep talking repeatedly about the "political interpretation of the gospel," or a "politically mediated theology," or a "theology that is public, critical, and praxis-oriented." Let me just say, once and for all, that the term "political theology" is my shorthand way of referring to a theology that has all those traits. It means exactly what those terms attempt to convey.

But should we talk about it in the singular or the plural, about "political theology" or "political theologies"? The noticeable differences in criteria and focus within this politically mediated theology would favor a plural reference. Indeed I used the plural in the subtitle of this book to suggest the range of subject matter under consideration. But there are enough shared features to justify the use of the singular noun for the sake of grammatical simplicity. I shall normally use the singular term "political theology" so long as it is not necessary to distinguish between the lines of thought under discussion. I shall use the plural "political theologies" when it is necessary to highlight differences within the general framework of the new theology. Defined in these general terms, then, political theology also takes in the theologies of revolution, liberation, exodus, hope, violence, and so forth. When I am referring specifically to the more restricted and specific "political theology" of Metz, I shall make that clear to the reader.

Metz himself has been challenged on the timeliness and appropriateness of the term "political theology." Even though we are going to broaden its scope in this book, we would do well to consider some of the main objections to Metz's use of the term; for if those objections were solid and compelling, they might also apply to our broader use of the term. The principle objection has been that the historical background of the expression hardly commends it for present-day usage. One hardly has to go far back in history if one is looking for political theologies that sought to involve God and revelation in government or the operation of the state. In 1922 Carl Schmitt published the first edition of his work, *Politische Theologie,* which had a great impact at the time. It provided ideological ammunition for German nationalist Catholicism and for positivist, order-bound Catholicism in general. Hans Maier has developed this terminological objection to Metz's phrase in detail, eventually turning it into a theological objection by trying to show that in the last analysis Metz's theology does not really differ from the old conservative political theology (273:5).

Metz has replied to that objection by pointing up the difference between his political theology and the earlier one. The big difference, as he sees it, lies in his theology's acceptance of the Enlightenment distinction between the state and society. Admitting that he had not perhaps paid due attention to the freighted historical overtones of the term, he feels that its use is still justified for want of a better word (301:268–70). Jürgen Moltmann came to Metz's assistance on this point by noting that while the term "political theology" was seriously undermined by its earlier use in history, its use by such people as Carl Schmitt is something that would bother the older generations primarily; it would not arouse the same connotations or objections in the minds of the younger generation (313:11).

The existence of a dispute over the very name of this theology makes it clear that the appellation "political" is ambiguous, or at least open to ambiguity. But to try to dispel that ambiguity before spelling out what is signified by political theology would be like working in a vacuum. Any ambiguity will be eliminated precisely through an exposition of the political interpretation of the gospel. Though it can give rise to errors and misunderstandings, the fact is that the term "political theology" is the least objectionable of the terms that might be used, and in that sense it is the best for our purposes here. It clearly indicates the injection of politics into the very discourse of theology as language.

It does not seem appropriate or satisfactory to talk about a theology "of the political" as Biot does (72), or "of politics" as Cox sometimes does (126:129). Sölle refers to such phrases as labels for "another theology of the genitive . . . " (396:68). Her point is well taken because such appellations seem to suggest that theology is simply broadening its themes or objects to include work, politics, art, progress, terrestrial realities, or what have you. In this case it seems to suggest that theology is going to concern itself with politics as a theme for its particular consideration. In fact, however, that is not what is happening or what should happen. Today the political realm is coming to form a part of theological discourse as such. It is entering into the *logos* of theology as an unavoidable mediating structure between theologal language (see chapter 7, section 3) on the one hand and the different themes theology must discuss on the other, these themes not necessarily being political at all.

9. FAVORABLE AND UNFAVORABLE REACTIONS

Like any new phenomenon, today's political theology is greeted with enthusiasm by some and animosity by others. Its enthusiastic supporters find satisfaction in the thought that political theology is tackling and resolving the present crisis in theology, and perhaps even paving the way for a restoration and reinstatement of traditional dogmatics in the face of the corrosive criticism of radically secular theology.

In later chapters of this book we shall throw a dash of cold water on such enthusiasm. This book is a *critical* introduction to political theology, not an enthusiastic initiation into it. Viewed dispassionately, political theology does not seem to be any ready-made formula, the mere application of which will remedy the present crisis of theology. It itself is a phenomenon symptomatic of the profound commotion surrounding theology today. Far from solving the problems raised by secular and radical theology, political theology finds those same problems arising within its own boundaries and still in need of solution.

It is even more clearly evident that the animosity and hostility toward political theology comes from dogmatic attitudes that correctly see that political theology is introducing important critical principles vis-à-vis traditional theology. The intensity of this hostility tends to increase with the severity of the criticism directed against the older theological tradition by the new theology. It tends to decrease, of course, insofar as the new theology is meekly submissive to received dogmatics and interested only in exploring the resonances of dogma in the political realm. In short, dogmatic minds can tolerate a theology of the political realm, but not with a theology that is politically mediated.

So both the enthusiastic and the hostile reactions to the new theology proceed from dogmatic positions, though they are evidently more open and flexible positions in the case of those who favor the new theology. Political theology itself does not possess any special treatment of its own to cure dogmatic paralysis. It is theological criticism in general which must prove the ultimate impossibility of dogmatic formulations and approaches (188; 189). But insofar as political theology does make room for a critical theology, its elaboration and exposition can and does chip away at the frozen wastes of a theology long refrigerated in dogmatic positivism. Political theology and critical theology dovetail with one another, presupposing and involving each other's existence.

The problems, weak spots, and possible criticisms that occur within theology will be given due consideration in their proper place. Right now I simply want to indicate the main kinds of general criticism and rebuttal that are directed against political theology. It is flatly rejected on the basis of one or more of these principles: on the basis of tradition and orthodoxy, on the basis of kerygma, and on the basis of existential thinking.

The principle of orthodoxy, understood in the most traditional sense, rejects the statements of political theology because they do not concur with those of traditional dogmatics. The kerygmatic principle attempts to reduce the gospel to some essential message such as God's reconciliation with man through Christ or Christ's wholehearted living for God and his work; it disdains any theology that does not restrict itself to a dispassionate commentary on that basic proclamation. Finally, the existential criterion looks back nostalgically to the era when theology spent its time speaking about existence, salvation from anxiety, the meaning of life, and so forth; it feels vague shudders when it hears talk about God and the gospel message couched in politically militant terms. Outright and complete rejection of political theology tends to be based on the combined use of all three principles just noted. The most general and common formulation of the objection might be put like this: Political theology betrays the Christian kerygma or message, a message that finds its obligatory and unsurpassable expression in the traditional orthodoxy and that is quite appropriately framed in the categories of personalist humanism.

Robert Spaemann provides an excellent example of how these principles are combined to reject political theology *in toto.* He reproaches political theology for its "ambiguity and indecision with respect to the content of the Christian kerygma" (398:484). He says that political theology has no right to pose as theology at all (398:493). To establish his opposition on solid grounds he has recourse to church tradition, in which he claims to find an "ecclesial relativism" and even a "political opportunism" that he elevates to a theological rule (398:485). The theology he champions vigorously possesses clear-cut existential features: It attempts to comment on the fact that "God is love" and that men need God; it proclaims an "indestructible joy" which "has nothing to do with politics." The integrism,* fundamentalism, and simplistic dogmatism of Spaemann's viewpoint are reflected clearly in the purely rhetorical flourish with which he ends his critique: "We have already thought a great deal about man; now it is time to think about God" (398:495). As if political theology had given up the idea of talking about God! As if it were somehow possible to talk about God *in se* without any mediating factor! Underlying the simplistic alternatives which he proposes as the only ones (either we contemplate man or we contemplate God) is the conservative will to alter nothing in the most traditional dogmatics.

The purely rhetorical attacks, devoid of critical value and grounded solely on dubious appeals to a now stale sensibility, discredit themselves. Such is the case, for example, with

---

*The Spanish word *integrismo* is used to designate a tendency or program or platform—political, religious, etc.—that seeks to maintain a tradition or existing state of affairs virtually intact and that tends to be opposed to anything but the most flimsy changes or reforms. Innovations and reforms are acceptable only insofar as they can be "integrated" into the existing structure. There are equivalent terms in several other European languages, alluding to the same basic notion.—Trans. note

the "ecumenical message" that was drafted by three theologians (Le Guillou, Clement, and Bosc) from different churches during the May 1968 crisis in France. Billed as an "essay in Christian discernment," it sought to shed light on the gospel attitude toward revolution. In that message the three theologians wrote: "We need authentic spiritual figures, paternal presences who share in the paternity of the Trinity, to speak to us in these times of boredom and empty palaver. They must speak the word that comes from silence and chisels the stone of the soul" (9:45–46). Those "paternal presences" are proposed as a valid alternative to any political interpretation of the gospel message. In that basic perspective Le Guillou presents Jesus as the "Suffering Servant" who is "infinitely above and beyond all politics" (9:15).

But where is the empty palaver? Is it in talking about God and Jesus Christ in the tangible terms of a concrete social situation, or is it in appealing to the "word that comes from silence and chisels the stone of the soul"? There is more than a trace of empty verbiage in a spirituality that thinks it has solved a question by mouthing words that idealize human existence ("paternal presences," sharing in the paternity of the Trinity no less!) and that give a false picture of real-life events and relationships (in our day cultural rebellion against, and emancipation from, every kind of father figure).

The appeal to an additional "supplement of soul," so often voiced since the days of Bergson, is on the same footing as the appeal to orthodoxy and tradition when it comes to forestalling contemporary growth in political awareness and the political mediation of theology. It will not work because it appeals to now discredited values. Such factors as the soul, tradition, and paternal presences cannot really serve as the foundation for anything, not even for objections. It is they, if anything, that are in need of solid grounding; and only the process of political mediation can convey some meaning and value to such terms.

Dorothee Sölle has challenged any purely kerygmatic theology that seeks to denigrate political involvement. She has pointed out that its alleged purity actually entails hidden political stances within it, stances which in the concrete entail conformism and accommodation to the existing social situation. "In these apparently apolitical phrases and concepts people find justification for the practice of politically desired attitudes and stances." "The more one reflects in purely theological terms, the more theology functions as a tool for social accommodation." Sölle presents examples of kerygmatic theology in which hunger or war are presented as tests devised by God for man, as situations which are in the hands of God and wholly outside of human will and human society. This depoliticization of social realities ultimately helps to consolidate the existing political authority: "Theological language thinks itself depoliticized, and has thereby served the interests of those in power." The serious thing above all else is that kerygmatic language, which is theologically pure and abstract, has nothing at all to do with the language of Jesus himself. Concentration on the kerygma obscures and waters down the real Jesus of history, denying his own political awareness (396:43–47).

10. THE QUESTION OF EXISTENCE PURSUED

Concern for preserving dogma and for preaching the kerygma can make it harder for people to accept a political hermeneutics of the gospel message. The same holds true for a third factor that began to be developed at great length by the generation of theologians who began their work between the years 1945 and 1965. The existentialist approach tends to de-emphasize or denigrate any political hermeneutics of the gospel, even though there is a clear and logical progression from existential humanism to politics.

Personal biographical factors contribute to the problem here. Most theologians over thirty-five years of age shared the zeal and enthusiasm for existentialism and incorporated it openly or discreetly into their own conception of theology. It is not easy to accept the impact of time's heavy hand on one's own work, especially when one's thinking and writing seems to date from only yesterday. It is hard to admit that work done no more than ten years ago is already theology of the past. Attachment to the past—to a very recent past—and the melancholic realization that what was ardently professed yesterday is no longer serviceable can operate on the emotional and prereflexive level to prevent one from moving towards a political interpretation of the gospel message.

I mention this problem because it undoubtedly must affect many theologians, and because I myself had to face this confrontation with earlier convictions and beliefs. The first book I wrote, which I thought would represent a personal contribution of some sort, dealt with faith. Its basic conception and makeup derived from classes held in 1965, and its title was to have been *Faith and Existence.* Various publishing factors altered that title and delayed its appearance in print until 1970 (187). It derived its inspiration from Pascal and existential currents. I dedicated it happily to Gabriel Marcel, whom I greatly revered at the time. The criticism that I would have to level at that work of mine today is the same criticisms that political theology levels at existential theology: i.e., that it poses questions and discusses them in an apolitical, individualistic, abstract, and highly idealized framework. Yet, for all that, I do not feel that my book is now wholly useless and out of date. The sensibility that shines through its pages may now be one that I have left behind, and its formulation of the problem of faith may be false—relatively speaking—in the light of present-day political awareness; but it also contains many elements that retain their full validity and that can, and even should, be incorporated into a politically mediated theology.

I make this personal reference for several reasons. First

of all, I want to make clear some of the difficulties, more of an emotional than a theoretical cast, that can make it hard for a person to accept a political hermeneutics of the gospel. Secondly, it seems somewhat strange to me that many theologians who began to express themselves in metaphysical and existential terms have moved on to political terms without a word of justification or explanation, as if nothing at all had happened to them and no break in continuity had taken place in their thinking. The fact is that the shift from a metaphysical and existential theology to a political theology is a decisive one. It is a shift in one's theological conception quite as important and major as the earlier shift to anthropocentrism in theology. If the earlier shift to anthropocentrism forced people to explain clearly what was left of the theocentrism of traditional theology, then the present-day shift to a politically mediated theology will also force people to explain exactly what has happened to the earlier humanistic and existential theology and its questions about the sense and purpose of life.

When Metz proposes "deprivatization" as the distinctive feature of political theology, one sometimes gets the impression that it represents nothing more than an addition or a corrective to the partialism of the existential viewpoint. For example, Metz says: "I take political theology to be a critical corrective to the excessive tendency of present-day theology towards privatization" (304:139–140). This would seem to suggest that political theology merely complements and completes the earlier theology, correcting it where that is necessary. In such a case political theology would be nothing more than a new or newly rediscovered "dimension" in theology, as some authors do in fact tend to view it (162). Does Metz himself view it in that light? There is no clearcut answer to that question in his writings, precisely because he does not explain in detail what now remains of scholastic theology, dogmatics in general, and the existential viewpoint in the projected work of political theology.

Herein lie the roots of the ambivalence and the relative lack of clearcut definition in Metz's proposal for a political theology.

It must be said clearly and straightforwardly: Political theology—that is, a theology mediated through the political—presupposes a break with all the theology that went before: i.e., scholastic theology (mediated through metaphysics), positive theology (mediated through exegesis and history), and existential theology (mediated through humanism dealing with existence). It is not simply a corrective to the one-sidedness of the earlier theology, nor is it a new dimension or space for amplifying the traditional and ageless dogmatics. It involves something more than a "deprivatization" grafted on to the otherwise unchanged and unchanging foundation of a theology of existence. Political theology is a distinct theology, a new and original theology that makes a break with all those theologies that have gone before—just as Greek patristic theology was not a straight-line continuation of earlier Judeo-Christian theology, as scholastic theology was not a straight-line continuation of patristic theology, as positive theology was not a straight-line continuation of scholastic theology, and as anthropocentric and existential theology was not a straight-line continuation of positive theology.

The fact that political theology is not a straight-line continuation of the earlier existential theology does not mean, however, that the question of life's meaning has disappeared. Dorothee Sölle makes it clear that the new political criterion of theology "does not mean that the whole question of individual existence is to be muted or left aside as something nonessential. Rather, it means that even this question can only be solved in terms of social conditionings and in the context of societal hopes and expectations" (396:70). How exactly are such existential questions to be rehabilitated and tackled in political theology? Sölle herself answers by saying that certain "existential" propositions (e.g., God's love and God's forgiveness) must be politically and socially mediated: "It just won't do to say simply and directly to someone, 'God loves you.' Since all reality is mediated through society and the world, that statement must also be politically mediated. It has meaning only when it signifies a movement to alter the status quo" (396:78).

Much the same is the case with divine reconciliation and divine pardon. Can one really imagine any direct pardon from God that would not be mediated through the pardon offered by other human beings? The reconciliation that God offers sinners has to be mediated socially in institutions and groups that will permit human beings to rehabilitate themselves in the eyes of society, work out their past guilt, and begin truly new lives (396:110–119).

The question of existence and the meaning of life does not disappear in political theology. Political theology goes beyond existential theology, but it picks up the legitimate questions of the earlier theology. Anticipating and paraphrasing a text in which Sartre tries to clarify the relationship existing between the philosophy of existence and dialectical theory (see chapter 3, section 1), we might view theological questioning about existence as an enclave or subdivision within a politically mediated theology. It is no longer acceptable or proper to propose such questions in isolation, much less to attempt to build an entire theology around them. But the basic question of existence does retain its own identity and relative autonomy within a broader political interpretation of the gospel.

The incorporation of the basic existential question into a political theology preserves it from a new or different kind of partialism and one-sidedness, one in which all other human differences and specific determinations would be dissolved in the political element. The clear perception that in man everything is mediated politically is not to be confused with the unfounded and totalitarian assumption that everything is politics. Not everything is politics: "There are realities which cannot be encompassed in all their aspects by the political dimension" (175:1064). Language, science, love, art, and so forth, are not political realities even though they are politically mediated. The danger facing present-day political theology is that it will equate the universal mediation of the political element with exclusive consideration of one and only one theme, thereby reducing theological reflection to a commentary on the political conditionings and consequences of the faith. It is a real danger, for in fact we are now witnessing an almost complete disregard for many critical and decisive theological questions: e.g., the linguistic analysis of Christian expressions, the psychoanalysis of the believer's consciousness, and confrontation with science in general and the various scientific disciplines in particular. It is as if the decisive role of political reality cancelled out other realities of a different nature—linguistic, psychogenetic, esthetic, cultural, and so forth.

The political formulation of theology does not rule out treatment of nonpolitical themes and topics: for example, theologal language, the relationship of faith to desire for the absolute, and the relationship of Christian "truth" to the truths of science. It does not eliminate the whole question of the meaning of life and death. It does not try to overlook the fact that concrete people are confronted with personal situations (e.g., love, vocation, parenthood, and moral decision-making), which are given configuration by the political sphere, but are not political in themselves. Political theology is not, and should not be, a simplistic reductionism that conveniently overlooks realities and questions that are not directly political.

The political awareness of people today does not rule out dedication to activities that are not political, such as science, art, technology, or simply love. It is somewhat disconcerting to see how some contemporary theologians seem to disdain any activity that does not have to do with liberty and societal change. There are traces of monomania in such an attitude. However modest grammar may seem by comparison with revolution, it too is necessary and useful. A new and different society will need teachers of grammar as well as leaders, to suggest just one simple example. The point is that a political interpretation of the gospel will not vitiate the relevance of questions dealing with theological grammar, syntax, and semantics (to keep the same example), however modest such questions may seem by comparison with the questions of freedom and the overthrow of oppressive power. There are ways of teaching grammar, fostering literacy, and analyzing language that are truly liberative and perhaps even revolutionary.

Political theology rules out earlier theologies insofar as the only possible theology today is one that is politically mediated, cognizant of its socioeconomic conditionings, and applied to making clear the social relevance of the gospel message. But that does not mean that all its questions must be directly and immediately political. Though mediated and conditioned by the political, many questions that are not directly political remain legitimate and unavoidable: questions of language, knowledge, the genesis of personality, the meaning of existence, and so forth. All such questions touch upon faith and prohibit theology from a one-track discourse about political praxis.

2

The Rejection of Christendom*

1. CONSTANTINIANISM AND CHRISTIAN INSTITUTIONS

The current focus on the political activity of Christians as a theme for theological discussion is a result of the demise of the Constantinian era—that is to say, of the long time span, symbolically opened by Constantine, during which Western civilization and Christianity formed one corpus in which civil power and ecclesiastical authority were closely linked.

"Constantinianism" is by now the conventional shorthand term for an ecclesiastical period that lasted for fifteen hundred years, from the Edict of Milan in A.D. 313 to the revolutions of modern history. Needless to say, it takes in a wide variety of situations and conditions in church history, including a time when the church served as the teacher of clerics in the various domains of the Goths, a time when empire and papacy vied with each other for power, and a time when national monarchs began to exercise political and religious absolutism. The generic term is used to cover

*Two terms, *cristiandad* and *cristianismo,* are now frequently used in theological discussions by Spanish-speaking commentators, and they are used in contrast to each other. *Cristianismo* ("Christianity") refers to the "Christian message" whereas *cristiandad* ("Christendom") refers to the social, political, and religious culture or complex that dominated the European and Mediterranean world for centuries. The latter term now tends to have negative connotations. —Trans. note and indeed obscure such historical vicissitudes as the shift from an age when popes amicably consecrated emperors to an age when bitter disputes arose over ecclesiastical benefices.

Indeed it is highly debatable whether the era of "Constantinianism" was inaugurated by Constantine himself, and so the appellation itself is open to some question. His role was mostly symbolical, rather than real and historical, though medieval popes often invoked the supposed Donation of Constantine. He himself can hardly be considered a Christian emperor, and he was followed by emperors who actually persecuted Christians. The Edict of Milan did inaugurate a period in which Christianity became the authorized religion; but of at least equal importance was the decree of Theodosius in Thessalonica in 380, which made it the obligatory religion and fostered the implacable suppression of pagan forms of worship. It was Theodosius, far more than Constantine, who resorted to religious unity as the chief recourse in attempting to overcome the crisis facing his empire.

Today we still find vestiges of the Constantinian regime in certain countries. Some, for example, still uphold Catholicism as the official religion of the nation. But for some time now people have felt that the dissolution of that basic system is virtually complete.

If we take "Christendom" to mean a society configured after a Christian mold or by Christians, then "Constantinianism" is merely one form of Christendom. The end of the Constantinian era has not meant the termination of the whole idea of Christendom, that is, of the direct and immediate translation of Christianity into concrete sociopolitical institutions. Quite the contrary seems to be the case. The dissolution of the Constantinian system seems to have brought the question into sharper focus and aroused attempts to deal with it. As the separation of church and state became a reality, Christians were confronted with the explicit issue of deciding how to act as Christians in the public arena of civil society. The question was more acute for Catholics than for Protestants, because the latter had for some time tended toward a purely private, interior religion. The Catholic bent was more directed to modelling society and culture, and hence it could not help but wonder what should be done, once the older system had crumbled, to give configuration to a political society now juridically independent of religious principles.

Alongside the older Constantinian idea there now arose a new, postconstantinian idea of Christendom. There is a danger that present-day political theology may be confused with either the older or the newer version, thereby losing its own real sense and thrust. While its differences with the older Constantinian notion are readily apparent, its differences with the more recent version of the Christendom ideal are not quite so obvious. The possible confusion is compounded by the fact that some present-day theologians feel that they are in continuity with the theologians of an earlier day who pondered the possibilities of a new Christendom. Hence it is most important clearly to distinguish between present-day political theologies and the theology of Christendom or New Christendom.

In the Protestant sphere political theologies arose primarily as a reaction against a theology of private, subjective religion. In the Catholic sphere, by contrast, political theologies must be viewed primarily as a reaction against the theological ethics of the Christendom system or ideal. Hence we should say something about the more modern ideal of a New Christendom and the institutions designed to make it a reality. The project had to do with Catholicism primarily, and so we must refer to it for the concrete details of the history and doctrine involved.

The Constantinian system was immediately followed by the rise of specifically Christian institutions. Around the turn of the twentieth century we see in Catholic circles the rise of the first institutions designed to provide a Christian model for a society that now saw itself as emancipated from the church. There arose such institutions as the parochial school, the Christian labor union or *syndicat,* and popular political parties that would eventually become the Christian Democrats. All these institutions were designed to pave the way for a New Christendom and to incarnate Christian policies and politics in a society now legally dissociated from the church. Their aim was to create a more Christian society, or a society that was in fact "Christian as such." The struggle for these new institutions was pushed most vigorously in those countries where the separation of church and state was effected more rapidly or more thoroughly.

Somewhat later, during the second third of the twentieth century, a different set of organizations arose to enlist in the crusade for a new Christendom. They were primarily concerned with the spiritual dimension rather than the political dimensions. It was the golden age of Catholic Action, the Movement for a Better World, and various *cursillo* activities in Spain and other analogous programs for Christian formation in other places. These movements and groups trained people for the apostolate, but it was taken for granted that those trained would move into their own proper sphere of activity and forge the guideline for sound Christian politics and soundly Christian institutions.

Political activity designed to build a New Christendom or a more Christian society did not seem proper for clerics. It was to be the work of lay people, and so the day of the laity had come. With the dissolution of the Constantinian system and the appearance of a society free from church tutelage, lay people would be needed to incarnate the ideal of a New Christendom in the political realm. To do this, however, they would have to be trained and given sound spiritual formation. Catholic Action provided both the people and the spiritual training, but it must not be forgotten that the political movement of Christian Democracy long antedated Catholic Action. The latter, therefore, served the aims of the former. The theology of the laity and the whole theory of the lay apostolate formed part of the idea-set of the New Christendom movement and was ordered to the aims of a Christian politics.

The postconstantinian ideal of a New Christendom waxed strong for just about a century. From the death of Pius XII in 1958, or perhaps more certainly from the end of Vatican II in 1965, it has virtually faded out of the picture. Not all Catholics are aware of that fact, and this has led to more than a little confusion and ambiguity. When some people now talk simply about the politics *of Christians,* others still take that to mean *Christian* politics. Confusion and conflict between the two groups is inevitable because seemingly identical terms actually entail very different practical procedures and operations by virtue of key differences in outlook.

To make the difference clear, it should be pointed out that present-day political theology does not in any way presuppose the existence or possibility of a Christian politics. In fact it expressly rules out that idea, as we shall see in section 8 of this chapter. The political praxis of Christians, a key theme of the current political theologies, has little if anything at all to do with the Christian politics envisioned by the earlier movement.

Today there is really no place for a Christian politics because the ideal of a new Christendom has lost all credibility and respect. The two ideas (a Christian politics and a New Christendom) are closely bound up with each other; they rise and fall together. Thus in the writings of Eduardo Frei of Chile, Christian Democracy is described as an effort to provoke a Christian revolution and to create a New Christendom (393:64).

Later on we shall consider the factors that led to the

collapse of this movement. Here we need only verify the collapse itself by considering the situation in the 1970s. Basically we are witnessing the expiration or the death throes of the movements and institutions inspired by the ideals of fashioning a New Christendom. Catholic Action is already past history. Christian labor-unionism long ago gave up its denominational cast. The bishops of France and the United States are less and less inclined to invest more money and personnel in the parochial school system. Christian Democratic parties, which held power in many countries up until quite recently, are now being displaced by Socialist governments (180). The dream of a New Christendom and its heyday have faded away. It now seems as unsalvageable as the Constanian era which it succeeded.

2. THE IDEA-SET OF THE NEW CHRISTENDOM MOVEMENT

The ideal of a Christian society, though now defunct, played an important historical role in its day and was instructive in many senses. Present-day political theology does not have the same idea-set as the New Christendom movement, nor anything like it, but it does incorporate the heritage of that earlier movement in some respects even as it opposes it or supplants it in others.

As the most recent tradition to be incorporated and supplanted, the theology of the New Christendom movement retains interest today. It has been abandoned by most, to be sure, but the newer theology derives from it even as it derives from the earlier anthropocentric theology. If we wish to know whither political theology is moving, we must know from whence it came and from what theology it has broken away. An examination of the doctrine of the New Christendom movement will serve the same purpose that our examination of humanist and existentialist theology did. It will help us to situate political theology in its proper relationship (of continuity and discontinuity) with the immediately prior theology.

The New Christendom ideal was "a concrete historical ideal," notes Jacques Maritain, defining it over against existing reality on the one hand and an unrealizable utopia on the other. It was "a prospective image, a viable possibility with the power to attract and combine the activities of human beings in a given historical moment" (245:134–35).

One sharp difference between the New Christendom ideal and that of the medieval age was that the former vigorously maintained the distinction between the spiritual and the temporal spheres. The Christendom of the medieval period was constituted as a sacral order while the New Christendom would only be a profane order, that is, "a lay city that was vitally Christian," or "a lay state constituted along Christian lines" (245:182). New Christendom, then, took for granted the desacralization of the political order, though this did not mean that there would not be an ethical and religious cast to temporal society (245:178).

It also assumed that Christians would be the chief officials of society and its main political agents. Otherwise it would be difficult to picture a politics of Christian inspiration. But even though this project, insofar as it was Christian, assumed that "Christians would assume the initiative in it, 'all men of good will' were called to collaborate" (242:271). Thus the New Christendom movement took its name from the fact that Christians would be the main motivating force and agents behind it; but its actual political structures would be lay structures because nonbelievers would participate in it on humanist and ethical bases shared by all people of whatever faith.

There were grave ambiguities, if not outright contradictions, imbedded in the idea of a state that was both lay and Christian in inspiration. How was its lay character to be reconciled with its Christian inspiration? Its proponents, however, did not feel disturbed by any such ambiguity, and so they sought to maintain three basic principles with equal assurance: (1) the lay character of political institutions; (2) the underlying Christian inspiration of the state; (3) the full incorporation of non-Christians into the state by virtue of its temporal aims as a civil society.

Christians could be the main protagonists as a majority group or a minority group. In principle it was assumed that the countries involved would be places where believers and baptized people constituted the majority of the citizenry. This was the sociological hypothesis that gave plausibility to the historical ideal of the new Christendom movement. As a majority group wielding the most power and influence, Christians would model society after their own taste —which is to say, according to their own consciences as molded by the gospel message. As one involved organization with headquarters in Assisi put it, they would work for a Christian city *(Pro civitate christiana)*. But of course non-Christians would be allowed to live and participate actively in this new city and its Christian politics.

"Tolerance" towards those who did not share Christian beliefs came to be an important principle in this movement, and it was not too difficult to find support for this principle in tradition. Medieval Christendom itself showed clear signs of flexibility in this regard as well as a capacity to incorporate believers in other religions. Religious intolerance and intransigence came to the forefront toward the end of the medieval period as heresies appeared on the scene. This was followed by the growth of absolutism and the linking of orthodoxy with national allegiance *(cuius regio ejus religio)*. The theorists of the New Christendom movement looked back past the modern age and the age of absolutism to earlier medieval times, and thus they did not find it difficult to reconcile the ideal of Christendom with that of tolerance. But the notion of tolerance itself made it clear what sort of society was envisioned: a society where

Christians represented the majority and permitted non-Christians to enjoy equal rights in society. In the New Christendom nonbelievers would occupy a place like that occupied by the Jews in medieval Christendom.

As the process of dechristianization proceeded apace in the world, it became increasingly difficult to maintain this basic formulation of the matter. Christians were increasingly turning into a minority faction in society. How could one envision the restoration of the medieval sociopolitical situation? The original ideal began to be whittled down, so that people began to talk more about a "more Christian society" rather than about a "New Christendom." One would not need a Christian majority to make society more Christian. All it would take would be a minority that was truly the "leaven in the mass" and that acted as such. This gave rise to an ideology suited to motivate minority Christian groups and make them aware of their leavening role in the amorphous multitude. Such groups could really infuse a Christian sense and Christian values into society. Moreover, the difference between a more Christian society and a New Christendom was one of degree rather than of kind. At the right moment there could be a transition from the former to the latter.

The basic tactic in the new line of strategy (a Christian minority acting as the leaven in the mass) was that believers would somehow come to occupy key positions in society. Chenu cites an episode recounted by Father Godin that provides a perfect illustration of how this would work. The personnel director of a large factory offered Godin a chance to have some dozen devout Christians placed in strategic moral, social, and spiritual positions in the factory. Godin refused, but note his reasons: "Let them remain a leaven in the pure state, as leaven intermingled in the mass. In three or four years, when their number has risen to thirty or forty, then you might propel a dozen or so into key positions." In short, he accepted the basic strategy of Christians occupying key positions, but he preferred to delay that step until the leavening process had proceeded further. Chenu, writing in 1944, remarks that "this is the gospel sense and approach" (138:118–19). It may well have been in the forties and fifties. It does not seem to still be that today, even though a few religious institutes are still motivated by the goal of occupying critical spots and posts in the social system.

3. A THEOLOGICAL ETHICS FOR POLITICS

The New Christendom ideal presumed it was possible to have a specifically Christian social doctrine. Christianity had its own distinctive solution to contribute to perplexing social problems. Over against the communist model on the one hand and the liberal model on the other, the Christian faith offered a third model of society with its own distinctive features drawn from the gospel message. Thus the heyday of the New Christendom movement coincided with the heyday of the church's social doctrine. For the latter did not just enunciate certain lofty moral principles about justice, peace, authority, private property, the family, and the common good. It also contained a concrete and fairly detailed image of the society that was to be fashioned along Christian lines.

The doctrine of the New Christendom movement was characterized by a welter of very specific details and descriptions. It did not allude in vague terms to some sort of society imbued with a gospel spirit. The New Christendom had a very distinct and precise physiognomy of its own; it was a distinctive social order and state of affairs with very concrete and specific features. Rather than being a vague label, New Christendom signified a clear-cut sociopolitical system with precisely defined institutions and functions.

The theoreticians of this New Christendom knew, or thought they knew, where they were going. They could describe in detail what this future society was to be like.

At the same time, however, it must be noted that their doctrine dealt directly with a Christian order, not with Christian praxis or political activity in general. This differentiated it clearly from other idea-sets concerned directly with practical ways of modifying society rather than with anticipatory descriptions of some future society. In this respect the idea-set of New Christendom represented a static conception of the social realm. It focused on how social relationships were or ought to be, not on the mechanisms of social change or on the transforming efficacy of action.

The New Christendom doctrine was not to be confused with the political theology propounded by Carl Schmitt. Maritain emphasized that very point, even though he allowed that his own position might be considered a political theology if that term was understood in a different sense. Maritain notes that Schmitt's political theology dealt with a political order that was sacred rather than profane (245:106–7). It was a theology for the older Christendom of the Holy Roman Empire, whereas his doctrine was meant for a profane Christendom. Viewed in these terms, we should distinguish three very different types of political theology: (1) a political theology for a sacral Christendom modelled after the holy empires of the distant past (Schmitt); (2) a political theology for a profane Christendom, whose social ethics and Christian politics is designed to establish and guide a lay state of Christian inspiration (Maritain); (3) present-day political theology, which does not include any Christian politics and which is not meant for a specifically Christian society.

Though in one sense the theology of the New Christendom might be considered a political theology, it is not a theology mediated through the political realm. In it politics makes contact with theology only via ethics, that is to say, through the ethical consequences of dogma. Rather than being a political theology, it is a theological ethics of societal life and politics. The structures of traditional dogmatics remain untouched and unaltered, only now they display and unfold practical consequences in society and public life. There is no political mediation of theology, no political interpretation of the gospel; there is simply an extension of theological ethics to political realities.

This ethico-theological cast still shows up clearly in such recent works as those of Paupert (335) and Coste (123), which in no way can be situated within the confines of what we undertand here by political theology. Both works deal with theology and politics, but neither offers a theology that is politically mediated. Theirs is still a theology of Christendom, or of a Christian society; and they share the conviction that there is a Christian or evangelical politics. Nothing in Catholic dogmatics is changed at all. This is clear, in general, in the books written by Coste. His ethical perspectives are in line with the most traditional dogmatic criteria. Adhering completely to what Catholics have always believed and expressed, Coste continues to talk about the two sources of morality—that is, natural law and the gospel (124:131–62)—and the existence of a Christian political ethics derived from obedience to God's divine commandments (123:71–72). In a book on international morality he can still talk about the "universal attraction of the risen Christ" (124:156) and Christ's Mystical Body (124:180). The basic timbre of such a theology of politics is therefore clear enough. It is caught ambiguously in the tension between a forthright recognition of the profane element in modern society and a nostalgic yearning for a society that is Christian in inspiration. This simple example illustrates a well-known fact: Not everything written on politics by theologians since the emergence of political theologies holds strictly to our notion of politically mediated theologies.

4. THE MEDIEVAL WORLD AS MODEL

The picture drawn by the New Christendom movement is essentially related to the past. Such a relationship is to some extent inevitable in any historical project. Prospective models of a future society cannot be built except on the basis of backward-looking models of past societies. Human projects of all sorts are composed of concrete experiences and memories. That does not mean we are incapable of projecting a future that cannot be reduced or equated with the past, but it does mean that our attempt to imagine some future must deal with materials already provided by earlier experience.

The inescapable role of past experience and historical recollection was not the only thing, however, which made the New Christendom doctrine turn to the past, and to the Middle Ages in particular. There was also a nostalgic yearning to recapture a lost paradise, a paradise which had almost been achieved in the Christendom of medieval Europe and which then crumbled under the impact of the modern age. Liberalism and communism represented the modern spirit that had come to birth on the ashes of medieval Christendom. To offer a third approach over against these two modern alternatives, one had to go back to the distant past and to reject the modern temper—though that was not always admitted outright. The Middle Ages offered the model and prototype that was now to be reproduced. That model had to be reworked and corrected in some respects, of course, because it certainly had not been perfect. The main corrective feature would be the desacralization of the political realm. To put it another way, one would have to affirm clearly the distinction between the sacred and the profane realms, between the spiritual order and the temporal order.

The renunciation of modernity, however, cost dearly. In configuring itself to a slightly corrected model of medieval

Christendom, the idea-set of the New Christendom movement ignored almost all the processes and situations that are typical of our own age: e.g., industrial development, the production system, the division between social classes, the anonymity of huge urban concentrations, the growing identity of political power and economic power, the manipulation of public awareness through advertising and political propaganda, and so forth. All such features that characterize the present moment in history were bypassed as if they did not exist at all. The picture of New Christendom—and the social teaching of the church which was closely associated with it for a long time—corresponded to a rural society of peasants and artisans that had flourished before the industrial age. In that earlier society each individual had his small piece of property, his family, and his guild. In that society the problems of authority were restricted to bringing the separate wills and wishes of all together into harmony, the presumption being that people were basically well disposed though sometimes in disagreement.

This optimistic and idyllic image contained large doses of naiveté and lack of realism. It was thus almost wholly incapable of offering valid alternatives to the existing social system in our own time. Indeed the social doctrine of the church was harshly criticized precisely because it was inoperable. It proposed goals that were alluring to some extent, but it totally lacked means to effect those goals. Its idyllic view of social relationships in the industrial age rendered it incapable of seeing the structures of oppression and domination that had warped the very fabric of the capitalist system. To be sure, the proponents of a more Christian society did notice and denounce some of the more flagrant injustices. But they viewed these injustices as passing episodes or accidental features of the economic system, failing to discern their structural character or even to grasp the many less patent forms of organized violence in the capitalist system. Hence the doctrine espousing a Christian society was reformist rather than revolutionary. It considered social justice to be possible within structures of bourgeois society, so long as these were properly corrected to diminish the inhuman situations to which they might give rise. Thus one can understand the point of the Marxist criticism levelled against Christian social doctrine. This doctrine, it said, rebukes capitalism in the name of an ideal that is linked up with an outmoded and superseded mode of production; hence, despite its good intentions, it is at bottom conservative (43:27).

5. A THEOLOGY OF CORPORATISM

This whole conception of society was bound up with certain specific theological representations. The notion of the kingship of God and Christ, for example, was brought forth for the purpose of producing specific political effects. The aim was not necessarily to legitimate a monarchical system of government, but it certainly was to vindicate the rights and perhaps even privileges of the Christian religion in society (the image of priests representing a God who ruled over and above civil governments, the rights of the true religion over those of false religions, and so forth). The notion that God himself had dictated positive precepts and hallowed the natural moral law was also invoked to immobilize the social structure in its most traditional forms and prejudices. The potential political clout and essentially conservative impact of those theological notions are familiar enough, though it is only recently that theologians have taken cognizance of them in a critical way.

So far, however, little notice has been taken of another link between theology and politics that has been of major importance. It has to do with the doctrine of Christ's Mystical Body and the clear-cut preference for some form of corporatism in the church's social teaching. Needless to say, there is no direct political thesis in the theological notion that Christians mystically form one body in Christ. This notion applies to the church, to an order of spiritual communion and communication, not to civil society and political organization. But one cannot fail to notice the fact that the theology of the Mystical Body attained its greatest development and splendor precisely during a period when the church was voicing its predilection for a corporatist solution to social problems. There is a basic and important similarity between the societal corporatism of *Quadragesimo Anno* (1931) and other papal documents on social questions on the one hand, and the mystical corporatism of *Mystici Corporis* (1943) on the other. I am not suggesting that the social corporatism of the one is deduced from the mystical corporatism of the other as its practical and political application. Nor am I suggesting that the later encyclical appeared as a posteriori theological justification for some sociopolitical stance. I am simply saying that they share some structural affinity and reciprocal relationship. They share one and the same vision of the human world, a vision applied in one to civil society and in the other to mystical communion.

Thus the theology of the Mystical Body, despite its seeming aloofness from social reality, betrays clear political connotations. It readily lends itself to a political reading. It makes very clear the fact that in the context of Christianity political attitudes do tend to be supported by religious ideas; and that religious ideas, for all their seeming detachment from the social conflicts of a given age, do play an intermediary role in those conflicts and instigate a specific line of praxis.

In the case of the New Christendom doctrine, the impact of mystical corporatism was to give rise to essentially conservative effects. The corporate image and principle consistently operated in the interest of conservatism and the defense of existing hierarchies and the standing order.

Once citizens were pictured as members of the same body, the old apologetic would immediately go on to note that there could only be one head and then a diversity of lesser organs. Each individual had an assigned role—as a hand, a foot, or whatever. Usually these explanations were addressed to those who, by some inexplicable and mysterious design of divine providence, were assigned to be the hands and feet performing the most thankless work. The appeal to social corporatism consistently was used to make sure that the members who performed the more lowly but necessary functions would not rebel. Here again the twofold corporatism of the New Christendom doctrine proved to be extremely conservative in cast.

This conception was linked up with another traditional Christian idea that was particularly emphasized by Protestantism and its ethics of vocation. God had placed each person in a particular place. There, in a social niche and a place within the divinely ordained social hierarchy, each person was to find holiness and salvation. Calderón spotlighted that notion in *El gran teatro del mundo,* and people looked to St. Paul for biblical justification of it: "The general rule is that each one should lead the life the Lord has assigned him, continuing as he was when the Lord called him" (1 Cor. 7:17). The celibate was to continue as a celibate, the married person as a married person, and the slave as a slave. But those who looked to this text tended to forget that Paul was expecting the imminent end of the world. Now, however, that end does not seem to be clearly in sight, and the possibility of a change in personal or social status is a real issue, one which Paul had not pondered and for which he would have felt there was not even enough time left. Paul's conception of the urgent need to prepare oneself for the parousia and not to waste time about changing one's social status certainly cannot be extrapolated into a theology wherein God clearly assigns a certain and unchangeable social status to each individual.

6. THE JESUS ERA

The heyday of the New Christendom movement was also a time of extraordinary optimism in the inherent potential of the Christian faith and its brilliant prospects for the near future. The middle years of the twentieth century were marked by high hopes for the future of Christianity. People seriously believed that the real evangelization of the earth was just about to begin. Freed of all traits of Constantinianism, the gospel message was now going to unfold all its formidable spiritual potential. These hopes and beliefs were fostered by the great Christian awakening that took place during those years. There appeared a generation of Christians who were keenly aware of their faith and their responsibilities to the world. The intellectual and spiritual level of the clergy rose sharply, attaining heights rarely reached in past history; and theology and other ecclesiastical disciplines also underwent a resurgence. All these factors helped to foster spectacular hopes.

The basic conviction was that the gospel message had so far only given a hint of its true potential, that now it would display its full power. Far from being outmoded or depleted, it was now in the bloom of youthful vigor. Christianity was still in its adolescence and only now would it bring about its own revolution in the world. In 1937 Chenu cited Sertillanges and Mauriac to make the point that we might still be primitive Christians: "We are still in the first springtide bloom of Christianity." A few centuries from now people might well view our age as "one of the very early stages of the Church" (139:81–82).

The apostasy of the laboring classes, which was a major preoccupation of the church at the time, seemed to have peaked and to be on the decline. The leaven of the gospel, noted Chenu, "is already at work in these masses, and working-class life as such is not impervious to the presence of Christ." Chenu predicted with bold assurance: "We are now entering a new era for Christendom; as the first Christians of this new era, we can sense its creative impulse and its air of apostolic youthfulness" (139:98–99).

This notion of a specifically Christian revolution seemed to go hand in hand with the conviction that the Christianization of society would require something more than cautious reformism. During the years immediately preceding Vatican II, not infrequent were proposals that, accepting the liberal and Marxist revolutions as accomplished facts, pointed to the coming of a third revolution that would be effected by Christians. In pointing to Christianity as "a revolutionary force" existing in any situation and capable of shaking the foundations of the social system by its perduring option for the oppressed, such proposals anticipated one of the most basic themes of the present-day theology of revolution. But they also remained firmly entrenched in the suppositions of the New Christendom movement and its hopes for the immediate universalization of Christianity insofar as they regarded this third revolution as a specifically Christian one (178:10–11, 85–86, 161–72).

Ardent hopes for a coming Christian era also were enkindled in certain people who were passionately interested in, or devoted to, apostolic action. Teilhard de Chardin envisioned and proclaimed the convergence of religions into a Christian focus (401:137–42). Father Lombardi broadened and broadcast the hopeful expectations of Pius XII, confidently stating that the coming era would be "the era of Jesus" (262:60) and formulating a manifesto for it (262:355–58). People recited the rosary for the conversion of Russia and, relying on the promises made at Fatima, felt that event could be dated for the very near future. It was a time of high hopes and great expectations shared by both the average faithful and Christian intellectuals. The former were offered preaching programs and populist Christian campaigns by such figures as Father Peyton and Billy Graham. In more sober fashion intellectuals formulated philosophies or theologies of history to give rational verisimilitude to these hopes. Berdyaev looked forward to a third "theandric" age, to an age or era of the Spirit (69:405–24). Even Maritain, little inclined to lyricism, was captivated by the themes of the moment: "Insofar as the effective implementation or realization of the gospel message in the socio-temporal order is concerned we are still in a prehistoric era." He, too, looked forward to a "third age" of Christianity that would be characterized by the humanism of the Incarnation.

7. THE FADING OF THE NEW CHRISTENDOM IDEAL

Having examined the basic stance and thrust of the New Christendom idea-set, one can readily guess where it has been open to critical attack and why it is now eclipsed. Its weakest point was precisely the social basis that sustained it: i.e., Christians as the majority force in society. The diminishing social and political weight of Christians made it impossible to expect any realization of a New Christendom. The dream seemed plausible only in a few countries where such a majority did in fact exist. But now, on the international scene or even in Western civilization alone, one could not really picture Christians as the leaders of a society leavened by their presence. Believers had lost the initiative, which moved elsewhere in society. The hoped-for era of Jesus had not arrived, and it seemed to be moving further and further away. In all likelihood it will never come. Confident expectations for the preaching of the gospel message were disappointed. There was no social base to give plausibility to the idea of a society sustained by Christian initiative.

Quite aside from the majority or minority status of Christians in society, there was a new problem with regard to doctrine and Christian awareness itself. Not long before it had seemed almost self-evident that Christianity had its own distinctive concepts and principles regarding the social order; now that point seemed less and less obvious. Such principles as peace, justice, liberty, and the common good, for example, seemed to be much too vague. What is more they were hardly peculiar to Christianity. However they might be interpreted or applied, they dovetailed with one or another nonreligious idea-set about human society.

The possibility of imagining a specifically Christian society seemed even more dubious. A society in conformity with the gospel message seemed to be an impossibility no matter how you looked at it. For Christians, it would be impossible ever to believe that the gospel message could be wholly assimilated into any given society; for nonbelievers, such an idea seemed devoid of sense.

Associated with the notion that no specifically Christian idea-set exists with regard to political matters is the current conviction that there is no "middle way" or third alternative way *(tercerismo)* over against capitalism on the one hand and socialism on the other. There is a wide gamut of capitalisms and socialisms, and in fact Christians adhere to different varieties of each. But it seems more and more clear to some people that there are no third alternatives or intermediate positions between the two economic systems. At least since the first convention of the Christians for Socialism movement in Santiago, Chile (April 1972), the failure of Christian social *tercerismo* and its illusory character have been recognized (2).

To these critical factors undermining the basic suppositions of the New Christendom idea-set from within have been added other factors operating from the outside. They are the result of historical and cultural processes bound up with the introduction of historical-materialist thinking into the West, and they will be considered more closely in the next chapter. The simple fact to be stressed here is that the theory of a New Christendom has been undermined and eroded just as much as, if not more than, the humanist and existentialist theology that waxed strong during the same period. Both have been succeeded by a political theology.

The abandonment of the New Christendom ideal did not imply any disdain for the positive values it embodied. The very fact that it represented a rejection of the Constantinian system was in itself a positive merit. To fully appreciate the progressive features in the thinking of someone like Maritain, for example, one must take a look at the polemical attacks directed against it. There is, for example, the incredibly obscurantist attack of Palacios in *El mito de la nueva cristiandad* (329), which admirably reflects the reaction of older Constantinian thinking against the novel proposal for a truly lay society. If Maritain should prove to be right in his forecast for the future, if it should be necessary for the church to go back to the catacombs, he would return to them "earnestly believing that the confessional State is superior to a lay State, that theology is a superior science to philosophy, and that the rights of Gŏd are the unique and authentic foundation for the rights of man" (329:155). The positive and progressive features in the notion of a secular Christian society must be judged in terms of the earlier but persisting notions of a sacral Christian society, not in terms of notions that came later on.

Furthermore, the New Christendom ideal had the merit of avoiding the "privatization" of Christianity that is rightly denounced today by political theology. The proponents of that ideal appreciated the fact that putting a purely private connotation on the gospel message would ultimately evaporate its impact and meaning; that if Christianity was to have solid and consistent import, it would have to be associated with societal praxis. At a time when most theologians, particularly Protestant theologians like Bultmann, were celebrating the "nonwordly" character of the faith, the New Christendom doctrine possessed a much more comprehensive theological vision even though it did not always consider itself as theology in the strict sense; for it attributed social, political, and cultural significance to the gospel message through the mediating public praxis of Christians.

In short, the New Christendom doctrine was a "political theology" in its own way and was presented as such. Its political theology was profoundly different from present-day political theology in content, social presuppositions, and plans for the future. It differed radically with regard to the possibility of politics playing a mediating role in theology. At the same time, however, its formal structure did a good job of framing the exigencies that must be met by every political theology and every theory dealing with the social praxis of Christians, whether or not the New Christendom ideal survives.

This formal structure underlies its principal themes and theses and includes the following elements: a historical model (medieval Christendom); theological symbols (the sovereignty of God, the Mystical Body of Christ); a prospective model (a profane Christendom in the future); and a theory dealing with the activity of Christians (a strategy to make society more Christian). Present-day political theology may have a very different content. But if it is to justify its name, it must give an account of those same formal elements, explaining the exact nature of its hermeneutic symbols, its retrospective and prospective models, and the type of action to which the new critical, public, and practical awareness of Chrisians leads.

8. FURTHER CONTRASTS BETWEEN OLD AND NEW POLITICAL THEOLOGY

Most of the objections against present-day political theology ultimately derive from mistakenly confusing or identifying it with the political theology of yesterday and yesteryear. It is erroneously equated with some sort of secular or sacral Christendom. Spaemann falls prey to this mistake or confusion when he asks accusingly: "What kind of secular world is one in which Christians cannot act politically without the blessing of theology and need some sort of theological construct rather than sociology?" (398:186). His objection is off the mark. Today political theology does not imply any need for the blessing or favor of theologians with regard to the political activity of Christians. It does not mean that social analysis is to be replaced by some sort of theological ideology. By comparing it with the theology of the Christendom outlook we will be able to dispel such mistakes and to specify the exact nature of present-day political theology in various respects.

Present-day political theology is characterized, first of all, by its rejection of all forms of Christendom, be they sacral or secular. All its proponents tend to point up the clear-cut difference between it and the political theology of people like Carl Schmitt, who sought to justify some sort of holy empire. Current political theology presupposes separation between ecclesiastical institutions and civil authority. It expressly rules out the notion that the church might engage in the direct or indirect manipulation of politics (347). There is to be no going back to some sort of ecclesiastical tutelage over social life. The explicit assumption is that society is emancipated from Christian regulation (301:271). Thus the temptation to reinstate clericalism in civic life is vigorously rejected.

But current theology does not just reject clerically controlled government and the embodiment of the ecclesiastical message in politics, which was espoused by proponents of sacral Christendom. It also rejects the notion of a Christian politics, the desire to flesh out the gospel message directly in social structures, and the more general notion of achieving a Christian or more Christian society. Current political theology, in other words, has also rejected the platform of the secular Christendom movement. This is not always brought out clearly. And when it is not clearly understood, people sometimes try to smuggle in the ideological trappings of the New Christendom movement under the cloak of credibility and favor now enjoyed by political theologies.

The touchstone of up-to-dateness on that issue is whether a given political formulation of theology does or does not expressly exclude a Christian or evangelical politics. The characteristic note of current political theology is that it is not associated with any specifically Christian politics. As Gollwitzer puts it: "There is no Christian politics, just as there is no Christian medicine; there are simply Christians in politics" (216:31).To phrase it in terms of the theology of revolution: "There is no Christian revolution, but there are people who are revolutionary by virtue of their Christian sense of responsibility" (357:156). The nonexistence of a Christian politics or a Christian revolution means in practice that there is no specifically Christian solution for social problems (396:69), and also that the church possesses no uniquely or exclusively Christian capability of its own to provide a concrete model of the future (54:230).

For this reason certain lines of effort must be regarded as inopportune and hapless. Such is the attempt, for example, of those who try to present the symbol of the kingdom of God as if it embodied a real "theory," in the strongest sense of that word, for some "potential social organization" irreducible to any sociopolitical model existing outside the Bible (49:127–46). In some proposals of that sort we find a surreptitious biblical fundamentalism of dubious critical value and a continuing nostalgia for a Christian model of society that scarcely fits in with the overall stance and general formulations of current political theology.

Present-day political theology is also distinctively characterized by its original focus on the relationship between theory and praxis. Christendom theology was primarily an ethics. It had to do with the ethico-political consequences of dogma, with Christian love and Christian action as consequences of faith; but it did not have to do with the faith itself. It was political theology insofar as it embodied a social morality based on dogma and logically flowing from it. It presupposed a separation between dogmatic theology and moral theology, which today is regarded as "ideology" in the worst sense of the term (59:89). Present-day theology thinks it is highly debatable to "reduce love to a consequence of faith" (396:90). It favors and supports the mediation of politics, but not a theologically based politics (396:66).

Current political theology has a different understanding of the relationship between theory and praxis. As we shall see further in chapter 3, it does not regard praxis simply as a consequence of theory but rather as an internal factor in the very formation of theory. This allows for a political theology that is not just the moral corollary of a dogmatic theology fashioned out of very different categories. Today political theology is equivalent to a "political hermeneutics" of the gospel message or of the Christian profession of faith (396:68). The political factor comes to form a "basic, hermeneutic theological category" (313:17); it is no longer merely an ethical category. In an important passage, cited earlier in a different context, Dorothee Sölle uses a concrete theological phrase to illustrate clearly what political mediation in theology really means and how it comes to form the fundamental interpretative category: "In terms of political theology it just won't do to say simply and directly to someone, 'God loves you.' Since all reality is mediated through society and the world, that statement must also be politically mediated. It has meaning only when it signifies a movement to alter the status quo. Just suppose we make that statement to a person who has lived in one of the worst urban slums for fifteen years. The despicable treatment he has experienced there makes that statement incredible. It does not permit him to believe in God's love" (396:78).

In other words love for human beings, and for the oppressed in particular, is not simply the ethical consequence of the dogmatic fact that God loves us. To be meaningful and plausible, the very proclamation that God loves us calls for the mediation of politics, for a practical movement that will alter the existing social situation.

Current political theology also differs sharply from older political theology by virtue of its different conception of the political realm. Metz alludes to this particular difference when he makes the point that now the political factor is understood in terms of the Enlightenment distinction between the state and society (301:269). In general we may say that the new theology is in line with a qualitative change in the very meaning of the political realm and in contemporary political awareness. This change will be considered in more detail in chapter 3. Here we might simply note that it entails a real break with the older conception of the political. As Marcuse puts it: "The new possibilities for a human society and its surrounding world can no longer be pictured or imagined as the continuation of the old possibilities. They do not run in the same historical continuum. In fact they clearly presuppose a rupture in the historical continuum and the qualitative difference that exists between a free society and the unfree societies of the present day" (279:7).

In this respect political theology has to do with the absolute novelty of a truly free human society, a society that is possible today for the first time in history by virtue of our technological dominion over nature and our awareness that society can alter its own institutions—even those institutions that hamstring us by appealing to some alleged essential nature. Thus current theology is in discontinuity with all previous theology by virtue of our newfound awareness of a newly possible social liberty.

All this does not rule out the possibility that the categories of present-day political theology might be abused and manipulated for objectives alien to its true spirit. Maier cites some examples of its "integrist" use in Germany (273:

20–21). Eyt warns against the dangers of a new Christian political mythology fed by the lexicon of the leftist. He is afraid that Christians seem to be looking for a new Constantine, embodied now in the guerrilla fighter rather than in an emperor. The demythologizing of Constantinianism would thus go hand in hand with a new and alienating mythologizing: "It runs in a long line from Charlemagne to Che Guevara. Man typically tends to give ever new form and shape to his alienations" (175:1074–75).

The warning is not without merit or timeliness. Some expressions and formulations of current political theologies do seem to be of dubious theological quality. But in any case it is absolutely necessary to distinguish between the import of a theory or doctrine and the use or abuse to which it is subjected. A political hermeneutics of the gospel message may be utilized or manipulated to fashion a Christian politics, to restore some form of Christendom, or to further ecclesiastical interference in civil life. But such manipulation is completely opposed and alien to the authentic thrust of that hermeneutics.

Present-day theology has given up the idea of fashioning a model Christian society. It holds no preconceived idea as to what the social order ought to be like, much less some picture of a social order shaped by the gospel message. In its eyes there is no Christian order, no gospel politics. There is simply the public and critical praxis of Christians. This praxis is not just a consequence of the faith. Rather, it is intrinsic to the faith as a factor that sustains and determines its meaning.

3

The Era of Dialectical Thinking

1. CULTURAL MILIEU AND THEOLOGY

Christians definitely have to get rid of the idea that the phenomena that arise within the church and theology are due exclusively or even mainly to factors flowing from the inner dynamics of Christianity itself. Though this idea is widely propagated by pastors and theologians, it is completely illusory to think that movements for Christian renewal derive purely and solely from a return to the sources, a greater fidelity to the gospel message, or a better understanding of the faith. To be sure, these and other factors do play a role in all ecclesiastical reform or theological innovation. But they should not be given greater weight than they deserve nor, in particular, should they be isolated from factors external to Christianity. Among these factors the overall dynamism of societal history is a decisive one.

Theology cannot select its problems nor derive them from its own immanent system (245:563). This has been the case with all the theologies of the past, but only a political theology can assimilate this fact with full awareness and then go on to explain it.

Suppose someone were to think that the existential and personalist turn of theology in recent years came from a better understanding of the biblical schemas of intersubjectivity: covenant, grace, reconciliation, love, and so forth.

Such a view would be abstract, partial, and ultimately false because the interpretation of the Bible in terms of those schemas became possible and necessary under the pressure of a culture preoccupied with personal existence. In like manner, to think that the social doctrine of the church resulted exclusively from a consideration of the ethical exigencies of the gospel or natural law would be to indulge in antihistorical fantasy. For in fact that doctrine appeared as a reaction designed to overcome the dechristianization of the working masses and to strip atheistic Marxism of some of its social claims.

This is not to suggest that personalism and social uneasiness do not have any foundation in the Bible and the most ancient tradition of the church. It is simply to question the notion that its rise to conscious awareness in the church was due simply and solely to a sudden turning back to the foundations of the faith. Though such a turning back did take place, it did not spring out of thin air; it was the end result of a whole complex of influences stemming from the cultural milieu.

Neither did political theology come from nowhere, or from factors internal to the Christian community. It is sheer fantasy to think that the rise of political theology right now is due simply to a reconsideration of the basic sources of the Christian faith. That reconsideration is real enough, and it is the most immediate root of present-day political theology. But why did it arise precisely at this time? If its origin and deepest roots are to be found exclusively in the gospel and tradition, why did it take two thousand years to manifest itself?

The recent appearance of political theology, then, is due not so much to the traditional elements of Christianity as to the contemporary historical and cultural situation. A political theology is possible because there are grounds for it in biblical and Christian tradition. But it exists and is necessary today because the contemporary configuration of culture outside Christianity is pressing for such a theology. This phenomenon, the genesis of political theology on the basis of factors extrinsic to the faith, deserves to be examined at closer range.

Close examination of the cultural determinants of political theology helps to make clear in what sense political mediation defines the *kairos* of current theology; it also clarifies the historical and social import of that theology. Political theology is a response to a specific cultural situation, which I shall characterize here as chiefly influenced by the incorporation of dialectical reasoning and historical materialism into Western thought.

Such a characterization may be partial and one-sided, and it certainly is not exhaustive. Both in terms of a sociology of knowledge and, even more, in terms of the flow of ideas today, one could well maintain that Western society has still not found itself. But that is not the point here. Dialectical reasoning and historical materialism are stressed here because, independently of the degree to which they have penetrated into Western learning, the very fact of their penetration is the most original and important phenomenon of recent years. It also is the decisive phenomenon in the appearance and formulation of a new political theology. The following pages will trace the general outlines of dialectical reasoning and its progressive relationship with the human sciences. This may not cover the whole of the contemporary cultural scene, but it will cover one of the key elements in that scene and hence the precise point where the extra-ideological discourse has come to press upon theology and move it toward a political mediation.

2. THE HUMUS OF MARXISM

The shift from existential and humanist sensibilities to political awareness, and more specifically to a dialectical and historical materialist outlook is evident in every sphere of Western culture: in philosophy, in the organization of learning and knowledge, in the theater and the literary world, and even in the patterns of conduct. The jump from the existentialist approach to this different vision could be illustrated by many kinds of data. But perhaps none is more indicative than the "conversion" of Sartre himself, the patriarch of existentialism, to reasoning of a historical, materialist, practical, and dialectical cast.

It is now customary and necessary to distinguish between the first or early Sartre of existentialist phenomenology and *Being and Nothingness* (1943) and the second or later Sartre who has focused on the Marxist theory of groups in action (*Critique of Dialectical Reason,* 1960). The shift was not due solely to personal biographical reasons, or to reasons inscribed in the very logic of his early thinking. Apart from those reasons, which are real enough, Sartre's philosophical itinerary is in line with the general trend of philosophy, learning, and culture in the West.

And so we hear the "later" Sartre making this solemn declaration as if it were his own profession of faith: "I consider Marxism as the unsurpassable philosophy of our times, and I regard the ideology of existence as an enclave within Marxism itself" (371:9–10). Thus the "existential ideology" maintains its relative and provisional autonomy precisely at the fault-line where Marxism has so far failed to concern itself with the questioning subject of knowledge (371:107). The philosophy of existence, then, is reduced to the level of ideologies and only dialectical-materialist analysis is accorded the rank of an authentic theory and authentic knowledge. Sartre says: "Today Marxism appears to be the only possible anthropology that is both historical and structural, and also the only one which takes man in his totality, that is to say, in terms of the materiality of his condition" (371:107). This explains the new vitality that Marxism has taken on in recent years despite its authoritarian sclerosis in some communist regimes: "Far from being exhausted, Marxism is younger and fresher today. It is still a child almost, and it has barely begun to bloom. So it continues to be the philosophy of our time. We cannot get around it because we have not yet gotten beyond the circumstances that engendered it. Our lines of thought, whatever they may be, must be fashioned on that humus; they must be contained within the framework which it provides for them, otherwise they will be lost in a vacuum or debase themselves" (371:29).

These valuations of Sartre apply equally to theology. In the last analysis current political theology is nothing else but the thoughts produced by faith on the humus of Marxism. Even though people may not like to admit it, it seems hard to deny the correspondence existing between the incorporation of Marxist thinking into the awareness of Western culture and the sudden flowering of a political hermeneutics of the gospel message. Political theology is a theology operating under the sign of Marx, just as truly as scholasticism was a theology operating under the sign of Aristotle and liberal Protestant theology was one operating under the sign of Kant. The present-day dialogue between Christians and Marxists bears much similiarity with that between scholastic thinkers and Aristotelians in the twelfth and thirteenth centuries. If no real scandal has resulted from a dogmatics based on the concepts and categories of a pagan Aristotle, there is little reason to be shocked by a theology nurtured on Marx's analysis. But this incorporation does admit of various degrees and shades, and only a detailed treatment of the themes of political theology will enable us to evaluate it correctly.

3. CONTEMPORARY HISTORY AND THE HUMAN SCIENCES

If one wants to explain the recent theological and practical rapprochement with Marxist positions, one must look to a complex of events that followed World War II. While that war may have signified the definitive defeat of fascisms, one big question still remained unanswered in the victorious countries: Would liberal democratic governments or socialist regimes gain the upper hand? This question of hegemony has not yet been decided, but certain important events and processes have helped to tip the balance in favor of a socialist configuration of the world: the failure of liberal democracies in their programmatic attempt to effect greater social levelling; the liberation movements of oppressed minorities even in developed countries (blacks in the United States and Catholics in Northern Ireland); the liberation movements against colonialism (in Africa primarily) and against economic imperialism (in Latin America primarily); the configuration of a Third World marked by underdevelopment in cultural and economic life; the weariness produced by a consumer society in the affluent nations and the impatient search for alternatives (student protests, counterculture movements, sexual liberation, and so forth); and the long war in Vietnam as a more localized and scandalous embodiment of the aberrations and contradictions imbedded in the world of our day.

All these facts have helped to rule out the possibility of a neutral, apolitical, and purely humanist attitude such as that which prevailed among theologians prior to 1965, most of them citizens of liberal democracies in the West. Insofar as those events had a profound impact on public awareness in the Western countries, they also affected the sensibility of theologians. They could no longer go on with existentialist disquisitions; they were constrained to undertake political reflection. And it would not be hard to prove that the birth of various political theologies in our day was closely bound up with the revolutionary activity of Christians in Latin America and Africa, the civil rights struggle in the United States, the May 1968 revolution in France, and the student protest movement.

Each concrete version of political theology corresponds very closely to certain precisely defined social processes and praxis, as we shall see in chapter 5. Thus the very course of history in the last twenty-five years has operated as a decisive factor in the appearance of a political theology. That history has also given rise to another fact of major importance: the appearance, or rather, the consolidation of a new concept of science, particularly in the realm of the human sciences, which have now come to be viewed from what is essentially a practical, critical, political, and dialectical standpoint. This new concept of science is the proximate factor that has determined the political form of present-day theology. We must not forget that theology is *logos* or discourse, a discourse about God. It belongs to the universe of word and representation, not to the universe of happenings and things. Hence it is most directly and immediately influenced by any alterations effected in the cultural realm of word, representation, and discourse.

The aforementioned historical events have not intervened directly in themselves to effect the formation of a political theology. They have intervened indirectly through the mediation of certain theoretical and interpretative instruments provided by the human sciences in their new organization and approach. Though theology is not a science, it does tend to model itself after the pattern of the sciences, of those sciences dealing with humanity in particular. Changes produced in the epistemology of the human sciences have almost immediate repercussions on theology.

The disposition of the human sciences has an immediate influence on the disposition of theology itself, and so there is every reason to examine those sciences closely. The historical import of a given theology is ultimately signaled by history itself. But the historical processes involved are concretely apprehended only through a human learning that itself is configured by these same processes. So it becomes evident that it is our knowledge about ourselves (i.e., the human sciences) that exerts the proximate and decisive influence on theology.

On another front, the relationship between the new political theology and the current world situation has been discussed in detail by many people. In particular they have explained in rich detail how a political and liberative interpretation of the gospel is closely linked to the scandal of an oppressive, iniquitous society in which the privileges enjoyed by a few are paid for by the misery of the many. Less well known and less studied is the relationship between such a theology and the epistemological situation of the human sciences, and hence it is all the more worthwhile and interesting to explore that point here.

A truly strict consideration of the human sciences should devote attention to two interconnected questions: first, the possibility of dialectical comprehension in the natural sciences, and, second, a new look at the distinction between the so-called natural sciences and the human sciences at a time when the former are deeply involved in the human world and offer the capability of altering it (through genetics, biochemistry, cybernetics, and so forth). But important as those two questions are epistemologically, they do not really affect our inquiry here. So we shall prescind from those questions and their answers, moving on to discover affinities between the delineated shape of political theology and that of the human sciences. We take the latter in its traditional scope, which would include sociology, political science, economics, linguistics, psychology, ethnology, history, and so forth. These disciplines are undergoing a serious transformation that we shall now consider.

4. THE DISAPPEARANCE OF MAN

The first and foremost transformation that has taken place recently in the human sciences has been the disappearance of man. There is no contradiction or paradox involved in saying that man as such has disappeared from the human sciences. It simply means that in the now prevailing model of science there is no place for man as such—that is to say for man considered in terms of essence or nature.

Man does not exist for the sciences. There are no suitable scientific propositions in which man as such, in all his real or potential universality, figures as the subject. The only thing that is real—i.e., that is a reality that can be the object of knowledge and a possible subject of scientific propositions—are human groups, social classes, races, national or linguistic communities, historical generations, and historical epochs. And the all-encompassing totality that exists in this sense is human cultures.

So what we can have, properly speaking, is a theory or science of human cultures or of a specific culture. Even sciences that seem to talk about forces and processes consubstantial with man, such as depth psychology for example, really are speaking about nothing more than a man who is culturally specified: i.e., Western man: but they speak at a level of historical depth that makes it seem that the analysis is valid on an indefinite scale. Take for example the psychoanalytic theory of the Oedipus complex. It does not refer to some presumed human essence. It refers solely to a concrete man who has been procreated and raised in the well-defined family structure that has prevailed in the West. In a tribe where child-rearing is carried out differently, one need not get any Oedipus complex; nor does it seem to show up in an Israeli kibbutz. To the extent that instincts can be modified by history, every theory about them has limited validity within the boundaries of a specific culture.

The evaporation of man in the human sciences has been masterfully described by Michel Foucault in *Words and Things,* which is subtitled "an archeology of the human sciences." His remarks, by virtue of their pointedness and diverting tone, have won deserved fame: "Man is nothing more than a recent invention, a figure scarcely two centuries old, a mere crease in our thinking which will be ironed out when that thinking has found a new shape and form" (192:15 and 398). "Man and God," he notes, "are so bound up with each other that the death of the latter is synonymous with the disappearance of the former" (192:353 and 396). These biting remarks have been viewed by many as clever "jests" designed to scandalize prudish humanists, or merely as ideological hypotheses in which the structuralist viewpoint seeks by hyperbole to highlight the formalist propensities of modern science. But they are no such thing. Foucault is not jesting or being fanciful; nor is he simply expressing a personal view. What he is doing really is verifying and solemnly endorsing what has been going on in the realm of the human sciences. His anti-humanism is not that of a philosopher or a prophet but rather that of an observer and notary public. Neither he nor structuralism has invented the dissolution of man in the human sciences. That dissolution resides in the human sciences themselves, in the methodological line they have adopted.

The same is true when Lévi-Strauss says that "the ultimate aim of the human sciences is not to construct man but to dissolve him" (259:357). He is not expounding structuralist philosophy. He is simply echoing the awareness that the scientific scholar has of his own work. The eclipse of man is not the provocatory thesis of a snob ideology; it is the natural result of the orbit being circled by science today.

From the standpoint of the human sciences "humanism" seems to be nothing but a chimera, a curious amalgam of ideas about man that are partly positivist and partly philosophical (192:15). As Foucault puts it, a quiet philosophical smile is the only reaction to those "who would still like to talk about man, his realm, and his liberation, . . . who would still like to pose questions about the nature of man and take man as their starting point for their approach to truth . . ." (192:353–54). Scepticism is rising with a malicious smile on the very frontiers of learning. The impossibility of knowing who or what man is precisely is clearing the way for the scepticism of people from Nietzsche to Cioran, who made fun of human essences. The general reaction of amusement that greets any attempt in the West to fashion an essentialist anthropology seems related to the smile of the Buddha. He, too, reacted with a scarcely transcendent smile when asked about man or God (332:121–34).

For a while Marxism was concerned to present itself as a humanism, and it then spoke of a "socialist humanism" (13). The aim at the time was, undoubtedly, to counteract and erase the image of Marxism as a dehumanized and dehumanizing system, the image conveyed to the West by the Soviet regime. But Marxists, too, have moved away from the ideals of humanism. From a strict Marxist standpoint, humanism can only appear to be ideology. Althusser, for example, has noted this point and energetically denounced the ideological character and inherent dangers of the concept of humanism: "It is not possible to *know* anything about human beings unless one is willing to reduce to ashes the philosophical myth about man." The only way to talk about man in the concrete is to regard him as a "complex of social relationships" (44:236 and 254). Althusser leads off his remarks on "Marxism and humanism" with a quote from Marx's *Das Capital* that scarcely favors a humanist perspective: "My analytic method does not start off from man but from the social period that is economically given" (44:225).

The abandonment of humanism in the scientific study of the human being is in no way equivalent to a lack of concern for man in real life. The antihumanism of the human sciences has nothing to do with a presumed disinterest in, or distaste for, human beings, as is sometimes suggested reproachfully by those who have a poor or erroneous comprehension of the matter. The "human" that is the target of antihumanist opposition is not the human being existing in real life or real human groups; it is "humanity" understood in abstract or essentialist terms, the "human nature" that is alleged to be verified in all men, and the transcendental human subject of idealist philosophy. The rejection and dissolution of that sort of humanism can be noted not only among intellectuals addicted to a structuralist approach but also in the whole praxis of contemporary science. Present-day science is what it is precisely insofar as it keeps chipping away at a generic humanist ideology. Such an ideology is in fact rather a humanism "by default." In other words, it is a humanism characterized by deficient knowledge about man. Only by being willing to give up the humanist idea-set is it possible to truly know what human beings are and have been.

The decline of the older "humanisms" does not mean that we have lost the valuable estimation of man that they introduced. The fact is that the so-called "humanist" values have become part of the implicit suppositions of Western culture and Western thought, so much so that continued stress on them serves no real or meaningful function.

Humanism is incapable of serving as the backbone for any knowledge or action. We all inject what we want into that term. Humanism is nothing more than an abstract, formal principle, like justice or brotherhood, that can be filled with the most varied content. At one point in history the humanist principle was the indispensable proponent of respect for the human person and the valuation of man over everything else. But today, when that principle and that respect can be considered an integral part of Western culture, humanism is redundant in cultural terms. It simply affirms a point that is now clear and widely taken for granted. An appeal to man, to the dignity of the human person, or to some form of humanism, adds nothing to what are already the tacit assumptions of Western culture. If it adds anything at all, what it adds now is a note of vague opposition to the scientific approach to the study of man or to the predominance of technique and technology in societal organization. But one cannot help but feel suspicious of humanist language when one realizes that it has come to be part of the rhetoric of conservative ideologies.

Existentialism is passing into history right alongside humanism. Some Marxist writers have directed most of their criticism against existential philosophy: e.g., Lukács (268), Garaudy (203), Marcuse (282:55–94), and Adorno (38). But the effectiveness of their criticism is independent of their underlying presuppositions based on historical materialism. Today we may regard the existential bent as something that has evaporated (323:143–44). We are living in a posthumanist and postexistentialist era.

5. THE ROLE OF PRAXIS IN THE PROCESS OF KNOWING

Along with the rejection of humanism there is a shift away from positivism, from the analytical and positivist ideal of science. Today the positivist or neopositivist outlook still prevails in the so-called natural sciences, where dialectical thinking has so far made little headway. Not long ago Monod could still picture Marxist dialectics as a quasi-mythological vitalism (314:44–50). The scene is quite different in the human sciences. There the dialectical focus has taken almost complete control of the scientific field, so much so that the human sciences are now tending to be regarded as specialized branches of the general Marxist theory. At the very least they are being understood in dialectical terms.

To think in dialectical terms means to think in terms of two basic presuppositions: (1) In every knowledge process or science the observer is implicated in the observation itself; (2) the relation to the objects known is an eminently practical one, so that real knowledge is bound up not with pure contemplation but rather with the practical handling of things. This leads to a new definition of the relationship between theory and praxis. Scientific knowledge now tends to set itself up as social criticism. Science comes to serve a revolutionary function by proposing historical alternatives that are very different from the existing reality.

The inclusion of praxis in the very process of authentic knowledge breaks with the positivist ideal of a pure science that merely observes and remains apolitical, that "leaves things as they were before," to echo Wittgenstein's view of philosophy (422:167). This model of science as an uncommitted spectator is fading into history. The final battles for its total liquidation are now being fought in the lecture halls and on the campuses of universities around the world, as students since 1968 have joined in the fight against that older model (17:135–216). The present university crisis signifies, among other things, the cancellation of science's positivist, speculative, and apolitical model (186:275–80).

Underlying this reformulation of the relationship between theory (or science) and praxis is Marx's second thesis against Feuerbach: "The question of knowing whether human thought can arrive at an objective truth is not a theoretical question but rather a practical question. It is in practice that man must prove and test the truth—which is to say, the reality, power, and earthliness of his thinking. Any discussion about the reality or unreality of thinking which is isolated from praxis is a purely scholastic discussion."

In the strains of ancient Chinese wisdom Mao Tse-tung makes the same point, using simpler language: "Whence come man's correct ideas? Are they innate in his brain? No. Do they drop from heaven? No. They derive solely from social practice: the struggle for production, the class struggle, and scientific experimentation. . . . If you want to know, you must participate in practice, in the transformation of reality. If you want to know the flavor of a pear, you yourself must transform it by eating it. . . . If you want to know the theory and methodology of revolution, you must participate in revolution. All authentic knowledge is born of direct experience" (277:157 and 13–14).

This thesis, that knowledge originates in praxis, cannot be considered specifically Marxist today, however. It is imbedded in the deepest presuppositions of present-day science and culture, because it represents a configuration of Western thinking that goes back to the Enlightenment. Introduced into more modern Western thought by Marx, it is now a common heritage rather than the private property of Marxism. For us today, truth is not a matter of representing things or of conforming to essences; it is a matter of the practical scope and transforming efficacy of our operative mental models. The concept of truth, which has had such intensely essentialist and idealistic connotations, is now being interpreted in terms of the validity of knowledge and is being progressively replaced by that less equivocal criterion (107:25–26). Here Marxism dovetails with the structuralist method, the philosophy of science, and the operational thinking that underlies many scientific theories (pragmatism, behaviorism, and positivist theories in general). The pretended claim of authentic knowledge is being replaced by a demand for valid and useful knowledge. The latter is not concerned with reality *in se;* it is aware that it is limited to real and effective interaction between human beings and natural or social reality.

We live in an age marked by the primacy of practical reason, which is to be understood not as an ethic or reason in line with some norm as in the Kantian model, but rather as an efficacious reason in line with the real and with an impact on the objective realm. Action is not merely a consequence of knowledge, a mere appendix to it. Quite the reverse is the case. "Praxis does not just depend on truth; truth depends just as much on the activity of human beings" (40:164). Today theory and praxis constitute the nerve-center of all critical knowledge (232).

6. THE CRITICAL AND SUBVERSIVE NATURE OF KNOWLEDGE

As we have just seen, a practical connotation is part and parcel of science, or knowledge, or theory (and also philosophy when and if it is accorded meaningfulness at all). This connotation confers on it a critical dimension as well. If authentic knowledge is not merely the gaze of a spectator, if it does not leave things as they were, the reason is that it offers realistic proposals to make them different. The realism of knowledge is not measured in terms of its conformity with what *is* but rather in terms of its investigation of what *can be*, thanks to human action.

The mission assigned to human intelligence and to intellectuals is to tell the truth and unveil deception, particularly the deceptions of those who govern (Chomsky, 143). Science, philosophy, and theory have the task of carrying out "a radical and thoroughgoing critique of present-day society and its alienating praxis." Their specific task is to "fight against everyday reality" and engage in the "merciless demythification of the world" (397:321). The science needed today is typified by its "resistance to the pitiful course of time today" (Horkheimer, 40:97). The essential task of philosophy is "denunciation," and its nourishing passion is "indignation." Philosophy comes down to nay-saying. It says no to the existing situation. But this is a theoretical nay-saying that requires the practical energy of the proletariat to make it effective in real life; and in its essence it is related to this practical implementation and efficacy (Lefèbvre, 253:25–27 and 151). In short, dialectical thinking is conceived as a capacity for negation on both the level of science or theory and the level of simple self-awareness. So it is seen by such people as Fougeyrollas (193), Adorno (39), and Habermas (232).

This dialectical and nay-saying understanding of knowledge is directly opposed to the analytic and positivist understanding of it. Intrinsic to it, then is a critical view of analytical philosophy and of logical and scientific positivism. The Frankfurt School stresses this point, but it is not alone in this. Horkheimer denounces "the cult of facts" that is characteristic of positivist thought, because it is in complicity with social conformity and blindly submissive to established authority (40:95–96). Marcuse labels positivist reasoning as "one-dimensional," as a discourse closed up in itself that proceeds by way of tautologies and conventional concepts instead of demonstrative judgments. As he sees it, it uses this approach to feign deep meaningfulness and to prove its own validity (280). Sartre reproaches positivist and analytical reasoning for its inability to comprehend what is new or novel, what humanity creates. And he also tries to show that dialectical reasoning, while it surpasses analytical reasoning, also includes it and fulfills it (371:148, 505–6).

The peculiar and proper feature of knowledge, science, and theory is its delineation of historical alternatives to the present state of affairs. The Hegelian notion that "the real is the rational" has usually been interpreted as a consecration of the present situation and a conformation of reason to the existing state of affairs. Now it is interpreted to mean something very different: "what is can never be true" (78:65). According to Marcuse both formulations now come down to the same thing. They both mean that there is a real antagonism between reality and the thinking process that tries to grasp it. The seeming contradiction between the two is resolved in some sort of synthesis like this: "The world of immediate experience, the world in which we live, must be comprehended, undermined, and transformed so that it may be converted into what truly is." Reason thus is the power which, running counter to the superficial appearance of the world and its immediate presence, guides all things to their reality and truth. Dialectical and critical reasoning is made up of this two-sided reality, that is, of the contrast and tension between that which "is" and that which "should be," between appearance and essence, real-life action and possibility. Dialectical thinking introduces a new dimension insofar as it presents the potentialities of the world as real historical possibilities (280:141–42). No immediate unity between reason and reality ever exists. Hence the notion of reason clearly has a critical and polemic character (283:14).

The critical and polemical character of knowledge vis-à-vis the existing world confers revolutionary capabilities on it. When understood in a dialectical way, science fulfills Gramsci's dictum that "the truth is revolutionary." Marcuse himself is quick to move to the logical conclusion of his own view of dialectical thinking. He talks about the "subversive power" of reason (280:141). The "great rejection" that he proposes as a reaction to existing social reality is merely the logical consequence of a critical theory of society (280:272; 281:218).

"All scientific knowledge ends up being revolutionary knowledge." That is how Castilla del Pino sums up the contrast between authentic and innovative scientific knowledge on the one hand and conservative knowledge (or mere erudition) on the other hand. In the latter case there is a tendency to leave things just as they are, to maintain the status quo. Hence "all erudition is a traditionalist form of knowing." It is a pseudoknowledge that changes nothing and disturbs no one. Genuine knowledge, by contrast, is problematic and creative. Free of myth, dogmatism, and prejudice, it is capable of introducing a new truth and therefore is often uncomfortable for those in power. Everything that a scientist does, "if it is authentic and valid, is also revolutionary," not only in his own particular field but also in the rest of reality in many instances. That is the great pleasure one derives from authentic knowledge and understanding: helping to undermine what is false, stupid, and cruel (107:29, 32–34, 45–48).

The same subversive potentiality is attributed to philosophy. Philosophic speculation virtually contains all manner of authentically revolutionary conduct insofar as it "liberates our awareness from empirical attachments and leaves it open to new and unwonted determinations" (89:147). Precisely because critical and scientific consciousness is not tied down to real life, it paves the way for surprising possibilities that will be liberative and even revolutionary.

7. DIALECTICAL TOTALITIES AND THE UNITY OF SCIENCE

Finally, dialectical thinking is characterized by the fact that it takes concrete and dynamic totalities for its object. It considers facts and events as elements of a historically defined reality from which they cannot be isolated (283:301). It is a method of comprehension focused on a totality and operating in that totality. It takes up and apprehends the parts in and through the whole. Strictly speaking, its true object should be the absolute totality of human history. But since that lies beyond our grasp, it devotes itself to relative and specific totalities. Goldmann points out that "the problem of method in the human sciences lies in dividing the empirical data into relative totalities that are sufficiently autonomous to serve as the framework for a scientific effort" (213:23 and 121). Sartre prefers to talk about totalities in the process of formation, about processes of totalization. Thus dialectical reasoning does not deal with finished totality but with a process of historical totalization that is carried through by human praxis (371:116 and 119). In the dialectical conception of reason, scientific knowledge is possible only as a knowledge of totalities; it is not present when reality is artificially dissected and split up into small pieces, which may well happen in certain particular "sciences."

This requirement, that scientific knowledge must take totalities as their only possible object, is not peculiar to Marxism. Structuralist analysis is in agreement that the concept of totality is the essential correlate of science. "Structure" specifically denotes the ideal of the intrinsic and self-sufficient intelligibility of some specific system that is characterized, among other things, as a totality (349: 6–10). In addition, structural analysis often assumes highly dynamic and operational features, as it does in the genetic or historical "constructivism" of Piaget, for example. When it does this, it becomes readily apparent, as Piaget himself has claimed, that structuralism has a dialectical character (341:71 and 101ff.).

The distinctively Marxist feature shows up when these totalities are viewed as erected on a material base involving production processes and relationships—more specifically, when concrete totalities are understood in terms of the relationship between structure and superstructure. The structure results from sensible and material necessity, from society's work to meet that necessity, and from the industrial and economic organization of that work. The rest of the human realm—politics, law, art, morality, religion, ideology, and culture—belongs to the domain of the superstructure, which is determined by the material-economic base.

Here we find ourselves at the very crux of the dialectical thinking proper to historical materialism: the functioning interaction between structure and superstructure and the relative autonomy of the latter within a dialectic totalization. Yet, oddly enough, Marxist theoreticians confess that such questions are still shrouded in obscurity and still in need of deeper theoretical exploration (44:113–44, 211, 219). To this we must add that there is hardly an investigator today who would not admit that the human realm, including its most "spiritual" products, needs an economic and laboring base. It thus is evident that there is a broad doctrinal zone between dialectical thinking in general and the more dogmatic Marxism that views the superstructure as a mere mirror or automatic reflection of the grounding structure. And so there is room for a real encounter between a critical but open Marxism and a scientific epistemology cognizant of the economic conditioning affecting all human reality. Surely it is this same open zone that leaves room for a political theology as well—as we shall see.

In devoting attention to totalities, dialectical thinking tends to re-establish communication between the different branches of knowledge dealing with man (psychology, economics, human ecology, linguistics, and so forth). This communication had been somewhat interrupted by positivist and analytic thinking insofar as it split them up into watertight compartments. Until very recently it was a commonplace that human knowledge had been seriously fragmented by the high degree of specialization required in the domain of a given science and by the differing scientific methods in use. Karl Jaspers spoke out on this fragmentation of knowledge, developing it into a philosophical thesis on the fragmentation of truth itself and a polyhedral notion of truth in which existential truth was ranged alongside scientific truth (240:305 and 320).

It was perhaps for an analogous reason—namely, in order to be able to squeeze Christian truth into the cracks arising out of a splintered knowledge—that Catholics proved to be well disposed to the notion that present-day science is and had to be fragmented (250:164–68). At times people equated an "interdisciplinary approach to the real" with the "fragmentation of knowledge," as if the latter could be directly equated with the former and as if the deabsolutization of particular sciences fostered by the interdisciplinary approach somehow would favor the creation of some space for theology (45:111–13).

Today a movement in the very opposite direction is evident. Based on the suppositions of dialectical reasoning, it is once again trying to restore unity to scientific knowledge and to get rid of the fragmentation. The most striking attempt at a rapprochement is that between dialectical materialism and psychoanalysis. Its importance lies in the fact that Freud and Marx are undoubtedly the two people who have left the most profound mark on our modern outlook. It should also be noted that for a long time official Marxism had rejected psychoanalysis as a bourgeois by-product while orthodox Freudianism, for its part, had rejected every socialist version of psychoanalysis. Their present-day rapprochement is a scientific and practical phenomenon of incalculable scope.

The integration of psychoanalysis into Marxism indicates quite clearly how a dialectical anthropology is forming today that seeks to give new unity to science amid the existing plurality of its methodologies and disciplines. Wilhelm Reich, an immediate disciple of Freud, was the first to discover that our society produces neurotics on an assembly-line basis, and hence that individual therapy was a useless waste of energy and resources so long as the repressive social mechanisms at the root of neuroses persisted. Reich also helped to point out how the family (the proximate psychoanalytic source in the genesis of neurosis) functioned in bourgeois society as the transmission line between the economic structure and the ideological superstructure.

Thus Reich laid the basis for fecund interaction and mutual enrichment between dialectical materialism and psychoanalysis (352). But he was shunted aside as heterodox by both Marxists and Freudians, who thereby delayed the impact of his thinking on the cultural situation. The incorporation of psychoanalysis into Marxism, as a cultural phenomenon, is of very recent vintage. The popularity of Hebert Marcuse's basic works has played no little role in this happening (280; 281). The works of Castilla del Pino, designed to fashion a dialectical anthropology, also illustrate the possibility of a Marxist hermeneutics of psychoanalysis (106; 108). Today it is generally accepted that Freud's analytic method can be inserted into practical-dialectical perspectives on society. Such rigorous theoreticians as Sartre (371:46–47) and Adorno (40:127–49) agree on the point. The term "Freudo-Marxism" is cropping up with increasing frequency (328). Even the antipsychiatry movement, though it may not necessarily allude to Marx, is doing nothing else but pushing its inquiry down to the socioeconomic roots of mental illness; it presupposes a dialectical conception. In the eyes of the "antipsychiatrists," and likewise in the eyes of the keenest critics of traditional psychiatric practice, mental illness ultimately is to be defined not as a quality inhering in the patient but as having a social definition; it entails some sort of dialectical interaction between the "sick" patient and society. This view is shared by people with such different basic focuses as Cooper, Laing, Hochmann, and Basaglia.

8. THE WEST AND DIALECTICAL REASONING

Today dialectical reasoning is much more than a method of analysis and interpretation applied to socioeconomic realities. While not replacing the epistemological instrument of the particular sciences, it is tending to set itself up as the unique and unitary viewpoint permitting a relative totalization or globalization of the human. There would be no particular value in trying to show in detail here how this is happening in the different areas of theory and praxis. So I shall content myself with three specific examples taken from fairly distinct strata of cultural life. Consider what is happening in esthetics, medicine, and the theater.

Esthetics is a science, but it deals with beauty. It deals with art and fruition. Thus it deals with elements of the human realm that would seem to be remote from, and impervious to, economic and material conditioning or determining factors. The noteworthy fact here is the appearance of a dialectical and materialist esthetics. It is not just that Marxist theorists are making passing allusions to esthetic themes. They are also formulating and elaborating a complete Marxist esthetics. That is what is being offered by people like Fischer (191), Lukacs (267), Dalla Volpe (418), and Rubert de Ventós (365).

This esthetics does not just operate through the concepts of dialectical reasoning, relating artistic products with the production modes and relationships of a given epoch. It also seeks to view art and the artists in terms of a critical and practical process of subverting societally given values. Thus the specific nature of a work of art is "to discover, in the concrete complex of immediately given class and national content, that new element that deserves to become a permanent possession of humanity and is effectively turned into that" (269:306). Thus we get the notion of "implicated" or "committed" art. Stress is put on "the revolutionary character of an art that does not so much try to *ex-plicate* the world as to *im-plicate* it and *be implicated* in it" (365:523).

The application of Marxist methods to the evaluations of works of art has led to some oversimplified procedures. Sometimes the work of art is related in a purely mechanical way with its socioeconomic conditionings while its singular and distinctive features are overlooked. But on the whole dialectical materialism has now abandoned such oversimplistic approaches and recognizes those specific features of art that cannot be reduced to determinations produced by the socioeconomic context.

Medicine will serve as a second example of a rather different character. Besides being a science, medicine is also a praxis. On the surface medical practice would seem to be totally apolitical, having nothing to do with social and economic power structures. But dialectical analysis goes on to reveal the political connotations of medicine. To begin with, the very illness of an individual and the nosological configuration of an age are determined by the labor regimen. Moreover, the overall relationship between doctors and patients, and also the whole organization of hospitals, reflects the authoritarian and repressive structure of society. The doctor, in other words, is a professional in the service of the public order and the system of production and consumption (1). Obviously when one takes cognizance of all this, there arises a "criticism of nosographic reasoning" (Hochmann) that has direct political repercussions: Medical practice takes on a critical and subversive cast vis-à-vis the "establishment." It should be noted that this example might readily be extended to the professional practice of lawyers, architects, social workers, and so forth.

A third example is furnished by the avant-garde theater of the present day. Here it is not a question of some scientific discipline, nor is it strictly a matter of some professional practice like medicine. But some relationship to critical awareness and a revolutionary praxis has become an essential ingredient of the contemporary theater. It is trying to reflect the contradictions of existing society and the conflicts of its audience, rejecting the false awareness nurtured by illusions and clearing the way for a clear-eyed recognition of the real world. The stage continues to be a place where some sort of rite is performed, but now that rite itself entails a transition to action and praxis—specifically to a praxis that will alter the existing order. This example, too, could be readily extended to other forms of artistic expression, involving them in a praxis that would alter the societal reality: e.g., literature, poetry, avant-garde film, and the plastic arts.

Strictly speaking, we must admit that the rapprochement between historical materialism and psychoanalysis, the formation of a Marxist esthetics, and the staging of theater designed to promote dialectical awareness did not just appear today for the very first time. Insofar as psychoanalysis and esthetics are concerned, we have already mentioned the names of Reich and Lukacs, whose early works date back fifty years or more. Insofar as the theater is concerned, the experimental theater work of Meyerhold and Piscator also goes back to around 1920. These people were precursors, but the political situation in the twenties and thirties prevented their pioneering thoughts and efforts from having any real impact on the cultural scene. Stalinism affected Marxist thinking, hardening it into the dogmatic authoritarianism of a police state. During the same period the rest of Europe was afflicted with the fever of anticommunist totalitarianisms. In such an atmosphere there was little chance for any real cultural understanding or implementation of dialectical materialism.

Since our object here is to analyze the sociocultural situation of theology, the important point is that for a long time—from the 1917 revolution until quite recently—Marx was confusedly associated or identified with Soviet Russia in the minds of many theologians. Stalinist Marxism was something outside Christendom, and it did not bring Christendom into any internal crisis. It represented the great power inimical to the Christian civilization of the West, just as the Turkish empire had posed a terrible external threat in an earlier day. But it did not represent a critical principle or force that might internally affect Christianity or the West. When communism was extended to other countries of Eastern Europe after World War II, persecution of ecclesiastical personnel and institutions rose sharply. People talked about the "church of silence" as they once had talked about missionaries and Christians captured by the Moors of Africa. The relationship between Christianity and communism was that of victim to executioner. Under such circumstances one could not even imagine theology agreeing to dialogue with Marxism or to take Marx's theoretical contributions seriously.

Culturally speaking, we are now witnessing the reception of Marxism in the West almost a century after Marx's death.

The phenomenon admits of quite a few different interpretations, needless to say. Not to be ruled out, of course, is the manipulation of Marxist thought by neocapitalist powers in order to "assimilate" it; nor can we overlook the application to Marxism itself of Marx's criticism of ideologies with the aim of going further than he did. But whether it is merely propagated, or manipulated, or critically transcended, today Marxism does present itself as a most coherent and totalizing theory. It is Marx who dominates the final third of our century as no one else does. Whether one wants to go with Marx, against Marx, or beyond Marx, the fact remains that no one can overlook him. Contemporary Western discourse bears the marks of dialectical reasoning, whether one identifies it or feels forced to treat it as an opponent.

9. CONTEMPORARY ISOMORPHISMS

Political theology is subject to the same impulse that has brought about a rapprochement between psychoanalysis and Marxism as well as the appearance of "implicated art" and a politically conscious practice of medicine. It, too, is a result of the new dialectical, critical, and political awareness that has recently appeared in the West. To put it pointedly and decisively: Political theology is the specific and proper form of theology in an epoch dominated by Marx. Some people might like to deny this assertion or water it down somehow—by claiming, for example, that political theology finds its true antecedents in biblical and Christian tradition. That is a sign of great naiveté, if not a dangerous illusion fed by the false awareness of a dogmatic Christianity. This fact has been seen clearly by conservative theologians who are more reserved toward political theology. (273:16; 387:36). They have pointed up the features it shares with Marxist social criticism, though of course it is no sign of clear-sightedness to interpret this affinity as something that discredits political theology.

If there is no connection between current political theology and the new disposition of science and also the awakened cultural awareness of the West, then it seems quite coincidental that people should suddenly start talking about the faith as a critical and revolutionary ferment precisely at the same time that others are saying the same thing about science, art, and professional practice. If this critical and revolutionary cast of the faith derives chiefly from the Bible, why is it that it has taken twenty centuries to appear? The points of similarity between political theology and other contemporary cultural phenomena are just too obvious to be disregarded.

The affinity is brought out by even the most cursory comparison of the features characteristic of postexistential theology (described earlier) and of present-day science with its dialectical approach. Let us recall that political theology is characterized as a public, critical, and practical theology. We have now found those very same features dominating current epistemology and dialectical theory. But we would do well to explore and highlight the isomorphisms in greater detail, getting beyond merely superficial resemblances. Of particular interest here is the posthumanist cast of current political theology, its relationship to praxis, its logical status vis-à-vis the positivisms of the given, and its ultimately subversive sense and thrust. These features enable us to see in greater and more rigorous detail that the outlines of current theology dovetail with modern science under the impact of dialectical reasoning. One question will be left unanswered for discussion later (see chapter 8): Is a historical-materialist theology possible?

The first thing that is readily verifiable is that theologians, too, are turning away from humanism. They are doing so with much reluctance, to be sure, because humanism had provided a solid base for apologetics, and it is not easy suddenly to abandon the supports provided by humanist values. But the shift away from humanism is already noticeable, and suddenly theologians are silent about it. The humanist emphasis has disappeared from theology books. This discreet silence itself proves that the values of humanism no longer count for much in the eyes of theologians; or at least they do not occupy the eminent and even hallowed position that they held only yesterday.

Directly critical remarks about humanism are rare from the lips of Christians, but some can be found. The Christians for Socialism attached the trait of "political naiveté" to those who still fail to take note of the structural mechanisms of society and the need for a scientific theory, and who therefore persist in deducing political considerations from certain humanist conceptions about freedom, the dignity of the human person, and so forth (2:20). Gustavo Gutiérrez is also critical of the inadequacies of a merely moralistic and humanizing vision of reality that fails to take due account of socioeconomic structures and the dynamics of history (230:79). Criticism of humanism, then, results from the adoption of a critical, scientific theory of society. Humanism comes to be viewed as myth and inertia, as the negation of real-life knowledge and the consecration of inefficacy in praxis.

In a different context, that of apophatic theology rather than political theology, Raimundo Panikkar invokes Buddhic wisdom, which seems to echo the link between the death of God and the death of "man" pointed up by Foucault. Panikkar tries to get beyond positivist dogmatics and relate his view of Buddhism with Christian theology: There "is" no God because in the last analysis there "is" no man either (330:156).

Of even more import than the criticism now directed against humanism is the fact that theology has ceased to talk about man—both man as a very general and universal notion and man as an isolated individual. These terms, characteristic of humanist discourse, have been abandoned in favor of concrete, collective reference to groups and social formations that are historically specified. The old humanist lexicon is being replaced by a new vocabulary whose main themes and terms are servitude and liberation, development and revolution, power and violence, production relationships, hunger, peace, civil rights, justice, and happiness.

Leaving aside a few theological discourses such as Augustine's *City of God,* which did attempt to offer a theological interpretation of fairly current events, we can say that now, for the first time in history, theology is seriously involved in talking about current situations and happenings. Theology books and articles, as well as Sunday sermons, offer a thematic treatment of such concrete events as civil war, terrorist acts, and worker strikes. Latin American theology in particular is now completely focused on what is really happening. Some works, particularly those dealing with the Latin American scene, seem to offer nothing more than a thin covering of theological hermeneutics over a content that is clearly derived from news events and political interpretations for the most part. See, for example, the works of Dewart (149), Vaccari (414), and Gozzer (223).

But real events are also much in evidence in European theology. For example, Tödt introduces a treatment of the theology of revolution by referring to the civil rights struggle in the United States, the social situation in South America, the war in Vietnam, and popular liberation movements (407). As contemporary history, these are the favorite themes of current theology; and they often are dealt with in great detail. There is now room in theology for very concrete events (209:286–91).

All these references help to make clear in what sense current theology is politically mediated. It is so mediated because it incorporates social and political realities into its discourse as judgmental elements for interpreting the gospel and also as realities that must be evaluated in terms of the gospel. Metaphysics and psychology have been replaced by sociohistorical analysis as the idiom and instrument of the theologian. Current political theology is opting for a knowledge of historical reality with the same care and attention that scholastic theology paid to the most subtle metaphysical distinctions and that existentialist theology paid to the analysis of depth psychology. Gospel message and political happening serve as principles of mutual interpretation.

This new attention to human groups and concrete human doings is the legitimate heir of the older humanism. Political theology maintains its continuity with earlier humanist theology insofar as it is still a discourse about man. There is discontinuity insofar as it no longer talks about some abstract, universal humanity or about the human individual isolated from concrete historical circumstances. Instead it now talks about concrete social classes, national income levels, sex, race, language, and all the other factors that define the real existence of human beings. It seems to be fulfilling the process that Engels prescribed for the humanism of Feuerbach: i.e., that the cult of man in the abstract had to be replaced by a scientific study of real human beings and their concrete historical development (287:292).

An impassioned comment of Cardonnel, which bids farewell once and for all to Feuerbach's type of abstract humanism, phrases the problem pointedly. It notes that once again we are dealing with the medieval problem of universals, of the unity and universality of the human species, but now we are considering it in terms of its "historical density" (101:71). Jesus liberates us from the devastating power of abstract humanity and reveals to us "a concrete, living, warm (human) universal": our neighbor (101:83). But to know this concrete neighbor and do something for him we must go through a sociopolitical analysis and then a sociopolitical praxis.

As we already noted in chapter 1 (section 5), current political theology embodies a reference to praxis. It is not just a vague reference of an indefinite sort, however. Like "theory" in Marxist thinking, this theology is essentially bound up with praxis insofar as praxis serves as a principle of knowledge and foundation. It is praxis, in other words, that provides theology with its point of origin and its legitimation. Moltmann stresses this in two of his theses on the theology of revolution. One has to do with theory in general: "Historical praxis, which seeks a freer and juster humanity, constitutes the horizon for the formation of theories." His other thesis deals specifically with theology: "The new criterion of theology and faith lies in praxis" (310:68 and 73). Or as Hugo Assmann puts it, the new element in theological reflection is to be found "at the point where theory and praxis come together as one" (54:220).

The resemblance to the Marxist concept of theory is even more noticeable in the fact that theology is now defined in essentially antipositivist terms—that is, as a discourse concerned not with what is or is happening in fact but rather with what can happen and be. As Moltmann sees it, hope determines the logical and epistemological status of theology. And the proper tense or time-frame of hope is the future. To put it another way, its modality is the negation of the present:

Doctrinal statements find their truth in their verifiable conformity with the reality that is there and that can be experienced. The enunciations of the promise, by contrast, must perforce clash with the reality we can experience in the present. They do not result from concrete experiences; rather, they are the condition which makes new experiences possible. They do not seek or pretend to illuminate the reality that is there; they illuminate the reality that is to come. They do not seek to copy the spirit of existing reality but to insert that reality in the promised change for which we are hoping. They do not wish to trail after reality but to run on ahead of it, thereby turning it into history (312:22–23).

Thus the logical structure of hope (and of theology) is characterized by its challenge to existing reality and its capacity to anticipate and create a new reality in history. This coincides exactly with the function that is assigned to dialectical thinking: i.e., to propose historical alternatives to the existing world. It has been said that in the theology of hope and political eschatology Ernst Bloch plays the same role that Aristotle played in the theology of an earlier day (284:486). This is true to some extent, but that role is shared by Marxist dialectical reasoning in general and by the Frankfurt School of criticism in particular. German political theology cites the Frankfurt School with the same gusto as it does Bloch.

Moltmann's proposals regarding hope, the promise, and theology correspond point for point with those of Marcuse noted earlier (see section 6) on bidimensional, critical, dialectical thinking. Insofar as logical structure is concerned, Moltmann's version of hoping is a modality or variant of Marcuse's critical knowing. Both are opposed to any positivist science that merely reproduces reality, and both define themselves in terms of their capacity to flesh out certain promises or projects in reality that contradict the already given universe. The positivist concept of truth is that of the mind's conformity with things. Moltmann, by contrast, maintains that the theological concept of truth, which is derived from hope and the promise, entails a definite lack of conformity with the given reality that is already present (312:110, 132, 155).

Lack of conformity with, or negation of, existing reality, then, has come to form an intrinsic feature of theology just as it has come to form an intrinsic feature of knowledge in the school of dialectical thinking—and the Frankfurt School especially. This is evident when one glances at the extra-theological citations of Moltmann and Metz. Besides Bloch, the people cited most regularly and faithfully are Adorno, Habermas, and Marcuse. This relationship with the Frankfurt School has been pointed up (274:78 and 81), and it contrasts with a general neglect of non-Marxist critical reasoning, which is also well represented in Germany today by such people as Karl Popper and Hans Albert. So whatever its real penetration into the West may be today, the fact is that political theology seems to be operating as if there were no line of reasoning but the Marxist one. With due respect for different nationalist overtones, the same observation would hold true for non-German theology, the Latin American theology of liberation for example, in which the reading and interpretation of Marx proceeds from different presuppositions, is not filtered through the Frankfurt School of thinking, and is usually closer to orthodox Marxism.

The subversive and revolutionary reach of the faith and of theology is the logical consequence of all that has been noted above. It should be noted here, however, that the revolutionary capability of Christianity is not necessarily bound up with a theology of revolution in the strict sense. In all its different versions "theology of revolution" serves as a convenient designation for certain specific interpretations of that revolutionary capability. But one must recognize a subversive factor in theology and the faith even though one may not go on to propose a theology of revolution in the strict sense.

In fact, the majority of today's theologians do talk about the aggressive or subversive character of faith, using different terms and giving them different emphases, usually without going on to proclaim a theology of revolution. For example: The faith "radically dislocates the believer" (258:49). "Eschatologically specified faith and revolutionary existence stand in an intrinsic and reciprocal relationship" (357:140). "The Christian faith is turning into a critical and revolutionary leaven" (2). "Faith demands revolution" (16:7).

A theology of revolution appears at the point when revolution is taken to be an inner moment or thrust of theology itself, described in terms of the revolutionary structure of the faith (177:111)—that is to say, when revolution is understood to be the mediation of theology. By the same token, one can point up the need for revolution and for the participation of Christians in it without directly implicating the faith of the gospel as such. Operating from a fairly conservative theological standpoint, Charbonneau, for example, affirms that "revolution is necessary" and that Marxists should not be allowed a monopoly on defining it (138:101). Here we come across a practical revolutionary attitude among Christians that is not theologically revolutionary. Finally, it should be obvious that one need not use the idiom of revolution to make clear the revolutionary dimension of the faith. That dimension is clearly recognized when someone calls the attention of the Christian community to its mission of "manifesting its opposition to what society takes for granted," making social institutions more "flexible and elastic," and "piercing through the immobility of society" (312:418–19).

All these approaches flesh out the revolutionary vocation of the faith, which thereby takes on features like those which dialectical thinking assigns to science and theory. The dialectical thesis that all authentic knowing has to end up being revolutionary is matched by the thesis of political theology that all genuine faith has to end up being revolutionary.

10. REFERENCES TO MARXISM IN THEOLOGY

The crucial point in the relationship between Marxist thinking and political theology, and the critical area where one has to decide whether there is any room for the latter within the former is to be found elsewhere, however. It resides concretely in the relationship of the religious fact to the socioeconomic structure and in its insertion within a specific human totality grounded on a material base. It is there, in the relationship of the religious fact to certain all-encompassing practical processes and their grounding on production relations, that one must consider the possibility or impossibility of any theology existing within a historical-materialist conception of man. It is there, too, that political theology must express itself with crystal clarity. Otherwise its other resemblances with dialectical thinking and Marxism could be a mere veneer and give a totally erroneous impression.

When theologians talk about faith as something that is politically implicated, opposed to existing reality, and revolutionary, they are certainly showing a willingness to get in tune with current sensibility. But might not this phenomenon be very superficial, entailing nothing more than the repetition of similar words and shibboleths? If that were the case then theology would not really be helping to change anything, except its own vocabulary.

The underlying question is the nature of the communication existing between historical-materialist thinking and political theology. It is quite clear that political theology, being theology, is not identical with Marxist thought. It is equally clear that the formal analogies between them do not establish anything more than a relationship of simple imitation. So what sort of communication or incorporation is there in reality between political theology and dialectical thinking?

The question can be drawn in sharper profile insofar as it is a fact that present-day theologians frequently cite Marxist theoreticians in their own support, as if the judgments and opinions of the latter can stand on their own feet in the discourse of faith and as if their presumed atheism did not represent any insurmountable obstacle to the utilization of their thought by theologians.

A few examples will suffice to illustrate the point. Throughout the course of a lengthy examination of Christian theology in a revolutionary world, Paul L. Lehmann offers reasons for his opposition to a "theology *of* revolution" and his approval of a "theology *for* revolution" by citing fragmentary remarks of Lenin in his own support—remarks containing Lenin's warnings about possible distortions and deformations of the revolution (255). In his attempt to validate the thesis that "no problems are created when one specifies history as the locale for rational rapprochement with God," Hervé Chaigne invokes Marcuse and his criticism of "one-dimensional" living (135: 106). Marcuse is also invoked by Metz in the same way. A text in which Marcuse notes that historical memory and recollection tends to generate a subversive attitude toward the establishment is used by Metz to support his suggestive notion of faith as "critical memory" (301:287). To develop that same idea further, Metz also alludes to Adorno's thinking on the significance of tradition as an internal feature of knowledge (301:290).

The basic procedure, then, is clear enough. Certain propositions originating in historical-materialist thinking are granted immediate validity in theological thinking, little thought being given to the rupture that faith occasions between the one and the other. This way of proceeding is so spontaneous in political theology that one would be hard put to find any theological text of extended length in which it did not crop up repeatedly. Marxist citations represent a whole literary genre in present-day theological literature. This book is no exception, and the reader will find abundant samples throughout it. So the matter of making clear what sort of communication exists, or can exist, between historical-materialist reasoning and theological thinking is important, not only with regard to other theologians, but for my book as well.

The use of Marxist citations in a theological text can serve various functions. It can serve as proof from authority, whereby certain theological assertions or criteria are supported by theses that are generally accepted outside theology. It can serve as a mere analogy between certain propositions that are valid in the realm of the human sciences and those that are being formulated in the realm of theology. It can be a way of using Marxist theory solely as a tool for apologetic purposes, wielding it to the advantage of theology insofar as it is serviceable and then dogmatically discarding it when it contradicts the Creed. It can represent the application of principles that prevail in dialectical reasoning to theology as if one were applying general principles to a more particular area. Finally, it can serve to present a common front, shared by both theology and Marxist thinking, vis-à-vis analytical-positivist reasoning.

Some of these functions overlap or complement each other. Others are mutually incompatible. But all of them can be found in one or another theologian. The citation of Marxism in political theology runs the whole gamut from obvious manipulation of Marxist texts to the argument from authority.

The precise function and import of incorporating Marxist suppositions into political theology is far from clear. Some sort of relationship does exist between political theology and historical-materialist thinking, but it is far from transparent and, most importantly, little clarified on the level of reflection. The only way to clarify it is to see to what extent Marxist criticism of religion and theology is accepted by the political theology that uses Marxist citations as a literary genre. When this point is not made clear, and unfortunately that is precisely what happens in the case of even the most lucid theologians, then it must be said that the public, critical, and practical idiom of theology is really navigating through a sea of ambiguities. A precondition for an unequivocal political theology is to clearly discuss the validity accorded to Marxist criticism of Christianity.

11. MARXISM ACCEPTED WITH RESTRICTIONS

There are certain decisive questions that must be considered if one is to make a meaningful comparison between political theology and Marxism and if one is to unmistakably mark out the real and ultimate contrast between them. Those questions are: Can theology adopt as its own the historical-materialist analysis of society? If it does do that, is it not contradicting itself? Is any theology possible at all in terms of Marxist presuppositions? Or is it a matter of accepting the Marxist analysis, but only in part? By what criterion, theological or not, are we to decide what is acceptable in Marxism and what is not? The affinities between political theology and dialectical thinking, or, more particularly, historical materialism, configure the latter as theologically relevant, but in what sort of configuration precisely? Is it as a necessary interlocutor, merely as a working hypothesis for theology, or as an indisputable thesis?

The complete response to these questions can only be outlined at the very end of this book. Right now all we can do is introduce some judgmental factors by considering the different ways in which present-day theologians answer those questions.

Many of today's theologians, and almost all those who have concerned themselves with political theology, seem to admit unreservedly the validity of the Marxist analysis insofar as socioeconomic realities are concerned. Current political theology takes for an accepted fact the historical-materialist interpretation of production relationships, social classes, political power, and the social processes of change. Up to that point a general consensus exists: Marxism is valid as a social and economic theory, and theological anthropology can count on it with the same assurance that it counts on the fact of phylogenetic evolution.

Now historical materialism includes an explanation of

the religious phenomenon that reduces it to a mere ideological superstructure engendered by relationships based on economic domination. At this point it seems that theology cannot identify itself with Marxism, except under pain of losing its own identity. It is at this point that the relationship of political theology to Marxist thought begins to grow obscure. To begin with, theologians are not unanimous in the way they try to evade the Marxist criticism of religion. Furthermore, no matter what way out they choose, they do not offer satisfactory reasons for their particular choice or explain it in clear-cut terms.

Some theologians restrict the validity of the Marxist analysis to the socioeconomic order, though they do not offer reasons why. In their opinion the Marxist method is valid only in the analysis of societal relationships, not in the realm of religious signification. This restrictive interpretation of Marxism, which rejects its pretensions to extend its criticism to religious reality, usually goes hand in hand with an ideological understanding of Marxism. Marx himself is then seen as one more link in the chain of philosophers who have criticized the Christian religion in ideological terms. He is viewed specifically as an epigone of Feuerbach, adopting his thesis about religious alienation and introducing certain modifications and complementary ideas by underlining productive, revolutionary praxis.

When Marxist atheism is understood along such lines, there is every reason to suspect a basic misunderstanding of some sort. The early writings of Marx in particular do indeed contain features of religious criticism taken over from Feuerbach. But they are not the typical features of Marxism, which specifically ridicules any desire to combat one set of ideas (religious ones) by using another set of ideas (atheistic ones): see 285:260. Marx takes for granted the fact that ideological or philosophical criticism of religion has been fully completed (287:41), and he is not interested in that. What he is interested in contributing is a set of principles for a practical criticism of the socioeconomic base.

Books written by theologians about Marxism prior to 1965 tended to fall into this misunderstanding and to interpret Marx's criticism of religion in ideological terms. Such was the case with the now classic work of Calvez, who describes and disagrees with Marx as a simple variation on Feuerbach and his ideas about man. Thus he feels he can come to this victorious conclusion over Marx: "The religious mode of existence contains within itself not only the key to various forms of alienation but at the same time the mediating principle that can eliminate those forms of alienation." And the principle comes down to "the relationship of created being to its creator" (96:111).

This misunderstanding is even clearer in the work of Helmut Gollwitzer on "the Marxist criticism of religion." Gollwitzer accords an important place to the study of Feuerbach in any exploration of Marxist atheism. At the same time he also tries to limit the validity of Marx's method to the socioeconomic realm: "Judgment of the realm of religion is the dividing line which marks off Marxism as a regional method from Marxism as an *ism* in the strict sense of that word (i.e., as a conception of the world)" (214:7). So Gollwitzer accepts the Marxist theory in the region of socioeconomic phenomena but deprives it of validity in the remaining realms of reality, denying it any right to set itself up as an overall conception of the world. As a strictly regional theory dealing with socioeconomic realities, the Marxist analysis cannot aspire to be a general theory about man and the world.

On the basis of its regional methodology, however, historical materialism considers itself authorized to elaborate a conception of the human realm and to move beyond the limits which some try to impose upon it. How can one deny the legitimacy of this extension without going into a polemical and convincing line of reasoning about its claim here and the reasons it offers in its own support?

Acknowledging the impossibility of separating Marxist economic analysis from its general concept of the human realm, some theologians accept the validity of Marxist criticism of religion. Raymond Domergue, who is very clear-eyed in interpreting that criticism, is quick to point up its qualitative difference from the merely ideological criticism of philosophers and scientific scholars. Domergue is quite right in pointing out that Christianity can readily digest ideological criticism, that only dialectical criticism would force it to recast itself in a basic way, and that this recasting would signal its self-destruction as a religion (154).

Many theologians, sharing this view, are taking advantage of the present-day theology of secularity to evade the blow dealt by Marxist criticism. If one starts off from the premise that there is a distinction between faith and religion, then one can say that the Marxist method dissolves the religious phenomenon but does not touch faith at all. The validity of Marx's religious criticism is one of the factors forcing us to accept a nonreligious Christianity, a secular faith. Such a secular faith would have the virtue of permitting us to evade the criticism levelled by Marxism against religion.

This way out, however, presupposes we can dogmatically assert that Christianity is a faith and a revelation, not a mere religion. Hence it can only be of use to those who are dogmatically convinced of the transcendence of the Christian faith over religious forms. The distinction, in short, is functional and effective only when used intramurally by Christians; it has no real apologetic or polemic value in confrontations with those outside Christianity (182:59–65). For Marxist thought, of course, this alleged distinction between religion and faith is an illusion without any real existence. Many religious traditions present themselves as revealed. Historical Christianity does not seem to be in a better position than any other religion to carry through a process of secularization to its ultimate conclusions. Hence the distinction between faith and religion, which is dogmatically asserted and valid for certain purposes, is irrelevant when it comes to evading the Marxist criticism of religion.

12. MARXISM FULLY ACCEPTED

One may go all the way in accepting Marx's criticism of religion. The Christian believer may accept the conclusion that all religion, including the Christian religion, is an ideological superstructure engendered by certain specific production relationships, but a superstructure which is capable in turn of reacting to the economic base and thereby demonstrating its relative autonomy.

That is the position of Marxist-Christians, who forthrightly state: "Our problematic depends entirely on the acceptance of historical materialism as an indubitable fact. As Marx himself puts it, 'In general the mode of material production dominates the development of social, political, and intellectual life.' " The natural conclusion, of course, is that religion belongs to the domain of ideology. Their only caution, one which they share with many present-day Marxists, is to rule out a mechanistic conception of the underlying structure: "The economic dialectics never operates in a pure state. On the contrary it is determined always by concrete circumstances, by the specific forms of the superstructure itself, and hence by the existing ideology." This point enables them to make room for the faith, even while taking for granted the presuppositions of historical materialism: "Thus even in its relationship with its material base, ideology enjoys a certain area of autonomy within which 'transcendence' can arise" (135:94).

This position seems much more realistic and sensible. Unfortunately it is not worked out or reasoned through by those who maintain it. Chaigne, for example, does nothing more than enunciate a thesis. He proposes a theoretical guideline that should be worked out in full. At the same time, however, it is to his credit that he clearly and consciously enunciates a position that many other Christians hold in some ingenuous or unconfessed form. An acceptance of historical materialism underlies many proposals of theologians who do not expressly refer to Marx.

There are few theological studies designed to integrate theology into a material-based dialectical anthropology. Marxism is tacitly assumed by many theologians, but there is no reflective or thematic treatment of that fact. The possibility of a theology based on Marxist theses or hypotheses still stands in need of full verification. In the absence of clear-cut theological precedents, theologians who want to work out this possibility must take a different tack if they do not want to start from zero. They must make use of both the elements implicit in present-day theology and extratheological works deriving from the Marxist camp and the sociology of religion.

Some Marxist theoreticians have attempted to lay hold of the fact of Christianity and theological ideology not in terms of dissolving them completely but rather in terms of critically recovering and rehabilitating the content embodied in them. Without meaning to slight the contributions of other contemporary authors, we might note here the work of Ernst Bloch and Lucien Goldmann. It is Bloch who has perhaps shown most earnestness and sympathy in trying to work out a historical-materialist theory of Christianity that would salvage its legitimate heritage. Bloch pictures Marxism, and Marxist hope in particular, as "religion in its heritage" (77:1521). And while Goldmann has restricted his study to a particular era of French Christianity, the Jansenist era, he has been most rigorous and methodical in concretely pointing up the relationships between the socioeconomic base and theological ideas of a period and a society (213). Here we might also include various Marxists who have in some way specialized in the Christian-Marxist dialogue (Garaudy, Lombardo-Radice, Luporini).

These and other studies based on sociology or social theory still await adequate transcription into theological terms. Theologians must still clarify whether and how believers can take over such analyses as their own. When all is said and done, only such clarification will eliminate equivocation from political theology and enable it to give a sound response to the demands and questions of dialectical thought. In this connection theology must spell out clearly its own anthropological suppositions, clearly stating to what extent it can accept a dialectical anthropology and where it must express reservations.

Assmann says that neither Hegel nor Marx have yet been digested theologically and that this will be a difficult metabolic process (54:218). This metabolic process, the assimilation of dialectical thinking and historical materialism into political theology, is the problem at hand. It will call for a lot more exploration and study, and it is still too early to say anything definitive at this point. In the last chapter of this book I shall try to offer a hypothesis that would give consistency and coherence to the program of political theology.

13. GROUNDING IN THE CULTURAL SITUATION

It is its insertion in the overall cultural scene of the present day and concretely in a dialectical approach to the understanding of that culture that provides theology with solid grounding and reinforces its validity.

When we are confronted with a theological thesis, and in particular when we are confronted with a whole system of theological assertions, we must ask ourselves certain basic questions: Is it legitimate and verified? What foundation underlies it? Whence does it derive its validity? Now positive theology takes it for granted that the grounds for its theological theses are to be found solely and exclusively in the data of tradition. A theological doctrine is well founded when it is found in the traditional documents and sources of Christianity: the Bible, the Councils, and so forth. In terms of such criteria, political theology faces a dilemma. On the one hand it may be honest enough to recognize what is contained in the data of tradition or "revelation" taken as a whole rather than in isolated or one-sided bits and pieces; in that case one would find it difficult to conclude that current political theology, with its essential reference to liberation and social change, is contained and well grounded in that traditional data. Or, on the other hand, political theology may indulge in a naive and one-sided exegesis of the Bible and tradition, pilfering the data that supports it and stressing the crucial nature of that data vis-à-vis other data in contradiction to the tenets of political theology. The fact is that political theology seems to represent a break with tradition more than it represents continuity with tradition. It seems hard put to claim solid grounding in tradition according to the criteria which tradition itself proposes as the proper basis for such grounding.

But the fact is that we must challenge and reject the notion of solid grounding which is maintained by the positive dogmatics of both Catholicism and neo-orthodox Protestantism (188). It is not certain that the foundation of a theology derives exclusively from tradition. This is obvious even if we maintain the habitual way of posing the question of theology's foundation. It is clear that any legitimate theology possesses not only traditional roots linking it with the past life of the faith but also certain cultural roots that link it to contemporary society. The validity of a theology derives both from its fidelity to original and traditional elements in Christianity and from its solid relationship with a specific cultural moment. Otherwise it is incomprehensible that different theologies have in fact succeeded one another during the course of history. If theological legitimacy is fixed exclusively by theology's identification with biblical and apostolic doctrine, then the variety of various theologies remains inexplicable—unless one assumes that only one of those theologies is legitimate.

The theologies of Thomas Aquinas, Augustine, and Origen are very different from one another. But they all are valid and solidly grounded not only because they are in continuity with the pristine roots of Christianity but also because they are faithful to their own age, meaningful at the time when they appeared, and in line with the suppositions of a given culture. It is this grounding on cultural bases that justifies their differences. It is this grounding that gives validity to any given theology insofar as it has distinctive traits of its own.

So the grounding of a theology also derives from its cultural connections, from its contemporaneity vis-à-vis the popular or scholarly conceptions of a given moment in history. The synchronization of a theology with its age provides it with solid grounding no less than does its continuity with tradition. It provides it with a different sort of grounding, but it is a grounding nevertheless. Synchronic grounding (or contemporaneity) plays just as important a role as does diachronic grounding (link with earlier historical traditions), the former being decisive in determining the distinctiveness and originality of a given theology. When one wants to look for the roots of a certain theology's distinctive traits, one cannot focus on its loyalty to traditional data; no distinctiveness derives from that source. Instead one must look to its synchronicity with a given cultural situation.

These observations, which seem obvious enough, will help us to clear up some points regarding the valid grounds of current political theology. The specific grounding of political theology precisely as "political," that is to say, as a theology that is mediated politically, does not derive so much from the data of tradition as from the society and culture in which it arises. The exact same thing was true for scholastic theology as "scholastic": Its grounding lay in medieval culture and the Aristotelianism then in vogue. So if present-day political theology does prove itself to be synchronized with the cultural universe of our day, then it is solidly grounded on that important front of contemporaneity. Of course it must also prove that it is solidly grounded on the diachronic front also, that it truly is in continuity with tradition. One must see whether the essential elements constitutive of the Christian faith do allow for the possibility of political mediation in theology. However, whether this possibility becomes a reality in fact will depend on cultural factors and determinants.

I am inclined to say, then, that one looks to tradition to ground political theology insofar as it is *theology,* but not insofar as it is *political* theology. This is not to suggest that biblical theology is devoid of political elements. But the theology contained in the Bible is not, or is not always, a politically mediated theology. (Indeed it is mediated more by Judaic mythology than by anything else.) If theology adopts some sort of political mediation today, that is due to cultural reasons rather than to biblical ones.

It makes no sense, then, to ask this sort of question as some suspicious authors do: "Are we to maintain, then, that the given cultural situation provides the only justification—a rather pragmatic one indeed—for the kind of discourse chosen by a theologian?" (163:379). It seems much more sensible to recognize that theology "can no longer determine the unity and peculiarity of its object in a purely theological way," that to do this it must also have recourse "to the canon of practical ecclesial awareness" (301:300). "The history of the church and theology is essentially a reaction of both to the historical situation of the world" (346:5). We must renounce the tempting dream of "theological purism" (59:51, 91, 116). Political theology finds one source of justification, not the only one, in the fact that it is related to the collective awareness of Christians (which is particularly sensitive to politics today) and reacting in a meaningful way to the contemporary world situation.

A theology is well founded, in part at least, when it is in synchrony with its age. This thesis takes on greater and even more decisive weight within a dialectical conception of reality. And precisely because current political theology does presuppose a dialectical conception of itself and of human realities, it views the problem of theological grounding very differently than does positive theology.

Traditional dogmatics imagined that Christian beliefs depended exclusively on biblical and apostolic teaching, having nothing to do with ideologies and cultures. It forged the myth of faith's independence from political regimes, social situations, and cultural conceptions. Faith, it said, or still says, transcends cultures even though it may take its forms of expression from them.

There is no such independence from the dialectical viewpoint. Nothing human is independent; everything is interdependent, with, as Marxism specifies, an underlying material base. Faith and theology are viewed as dependent on a social and economic base, upon which they may actively react in turn. The current political cast of faith and theology depends on the same socioeconomic determinations that have also produced a shift towards politics in science, medicine, the arts, and personal activity. To ask whether a political theology is well grounded today is equivalent to asking whether an implicated or committed art is justified today. Both are justified or well grounded insofar as they are legitimate products on the superstructural level of a specific situation at the level of the material infrastructure.

Thus, by virtue of its dialectical premises, political theology has its own peculiar viewpoint regarding what is and is not well founded in theology. It entails a new concept of theological validity and legitimation. The depth and solidity of theology's validity now rests upon its relationship to a social situation. A theology is well grounded when it makes the gospel of Jesus Christ meaningful to its contemporaries. And according to this new concept it has contributed, political theology itself is well grounded.

Up to the present day Christianity has in fact transcended different cultures. It has transcended them insofar as it has been capable of passing from one to another without losing itself. This is a datum of history, and in that sense one can and must talk about the transcendence of the faith vis-à-vis cultures. To a theology with a dialectical viewpoint, however, this does not prove the independence of dogma from society. It simply proves the perdurance of a theologal dimension through history, a dimension that has taken on different concrete manifestations depending on the nature of the societal base. The transcendence of the faith vis-à-vis culture is a matter for factual verification in terms of past history. It is not a de jure thesis that can make any claims with regard to the future. A critical theology cannot permit itself to engage in predictions about the future. To state with confidence that the Christian faith will perdure no matter what sort of underlying social relationships prevail is to make a dogmatic affirmation. Such an affirmation is quite understandable within the framework of traditional theology, but it exceeds the assertive capability of a critical-dialectical theology such as a sound and consistent political theology would be.

Consistent with the society in which it arises, political theology sees itself solidly grounded on that front. It views the relationship between religious ideas and social structures as one of dependence or dialectical interdependence. This enables it to comprehend the rise and disappearance of theological systems in the past as something based not on mere chance but on relationships with the social base. By verifying the fact that the faith has proved to be possible in very different situations and cultures, it feels justified in looking toward the future with confidence. It does not presume to be able to make dogmatic assertions about that future and it does not see any sure guarantees for its confidence. But it has real hope that the faith will continue to show the same capacity to perdure in the cultures of the future.

PART TWO

PROGRAM

4

Looking at the Past: Liberative Memories

1. OUTLINES OF A PROGRAM

Political theology, or a theology that is politically mediated if you prefer, is one that defines itself basically as a critical, public, and practical theology. To these basic structural traits can be added several others that circumscribe it historically: its involvement in a dialectical anthropology, its adoption, to a greater or lesser degree, of the Marxist critique, and its rejection of the New Christendom ideal. These common features, which are shared by theologies as different as the theology of liberation, the theology of revolution, and the theology of hope, make it clear that the term "political theology" is more than a convenient label for theologies of different inspiration, that there is a relatively homogeneous theological space that corresponds to the label.

Despite these shared features actually current efforts to shape a political theology do not always display any clear-cut unity. Analysis may sometimes uncover irreducible discrepancies (see chapter 7). At other times, however, in-depth study enables one to see deeper underlying affinities between theologies that seem very different on the surface.

The impression that political theologies are fragmentary and disorderly derives first from their literary presentation. Most of the writings in this field are in the form of essays: articles in magazines, chapters in books dealing with various topics, and anthologies of disconnected essays by different authors. There are relatively few books on political theology that have been written by one person and that treat the matter in a fairly extensive, unified, and systematic way. That is why the works of Gutiérrez (230), Assmann (59), Xhaufflaire (424), and Biot (72) are of particular interest. They do attempt to work out a fairly complete program of political theology and to compare their results with more or less similar efforts.

Unfortunately repetition rather than in-depth treatment is the characteristic feature of most political theologies. The work of Metz, for example, is very repetitive. What he says in two or three works seems to be repeated ad infinitum in all his other writings. Some articles seem so similar to each other that the reader can only wonder whether one and the same text has been slightly corrected by the author, whether he is dealing with different versions of the same text, or simply whether the author is being exploited by his publishers. And that does not take into account the authors who merely reiterate the theological views of others as if they were certain formulations.

In short, the fragmentariness of the essay form, the excessive repetition of the same ideas, and the lack of in-depth treatment means that political theology is suffering from grave programmatic and methodological deficiencies. On the one hand it lacks a comprehensive vision and a full development of the theological interpretation of the gospel; it is defective in its program, its content, its line of argumentation. On the other hand it also lacks in-depth critical reflection about itself; it is defective in theory and method.

Is it possible to repair these programmatic and methodological deficiencies? I think it is, and it must also be said that not all the literature of political theology suffers from the defects mentioned. In any case, a critical introduction to political theologies must direct its attention to those two aspects, attempting to arrange its themes into some unitary form of discourse and then to reflect on the ultimate sense of that discourse. The programmatic task is what will occupy us in Part Two. The critical and theoretical task will concern us in Part Three.

The programmatic problem might be put as follows. Some theologians talk about political theology in connection with eschatology and God's promises. Some link it with evangelical charity, interpreting this as political charity that calls for a class option in favor of the oppressed. Some conceive political theology basically as a theology of the Exodus, or else associate it with Jesus' polemical attitude toward the political powers of his own day. Sometimes this critical and political interpretation of the faith is presented as if it were grounded exclusively on one biblical idea: e.g., hope, or conversion, or the new man and the new earth. Moreover, predilection for one theme seems to entail not only the subordination of other themes but their total neglect. And there are also one-sided and intolerant positions that maintain a true political theology has to be a theology of eschatology or conversion or whatever.

Such one-sidedness and single-track thinking seems to be most unfortunate. Against all such one-sided views, we must maintain firmly that political theology, like all theology, is proven to be consistent only when it addresses all the questions. Against all such forms of theological astigmatism we must propose and work out a truly multidimensional and comprehensive vision, exploring the question of God through the whole universe of reality and the totality of Christian witness (188: 7–8).

In this and the two following chapters I shall attempt to present the program of political theology as completely as possible. My treatment will not be exhaustive, needless to say, but it will try to set forth the content and themes of political theology. Specific themes will not always be worked out as much as they might be. That has been done in some studies, though at times in a somewhat disconnected way, and it goes beyond the bounds of a general introduction such as this book purports to be. What has not been done for the most part, and what deserves particular attention right now, is the job of linking one set of themes with other sets and fashioning them into a relatively complete program. I shall try to trace out such a program in Part Two of this book, with several aims in mind: (1) to prove that political theology can go beyond the essay level and be developed systematically; (2) to make it clear that political theology does adopt the traditional categories of theology and reinterpret them in a new key, so that its connection with Christian tradition can be seen; and (3) to establish some coherence and unity between the different points of view that have been expressed in essays on political theology but that have not been satisfactorily compared and contrasted with one another.

The program of political theology can be worked out according to a variety of schemas. Here I shall use a historical reference as the base point, considering how political theology looks at the past, the present, and the future. In the concrete, political theology finds its model in certain historical paradigms from the past that are offered it by biblical tradition, then tries to establish ties with some sort of historical praxis that will be effective in the present, and looks forward with hope towards some promised future. This basic framework, then, enables us to recapture the threefold dimension of Christianity in the framework of a political theology. It enables us to focus on faith as the evocation and remembrance of certain testimony, on charity as a praxis that can and does alter existing reality, and on hope as an openness to the promise that is yet to be fulfilled. This threefold dimension is what gives specific identity to the Christian conscience (182:149).

This basic schema will also enable us to consider the three

vectors that we said a political theology must have when we were discussing the idea-set of the New Christendom movement. We then noted that this movement had a historical model, a prospective image of the future, and a doctrine defining Christian activity in the present. Without these three references a political theology could hardly regard itself as complete. Insofar as any current political theology seeks to replace older political theologies, it must spell out its foundational models in Christian tradition (chapter 4), its operational thrust in the present (chapter 5), and the future horizon to which it is open (chapter 6).

2. MODEL EVENTS, SECTS, AND PROPHETISM

Political theology is rooted in certain historical paradigms that make it possible. It considers its theses to be authorized by certain precedents in biblical and Christian tradition. These precedents are not really ideas, doctrines, or sayings contained in the Bible and tradition and available for the use of political theology; all these could be used to interpret not only the historical past but also the present and the future. The precedents in question are events or happenings, wondrous deeds inscribed in time and history that give support and legitimacy to the practical, political, and critical thrust of political theology.

Connection with the past is absolutely essential. It is particularly necessary in theology. If a theology wants to go on considering itself Christian, it must demonstrate its connection with the constitutive or foundational moments of Christianity—though this should not be equated with any overly simplistic summons to "get back to the sources." The same link, however, is also required of any theory or praxis that does not want to end up in mere fantasies. No one lives without a past, not even revolutionaries. The past makes its presence felt in the methodology, the practical plans, and even the lexicon of revolution. In that particular context it is the revolutionary past that provides concrete shape to what might otherwise remain a passing fancy. When a cultural revolution is seen as a long march through institutions (167:130), for example, it is being viewed along the lines of the "long march" taken by Mao Tse-tung and the Chinese Communists in 1935. When the May 1968 student revolt in France is referred to as the "takeover" of the word (115), there is either an explicit or implicit allusion to the takeover of the Bastille in 1789. The events of 1968 will in turn serve as a paradigm for future revolutionary acts, which will be viewed as another "French May," or "Prague Spring," or "American hot summer."

When one selects certain events from past history, then history itself seems to take on sense and direction. A particular line of action seems to follow, and the outlines of a future can be glimpsed. By choosing certain happenings as models, we convert the past into history and endow it with meaning. Unless we choose such models, there is no history at all and no real meaning for human praxis. Time becomes an indistinct flux, and the future ceases to serve as a compass for our concrete activity.

The Christian is not a person without history. To be a Christian, in fact, means to have adopted as one's own a history and tradition of witness that is focused on Jesus Christ. Faith presupposes an ordering of the past in which certain specific happenings are regarded as highly meaningful; they form Christian history. But in the context of this overall history each brand of theological discourse makes a further specific selection and arrangement, stressing certain Christian events rather than others.

In the history that goes to make up the Christian faith, a history narrated by the Old and New Testaments, political theology has a predilection for three exemplary situations or happenings: the Exodus (or liberation) of the Hebrews from bondage in Egypt; prophetism as a methodical critique and criticism of existing institutions; and the mortal conflict of Jesus with the social authorities or power-centers of his day. The solid grounding of a theology in tradition has two aspects: a foundation (1) in tradition that is also (2) in line with the traditional criterion as to what gives grounding to a theology. Political theology is solidly grounded on this front insofar as it remains faithful to those three historical precedents and accepts them as archetypes.

To these three biblical archetypes we would do well to add a fourth extrabiblical reference point: the long line of Christian millenarians, utopians, and revolutionaries who have dotted the pages of Christian history over the past twenty centuries. They, too, are part of the tradition that the theologian can and should claim as ancestral witness to the faith. They, too, furnish historical paradigms worthy of serious attention by political theology. So far, however, theologians have paid hardly any attention at all to past messianic revolutionary movements that were Christian in inspiration. In all likelihood, two reasons account for this neglect. First of all, those movements do not form part of the essential, constitutive elements of Christian tradition as do biblical and apostolic traditions; hence they are regarded as irrelevant insofar as the grounding of a theological position is concerned. Secondly, such movements have almost always been heterodox, and this makes them look rather unsalvageable in the eyes of theology. As a result it appears that messianic Christian movements in history have been given closer study and better appreciation by non-Christians than by Christian theologians.

This is particularly true of Ernst Bloch, who has devoted a book to Thomas Münzer (79) and other studies to radical Christian movements (76). The positive evaluation arrived at by Bloch should not be lost sight of by political theology. Bloch suggests that the revolutionary theology of Christian millenarianism represents the youthful dream of incipient socialism, which can now be brought to fruition for the first time by scientific socialism. That earlier theology entertained ideals it could not flesh out in reality because it lacked an adequate methodology.

Among the theologians only Richard Shaull has taken the phenomenon of revolutionary Christian sects into serious account. He interprets them in line with the typology of Troeltsch, which makes a distinction between church and sect (409). In this view churches exert their influence through existing power structures whereas sects react against compromise and entanglement with the established social order. Shaull maintains that the time has come to rediscover the heritage of such Christian sects as "agents of revolution" and daring dissenters. He goes so far as to propose that the church be given a new configuration along the lines of a sect, and that ecumenism be based on an "International" of sects (391:38).

This proposal, which ultimately comes down to calling for a dissolution of "church" in favor of a communion between "sects," calls for some comment. If a church is defined as such sociologically by virtue of its integration into a given culture and its ties with existing social institutions whereas a sect is defined by its refusal to accept inculturation and commitment to the established order, then obviously a theology of liberation or revolution must be grounded sociologically on the basis of the sect just as the earlier theology of Christendom was based on the church. Only sects, understood in the sense just described, can offer a sound social and practical base for a theology of dissent, protest, and counterculture.

On the other side of the coin, however, sect has customarily been differentiated from church by the fact that the former represents a group of people seeking to flee from the world and social responsibilities. In that respect there is some question as to the validity or propriety of attributing a Christian political praxis to sects. It would be better to say that a praxis of liberation and revolution inspired by the gospel message would properly be found in Christian groups who shared some of the traditional features of churches and other features characteristic of sects. From the former it would derive its involvement in society and culture; from the latter it would draw its praxis of critical discernment and dissent.

This would lead to a redefinition of the Christian community in terms equally far removed from the older model of sect and the older model of church. To be sure, this possibility has not escaped the notice of those concerned with the sociology of Christianity. As early as 1929 Richard Niebuhr introduced the notion of a dynamic interaction and mutual relationship between church and sect (324). What we see occurring today among some groups of Christians in conjunction with the new critical and public theology is the dropping of certain traits traditionally associated with "churches" and the adoption of certain traits characteristic of "sects."

This repositioning of the Christian community somewhere midway between "church" and "sect" produces certain important consequences. It means that the common theology and praxis of Christians must adopt the heritage of the old dissident and heterodox sects, respecting it as much as it respects the orthodox heritage of the churches. A general thrust toward rehabilitating heterodox figures of an earlier day and recovering the truths they defended with greater or lesser success comes naturally to current political theology. It is well within its rights in trying to recapture the heritage of heterodox revolutionaries and justify its claim to be Christian. Present-day theology of liberation and revolution should take possession of its full and complete history, which would have to include the following: thirteenth-century Franciscanism as a protest movement of lay people, Bartolomé de Las Casas's defense of the natives of America (104, 165:65–81), the evangelizing and socioeconomic reality of the Jesuit Reductions in Paraguay, and Christian utopian socialism of the nineteenth century. However, it would also include the activities of others whose approach was regarded as heretical: Joachim of Fiore, John Wyclif, John Hus, the Waldensians, Thomas Münzer, and others whose program called for the creation of a very different society (186:128–35). It is certainly true that these earlier figures usually envisioned their different society as some form of evangelical Christendom, a model that has now been discarded. But it is not a matter of hearkening back to their dreams; it is a matter of extracting anything that might be of practical significance for us today.

Though it does form part of biblical tradition, prophetism has not been subjected to thorough or rigorous study by political theology. This is not to say that there is no talk about prophetism. On the contrary, the lexicon of prophetism is very much in vogue right now. People frequently talk about the prophetic character of Christian speech and Christian praxis, usually associating this with the denunciation of collective sinful situations. That is even true of some episcopal documents: e.g., the documents of the Medellín Conference in 1968 or the remarks of the Spanish bishops on the church and the political community in January 1973. Both of these approach social issues in terms of the "prophetic denunciation" of unjust situations.

Present-day consideration of the prophets has so far focused on their critical and practical stance, on their role as public provocateurs. It has also focused on the anticipatory thrust and import of their gestures. The biblical prophet is seen as a person of the future (which is a perfectly traditional view) and as a person lashing out at established conventions and existing social institutions (367)—an aspect akin to the novel character of current political theology. This backward look at biblical prophetism leads to a stress on the prophetic duty of the Christian. This duty is described in terms of the biblical model. It includes prophetic denunciation, prophetic gestures, and a whole literary genre of religious and political prophetism that is extensive enough to have already provoked critics (54).

However, the attribution of a prophetic impulse to Christianity and, to an even greater degree, the allusion to the biblical prophetic paradigm seem to be a relatively secondary and marginal element in current political interpretation of the gospel. Prophetism is not a basic principle in political theology, a substantive principle that is fully worked out to a set of ultimate conclusions. We do find relatively well developed theologies of the Exodus and of messianism, but we do not find any well developed theology of prophetism. The use of prophetic language in current theology is not accompanied by any careful working out of the theological sense of the prophetic paradigm. Though a theory of prophetism is of vital importance in grounding political theology, this theology has not elaborated any such theory.

On every side biblical prophetism is related with political theology. Though prophetism is predominantly orientated towards the future, it is in fact bound up with all three temporal dimensions used here to schematize political theology. In the biblical prophets we find an eschatological, apocalyptic, utopian horizon pointing toward a promised messianic future. The book of Isaiah offers the best example of an eschatological utopia where ultimate reconciliation is promised: "Then the wolf shall be a guest of the lamb, and the leopard shall lie down with the kid; the calf and the young lion shall browse together, with a little child to guide them" (Isa. 11:6). In the biblical prophets we also find a practical interpretation of the events and situations they are compelled to live through: the misfortunes of the Hebrew nation, the exile in Babylon, and the expectant yearning for a return to Israel. By virtue of their attention to the historical vicissitudes of the present, the hermeneutic categories of the prophets are valid and useful for a politico-theological interpretation of the present by every generation of Christians. When it comes to the dimension we are considering specifically here—i.e., exemplary happenings in past history—it is the acts and symbolic gestures of the biblical prophets that deserve particular consideration, not their sayings, promises, or interpretations. For example, Jeremiah purchases a field when all seems lost for Judah (Jer. 32), Hosea contracts marriage with a harlot (Hos. 1), and three young men refuse to worship the golden statue set up by King Nebuchadnezzar of Babylon (Dan. 3). Their actions are historical paradigms that form an essential part of Christian faith and summon us to a public, critical praxis with a corresponding political theology.

Many of these model precedents from the past, such as the various Christian movements of protest and prophetism, have not been studied very seriously as yet. But a few have been worked out in greater detail by political theology. This is true of two paradigms in particular, which we shall consider in detail throughout the rest of this chapter. They are (1) the Hebrew exodus from Egypt and (2) Jesus' confrontation with the public authorities of his day. So far they are the two paradigms that have been extensively studied by recent theology and that constitute the two most important chapters in its retrospective glance at its own grounding in past history.

3. EXODUS THEOLOGY

Included in current political theology is an Exodus theology. The image of the church as an "exodus community," which was made popular by Moltmann, has social and political connotations: "Christendom must dare to undertake the Exodus, viewing its societal roles as a new Babylonian captivity." A Christendom on exodus means a group "that is not capable of being assimilated or conquered," that is ever ready to "flee the social roles that have been set for it by society"(312:418–19). Most importantly of all, it means that Christendom, as the bearer of the gospel hope, "enters into a polemical and liberative relationship not just with the religions and ideologies of human beings but even more so with everyday life." The hope of a Christendom on exodus entails "practical resistance" and "creative refashioning" that calls into question the existing order and serves what is to come in the future (312:425–26).

In Moltmann's thinking the Exodus is nothing but a theological category or a theological representation. Of course it contains an implicit reference to the historical fact of the Hebrews' liberation from Egypt, but the weight of his ecclesiology bears down more on the present moment than on the past historical model. His theology is a theology of hope more than it is an Exodus theology. In it the Exodus is simply one among many images serving to outline the community's attitude of hope.

Some other theologians have put more stress on the Hebrew Exodus as an event that really happened in past history. They forcefully underline its historical reality, its value as a model for Christian praxis, and its importance for the possibility of talking about God in terms of a liberation theology. Thus they formulate an Exodus theology in the strict sense of that term. The departure from Egypt is much more than a mere image designed to enrich theological representations; it becomes the primeval and fundamental happening of the history of divine revelation itself. The Exodus comes to constitute the prototype of divine revelation, the privileged moment in which God once manifested himself and now continues to do the same. At the same time the Exodus of history did not just signify a withdrawal from socially assigned roles. It was a liberative revolution in the strict sense, a socially subversive act comparable to slave rebellions or other struggles of oppressed peoples against imperialism. The significance of that act for the theologian lies in the fact that it was carried out under the inspiration of faith and interpreted as the portentous result of a divine revelation; even more importantly, it brought into existence a nation of people, the Israelites, who thereby began to serve as the bearer of God's promises.

The connection between the Exodus and the original divine revelation is clearly brought out by Harvey Cox. He sees it as the focal point of the theology of desacralization. It simultaneously symbolizes and realizes man's liberation from a sacral political order so that he may involve himself in history and social change. Picking up a traditional theme of biblical exegesis that underlines the fact that the God of the Bible reveals himself in the events of history rather than in physical or cosmic phenomena as other cosmic or nature deities do, Cox goes on to point out that the first and foremost event in which God spoke decisively to the Hebrews was a liberation event that brought them out of Egypt. He thinks it is of the utmost significance that the event in question brought about a major social change, that it was what we today would call a mass act of civil disobedience. Thus the Exodus, seen as an "act of insurrection," can support a theology of revolution. In his early work Cox prefers to talk about a "theology of rapid social change" rather than about a theology of revolution (126:47–48). In Christian praxis the import of the Exodus is to encourage the abandonment of older immobilist attitudes. Once Christians are courageous enough to move out of the paralyzing structures of the present, God himself will furnish them with new ones. They do not need a detailed plan of the promised land before leaving Egypt (126:258).

Latin American theology also stresses the fact that liberation from Egypt was a political act, noting the link between it and creation in the Hebrew experience; those two events are almost completely identified in the mind of the Israelites (230:203–4). To be created by God is equivalent to being free. Indeed the very possibility of appreciating life and the world as creation depends on the concrete experience of liberation. People begin to see their own history as an exodus before they begin to see the universe as the creative work of God. Divine revelation, including the fact that the world is God's creation, begins with the freedom inaugurated in the Exodus. As Jean Cardonnel says:

> Sacred history, the conscious history of a people, does not begin in Genesis but in Exodus. The concrete experience of liberation is the only way to discover the fact of creation. It is only the deeply lived experience of oppression that prompts man to work toward his radical liberation, in which process he can come to discover that the world is a creation (100:123).

It is in the work of Cardonnel that Exodus theology finds its fullest elaboration and its most passionate tones. As he sees it, God makes himself known precisely by making the cause of the oppressed his own and intervening on the side of their liberation. Here the Exodus theme links with another theme of major importance in current political theology: the need to opt for the poor and oppressed because the gospel message is a proclamation of liberation addressed primarily to them. God's revelation is the announcement of his identification with the subjugated:

> It is first and foremost in making the cause of the oppressed his own that God does his work and manifests the fact that he is God. He reveals himself as the one who rouses and creates a people who had not existed as such before. Whereas other deities simply endorse the victories of their people, the specific character of the one and only God is the fact that he intervenes in the very midst of abandonment and dereliction. His divine revelation begins with the liberation of the most oppressed and tortured people, who thereby move prophetically from oppression to liberation (21:81).

That is what specifically identifies the God of the Bible and distinguishes him from the deity of metaphysics. In the outlook of Cardonnel an Exodus theology is what clarifies

Christian theology and gives it its essential and distinctive character. Either theology is an Exodus theology or it is not Christian at all:

> The revealed God to whom I offer my faith is infinitely different from the deity of deism. He is not a "supreme being" whose loveless benevolence derives from his arbitrary power. Rather, he it is who intervenes in the history of human beings. The originality of revelation lies in the fact that God makes himself known by quickening the spirit of a people threatened with total defeat. That is the real meaning of Israel's destiny, which anticipates the passover of all peoples from a fatalistic order to an order of freedom. There is some undeniable affinity between God and weakness. The eternal one is revealed in the despised and oppressed in order to confound the powerful (21:80).

So the Exodus is the first event of revelation and salvation. For the first time human beings realize that they have been saved by God through their concrete experience of liberation from oppression and the attainment of a new freedom. The Exodus experience was a liberation experience (369:118–21), and it constitutes the archetypal event in the historical self-awareness of the Christian faith. Its profile gives form to the other historical commitments of the believer. When theology tries to understand itself through its recollection of the Exodus, it is proceeding as revolutionary theory does when it recalls the historical precedents set for it by the French or Russian or Chinese revolution. The memory evoked in this process is then incorporated into the praxis of the present and its prospective hopes for the immediate future. It becomes an image and a standard accompanying one's revolutionary understanding of the time. In the case of theology, the Exodus is a symbol of throwing off the yoke, breaking away from established institutions, and evincing the ability of a people to fashion or refashion a life for themselves. They throw off the suffocating convenience of their age-old situation, lured on by the enticements of a new promised land. The Exodus symbolizes a theological grasp of history as the possibility for change and discontinuity, as malleable material in human hands, as a line of action based on the awareness that one has been liberated by God.

At this point one thing should be noted, however: Before it was an image or symbol that might be used like any other theological representation, the Exodus was a historical fact. When one talks about "conversion" or "charity" or "salvation," as we shall do in the next chapter, one is utilizing theological categories that are not empirical realities in any immediate or direct sense. There should be some material, tangible facts underlying these terms and giving them substantive reality, but the terms themselves are primarily theological categories; they are keys for representation and interpretation, not facts or happenings. The Exodus, by contrast, is a *matter of fact,* not a key for representation and interpretation. It must be considered in terms of its historical reality before one attempts to speculate on its symbolic import.

The same point holds true for the other historical paradigms cited here: prophetism as the historical stance of certain individual human beings and Jesus' clash with the public authorities of his day. The conclusions we arrived at concerning the Exodus apply equally to the other historical paradigms.

4. INTERPRETATION AND EVENT

Biot has made some sound and useful criticisms of Exodus theology. But if we stress the point that the Exodus must be viewed as a real event before being used as a theological category, we can narrow the scope of his objections. There is a twofold thrust to his objections. First of all, he wisely warns us against the precritical ingenuousness of some versions of Exodus theology. Biot reminds us that we must not make the mistake of extrapolating the biblical account of the Exodus in attempting to interpret its political import here and now: "It can be legitimate to view the Exodus happening as the prototype for present-day revolutionary activity, if we make sure to point out that no biblical author interpreted it thus." The legitimacy of such an interpretation is greatly diminished by Biot, however, as he makes it a matter of individual taste or preference: "As a matter of personal taste, someone may come to view the Exodus story as a confirmation of his own revolutionary commitment; but he must recognize that this interpretation itself is not biblical."

In addition to this criticism of an exegetical nature, Biot has another of a theological cast. Even if the Bible itself were to offer the aforementioned interpretation of the Exodus, "that in itself would not hallow or canonize revolution." His line of reasoning is based on an indisputable premise: "The historical events narrated in the Bible cannot constitute moral norms." Thus the fact of the Exodus does not point of necessity toward a theology of revolution (72:129).

These criticisms are healthy warnings against oversimplistic versions of Exodus theology or a theology of revolution. But they also embody serious misunderstandings, an analysis of which will help us to see more clearly what the true import of the Exodus is as a historical model for political theology.

Insofar as Biot's first criticism is concerned, it is up to exegetes to decide the question. The interpretation of the Exodus event as an act of resistance, insurrection, and liberation is highly suggestive, but is that the biblical interpretation? It may well be that theologians of the Exodus have been too hasty in assuming a "yes" answer to that question. But Biot himself seems to be rather hasty in assuming a "no" answer without spelling out his exegetical reasoning on the matter. There is every reason, of course, to try to find out exactly what the Bible thinks about the Exodus as a possible archetype for civil insurrection motivated by Christian hope in a new earth. But even here it is worth pointing out that the critical issue is not so much the Bible's interpretation of the Exodus happening as *the happening itself* which is related by the Bible. The important issue is not whether a political interpretation of the Exodus has a solid basis in the Bible; it is whether the happening itself is biblical. In short, it is a question of historical fact, not a question of hermeneutics.

If we consider the Exodus as a historical reality, then it is more or less beside the point whether the Bible does or does not interpret it along the same lines as current political theology. The fact that the biblical authors might not have taken account of the subversive political significance of the flight from Egypt is not a crushing blow. The crucial point is that from the way they relate the event this subversive political significance seems to be clear and obvious. It flows from the very nature of the event itself, whether those who reported the event in the Bible were aware of it or not. The Exodus from Egypt was a political act, clearly bearing the stamp of resistance and rebellion. And if an action of that sort lies at the very origin of biblical tradition, then on that score there is justification for an Exodus theology and its prolongations in a theology of liberation. Political theology relates to the event of the Exodus itself, with the escape from Egypt as history, not (or not only) with the understanding and interpretation of that event by the biblical writers.

There is a real core of truth in Biot's second objection. Biblical facts and events do not give rise to moral norms; in fact they are not always exemplars either. This is obvious enough when the Bible itself condemns them as sinful. But even those deeds it regards positively or applauds loudly do not necessarily possess exemplary value by virtue of that simple fact. It would be naive to try to construct a theological or moral teaching on the story of Judith, for example. To that extent Biot's objection is very much to the point. But here again we find that it, too, has limitations and cannot be pushed further.

It is misleading to talk in generic terms about "the historical events narrated by the Bible," as Biot does, placing them alongside each other indiscriminately and then adding that they do not canonize anything. The Judith event is not on the same plane as the Exodus event; hence the former cannot have the same exemplary value as the latter. If we are talking about the most fundamental events of what is called salvation history, we cannot rightly say that they do not contain any import as models. Like the cross, the Exodus does have archetypal significance. Of course it would be a very different matter if one were to claim that they give rise to moral norms. Neither the cross nor the Exodus can be said to establish any moral norm.

The cross, for example, does specify a general moral attitude, but not a concrete norm. There is a theology and also an ethics of the cross, but there are no precepts arising directly out of it. In like manner there is a morality and a theology of the Exodus, though one cannot derive codifiable norms from it. The Exodus has exemplary and paradigmatic value, though it has no normative value in a case-book sense. This conclusion follows from the very nature of the sequence of events that faith accepts as salvation history. If salvation history, viewed as an overall process and in terms of its cardinal happenings, does not have any value for the Christian as exemplar and prototype, what possible import could it possess?

Let us grant, then, that the Exodus does not give rise to any moral norm prescribing and sanctioning revolution or any other social change. No obligation to revolution, and indeed no obligation whatsoever, follows from the fact of the Exodus. There is no moral precept to engage in revolution, or liberating insurrection. Moreover, one is making a gratuitous assertion if one claims that political theology tries to defend the existence of such a norm flowing from some event narrated in the Bible. But that does not mean that the Exodus does not possess exemplary value as a paradigm and archetype. The Exodus is not a norm-giving memory, it is an example-giving memory. While evocation of that event does not create obligations, it does nourish Christian consciousness, give inspiration to the imagination of the faith, and prompt people to liberative action.

The same holds true for other facts and events in the Bible. They are not normative; they are sources of inspiration and liberation. They give rise to a possibility, not to a necessary obligation. In presenting certain actions performed by our forefathers in the faith as an integral part of history in which God is a participant, the biblical account authorizes us to take analogous action on the basis of our faith. To put it concretely, the Exodus is a liberative memory with regard to the possibility of insurrection. The biblical narrative of the escape from Egypt liberates people from fear of revolution. It takes away the fear that rises in us when we advert to the illicit nature of disobedience or insurrection against political authority. Should we be afraid that affiliation with a revolution is incompatible with our faith, the example of the Exodus is there to dispel that particular fear. The Exodus certifies that insurrection is a stance or line of action that is possible for one who has faith.

The same basic interpretation holds true for the sayings of the Bible. They are liberative pronouncements, not constraining ones. One cannot rigorously deduce political norms or even general norms of action from them. The belief that the biblical text contains precepts of divine law in the strict sense is bound up with the myth of the Bible as a revealed oracle. But as soon as Scripture ceases to be viewed as such an oracle, the notion that its precepts are the precepts of God himself disappears (190:179–94).

It must also be pointed out that in the Bible we find not one but several different models of political behavior. Smolik, for example, has been able to detect three models of Christian social life in the New Testament: (1) a prepolitical model in the gospels; (2) a conservative model in the writings of Paul; and (3) a revolutionary model in the book of Revelation (395). Which of these would be obligatory? Since there is a variety of political paradigms in the Bible, there is clearly no room for a constrictive interpretation. They cannot all be normative at the very same time; hence none of them is normative. With its doctrinal pronouncements and its historical narratives the Bible offers inspirational models, not prescriptive standards.

In that sense Spaemann is quite correct when he makes the following observation in the course of criticizing political theology: "It is not possible to deduce concrete maxims of political conduct from theological pronouncements" (398:488). That is true, of course. But political theology definitely does not try to derive political maxims from theological assertions; it does not propose a theologically grounded politics. Spaemann's objection might well apply to the older theologies of the Christendom outlook, but it does not really apply to current political theology. In the latter there is no causal or logical connection between adhesion to the faith and political affiliation, much less between specific dogmatic theses and specific civil attitudes. As Blanquart points out, the believer "is not a revolutionary because he is a Christian; rather, being a revolutionary is his way of being a Christian" (74:147). François Biot, who also stresses the fact that the road from faith to politics is a complicated one rather than a matter of straightforward deductive reasoning, spells out the deeper reason that rules out any deductive reasoning of such a kind: "People are political beings before being Christians, if they are Christians at all." Thus any such formula as "I am a socialist because I am a Christian" is objectively unacceptable, even though it may sum up the personal path of some people who went on from their faith to discover socialism (72:191–212).

Let us get back to the Exodus for a moment and its potential value as an exemplar. Insofar as it is an event that was prior in time to Jesus Christ, our valuation of it will depend on our valuation of the Old Testament in general. Some time ago Ernst Bloch called attention to the fact that all Christian rebels have appealed to the Old Testament (79:47). Thus there is nothing peculiar in the fact that current political theology should do the same thing, since it too is critical and rebellious towards the prevailing social order. The current rehabilitation of politics in theology goes hand in hand with the corresponding rehabilitation of the Old Testament and its earthy realism (186:137–38). On a certain methodological level the current debate over political theology is also a debate over the present-day relevance of the Old Testament. Hans Maier, for example, fears all the current versions of political theology because he sees them bringing back the pagan and Jewish formulations of an ancient day (273:6). Such a rehabilitation, however, does not disturb the proponents of political theology at all. Sölle echoes the common feeling when she reproaches Bultmann for having neglected "the primary Jewish form (of hope) with which all political theology must be linked" (396:62).

Political theology is particularly deserving of a high credit rating if in fact there is not direct access to the faith of the New Testament and if the thrust of the Old Testament, with its tenacious hold on earthly reality and political history, continues to be a factor intrinsic to the adherence of the Christian. But political theology does not draw its models exclusively from the Old Testament. It also finds them in the New Testament, and in particular in the person of Jesus himself.

5. FROM AN APOLITICAL JESUS TO A CRITICAL JESUS

The attitude of Jesus toward political authority is of the highest importance for the Christian and for theology. Was Jesus purely religious in outlook and spirit, wholly uninterested in civil society and its institutions? Did he stand above the political struggles of his time, evincing some higher and loftier impartiality? Did he take a stand vis-à-vis the power structure? Was he even a revolutionary?

Traditionally exegesis and theology have answered these questions by stressing the impartiality and apolitical attitude of Jesus toward civil society. Theologians maintained that he always stood far above political realities, and various exegetical arguments were adduced to solidly underline his apolitical outlook. The chief support for this conclusion was the fact that Jesus clearly refused to accept the political expectations bound up with Jewish messianism. His rejection of political messianism is apparent throughtout the gospels, and it is highlighted both in the account of his temptations (Matt. 4:1–11) and in the report of his flight from those who would proclaim him king (John 6:15). This rejection would seem to give real verisimilitude to the image of an apolitical Jesus.

But the biographical apoliticism of Jesus has not prevented the politicization of christological dogma. Indeed, even within the Catholic orbit, there has arisen a curious dissociation between the Jesus of history and the Christ of faith. On the one hand every effort has been made to erase from the biography of the historical Jesus not only any desire for kingship (an effort well founded exegetically) but also every trace of political messianism and political interest in general. On the other hand, however, the Christ of faith was simultaneously exalted as a king. To be sure, he was regarded as a king in some transcendent sense. Yet this

King Christ of dogma gave rise to political effects: Emperors and kings governed in his name. Thus the apoliticism of the historical Jesus has been linked with a political Christology; and, as Schmidt points out, the image of this political Christ has obstructed our efforts to comprehend the political import of the public life of the historical Jesus (383:472). If we wish to rediscover the political messianism of the historical Jesus, we must forget Christ the King; because here Christology has obscured history.

The stress on the apoliticism of Jesus by traditional theology was to a certain extent an indication of healthy good sense. As it was, theology tended to go overboard in its reverence for the established order, going so far as to see that order grounded on the will of God. It would have been even more servile towards the established order if, in addition, it had attributed imperial designs to Jesus and invested him with the desire to make himself king. In this respect traditional theology deserves our appreciation. While it had a propensity to exalt authority and to formulate theses about Christ the King, it did at least refrain from seeing designs for terrestrial rule in the Jesus of history. It is quite clear that Jesus did refuse to be a king. And since politics was traditionally viewed as the exercise of institutional power, the portrait of an apolitical Jesus was correct in that sense.

Crespy tells us that "it is too early to speak unequivocally and unmistakably about the real political import of Jesus' life and death" (130:102). His comment may well be prompted by the meaning and connotations associated with the word "politics" up until very recent times, and the attendant ambivalence to which it gave rise. But isn't every political theology subject to the same ambiguity? The possibility of misunderstanding and equivocation is not enough to justify avoidance of the issue. It simply forces us to dispel the equivocation before we engage in political theology.

The fact is that traditional theology never got around to

considering another possible aspect of the political import of Jesus' life: his criticism of, and opposition to, power. Concerned wholly with the task of ruling out any identification of Jesus with the public authorities and power-centers and any pretension to political dominion on his part, traditional theology never considered the opposite side of the coin: i.e., his possible opposition to those very authorities and powers. And it is in terms of this latter focus that the question of Jesus' political attitude is being raised again today.

Even now some continue to defend the apoliticism of Jesus, adding that one cannot deduce from that fact that Christians are obliged to be equally apolitical. Le Guillou, for example, says: "Christ voluntarily manifested himself as the 'suffering servant' infinitely above all politics" (225:15). The apoliticism of Jesus is equally self-evident to René Coste: "He chose to be strictly apolitical, in the sense that he considered himself above politics at all times." Coste bases his line of reasoning here on Jesus' "categorical opposition to political messianism" (123:11 and 27–29). The ground of this line of argument is itself highly debatable, as we shall soon see. Even aside from that, the apoliticism he defends in his argument would only be valid if the term "politics" is taken in the old sense. It does not really apply to the more modern understanding of the term. Moreover, Coste himself goes on to say that the apoliticism of Jesus, paradoxically enough, can prompt Christians to assume the responsibility of fashioning a new approach toward public life and adopting a political stance (123:41).

Insofar as this basic outlook is concerned, it should be noted that it mechanically repeats a traditional thesis about the apoliticism of Jesus without adverting to the fact that there has been a profound change in the meaning of both the term "political" and the term "apolitical." When one fails to note this change, one leaves the meaning of both terms wrapped in obscurity.

Neither Le Guillou nor Coste explain what it means exactly to "be above politics." What is "politics" in their view? Though we may easily enough figure out the answer to that question, they themselves do not spell it out for us. Thus the apoliticism of Jesus remains a vague concept embracing some sort of ill-defined allergy toward the civil realm and the arena of social and economic conflicts. Their apolitical Jesus is a purely religious prophet (the "Suffering Servant") who never got involved in earthly affairs and the acute human tensions of his time. That apoliticism reflects a conservative theology that is deeply concerned to preserve the existing political and dogmatic order. Its political conservatism is reflected in the fear of seeing Jesus as an active opponent of existing public institutions because that would somehow diminish his stature. Political activity is looked down upon as something unworthy of Jesus or any great-spirited person. The dogmatic conservatism of this viewpoint is evident in its desire to maintain a few hoary assertions about the apoliticism of Jesus without adverting to the fact that a real semantic change may have turned their ultimate meaning completely upside down.

In any case it seems very hard to conceal the apparent fact that Jesus engaged in a confrontation with the public powers of his day. The point is made clear through the gospel narratives, and particularly in the fourth gospel. The confrontation grows more pointed and acute as it approaches its tragic denouement, so much so that any assertion about Jesus' apoliticism seems untenable and devoid of sense. Its only valid point would be its stress on the fact that Jesus did refuse to accept kingship.

The ultimate condemnation of Jesus, which was both a civil and a religious process, dispels any lingering doubts about the political thrust and scope of his public activity. The picture of an apolitical Jesus crumbles when we advert to his final destiny on the cross. Only two classes of people were executed in those days: common criminals and political enemies. And since Jesus was not a common criminal, his execution can only be explained as a government action prompted by political motives. To allege that reasons behind Jesus' crucifixion might have been exclusively religious is to forget the fact that religion is not just religion when it has a say in people's life and death; in such a case it is also a political institution. And that leaves room for some modified political view of Jesus' ministry at the very least.

This modified view accepts the fact that Jesus did clash with the political powers of his day, but it views this clash as an indirect one mediated through the religious issue. Jesus' criticism was itself religious in nature. It focused on the institutions of Judaism as a religion, attacking them because that religion had fallen into the trap of ritual externalism and formulism. But in a social system thoroughly suffused with a religious tradition and in a governmental system where priestly dictates form part of state policy, such criticism of religious cult becomes political criticism as well. So Jesus' polemics against political institutions and political authority flow indirectly from his polemics against religious institutions and authorities. Thus Jesus' attitude toward such things as the temple, the Sabbath, and the forgiveness of sins would indirectly lead to political repercussions, bringing him into confrontation with the civil authorities and hence to death on the cross.

This viewpoint underlies the statements of some people such as Weth, who says that "the revolutionary aspect of Jesus is his forgiveness of sin" (421:96). Statements of this sort provide for a political dimension in Jesus' work, but put their stress on a religious fact as the more direct and immediate focus of it.

This stance in Christology corresponds to another in ecclesiology that regards all criticism of religion as already political criticism (154:9). In this view theology takes on a political dimension by virtue of its ties with the church and its duty to engage in ecclesiastical criticism. Rendtorff put it this way: "The ecclesiastical ties of theology possess a political character as such, insofar as the ecclesiastical institution is a prime political factor; by the same token, then, criticism of the church as an institution is political criticism as well" (355:217).

I would voice two reservations about such a view. First of all, it is extremely vague and ill-defined. The political character of the church is clear enough when it constitutes an institution concerned with public order in a direct way—that is to say, in a sacral society. It is not so clear in a different type of social or ecclesiastical organization. Whether ecclesiastical criticism is also political criticism will depend on various factors and will admit of different modalities that should not be overlooked by a vague general statement. My second reservation has to do with the very nature of Christian commitment and that of political theology. Is Christian praxis revolutionary only insofar as it includes intraecclesiastical activity? Does theology possess a political dimension only insofar as it is criticism of the church as an institution?

The interpretation mentioned does have the merit of spelling out clearly this much: that the public activity of Jesus manifestly had a political thrust and was not apolitical. That in itself would be enough to solidly ground any political theology. If Jesus did engage in open conflict with the political authorities of his day precisely because of his good news—even though that may have been a secondary result of his main conflict with the religious authorities—that would be basic justification for a theology concerned to confront authority and power, for a public, critical, praxis-oriented theology.

But the data of the New Testament oblige us to go further than that. The aforementioned moderate interpretation plays down the data too much, as if it were afraid to taint the image of Jesus by implicating him directly in political debate. Such a desire to de-emphasize the political import of his public life and to regard it as a secondary offshoot of his work can only derive from a tacit deprecation of political realities. If man is essentially a political animal and if Jesus found self-fulfillment by leading a full human life, then what is wrong with attributing to him a line of activity that had directly political import? If the gospels had reported information about Jesus' poetic or artistic activity, would people be afraid to demean his religious import by viewing him as an artist or poet? Why is there so much scandal and panic about his political activity? The a priori stance that Jesus' ministry could not possibly have had any directly political import clearly derives from some sort of disdain for the political dimension in man.

6. THE CONFRONTATION WITH POWER

Viewed without any prejudices regarding political activity, the public life of Jesus takes on a more direct and immediate political dimension. In Jesus we find an explicit criticism of civil authority and a direct confrontation with it, quite apart from any indirect consequences arising from his religious criticism. To mention only one point, the moment when this confrontation reaches its apex, Jesus stands defiantly silent before Herod and sternly admonishes Pilate that his authority comes from above (186:120–22). That alone proves that Jesus stood toe to toe with the civil authorities and challenged them personally and directly.

So it would seem that theology cannot rest content with a view that sees only indirect political import in Jesus' public activity. It is wholly justified in seeing in the gospel story a happening that is both directly political and directly religious. That at least is the view of a fair number of theologians who regard the political import of his message as just as essential and primary as its religious content. Metz writes: "The salvation toward which Christian faith and hope direct its gaze is not a private salvation. The proclamation of this salvation led Jesus to a fatal conflict with the public authorities of his day." He then goes on to point out that the cross was not framed in a purely religious context (297:391), which would indicate that the mortal collision between Jesus and the public authorities lay above and beyond any neat distinction between the religious and the political.

Even more clear-cut on this particular point is Leslie Dewart. He forthrightly and explicitly rules out as inadequate the interpretation that the gospel message is revolutionary only in the vague sense that the rehabilitation or restoration of the human condition as a whole implies certain consequences for the ongoing march of political affairs. Dewart unflinchingly advocates the political messianism of Jesus, in the sense that Jesus was engaged in the "politics of God" and that political tasks possess a religious import (and vice-versa). With regard to the life story of Jesus, Dewart says a political connotation was inscribed in the very core of the Christian happening. It is no accident that throughout his public life Jesus was the storm-center of political controversy, that he was accused of political offenses on more than one occasion, and that his condemnation and execution were directly related to political problems (150:491–92).

The direct conflict between Jesus and public authority seems to be sufficiently important and serious to rule out the idea that it was accidental and secondary. It has value for the Christian as a model, and it serves to define the outlook and attitude of faith. As Domergue puts it: "The faith that centers on Jesus Christ does not perceive him as an object of knowledge but as a witness, as the witness to a concrete and exemplary experience of liberation that can and should be lived today" (154:30).

This liberation experience was emancipating, not only vis-à-vis the age-old religious sacral order but also vis-à-vis civil bondage. In political theology the gospel story, as a confrontation with power, is a paradigmatic history just as the Exodus story is. Taking the liberation of the Hebrews from Egypt as a model event, political theology includes in it an Exodus theology. Similarly, taking Jesus as a model, it includes a theology of messianism. This messianic theology has been worked out mainly by Paul L. Lehmann, who makes it a fundamental category of interpretation not only in Christology but in theology as a whole. In his view the messianic image is the crucial image that sheds light on what God is doing in the world. In line with that image, a theology of messianism is one that stresses the politics of God—that is to say, what God has done and is still doing to keep human life truly human (256:112–13). According to this outlook, Jesus is Messiah insofar as it is through him that God carries out his political program of making human beings more human.

The observations made earlier with regard to the meaning of the Exodus also apply to Jesus' criticism of power. The theology concerned with Jesus' political messianism is wholly akin to Exodus theology, imposing analogous criteria on current political theology. To put it better, it does not really impose them; it suggests them, inspires them, and fosters them. The political attitude of Jesus does not create moral precepts any more or less than does the Exodus. It is exemplary and revelatory rather than normative in the strict sense.

7. A ZEALOT MESSIANISM?

To fill in the full picture of Jesus' political messianism as a paradigm, we must consider one more feature: his relationship and contact with Jewish political movements seeking liberation from Roman rule. Where did Jesus stand in the agitated political atmosphere of his day?

We know that during the years of his public life there was a growing and active nationalist faction known as the Zealots, who engaged in subversive activity against Roman rule. The desert was the ultimate refuge for those engaged in this guerrilla resistance. In recent times the whole question of Jesus' relationship to Zealot groups has been raised quite concretely. Previously it had hardly merited any attention at all, though early in this century Kautsky (246) and Eisler (170) agreed in viewing Jesus as a political rebel.

Its reappearance today is due to two circumstances. First of all, it is of burning relevance in an age marked by liberation movements against imperialism that bear striking resemblance to the Jewish Zealot movement. Secondly, the discovery of the Dead Sea Scrolls has shed new light on the civil and religious milieu of Jesus. There seems to have been an uninterrupted chain of contacts running between Jesus and John the Baptist, between John and the Essenes in the desert, and between the Essenes and the Zealot guerrillas also hiding out in the desert. Since there is no room here to discuss this matter fully in historical or exegetical terms, the best way to present the state of the question today is to summarize two contrasting opinions.

Though he does not refer to them directly, Michel Dutheil follows the line of thought expressed by Brandon (85) and Carmichael (102). His view is that amid the complex mosaic of possible political positions in his own day, Jesus was clearly "on the side of the resistance." His argument starts from the negative side, noting that the people to whom Jesus was most clearly opposed were the Sadducees and the Herodians—i.e., those who were collaborating with Roman rule. He then presents a collection of incidents and actions that would indicate that in all likelihood there was some link between Jesus and the Zealots, or between Jesus and those who were involved in resistance against Rome. His purification of the Temple and his beating of the merchants could represent a typical act of subversion and reprisal. The apostles had two swords when Jesus was arrested in the garden of Gethsemane. The whole city was stirred up when Jesus made his triumphant entry into Jerusalem. One of his disciples, Simon, bore the further appellation, "the Zealot." Moreover, some of Jesus' statements clearly have guerrilla or subversive overtones. Jesus remarks that the kingdom of heaven has been subject to violence from the time of John the Baptist until the present moment, "and the violent bear it away." He tells people that he has not come to bring peace but the sword. Dutheil stresses the political significance of John the Baptist and then tries to show that Jesus took over his functions when the Baptist was imprisoned. His conclusion is clear. The messianism of Jesus is not just political; it is a Zealot messianism. That does not mean that Jesus was just another political activist: "In all likelihood the messianic awareness of Jesus was not confined wholly and exclusively within the boundaries of the Zealot movement, though it operated easily and readily in that milieu and did not reject its chief objective" (166:55–63).

The exegetical reconstruction of Oscar Cullmann is rather different. He retains the whole series of gospel incidents that would seem to indicate Jesus' Zealotism. But over against them he sets an equally rich series of gospel incidents and data that present Jesus as someone opposed to violence, little interested in institutional reform, and wholly concerned with the conversion of the human heart (132:22 and 38–41). The Zealot political conception of the Messiah is one that Jesus found to be a particular temptation for himself. When the devil shows him all the kingdoms of the earth during his stay in the desert, he is proposing the Zealot ideal to him. And since we tend to be tempted most by that which lies closest to our own heart, we can assume that Jesus at one point thought about adopting some form of political messianism but eventually rejected that idea vigorously (132:52). Cullmann admits that Jesus was condemned to death for being a political rebel, for being a Zealot, but he says that the accusation of Zealotism was a judicial error. The Romans mistook the true intentions of Jesus and wrongly viewed him as a Zealot (132:43–47).

Cullmann's version coincides with that of Martin Hengel (235) for the most part, and it is more generally accepted by theologians than is the picture of Jesus as a Zealot. Gutiérrez reiterates it when he says that Zealots were among the innermost circle around Jesus, but that Jesus himself stood apart from the Zealot movement and was opposed to all politico-religious messianism (230:299–307). Segundo Galilea also espouses this view, rejecting both the image of Jesus as ingenuous and the image of Jesus as revolutionary (195). Dumas takes a stand against the political and revolutionary depiction of Jesus in Pasolini's film, *The Gospel according to Saint Matthew.* As Dumas sees it, Jesus' contemporaries did not view him as a revolutionary Zealot on the one hand or as a merely passive victim of the world's injustice and violence on the other (158:14).

By contrast, other exegetes do not distinguish Jesus from the Zealots in terms of his attitude toward violence but rather in terms of his attitude toward Jewish nationalist pretensions and the desire to restore a politico-religious state in Israel. The Zealots saw such power as a valid alternative to Roman rule, according to these exegetes, but Jesus regarded both Roman and Jewish power as corrupt (219:37).

Whether Jesus was adherent to the Zealot movement or not is a question of fact to be decided by exegetical and historical investigation. Sometimes, however, the question is decided on the basis of some dogmatic conception or some ideological line of reasoning. That is what Comblin does, for example, when he argues that it is unthinkable that an exceptional person like Jesus would ever associate himself with either the Zealots or the monks of Qumran (121:236–37). His line of argument is devoid of logical consistency, and is based on some a priori notion of what being "exceptional" entails. One might just as well argue that an exceptional human being should not have lived in Palestine or in such an obscure age. Comblin himself decries the fact that "Jesus and his life have been treated like some sort of icon, . . . his personality reduced to a stereotype of certain theological themes" (121:236). But for some inexplicable reason he falls prey to the same sort of iconography. In order to keep Jesus enshrined in some lofty niche as an "exceptional" person, he starts out with the prejudice that Jesus could not possibly have associated himself with a monastic community or with a political resistance movement.

The debate over the possible Zealotism of Jesus is important, but it is not of transcendental importance. Did Jesus participate directly and actively in a movement entailing armed resistance to Roman power and seeking the political liberation of Israel? Was he a revolutionary? The concrete details of Jesus' political behavior are not our main concern, as Sölle brings out: "the point for us . . . is to come to know the basic direction of his behavior and to turn his goals into a reality in a fresh way in our own world today" (396:74). It seems difficult to deny that Jesus clearly adopted a critical attitude toward political authority and power. Assuming that, the further question as to whether he was a member of the Zealot movement does not seem to be a crucial one for theology. Clearing up that issue is more a matter for exegesis and biography than for theology. The possibility that Jesus was a Zealot is one that would add sharper outlines to his life story, but in no essential way would it alter the paradigmatic and theologically decisive fact that he did engage in a confrontatiton with the public authorities of his day.

Needless to say, the picture of Jesus as a guerrilla fighter is a source of flattery and inspiration to Christians involved in armed liberation movements. If exegesis did manage to prove that there was a close and clear-cut tie between Jesus and the Zealots, then one would not have to appeal to such figures as Camilo Torres to prove that guerrilla warfare can be supported by Christians. The example would be provided by Jesus himself. The image of the guerrilla priest, so deeply rooted in Spain (103) and Latin America, would not seem so odd or contradictory.

But even though a Zealot messianism would provide political resistance movements and guerrilla warfare with new titles to possible legitimacy, it does not canonize them or make them obligatory. The same would hold true, of course, should the opposite hypothesis prove to be true. Even if it were shown that Jesus was wholly and completely detached from the Zealot movement, that would not justify the rejection of armed resistance and guerrilla warfare. It should be repeated here that there is no easy and simple way to deduce political maxims from biblical statements and events. Concrete political affiliation ultimately depends on historical circumstances that have nothing to do with theology or exegesis.

8. HISTORY AND EVOCATION

In the debate over the possible Zealotism of Jesus, all theologians and exegetes work with the same biblical data; but they all organize that data in their own way. This makes it clear that exegesis does not specify or determine theology in a univocal or constrictive way. The conditioning is flexible, and also reciprocal. It is not correct to say that theology follows, or should follow, in the wake of exegesis. The criterion that theologians must submissively accept and appropriate the results obtained by exegetes does not correspond to the process of exegetical activity; for the exegetes themselves are influenced by theologians in the course of their investigative work. Biblical "discoveries" themselves are prompted by the needs of present-day faith, which are discussed by theologians.

Insofar as Jesus' relationship to the guerrilla partisans of his day is concerned, the exegetical and historical data is so fragmentary that the pieces can be brought into some sort of unity only with the help of theological presuppositions. It is not easy, and perhaps not even possible, to identify Jesus' "political line" (399:84) with any precision. All writers try, or think they are trying, to offer a scientific, objective exegesis devoid of presuppositions; but in reality their efforts flow from some prior theological and political stance. Dutheil finds a Zealot Jesus in the gospels and other contemporary documents because that is what he is looking for. Cullmann does not find that Jesus in the same sources because he rejects that image.

It is clear, then, that the relationship to Jesus is quite different from the way in which it is usually imagined. It is not the historical or exegetical Jesus who gives shape to a concrete theology and Christian praxis. Rather every particular theology and every specific Christian outlook molds Jesus' image according to its own needs, thus giving form to the rather indistinct image of the historical Jesus. In concrete practice historians and exegetes approach the interpretation of the Bible on the basis of certain political presuppositions that are usually unadmitted and masked and that underlie their allegations of impartial objectivity.

This is another version of the old problem dealing with the Jesus of history and the Christ of faith. Only now the problematic relationship is not between the Jesus who really lived and the image formed by the authors of the New Testament; it is between the historical Jesus and the image we can and do form of him on the basis of our writing or unwitting partisanship. Like it or not, intentionally or not, people today fashion their portrait of Jesus on the basis of their own social and political options, which have a real influence on the outlines of his image.

Dutheil himself is quite clear on this point: "In every epoch the Christian must go back and sketch an image of his master that will enable him effectively to maintain his own hopes while still remaining faithful to the events of his own day and carrying on the model of Jesus" (166:66). In short, the image of Jesus is not traced out in advance for the Christian and the theologian by the historical evidence or by exegesis. The gaps in our knowledge of Jesus' real life are, within certain limits, subject to the freedom displayed by various theological interpretations. It is the historical Jesus who serves as the paradigm for political theology. But the final touches of our portrait follow from a pattern based on our concrete experience of the faith here and now, insofar as there is no certain biographical data to constrain us.

Needless to say, our model of Jesus cannot be based on mere whim. We cannot give him the features of a Don Juan or an Attila, for example. Nor is it possible to confuse him with other religious reformers such as Buddha or Mahomet. The certain data of history are sufficient to rule out many interpretations and any attempt to manipulate the facts. But once we give that data their due, there is room for personal discretion in drawing up his portrait and highlighting different details. The whole process would seem to involve two basic aspects. The certain data oblige us to base a faithful memory of Jesus on a certain substratum that is truly in continuity with him; the gaps in our historical knowledge leave room for great variety in filling in the details of that portrait so that it may be meaningful and evocative for a given age. The basic problem is to figure out how much symbolism and hermeneutic variation that image can sustain.

From everything said above one can deduce that historical facts and events are paradigmatic for theology, not insofar as they have really taken place but insofar as they are evoked. Even when we are trying to seek out the historical messianism of Jesus, we are faced with a Christ of faith who can be interpreted in ever new ways and from endlessly different starting points. It is the evocation of faith, not the hard news of history, that takes Jesus as the witness to an exemplary messianic experience of liberation vis-à-vis the power structure. This evocation is a transfiguring one; without being unfaithful to the data of history, it fills in the gaps in that data and wraps the data in a higher meaning. It is this evocation more than the hard data that decides whether Jesus did or did not take a direct stand against political authority, whether he did or did not affiliate himself with the Zealot party, whether he did or did not adopt the messianic expectation of national liberation. And this fact is not peculiar to political theology. All Christology and all theology of salvation history operates with evocations much more than with hard historical information.

When we evoke the past to find meaning for the present or the future in it, when we extract models from it by spotlighting certain events over others and endowing them with singular, unique, definitive value for all time, then our work of evocation transforms history into epic and gest. To borrow an idea from Lévi-Strauss which will put the matter more pointedly, we can say that evocation turns history into myth (259:368–77). The historical story of Jesus, and of the Exodus, becomes a paradigm of transcendent and singular exemplarity insofar as it is mythified history. What really happened back then is combined into one whole with our current interpretation and the stimulating function it is meant to fulfill.

Theologians should learn to call things by their right name, even though that name may not always enjoy a good press. In particular they must learn to acknowledge the presence of myth where it truly is present, however much myth may be discredited at the moment. Theology should talk about myth in purely descriptive terms before it goes on to talk about it in critical and judgmental terms. At the descriptive level, avoiding both pejorative and panegyric tones, theology has to recognize that there are Christian myths and that Christian theology itself works with myths. At a later stage we may use faith or dogma to justify or semantically modify elements that are mythical on the purely phenomenological and descriptive level, but that is a different matter. We must respect the identity of things as they present themselves to us, refusing to assume from the start that things are essentially different when on the surface level they seem to be identical in outward appearance.

On this phenomenological level, dogmatic evocation in Christianity takes on all the outward features of myth. In contrast to those who start right out by opposing Christian dogma to myth, we must realize that at least on first appearance dogmas constitute mythical representations. For the believer, this is true only on the level of first appearance; for the nonbeliever, it is true on every level.

In this connection Bultmann has been exceptionally frank in stating that the religious representations of the Bible have a mythic character, though he operates from a different concept of myth. He has also been honest in saying that faith and theology do not work with a news chronicle of historical facts *(Historie)* but rather with a history endowed with meaning and interpreted through human understanding of history *(Geschichte)*. Richard Kroner admits this interpenetration of history and myth in biblical tradition without recourse to euphemisms. He notes that in biblical history myth is not and cannot be differentiated from real-life history, and that history in turn should not be separated from myth. There history is turned into myth because it is experienced under the impulse of the pious imagination rather than being the result of objective questioning and scientific investigation (248:46–47).

On the phenomenological level the only justifiable way to separate Christian dogma from the general realm of myths is to stress the historical support that the former enjoys.

Taking advantage of the fantastic and fabulous character of myths in general, theologians customarily point out that Christian dogma contains an essential reference to real history. Thus, insofar as it does relate to historical facts, the Christian faith would cease to be myth. This viewpoint overlooks two points: (1) Many myths outside Christianity also rest on some solid historical support; (2) in its dogma the real history of Christianity is a mythified history that has been poetically shaped by faith. On that front, then, the difference between Christian history as evoked by dogma and myths with some historical base is greatly diminished. It may well be that the Christian myth rests upon a thicker layer of historical reality, but that does not change its mythical nature. It might be well for theology to make use of the concept of "mythistory" that Van der Leeuw and Duméry have elaborated in the philosophy of religion. Thus Christianity would be a "mythistory" insofar as it is "a myth supported by a history, or better, a myth called upon to elucidate the significant aspects of the real content of a real history" (161:167).

The public life and death of Jesus and the Exodus event are models in political theology insofar as they are "mythistory"—i.e., insofar as they are history evoked, transformed by recollection, and mythified. Myth is the only way in which a past fact or event can come to constitute a paradigm for action, a springboard for liberty, an opening for glimpsing into mystery. History ever exerts its weight on our lives. Thus the history of Jesus, like that of so many other people, still exerts its weight on present society whether Christian or not. But as soon as historical consciousness focuses on certain fragments of past history to give them privileged significance, it dresses them in the raiment of myth. Faith lives from memories, but from memories that it itself selects, elaborates, and transfigures. Political theology finds its inspiration in certain original experiences of liberation (the Exodus, the gospel proclamation); using a political mediation and syntax, it organizes the documentary information that itself is somewhat indeterminate and that has come down to our day from those experiences.

9. CHRISTOLOGICAL POETICS

The transfiguration of history when evoked by faith can be seen concretely in the basic turn of theology's language (which should be discursive and reflexive) toward poetics. It clearly leans toward being a Christian lyricism or epic. This poetic expression betrays the mythical content of the evocation. The phenomenon itself, the poetic transformation of language in the service of a mythical transformation of history, is visible in many theologians. Here I should like to examine it in the work of two distinguished and quite representative theologians who exemplify a certain kind of poetic evocation that is not infrequent in political theology.

We find abundant samples of this in the work of Jürgen Moltmann. Indeed let it be said right here that Moltmann is demonstrably one of the greatest Christian poets of our time. His theology of hope is often theology as poetry, a theology of poetic expression rather than a theology of reflexive and critical discourse. That is both a compliment and a censure because theologians, before being exegetes, poets, preachers, or whatever, should be critics of official ecclesiastical expression and their own.

Moltmann often shows himself to be uncritical about his own use of language. His theology moves back and forth between exegesis and poetry; it is partly a biblical theology and partly a poetic theology. On the one hand it may correspond very precisely and scientifically with what the biblical authors thought and expressed; but he seldom asks himself whether we today can make the thinking of the Bible our own. On the other hand it unfolds a lofty poetics of faith and hope; but this poetics seldom manages to reach the level of critical reflection. Here, then, are some samples of Moltmann's poetry from different works of his: "Christ is not only consolation *in* suffering, he is also the protest of God's promise *against* suffering" (312:27); "In the presence of slaves Christ incarnates in his person the future of freedom" (310:72); "In the crucified one liberty and life turn their countenance toward the impious and the enchained" (309:316).

The same poeticizing propensity is evident in Jean Cardonnel, whose work is predominantly an epic of liberation effected by God. This epic is evident in his commentary on the Exodus, some passages of which were cited earlier (section 3); and it reappears in his Christology. Here are some refrains of his poetic Christology: "Christ, carried by a prophetic people and actualized by the convergence of insane gestures that go to make up the universal people, brings freedom and radiates absolute originality" (101:84); "Jesus Christ is the imagination, liberated to the fullest extent possible, taking over power" (101:87).

The style of these passages by Moltmann and Cardonnel clearly demonstrates a procedure that occurs quite frequently in theology in general and political theology in particular: i.e., critical discourse is displaced by rhetorical discourse or by poetic evocation. The texts are on the level of poetry, belonging to the same basic literary genre as the psalms and the *chansons de geste*. If the psalms are often *chansons de geste* about God, the political theology of the authors cited here are often *chansons de geste* about Christ. Their poetic language is not identical with that of the psalms, of course. It has changed to a modern idiom talking about "protest," "liberty," and the "future." The last text cited even included such recent allusions as the slogans of the French student revolt in May of 1968: "Liberating the imagination" and "the imagination in power," for example. Aside from that more modern idiom, however, the literary tenor of the texts resembles the psalter and the poetic passages of the prophets more than it does anything else.

We are witnessing the elaboration or creation of a new Christological language. It hardly need be pointed out that before it reached theology books, this language had shown up in worship. In particular it had shown up in liturgical chant where, it should be noted in passing, it had its own very proper and most suitable place. This new language is a political language. To be more precise, it is a language that gives poetical expression to political liberation. It replaces the age-old ontological and cosmological language used to express faith in Jesus Christ. Previously theological language spoke about Christ as the Word, the substantial image of the Father, the incarnate Son of God, and the firstborn of every creature; now it refers to him as God's protest, as the incarnation of the future of liberty, as imagination personified.

This transformation of language explains why the words in which political theology expresses its liberative recollection of Jesus do not have much to do with the terminology of Chalcedon and Christological dogma in general. The statements of Cardonnel, Moltmann, and other present-day theologians belong to a universe of discourse that is quite different from the one that served as the framework for the dogma elaborated by the Council of Chalcedon. They have to do with traditional Christological dogma insofar as they refer to the same historical personage (Jesus of Nazareth) and evoke him in an interpreted, transfigured, mythified way. But current Christology of liberation is not deduced logically from Christological dogma; it is independent of that dogma to some extent. It is not an orthodox Christology but rather a parallel Christology. What traditional dogmatics understood concretely by the divinity of Christ is outside the perspectives of liberation Christology. The witness that Jesus bears to an exemplary experience of liberation does not seem to preserve any relationship with the traditional attribute of a divine nature. Indeed there is much significance in the fact that the newer liberation Christology fails to make explicit mention of Jesus' divine nature. Lest there be any doubt on this, Cardonnel makes the point very clear: "To say that Jesus is God in the sense of a pre-existing divinity is to complicate and falsify everything. The only reality comes down to the fact that Jesus is the Christ, the Messiah" (101:83).

The appearance today of a parallel Christology that cannot be reduced to the traditional one helps us to appreciate better how Christological dogma arose in the first place. Exegetes stress the fact that the major Christological texts of the New Testament (especially Phil. 2:6–11) proceed from liturgical hymns (199:230). It is in the milieu of cultic exaltation and its sustaining emotion of song that the major Christological attributes arise. But neither exegetes nor theologians have gone on to draw a rather obvious conclusion from that fact. It is that dogma shows up first as poetry and chant. The statements of dogma were first lyrical, epic, or dramatic expressions with which Christians, moved by their own enthusiasm and without any cognitive aim, celebrated Jesus. Dogma appeared when those hymns were changed into doctrinal prose. Christological dogma issues from poetic and hymnic material in honor of Christ, material that was then transformed into stereotyped propositions with a cognitive purport. Dogmatics is poetry that has become stereotyped, that has been turned into prose and doctrine with all the appearances of authentic knowledge.

The strong poetic density of the fresh expressions of the nascent political Christology does a fine job of reproducing the primitive flavor of the ancient expressions in traditional Christology. When the early Christians heard that Jesus was the Word made flesh, the statement probably sounded to them much like it sounds to people today when someone says that Jesus personifies the future of liberty or is imagination liberated to the highest degree possible. Those are not cognitive statements; they do not contain knowledge. So analysis of the poetic genre evident in contemporary Christological texts brings out two points: (1) the evocative process used by political theology to recall the history of Jesus, and (2) the original genesis of Christological dogma in the first centuries of church life through the same sort of process.

10. THE QUESTION OF GROUNDING

There are lines of continuity between the ontological and cosmological Christology of traditional dogma and current liberation Christology, but there is also a break in continuity. The discontinuity appears in statements and expressions, and also of course in the concepts and meanings of words. There the break is complete. Only great naiveté or some sort of dogmatic prejudice could prompt one to think that the aforecited formulas of liberation Christology and other similar current Christologies mean the same as the formulas of Chalcedon or the New Testament. But there is a link of continuity between them too insofar as both proceed to attribute to Jesus certain absolutely singular predicates that he does not share with anyone else. It is the same identical mental processes or mechanisms that lead people to exalt Jesus as the Son of God or as the Future of our liberty.

The root question, then, has to do with the functioning and grounding of these processes. What entitles us to view Jesus in terms of such singular and surprising attributes? Why see him specifically as *the* exemplary witness to liberation, and not Socrates or Spartacus or someone else? Why search at all for some privileged exemplar who is incommensurable with the rest rather than taking note of the many different exemplary witnesses who glimpse history in some way, without focusing in a special way on any one of them in particular?

The answer cannot be that Christological dogma obliges

us to do all that. First of all, current liberation Christology definitely does not flow at all from traditional dogma. The dogma that in Jesus God has become man does not give rise to a theology of the future any more than to a theology of the past, to a theology of liberation any more than to a theology of authority. Everything depends on what one understands by God and how one defines human existence. In short, everything depends on extra-christological presuppositions prior to any Christology. What is more, traditional Christological dogma itself arose as the result of the mechanisms that we are now asking about.

For that very reason we cannot answer the question adequately by saying that it is faith that assigns these attributes to Jesus. That answer will not do either. Of course it is faith that does that, assigning unique and wholly singular attributes to Jesus; but faith is precisely that process of assignment, and it does not exist prior to it. To ask why Jesus rather than Socrates is taken as the exemplary witness to liberation is to ask about the reason for faith.

Now one might say that this question is not specific or peculiar to political theology. I agree completely, but political theology cannot delegate the task of validating its principal theses to traditional dogmatics. From its own proper perspective it must concern itself with all its underlying principles. The discontinuity that separates it from earlier theology means that the traditional grounding cannot continue to be valid for a political hermeneutics of the gospel message. So that leaves standing the question as to how political theology justifies the fact that it takes Jesus as the unique exemplar of liberation, the fundamental principle and criterion that is taken for granted in theological discourse.

For the moment we must interrupt this line of reflection, leaving suspended the whole question of the ultimate grounding and support for the believer's conviction that

Jesus is the exemplary and unique witness. It is a question, however, that calls for detailed examination and that has been inexplicably overlooked by both political theology and theology in general. This oversight must be repaired by theology; it must reflect deeply on its own basic roots, paying critical attention not only to the consequences of faith but also to the very fact of faith itself and its genesis.

Granting all that, we can still say that political theology's reference to an exemplary historical tradition, one that includes the Exodus epic and the public life of Jesus as highlights, does give it a certain measure of grounding and validity—at least within the precincts of faith and the church. If we presuppose faith in Jesus, then political theology is grounded and legitimized insofar as it has recourse to Jesus as the original witness to liberation. If we presuppose belief in some sort of revelation, then political theology is valid insofar as it harkens back to the first and primary revelation event (i.e., the Exodus) and hones in on its political content. Of course that does not justify political theology on all fronts because it involves a presupposition of faith that must also be justified in turn. But within the context of the Christian community it does furnish one of the elements for its own justification: the traditional element of a link with the foundational grounding factors of Christianity. This traditional element, together with the element of solid grounding in the cultural situation (see chapter 3, section 13), does provide an adequate and complete legitimation of political theology within the confines of Christianity.

When theologians and Christians demand that political theology show its rights for accreditation, one need only refer them to those two elements. One can show that political theology is faithful to the history of Israel and of Christ on the one hand, and to the present cultural situation or society on the other. Insofar as believers are concerned, political theology is legitimate as *theology* because of the fact of its relation to Christ; and it is legitimate as *political* theology because of its relation to today's cultural situation.

The situation is very different vis-à-vis nonbelievers, and insofar as the ultimate justification of political theology is concerned. Here, as we noted already, one must look to some other sort of validation in order to legitimate and give real meaning to theology's approach. That validation is bound up with an epistemological theory and criticism of political theology that we will not be able to outline until Part Three of this book.

11. CRITICAL MEMORY AND DOGMA

The preceding comments on political theology's reference to the past as a process of liberational recollection merely represent an elaboration and application of an intuition provided by Johannes Metz, an intuition that seems to be extraordinarily suggestive but rather imprecise and not worked out fully. He has remarked that faith can and should be interpreted in terms of recollection or memory. Borrowing in turn from Marcuse, he says that this recollection or memory should be considered critical or subversive, its opposition to the present status quo liberating people from the one-dimensional and bewitching spell of the dominant consciousness. Tradition is thus mobilized as a critical and liberative potentiality. Metz believes that this specification of faith as memory explains why faith is and must be linked up with some content, and hence is necessarily a "dogmatic faith" (301:286–88).

Now that viewpoint would seem to be a fruitful one, open to excellent possibilities on the theoretical level. At the same time, however, it is pockmarked with holes and open to equivocation. To begin with, the appeal to Marcuse would seem to be of dubious validity. It does not seem right to put forward a theoretical category proposed by someone else and then give it a completely different meaning than it had in its original context without justifying the alteration in meaning—as much as to say that Marcuse himself was talking about the critical and subversive capability contained in a sacred history.

Even more serious is the fact that Metz depicts the relationship between past tradition and present day in terms of one single sense that runs in only one direction. He makes tradition the critical principle vis-à-vis the present without noticing that the relationship between the two is critical and dialectical, that the present also operates on tradition, dismembers it, and renders it out of date. Moreover he talks about faith as critical recollection or memory but he does not spell out what is the precise content of this recollection, how it is actualized right now in faith, and how memory comes to work critically and effectively on the present. Nor does he explain why certain specific memories linked to Christian tradition are selected while other memories are not. These points, which are vague and imprecise in Metz's presentation, become fully precise through the criteria that have been presented here.

Insofar as the content of the recollection is concerned, it is certain events and facts of Judeo-Christian tradition—not dogma or orthodoxy as such—that contain a critical and subversive capability. Christian dogmas, in their official formulation, do not subvert anything; they do not proffer any liberation, nor do they unlock any doors to the future. It is not dogmatic orthodoxy that is mobilizing Christians to undertake a liberative political praxis and theologians to work out a political interpretation of the gospel message. Indeed that orthodoxy is invoked instead to immobilize and hallow the old order of things. Dogmas have not served as vehicles for a critical and subversive memory. If the Christian does live with liberative memories, that is not due to any dogmatic formulation; it is due to the possibility of linking up with the actual events of an exemplary and grounding history without the mediation of dogma.

Insofar as the way in which the past becomes memory is

concerned, it does not happen simply through historical information, scholarship, or knowledge—not even through knowledge grounded solidly on some positive revelation; it happens through a truly lived process of evocation, through poetic transfiguration and the mythical interpretation of history. Exodus theology and liberation Christology arise as *chansons de geste,* as epic poems in honor of Moses and Jesus respectively, as liturgical hymns and messianic psalms. They are sung before they become discourse. Moreover, it is this epic and mythic recovery of a history that makes this history operative and vital today, for only myth enables the past to exert some influence on the present above and beyond merely chronological priority or material causality.

The biggest mistake in Metz's presentation is that he adds a questionable note to his view. After perceptively and correctly noting that the notion of faith as memory does demand some content for that faith, that is to say, a *fides quae creditur* or credo, he goes on to say that this calls for some sort of "dogmatic faith" (301:287–88). What does he mean by dogmatic faith here? One cannot help but suspect he means some sort of positivist faith determined authoritatively by every one of the traditional Catholic or Christian dogmas. Does Metz assume perchance that those dogmas are subversive in themselves? Does he really believe that if the recollection process of faith is not to be a will-o'-the-wisp, it must be a specifically dogmatic form of recollection? Why does he equate the content of faith, the *fides quae creditur,* with dogmatic faith? Is the way of orthodoxy and dogma the only way to give content to faith? Are there not forms of belief that are not dogmatic?

It is not clear how Metz would answer those questions. But the basic approach of a politically mediated theology would certainly be to answer them in a way that was far from traditionalist or dogmatic. On this point the theologies of liberation and revolution are moving in the same general direction as modern theology in general—that is to say, toward a nondogmatic and nonpositivist theology dissociated from orthodoxy (188). Giuseppe Vaccari has given clear expression to the need to break away from classical, dogmatic Christology: "As a universal figure belonging to all human beings, Christ cannot be recovered with the instruments of traditional theology and the one-track interpretational guidelines that tend to flesh him out in an acritical and mythical milieu. We must go back behind the mediating influences of Greek and Latin culture, fleshing out his figure by somehow recovering his human actions" (414:329).

The ultimate limits at which a liberation Christology such as the one outlined here might arrive eventually would amount to the diminution of Jesus' absolute singularity. Here again I shall let Vaccari speak: "Hervé Chaigne is correct in talking about an analogy between the figure of Guevara and that of Christ. Both were extremists. Both wanted to save their own people. But Manzoni is wrong when he says that Christ 'is just one person and nothing more.' Incarnated in Christ are all those who fight and die for the liberation of the people" (414:16).

5

Looking at the Present: Political Praxis and Theological Representations

1. THE PRESENT AND PRAXIS

It is in praxis that political theology finds its matrix and nutritive soil, for it is a theology that is faith's reflection on political praxis in our day—on the praxis of Christians in particular. On this front it addresses itself essentially to concrete life here and now. Note that the present in question is not a metaphysical present; it is not the fleeting instant of time lived out in freedom and decision-making that is discussed by existential philosophy and theology. Rather, it is a social and historical present that in its here-and-now reality includes a certain layer of the immediate past and the imminent future. In the view of political theology present praxis includes both those past events that still give character to the present historical moment and the most proximate tasks called for by the social dialectics.

Insofar as it is reflection on an already given praxis, though that praxis still is relevant to the contemporary historical situation, political theology is a retrospective *post factum* interpretation, a reflection dealing with a prior praxis. Insofar as it is reflection on a praxis yet to be performed, political theology is prospective, anticipatory, and directive; it is a reflection geared to some subsequent praxis. Both before and behind, then, it relates with collective, political praxis; for it is a theological reading, interpretation, and recovery of the real-life praxis of our day and also a compelling anticipation and theological motivation for a new praxis. It gathers in the more vital concrete experiences of collective activity and explores their dynamic thrust into the future. The indicative joins with the imperative in political theology. As social theory, then, political theology is an intellectual and critical mediation between two moments of praxis: between the most recent praxis of the past and the most immediate praxis to be undertaken in the future.

The present realities of praxis considered by political theology are the same analyzed by other types of reflection such as social theory, sociology, history, and political science; but political theology approaches them through its own distinctive representations. It is important, therefore, to distinguish between the events or situations with which it is concerned on the one hand and the categories or representations which it uses as interpretative tools or hermeneutic instruments. Any critical discussion of the bond that links political theology to present praxis must take the form of debate over every one of those aspects and start right at the very beginning.

Political theology has to do with action, but with collective action rather than individual action. It is concerned with the action of peoples, human groups, and social classes. Thus it would seem to be a bit off the mark to bring up, for example, Blondel's philosophy of action as proof that there is a close link between more recent Catholic thinking and praxis (230:31). The analogy is superficial, because the action analyzed by Blondel, and then given new consideration in Catholic theology subsequently, is the action of the individual—though of course such individual action may end up cooperating with that of others at some point in its dynamic course and thus become collective. Moreover, the action considered by Blondel is contemplated in idealistic terms; it is viewed in terms of the basic principle of the infinite capacity of a spiritual subject. By contrast political theology is concerned with a collective praxis, with a concrete and historically determined praxis based on what social classes or human groups do in fact do or might be capable of doing.

Here it is obviously a political praxis that is involved. It is in trying to define "political," however, that the real problems begin. With what kind of "politics" is political theology concerned? At what semantic level is *polis* taken over by this theology? Sad to say, theologians are often far from clear on this point. We hear them tell us that theology is bound up with some sort of social praxis, that it has some function vis-à-vis society, or that it proclaims the future awaiting human liberty; but we are seldom told precisely what sort of praxis, society, and liberty they have in mind.

Only one thing seems clear and generally acknowledged: The "political" element is not to be equated with the state or the government. It is here that currrent political theology differs clearly from older political theology. The latter was inclined to fall in with the ideology of the royal court and the aristocratic council, to bow before the king and attempt to give solid theological grounding to his sovereignty and rule. Current political theology reveals itself to be extremely critical toward the established centers of power and authority. If anything can be stated with certainty, it is that the "politics" that is the present object of theological reflection is not the official activity carried out by public magistrates; or even if it is, it is not that activity exclusively. Such official activity constitutes at best only part of "politics," and it is always viewed in critical contrast with other types of political action.

Moreover, current political theology focuses on the dynamism and mobility of the political realm, on its future possibilities as a result of collective action. This is suggested by its reference to action or praxis, and it is a feature shared by all the theologians in this area. Political theology is not a theology of the status quo but a theology of change and alteration. It is a theology of a history made by human beings, a theology of society insofar as society is capable of being shaped by different possible alternatives to the present situation.

It is at this point that the discrepancies or vague points begin to appear, both with respect to the political realm as such and the kind of change that people seek to effect.

2. THE POLITICAL REALM AND ITS ALTERATION

Insofar as the political realm is concerned, we find elucidations and explanations that are terribly imprecise. It is somewhat disturbing to find that Metz, who more than anyone else has propagated the basic formula and category of "political theology," does not state what he means by "politics" with the desired clarity. He does say that the new concept of politics takes for granted a distinction between state and society (301:269), a point typically made in all current theology as we noted earlier. But apart from that, Metz's only other contribution is amazingly vague: "It may well be . . . that the new name for culture is politics" (301:275). The indecisiveness of "it may well be," together with the problematic nature of the very concept of culture, leaves us without any certain knowledge of the way in which the political realm is understood in Metz's political theology. In any case his attempt to bring politics and culture closer together is indicative of a more pervasive tendency to equate vaguely the political realm with the social and cultural realm, the only distinctive connotation being a clear awareness that society and culture depend on decisions made on the level of official power. Thus political theology would be more or less equivalent to a theology of society or culture.

At the opposite extreme are those theologians who interpret politics in its most strict sense. In Max Weber's terms it can be described as an "orientation toward power" (145:126–27). Here we can group both those who are elaborating a theology of violence and those who are asserting that evangelical love demands taking sides with the oppressed in the struggle between social classes. The theology of violence has to do with politics in its strictest sense because it seeks to subvert established power through revolutionary violence. To be more precise, it seeks to subvert the latent violence of an oppressive juridical order through a revolutionary violence that itself aspires to take over the reins of power. Other theologians look at a world divided up into exploiters and exploited and say that evangelical charity obliges us to take sides with the latter (see section 11). It is clear that they, too, take politics in the strict sense, closely akin to the meaning it has among political parties and syndicalist movements. The theology propounded by the Christians for Socialism well exemplifies this second tendency, in which political praxis is not some vague collective action on society and culture but rather an action framed in terms of the struggle for official power—hence a partisan action of a combative sort.

With regard to the kind of change to be effected in society, once again we run into a wide range of positions and a great deal of ambiguity. We find much ambiguity in Cox's use of language in *The Secular City,* where he advocates "rapid social change." Cox hurries over the term "revolution" as if he were walking on live coals; he is simply afraid to use it at all. Yet he himself recognizes that his term is a euphemism for "revolution" (126:129). It is true enough that on the surface it would seem that rapid social change might well be an emancipatory revolution. But the fact that he makes every effort not to use the latter word and resorts to the euphemism leads one to suspect that the two are not identical. One senses that it is not just a matter of linguistic caution, that his avoidance of the lexicon of revolution stems from the fact that his own doctrinal stance is a progressivist and developmentalist one rather than a revolutionary one. Cox's secular city seems to evolve and change simply through the process of technological development and progress. His empirical model is clearly Yankee society and the great megalopolises of North America in particular. In his eyes it is industry, technology, and urbanization that impose rapid social change. The enthusiastic and idyllic tone in which he describes urban society and its functional approach to human relationships indicates clearly that he has not really grasped the phenomena of alienation and exploitation that underlie the social change effected by that kind of progress and development. The inhabitant of the secular city, of the technopolis, is not bourgeois in the etymological sense of the term, which is the only sense Cox uses; he is not the inhabitant of a *bourg*. But he continues to be bourgeois in the Marxist sense of the term—that is to say, the superdeveloped bourgeois inhabitant of Yankee neocapitalist society. To do justice to Cox, however, we must note that he has written subsequent works that are far less Yankee in tone and forthrightly allude to the lexicon of liberating revolution (125; 129).

Cox's ambiguous and bourgeois theology of social change bears strong resemblances to the Catholic theology of development, which has arisen around the encyclical *Populorum Progressio* and its central theme that "development is the new name for peace." It has found favor among many Catholics who regard it as a panacea for social problems. This theology of development (65; 251) is associated with an optimistic theology of progress (41; 323), which in turn is inscribed in a general theology of terrestrial realities that was first formulated by Thils (404).

Development, too, is a type of social change; and of course it can take place rapidly. But all developmentalist theories characteristically believe that the necessary change can come about without altering the underlying presuppositions of the social system—the web of production relationships specifically. As for various theologies of progress and development, they evince a historical optimism and other traits quite similar to the theology of the eighteenth-century Enlightenment so masterfully described by Barth (64). In other words, they are theologies concerned with good bourgeois order and its ability to bring happiness to the world.

A good number of theologians are currently challenging this optimistic view, feeling that development and technology are incapable of creating a just society in and of themselves. In general it could be said that they vigorously and harshly reject mere reformism. Gustavo Gutiérrez has given a detailed and forceful explanation of the reasons why the ideology and technology of development, which had aroused such high expectations during the decade of the fifties, has subsequently fallen into great discredit. His own theology of liberation is in direct contrast to a theology of development (230:43–49, 113–33; 226:29–42).

But not all theologians or Christians pass such severe judgment on the technological or developmentalist approach. At the 1966 Geneva Conference of the World Council of Churches, which dealt with the theme of church and society, there developed a clear opposition between "technologists" on the one hand and "revolutionaries" on the other (420). Although no one waved a flag for any reformist or purely evolutionary solution, there were people who felt that "the alternative between technological revolution and social revolution is resolved by rational arguments, not theological ones" (408:96) and that theology could reject the supposed dilemma of revolution versus evolution (421:107).

These latter viewpoints, however, do not seem to be very consistent. The alternative between evolution and revolution may have been superseded in a few countries that have already entered into a process of social revolution; but in most countries it remains a very real alternative that cannot be eliminated. By the same token no one doubts that the solution or resolution of this problem must be rational rather than theological. The point at issue is that if rational analysis should discover that revolution is the only real solution, then a theology of revolution becomes both possible and necessary.

But the possible alternative to mere developmentalism and technology as well as the definition of social change as a thoroughgoing alteration of the socioeconomic system and its structures cannot be reduced to one single format. People may adopt different models, which would be matched by theological approaches of an equally distinctive stamp. In the concrete, proposals for some sort of social change that would not merely be developmentalist or reformist, as well as the corresponding theologies that attempt to reflect on such change from the standpoint of faith, tend to be organized around one or more of the following themes: liberation, revolution, protest, and violence.

3. LIBERATION

The favorite theme of Catholic theologians, of Latin Americans in particular, is liberation. That is understandable enough. Those western countries with a predominantly Catholic population tend to be far behind those with a predominantly Protestant population insofar as development is concerned. Moreover, Latin America as a whole is still suffering from a basic situation of economic colonialism. The theology of liberation is grounded on a social experience, lived in and with faith, wherein a colonized people feels it must be liberated externally from the forces of imperialism and internally from the grip of domestic economic oligarchies. As J.A. Hernández puts it: "My starting point should be clear. It is . . . Latin America under domination" (59:41). The world of this theology is the Third World, the world of Fanon and his "wretched of the earth" (176). Moreover, in the part of the Third World that is predominantly Catholic, for a long time the church has helped to bring about the consolidation of colonial structures. Current disengagement from those structures inevitably takes the form of theological self-criticism by a now repentant church. Thus the theology of liberation is presented as a critique and criticism "of the church's activity in Latin America" (198).

It should be noted that the term "liberation" signifies two different things in theology. First, it alludes to the empirical, sociohistorical fact of the emancipation of certain human groups. Second, however, it also constitutes a theological category that has to do with the work of Jesus Christ and that realizes or actualizes the traditional Christian idea of salvation for oppressed peoples. The theology of liberation specifically attempts to link the two connotations, trying to make it clear that the distinct levels of meaning associated with liberation are part of "one single complex process that finds its ultimate meaning and full realization in the salvific work of Christ" (230:68–69).

To liberation theology we must append another theological theme that is older than it and that is also highly relevant today. It is the notion that evangelical love is on the side of the oppressed and that this partisanship gives it an impact and effectiveness that is socially subversive. This theme has been picked up by liberation theologians, but it comes to us from an earlier day and it can be propounded from outside the borders of liberation theology in the strict or current sense of the term. In 1959, when there was yet no talk about a theology of liberation or a theology of revolution, Fernández de Castro anticipated them with his basic assertion that "the position of the Christian is to be found on the side of all the oppressed of the earth" (178:85–86). Christianity has a liberative and revolutionary power in any situation imaginable because "it is ever on the side of the victims, ever identified with those who are suffering oppression, with those who possess the power of revolution in a given society" (178:169–70). It was also some time ago that Paupert wrote these words: "The gospel message bids us be wholly and unconditionally on the side of the lowliest. . . . If that means being on the left, as it seems to, then the gospel message is on the left" (335:149). By now the theme has become commonplace. The gospel demand for justice is governed by a very concrete criterion, by the situation of those who are most dispossessed (238:490).

From this premise Jürgen Moltmann draws a cardinal thesis for theology. He spells it out thus: "In the present struggle for liberty and justice, Christians must side with the humanity of the oppressed" (310:75). Girardi, for his part, derives the same principle from the concept of love and its universality. He explains how the universalism and partisanship of Christian love come together in these terms: "Universalism is not neutrality. It implies a class option, an option for that class which upholds the interest of humanity and which will free the world in freeing itself. Hence one must love all, but not all in the same way. One loves the oppressed by liberating them from their misery; one loves the oppressors by liberating them from their sinfulness" (208:94–96).

The same basic position can be enunciated from another point of view. As Gérard Lutte likes to put it, "the church belongs to the poor." It is no accident that he was discharged from the Salesian Atheneum in Rome the same time as his confrere Girardi. Both have asserted that impartiality is impossible for the Christian—Girardi starting from a theology of love, Lutte from ecclesiology. In some of its propositions, Lutte's ecclesiology seems to be as elementary as the following remark might suggest: "The kingdom of God, and hence the church, belongs only to the poor" (271:16). To the usual criticisms made of the term, "church of the poor" (205:190–201), one must add the fact that Lutte's version is oversimplistic on two fronts. On the one hand he does not pay heed to the important qualification that the church is a community of those who are poor and lowly by vocation, not by condition. On the other hand he also uses the term "poor" without sufficient analysis and concrete realization, ultimately giving it a sentimental and populist sense (186:252–53).

This does not undermine the fact that Gérard Lutte is right on target with some of his remarks and evaluations, agreeing with those of other authors cited above. He says, for example, that "the Christian will necessarily be a class person." At other times he makes statements that are preeminently metaphorical (taken from the Bible with particular reference to the *Magnificat).* Yet these, too, have an acceptable sense: "God is not impartial. He has taken the side of the poor against the rich, the weak against the powerful, the ignorant against the wise" (271:21).

The common people and the poor come to constitute a theological locus, the privileged locale for God's manifestation. This is the fundamental intuition of the "grassroots" or "base line" theology *(teología de la base)* preached by González-Ruiz. The base line is the amalgam of social strata that support the heavy weight of goods production without sharing in its control or even in its consumption for the most part. Base-line theology, then, is a process of theological reflection that "focuses its gaze first and foremost on that zone of human reality." To express it more clearly, and in partisan terms as blatant as those of the *Magnificat,* one could put it this way: "God is there at the base line. The great locale for theophany is to be found among the poor, the hungry, the exploited, the imprisoned, the oppressed, and the lowly" (221:7–8).

The logic of commitment to the oppressed leads political theology not to be satisfied with being a discourse *about* the poor and exploited in the process of emancipation. It logically aspires to be their own voice when they finally reach the point of being able to express themselves in freedom. Gustavo Gutiérrez quite rightly points out that the qualitative leap to a new theological perspective will take place only "when the oppressed themselves can express themselves freely and creatively in society and among the people of God," only when they become the artisans of their own liberation and make their own voice heard directly and without intermediaries (229:30–31). A theology of liberation, then, is the voice of the people themselves in the process of self-liberation.

4. REVOLUTION AND PROTEST

Whereas the theology of liberation tends to be the work of Catholics, and of Latin Americans in particular, the theology of revolution as well as the debate over it has cropped up in Protestant communities and the highly developed countries for the most part. Some Catholics, particularly in France, have contributed to it; but the basic formulation of a theology of revolution does not go well with Catholic orthodoxy.

The theology of revolution does not consider a given historical situation of dependence among a particular social class or in a given country as a whole. It focuses on revolutionary movements in general, including those that arise in highly developed countries. The basic historical experience underlying it seems to be the French student revolt of May 1968 and other similar subversive movements, not just liberation movements in the Third World. Of course there had been some talk about a theology of revolution even before May 1968. Shaull spoke about it at the 1966 Conference in Geneva, and Ernst Bloch published his book on Thomas Münzer in 1921 (79). But the French happenings of 1968 gave concrete features to the vague possibility, filling in the purport and strategy of revolutionary activities in countries that might be culturally and industrially advanced. On the other hand the theology of revolution, which had blazed up like a comet, already seems to be on the way to oblivion. Since 1970 it hardly has been mentioned.

The relationship between the theology of revolution and liberation theology might be made clear by the distinction Hugo Assmann draws between "a permanent theology of revolution in general, which deals with the whole question and its context at its roots, and a specific theology of revolution that focuses on the concrete circumstances of an acutely revolutionary situation" (54:221). It is Assmann's opinion that most of what is regarded as political theology and theology of revolution falls under the heading of a general theology of revolution, i.e., a theology concerned to show that the ultimate questions of the faith are real only through the mediation of the penultimate questions of politics. He then defines a specific theology of revolution as one which has to do with a situation in which concrete, penultimate questions are the only ones formulated—so that one would be suspected of evasiveness if one attempted to formulate ultimate questions here and now (54:221–23). Following this standard of division, we can characterize European theology of revolution as a general theology of revolution, and Latin American theology of liberation as a specific theology of the Latin American revolution.

Needless to say, the concept of revolution should be specified. Theologians must spell out clearly what they are referring to. They do not always do that, and so we must set high value on such works as those of Martin Lotz (264), which deliberately set out to give historical and conceptual definition to revolution from the standpoint of theological reflection.

Revolutionary action proposes to change the prevailing system (370:226). At this point theologians debate whether it is possible to speak strictly of a theology of revolution, or whether one can only speak about a theology for a time of revolution. Paul L. Lehmann opts decisively for the second alternative, quoting a comment of Hromadka in his own support: "I do not have a theology of revolution, but I do have a theology for the revolution" (255:174). De Certeau is of the same mind. After indicating some of the methodological difficulities facing a theology of revolution, he goes on to suggest what might possibly be a theology "in this age of revolutions" (116:134–47).

But over against this position there is another more rigorous stand concerning a theology of revolution. It characteristically purports to "comprehend revolution by an appeal to the revolutionary structure of Christian faith as an intrinsic element and motivating factor of theology itself" (177:111).

The structure of the theology of revolution is analogous to that of liberation theology. It connects a historical praxis with certain theological representations. The theology of revolution tries to ascertain the relationship between the revolutionary activity of human beings and that of God (421:93 and 105), and it does so by "establishing a critical and liberative correlation between the revolutionary aspect of the gospel and the revolutionary aspect of the world situation" (5:XI). In this theology, the kingdom of God is viewed and understood as revolution. To be specific, it is understood as "the eschatological revolution, the revolution to end all revolutions" (215:50); or, to put it in other words, it is viewed as "the revolution in the revolution, the salvation of the revolution from its alienated form"

(310:81). Contrary to what some critics have understood by it (370:239), the theology of revolution does not entail any "Christian revolutionism."

Although theological interpretation of revolution lends itself to various focuses, it obviously represents a most felicitous principle for a thoroughgoing reformulation of theology. The sharp break with traditional dogmatics shows up more clearly in the theology of revolution than in other forms of political theology. The fact is that under the banner of liberation theology, and side by side with truly daring attempts to rethink the faith down to its roots, we find dogmatic propositions that fully maintain the traditional orthodoxy of Catholicism without any critical distance being established from that orthodoxy. One brand of the theology of liberation and the political theology of Metz are subject to very ambiguous treatment whereas the theology of revolution, by its very nature and purpose, seems to be able to avoid such handling with greater effectiveness.

There is no doubt that one might well try theologically to apprehend the fact of revolution from fairly traditional theological bases. But ultimately one is forced to ask oneself whether that manner of apprehension gets to the bottom or not. A deep and thoroughgoing comprehension of the revolutionary fact seems impossible unless one grasps its critical dimension vis-à-vis religious dogmas—which is to say, unless one alters traditional dogmatics. Cazalis pointedly asserts that "the theology of revolution implies a revolution in theology" (114:59). Moltmann says the same thing and adds: "The church has no right to a theology of revolution so long as it has not undergone reform from the roots up" (310:68). Thus the theology of revolution presupposes a revolutionary ecclesiology and a revolutionary ecclesiastical praxis.

The relationship between a theology of social change (not just of revolution) and a theology of ecclesiastical change is presently a serious point of contention. Christians in Latin

America and Africa are wont to criticize European Christians for an excessive preoccupation with ecclesiastical reform. That is the reproach the Third World levels against such concrete efforts as those of the Dutch church and its deliberations. Consider these words uttered by Dom Helder Camara in a discourse delivered in Münster: "For the love of God I beg you not to suffocate yourselves with the internal problems of the church while the truly major and urgent problems of humanity challenge us." The archbishop of Recife seems to be well aware of the opposing point of view: "If the church does not have the courage to touch its own structures, it will not have the moral strength to criticize society" (98:21). Yet he is a moderate representative of a tendency which, when carried to the extreme, would be content to put through timid administrative reforms within the church (dealing with parishes, curias, hierarchical relationships, and so forth) while demanding incisive changes in society. As one commentator has remarked ironically, "The bishops prescribe much more energetic remedies for society than for the church itself" (390:205).

In this emphasis on the great problems of humanity that sets aside intraecclesiastical reform as irrelevant, one must note and criticize a defensive reaction of a conservative and dogmatic cast that is very much in line with Roman Catholic order. Of course the problems of humanity are more important than those of the Christian community. But courage to face up to church problems will do much more than provide Christians with the moral courage to engage in political criticism. Self-criticism is the touchstone of veracity and realism for all criticism. If a church does not place itself and its allegedly divine institutions in the scales of judgment, then it cannot weigh social institutions on those same scales; for the latter are grounded just as solidly on allegedly divine or natural laws. In that case its potential denunciation of an unjust society would be merely rhetorical. Without denying that European Christians are sometimes excessively preoccupied with internal questions, we can say that the reproach of the African and Latin American churches is also unjustified. It is as if one were to censure the worldwide university movement for paying particular attention to the problems of the university within the general political context. Christians can and should discuss ecclesiastical questions just as students can and should discuss university matters. The only condition would be that such "sectional" or "internal" problems should be framed in the broader context of political society.

The theology of revolution is hardly related at all to traditional dogmatic categories, very free in its use of the Bible, and harsh in its judgment of the official churches. Its overall radicalism has made it the target for much criticism, even from theologians who advocate a practical, public, critical theology. The radical nature of some theologians of liberation (e.g., Assmann, Richard, Alves in some respects, and a few others) scarcely seems less. But the fact that under the rubric of liberation theology we find proposals that are very conservative in terms of theology, though progressive in social terms, tends to undermine the critical capacity of that theology when taken in overall terms.

The fact is that the theology of revolution has not been assimilated and digested by the official, orthodox theology of the churches whereas political theology and liberation theology have quickly been incorporated into the most traditional dogmatics. Much reserve and suspicion is shown toward the theologians of revolution even as the theologians of liberation are beginning to be accepted and quoted ever so timidly by the episcopal hierarchy.

As has already been noted by the most clear-eyed theologians of Latin America (59:111; 376:252; 417:427), the assimilation of the idiom of liberation by the ecclesiastical order entails the danger that it will be emptied of all real meaning. But this process is actually helped along by the conservative ecclesiastical tone of much Latin American theology. It might well be in order to ask whether liberation theology does not need an idiom that is more clearly revolutionary and dissociated from the past in order to preserve its radical import over against other possible versions that would maintain its complicity with traditional orthodoxy. Perhaps the quick fall of the theology of revolution into oblivion is due specifically to the greater resistance it offered to any attempt at manipulation by the churches. If that is so, then it would have to be rehabilitated in order to eliminate the equivocation that now compromises other political interpretations of the gospel.

The theology of revolution, or perhaps we should say certain versions of it, is open to criticism from different points of view. In fact some critics have brought out that it sometimes operates with an image of revolution that is romantic, mythical, and unrealistic (54:225). It has also been censured, and Shaull in particular, for forging a naive and precritical representation of God's revolutionary activity in history; this particular criticism and its underlying basis will be considered in detail (see chapter 7). But these criticisms do not properly apply to all the theologians of revolution, and they might also apply to theologians of liberation. Don't many of the latter offer an equally romantic image of liberation and an equally ingenuous idea of God's liberative action? The general air of suspicion that surrounds the theology of revolution really comes from another corner; it stems from dogmatic prejudice and a resultant panic over the possibility of revolutionary changes in theology and the church.

In contrast to the movements centered around revolution and liberation, those concerned with rejection and protest have not found much of an echo in the work of theologians. That is not to say that they are wholly absent from current theology. For example, Girardi recognizes that "contemporary worldwide protest is in continuity with the gospel protest insofar as it entails a denunciation of collective sin" (208:45). His comment, let it be noted in passing, is entirely in line with other remarks already cited that point up the correspondence or continuity between contemporary liberation and revolution on the one hand and the liberative-revolutionary thrust of the gospel on the other.

Despite the neglect of protest movements, the fact is that the political praxis of Christians does call for a theology of combativeness, dissent, nonconformity, and rejection. Especially during the years just prior to 1968, a posture of rejection and overall challenge prevailed among many Christians, a position that Aldo d'Alfonso has illustrated with texts and documents relative to the attitude of dissent and protest among Italian Catholics (42). On the level of theoretical reflection we find that not infrequently "gospel politics" is described in terms of a series of vigorous protests and rejections (36:625, 631).

To these judgmental elements intrinsic to Christianity must be added the necessity of reflecting theologically on the "great rejection" proposed by Marcuse and others, as well as on certain other movements that are specifically oppositional: e.g., the counterculture, antipsychiatry, neo-anarchism, the deschooling of society, and so forth. While Fanon has been picked up by theologians and incorporated into liberation theology, people such as Alan Watts, Marcuse, Goodman, Illich, Cooper, Laing, and other counterculture theoreticians protesting against institutions have not been taken into account by theology. In general one can say that current movements of anarchist inspiration—anarchism now being rediscovered as counterculture protest against a society that crushes freedom—have not been the object of serious consideration by theologians. Whatever weaknesses such movements may have in terms of epistemology and praxis, this lack of attention is not readily explainable, for there is clearly an analogous attitude to be found in the basic thrust of anarchism on the one hand and the basic animus of dissident Christian sects and groups of every age. This analogy would seem to call for explicit consideration and reflection.

So there is a lacuna in the discourse of political theology. Missing from it is a theology of rejection. We do not find in it the great no of total rejection nor, should that be impossible (396:95), the no of concrete and specific rejections. Contrary to what many think (273:16), such rejections would not represent vague abstractions or bitterness or even resentment toward industrial society; rather, they would indicate clear-eyed awareness and a real critical sense nurtured by a scientific analysis of social reality.

In order to sketch out a theology of protest, I must refer to one of my own works that dealt with protest and Christianity (186:165–92). In it I tried to reflect theologically on certain aspects of contemporary social criticism that are not readily grasped from the standpoint of liberation theology or the theology of revolution. The sociological basis of that reflection was provided mainly by the student protest movement, while my theoretical perspective was taken over from Marcuse. These elements were then worked out theologically through a political hermeneutics of a particular gospel theme: the theme of not belonging to this world. It was a very general and rudimentary effort, but it opened the way for a more systematic study that still remains to be done. That study would be a detailed theological reflection on various current theories and movements that typically espouse nonconformity and nay-saying vis-à-vis the existing order.

5. VIOLENCE

Neither liberation, revolution, rejection, nor protest can take place without some sort of violence in the broadest sense of the term. Violence is shared by all movements of liberation, revolution, or protest. It gives them concrete form, fleshing them out in the real world. Without violence they lose themselves in abstraction, unreality, and ineffectiveness. The only way to subvert the dominant powers of oppression is to oppose them with an antagonistic power. Conflict and a clash between powers—in a word, violence—is inherent in any serious social change. When Marcuse proposes an ethics of revolution, he means by that an ethics of violence (282:143–45). The most realistic theologians recognize that there is a close correlation between a theology of revolution and a theology of violence. I myself at one time was inclined to defend the notion that revolution could be separated from violence, but realism forces us to reject that point of view. As Vaccari makes clear, a distinction between a theology of revolution and a theology of violence is untenable (186:159–61).

In Christian analyses of violence it is now commonplace to find Helder Camara's description of the chain or spiral of violence. As he describes it, "violence number one" is the institutionalized violence imbedded in and underlying the oppressive power structure. This original violence provokes and unleashes "violence number two," which is the violence of the oppressed or the young or revolution in general. The authorities then try to restore public order by resorting to repressive measures; that is "violence number three" (97:19–23). Violence breeds violence, provokes violence in return. That is the common thread that runs through papal and episcopal statements on the general subject.

The prevailing tone sounded in the theology of violence is an ethical one. The abundant literature that falls under that heading belongs almost completely to the genre of moral theology, and its talk centers around the conditions that make violence licit. What is more, and also somewhat surprising, this discussion tends to remain within the context formulated by classic moral theology; and that hardly seems to be very revolutionary. To be specific, it tends to adopt as its basic criterion the age-old moral principle of legitimate defense and its proper proportions. Thus the current theology of violence tends to be no more than a new application of an old principle; it takes the classic principle of the individual's right to defend himself by violence against an unjust aggressor and then applies it to revolutionary violence perpetrated by a group. Almost everything that has been written by Christians on this topic, including one of my works concerning an ethics of violence (186: 223–37), remains within this relatively traditional framework.

Another traditional thesis utilized a great deal has to do with the legitimate killing of tyrannical rulers. The licitness of tyrannicide under certain conditions was considered by more than one moralist in the past: John of Salisbury in the eleventh century, Thomas Aquinas in the thirteenth century, and Mariana in the golden age of Spain. Utilizing their thoughts, modern writers reach the conclusion that armed insurrection is now legitimate against modern tyranny —not tyranny personified by some individual but tyranny institutionalized in a particular social system (133:186; 414:123).

So it is somewhat paradoxical to find that the theology of revolutionary violence is a theology that remains fairly loyal to tradition and is hardly revolutionary as theology. Its intent is described by one author as an effort to understand "in present-day terms, in terms of the masses, in truly dynamic and democratic terms, the classic teaching on the right of revolution" (133:187).

Even granting that the classic moral guidelines concerning legitimate defense and tyrannicide leave room for quite revolutionary applications to oppressive regimes of the present day, one cannot help but raise a question about this traditional ethics. It seems capable of subverting everything except itself. It seems to suggest that a few unalterable moral principles inherited from the most ancient past can give legitimacy to a complete alteration of society. It seems doubtful, however, that a consistent theology of revolution could take for granted certain moral criteria established centuries ago and closely allied to a static concept of society. Those criteria were worked out to restore a given order that might be upset by injustice for a fleeting moment; in itself, however, it was a stable and perduring order. Today we need an ethics of the liberating process and of permanent change, an ethics designed not to preserve or restore some threatened order but to create new forms of societal life.

And so we must ask ourselves whether the traditional principles concerning legitimate self-defense are necessary and adequate for an ethics of revolution. Two other possible answers are found on the fringes of the more traditional approach. One says that the traditional principles are no longer needed; the other says they are inadequate. Both agree in regarding all violence as immoral; but whereas one goes on to deduce an imperative obligation to nonviolence, the other maintains that the binomial violence-revolution, once triumphant, forces us to redefine social morality. And so we find two new principles proposed over against the old principles maintained by most theologians and moralists when they consider the phenomenon of revolutionary violence. On the one hand we find the principle of nonviolence defended by many Christians today; on the other hand we find an ethics of revolution that views the opposition between moral and immoral in dialectical terms (Marcuse).

In the eyes of some Christians who profess nonviolence, violence itself is regarded as antievangelical. That would also hold true for the classic moral principles on the legitimate use of violence for defense and its modern counterparts (52). These Christians try to present a nonviolent Jesus who is the direct opposite of the Zealot Jesus presented by other exegetes. But the proponents of this particular nonviolence are not to be confused with people who are against civil violence but continue to uphold the licitness of wars and a high death toll as the price to be paid for safeguarding the "values" of Western civilization (142: 137). Nor are they to be confused with those who have a somewhat hypocritical view of the situation, who are scandalized by revolutionary violence but not by the violence imbedded in the established order.

In Christian circles those who hold a strict nonviolent view typically tend to see nonviolence as the distinctive trait of the gospel messsage. For them the principle of nonviolence itself embodies and effects the revolution inherent in that message; for it introduces a liberating principle that stands in sharp contrast to the principle of power that presently rules societal relationships (152:212). Some Christian spokesmen for nonviolence, such as Helder Camara and Martin Luther King, Jr., have made a personal option for nonviolence but have not gone on to say that violence itself is against the gospel message. Those who hold a strict nonviolent view, however, do not regard nonviolence as a counsel or charism; rather, it is an intrinsic part of the revolution wrought by the gospel message (233:17–25). Thomas Merton goes so far as to present the principle of nonviolence as the underlying "theory of Christian effectiveness" in the political order (294:189).

The theology of nonviolence has been criticized from different standpoints. The first objection raised consistently is that violence is everywhere (243:3) and that nonviolence is an unrealistic, fictitious alternative. Domergue puts it thus: "The phrase 'opting for violence' is itself ambiguous; one cannot opt for something in which one is already enmeshed" (153:88). Along the same lines, some point out that no real option for nonviolence exists; one can only opt for different kinds of violence. Hence Moltmann states: "The problem of violent action versus nonviolence is a false problem. The only real issue is between justified violence and unjustified violence" (310:77). Since a closer analysis of reality suggests that "humanity is groping for ways to replace violent means by nonviolent ones," Christians too must try to abide by the principle of less and less violence (153:89–90).

Moreover, stress is laid on the fact that "the great precept of the gospel is not the precept of nonviolence but the precept of charity, the summons to display a truly and effectively operative love" (186:229). Chaigne believes he can detect in the tenet of nonviolence a disguised attempt to reinstate the Christendom ideal, to inject an element of religious ideology into the social process instead of letting it operate on its own forces—which would include violence (134; 136).

Finally, criticism is directed at Helder Camara's phrase, "I would rather be killed than kill." The generous spirit underlying this principle is not questioned. What is criticized is the concept of violence that it takes for granted, suggesting that only killing is violence (54:242).

Moving in the opposite direction to the morality of nonviolence, and also away from the traditional criterion, is Marcuse's ethical reflection on revolution. In his opinion the fact of revolution, judged by the concepts prevailing in the normal state of affairs, is always immoral by very definition; for basically revolution attacks the legitimacy and morality of the established order. But revolution is designed to do just that; it seeks to generate some new moral presuppositions, to tear down the prevailing moral order and set up a different moral order. The ethics of revolution decides between the "right of the existing order" and the "right of what might and perhaps should be" on the basis of a "historical calculus" that is rational and basically empirical. It is an inhuman calculus insofar as it operates in quantitative terms, counting up the victims of the revolution on the one hand and those of the established order on the other; but its inhumanity is the inhumanity of history itself (282:148–51).

Aside from some purely expository remarks on the arithmetic of Marcuse's historical calculus (355:286–88), theologians have not paid much attention to his reflections. In particular, they do not seem to have adverted to the fact that revolution itself necessarily entails a subversion of moral values, so that an ethics of revolution itself must end up being revolutionized. Only Trutz Rendtorff seems to echo Marcuse here, when he quotes him and then adds his own comments. Rendtorff says: "Change itself is an ethical category, a category of the morality that is possible and real here and now" (354:101–3).

But a quantitative calculus of suffering and its victims is not wholly overlooked by Christian ethics. A sociologist and moralist as reserved as Díez-Alegría is bold enough to set forth the following thesis: "Even though a revolution may entail a certain measure of injustice and establish an order that itself has elements of injustice, its overall licitness would still be ensured so long as it represented a step forward toward greater justice" (151:80).

6. TRANSITORY THEOLOGIES

Such, then, are the contemporary social phenomena on which political theology reflects more or less deeply and precisely: liberation, revolution, protest, and violence. Certain critical observations are now in order concerning the way in which these phenomena are incorporated into theology. Here I shall confine my remarks to the theology of liberation for two reasons. First of all, my observations about that particular theology can readily be applied to other approaches. Secondly, I have already written at some length about the themes of revolution, protest, and violence in another book (186).

The first cautionary observation concerns the transitory character of any theology of liberation. We simply must discard the notion that seems to be cherished still by some Christians and theologians—namely, that once we now put together a political theology of liberation and revolution, we will have finally come up with the *quid* of theology, with its ultimate and definitive configuration, and perhaps even with the recipe that will guarantee theology's survival in any culture or society whatsoever. Nothing could be further from reality. Precisely insofar as political theology has assimilated a dialectical understanding of man (see chapter 3), and has done so well, it knows for sure something that no prior theology could have even guessed. It knows that it is itself destined for abolition some day, that it will disappear along with the socioeconomic conditions that presently called it into being and made it topical.

This point would seem wholly superfluous and even ridiculous with respect to any other discipline. If one were talking about Paulo Freire's pedagogy of the oppressed (194), which has so many affinities with liberation theology, it would hardly make sense to point out that it only had transitory value and validity. That fact is taken for granted in educational pedagogy and countless other human sciences. Yet such is not the case in theology, however conscious it may now be of its own historicity. Theologians are wont to stress the historical relativity of past theologies, but not the historical relativity of their own particular version. The centuries-old habit of thinking that theology worked with eternal, immutable truths continues to weigh down upon current theology. Today some theologians talk about the theology of liberation with an air of conviction suggesting that they have found the secret essence of theology; it is the same air of conviction that once surrounded their remarks on existential theology.

And so we meet all sorts of exclusivist and forceful statements. We are assured that the term "theology of liberation" is not meant "to designate one segment or sector of theology but theology as a whole." What is more, it does not designate theology simply from "*one* possible angle of vision but rather from *the* angle of vision that the Christian sources point to as the only authentic and privileged one" (author's italics, 388:403). Faced with such assertions, we would seem to be perfectly justified in warning against theology's persistent and age-old mania of believing that it has hit upon what is truly authentic and absolute. Assmann's remarks on "the provisional character of theological activity" (59:116) are very much in order and to the point. He has this shrewd observation:

> The classic temptation facing theology has always been the temptation to operate from an all-encompassing horizon that takes in everything, with the result that it rejects provisional historicity however real and concrete it may be. . . . This temptation has never disappeared; it may remain beneath the surface but it almost seems to be woven into the structure of theology. . . . So we should not be surprised to find that same temptation arising now and then in current reflection on the process of liberation . . . . We do well to remember that the temptation to engage in absolutes is still very much alive in theology, whether people advert to it or not (58:11–12).

We need only add one further observation to fill out Assmann's insightful commentary: The only effective way to combat the unconscious vestiges of theology's absolutizing past is to make a conscious, deliberate decision to fashion a theology for here and now which makes no claims about holding true for other times and situations. Echoing Geffré (207:304), we must acknowledge forthrightly that a general and universally valid theology of liberation would be wholly meaningless.

As Cox has pointed out, the imprisoned and the oppressed do not yearn to fraternize with their keepers; they yearn for the abolition of their bondage. They seek freedom from captivity, not better relations with their captors (126:166). In the meantime there is such a thing as liberation theology because there are captives, slaves, and oppressed peoples. There is room for beneficence now as before because there are poor people disposed to be the object of such beneficence. But what will happen when oppression disappears and there are no more people to liberate? For we must assume that liberation theology aspires to the effective realization of liberation; otherwise we would remain in the contradictory situation embodied in traditional beneficence, which required the presence of poor people so that virtue might be practiced. Right now theologians need captive peoples in order to be able to talk about the gospel as liberation.

The ambiguity of a theology that sees in poverty and oppression both evil to be eliminated and the possibility of a particular theological idiom is evident in such statements as this: "The real epiphany of God's word is the word of the poor man who says, 'I am hungry' " (164:346–47). Such a statement by itself obviously does not entitle us to assume that its author, Enrique Dussel, entertains the idea that the cry of hungry people is the only real manifestation of God's word. But that idea, with all the contradiction entailed in it, does hover temptingly around the portals of some versions of liberation theology.

But if the word of God does sound out in the voice of the poor, where will it resound when the poor cease to be poor? If a theology of God's word is grounded on that idea, will it not have to take for granted that the symbol of God will be superfluous insofar as there are no injustices to castigate in his name? And is it not caught in the contradictory position of having to affirm the existence of social evils like poverty and bondage as the precondition for its own existence as a theology *of liberation* while at the same time aspiring to see them eliminated?

This should indicate a very real danger for any liberation theology. It may unwittingly be glad to see the continuing presence of oppressed people so that it may be able to present the gospel to them as a message of liberation. Once upon a time apologetics required the presence of irreligious people to whom it might offer the fullness of the Christian religion. Now a similar danger threatens the new apologetic approach, though it may not be consciously adverted to. It may have to feed on the yearning of oppressed peoples for freedom in order to be able to offer them something substantive from the gospel message. But what will theology say when there are no people to liberate? What theme, what nostalgia will it look to then? These questions gnaw at some Christians, buried deep inside as unacknowledged fears. When they are faced boldly and clearly, they lead us to the obvious conclusion that liberation theology as such is destined to disappear, that its most beneficial result would be to stimulate a real-life praxis that made it superfluous and no longer workable.

Some are wont to respond to this line of thought by pointing out that freedom is not something attained once and for all, that liberation is a process coexistent with human history itself rather than a single moment in history. Gutiérrez states this emphatically when he proposes that we "conceive history as a process of human liberation" (230: 68). On that assumption it will always be possible to have a theology of liberation, a theology concerned with the slow and ongoing attainment of human freedom. In response, however, we must point out that it is we, the people of the western world today, who picture history that way. People of other times and places have not pictured it as such, and we cannot be sure how people will see it in the future (189). We assume they will go on being concerned with their personal and collective liberation, but that supposition is merely an extrapolation of our own present experience and our acute sense of liberty.

The analyses and predictions of futurology tend to show us human beings in the future who will be less preoccupied with liberty than we are today—whether or not they will be more or less free than we today are. To picture all of history as a process of liberation is to make a wager: Perhaps today's Christian must make that wager, but only future history can prove that it was well grounded.

7. A RELIGION OF THE OPPRESSED

Another point deserving attention has to do with the possibility of establishing a solid connection between current liberation movements and the liberating gospel message. More generally it has to do with the possibility of discovering and establishing some real correlation between social change (which would include revolution) and the true concerns of Christianity (5:XI; 357:140).

Some theologians think the correlation is clear-cut and obvious, and they view it in the following light. The gospel and the Bible, they say, show a clear preference for the poor and the oppressed; to them they proclaim liberation and urge them on to it. Thus God (or Christ) is on the side of the oppressed, inspiring and abetting people's liberation; for that reason a theology of liberation is possible. So the argument goes. Now it would all seem to be correct, so long as one accepts the basic underlying presupposition that the gospel and the Bible itself directly constitute the word of God. In short, one must assume at the start that the praise of the poor in the Bible was uttered by God himself and hence objectively manifests a divine predilection.

At this point we do well to recall other possible interpretations of a different cast. The affinity between the gospel message and the oppressed has been noted by people outside the faith also. Nietzsche, for example, regarded Jewish morality as a slave ethic and interpreted Judeo-Christian life as the long history of slave rebellion in the field of morality (325:287–308). Nietzsche's evaluation of that history was a very denigrating one. But even a positive evaluation of it does not mean automatic support for liberation theology and its point of view. One strain of Marxist tradition, for example, goes back to Engels and agrees with Nietzsche in seeing the rise of Christianity as a religion of slaves; but it does not follow Nietzsche in his negative evaluation of it. Engels stresses the fact that "in its origin Christianity was a movement of the oppressed," a religion of "slaves and freedmen, the poor and those deprived of rights" and he notes its "points of contact with the modern movement of workers" (287:310).

Ernst Bloch observes that if one starts from its economic base, one can see that Christianity differs from all other religions in that it began as an ideology of the oppressed (76:112). This singular feature of Christianity is what makes it superior to other forms of religion in his eyes. For even though it took a dreamy, mythological, and rather adolescent form, it did identify itself with the historical movement for the emancipation of the poor, which only socialism can tackle scientifically and bring to concrete realization (76:104–5).

Finally, Gilbert Mury writes: "Christianity was built on the foundation of a universal protest against the exploitation that had become universal. It was the first universal religion possible, since universalism is based on a complete inversion of values" (318:126). Needless to say, this positive evaluation of primitive Christianity by these Marxist writers does not in any way favor anything remotely resembling a theology of liberation or revolution. The mere fact that the Christian message corresponds to emancipation movements does not give any doctrinal validity to the former. Many different theses can be derived from that correspondence; it does not lead automatically or univocally to a political theology.

Strictly speaking, the possibility of establishing harmony

between the New Testament and the yearning of people for freedom only points up the similarity between the situation of certain Christian communities today and that of the primitive Christian community. The first Christians came to believe in Jesus and worship him in a situation of poverty and oppression quite like that experienced today by millions of human beings and Christians in the Third World and elsewhere. Yet the similarity itself remains ambiguous, open to very different and even contradictory interpretations. A critical theory of religion finds proof in the fact that Christianity arose as an ideology of the oppressed —whatever valuation might then be put on that fact.

Some theologians of liberation, on the other hand, seem to assume that this proves the limitless capacity of God's word to meet human beings in any given historical situation whatsoever. But notice the dogmatic character of that assumption. It depends entirely on an act of faith, not only in Jesus but also in the content of the Bible as revelatory and revealed. Notice also that such a theology of liberation does not tend to make any attempt to give solid grounding to that assumption. It simply leaves its position ungrounded, or else it simply adopts the traditional dogmatics. In the first case it is left hanging in mid-air; in the second case its whole validity depends upon the validity of traditional, age-old dogmatics. Once again we are faced with the question of the grounding of political theology, and specifically with its lack of any reasoned foundation (see chapter 4, section 10).

From a different standpoint than the one we have been using, Pannenberg makes some comments that clearly illustrate the ambiguous relationship that arises when the New Testament is regarded as a theology and morality of the oppressed. He begins by viewing the New Testament commandments of obedience as typical expressions of a morality for downtrodden peoples, a morality of sheer passivity. This passive attitude, he feels, stemmed from a conviction that the end of the world was imminent, so that "there would be no time for institutional reforms." Not all theologians or exegetes would lay such great stress on the passive character of New Testament morality of course; but once Pannenberg has done that, he finds himself in an uncomfortable position. How can one justify an activist ethics that promotes participation in a process of social change?

It is not too difficult for him to get out of that particular corner. He resorts to the same principle which was brought out earlier in this book (see chapter 4, section 4): i.e., the nonobligatory character of biblical pronouncements and imperatives. He says: "The purely passive and submissive morality of the New Testament cannot be falsely interpreted as perpetually binding on all Christian conduct because it was conditioned by a situation of submission and subjection that was wholly removed from any sense of active political responsibility" (333:237). Thus the ethical representations of the Bible are treated in the same way that the cosmological representations are; and no one regards the latter as being obligatory in any way. The morality of the oppressed found in the New Testament is put on the same plane as its cosmology of the heavenly bodies; it is simply an ideology conditioned by the sociocultural situation.

Now Pannenberg's assertion that biblical theology and its morality of the oppressed are historically conditioned and therefore not perpetually binding sets a major critical reservation in the path of liberation theology. There is no doubt that the New Testament presents itself as a proclamation of good news to the poor and the enslaved. It also addresses to them a message and a moral code of liberation that is not as passive as Pannenberg thinks. So there is a biblical theology of liberation. But now we run into the problem: that very theology is conditioned by the status of the early Christians. To what extent, then, can it be regarded as binding? Is liberation theology the only legitimate one because it is found in certain biblical texts? The answer seems to be no.

In this instance, as was true in the case of Exodus theology and the theology of political messianism, the Bible's remarks open up a possibility; they do not define an obligation or necessity. A theology of liberation is possible and legitimate since the biblical witnesses themselves had one; hence it is clearly possible to relate faith in Jesus to an active yearning for liberty. But one must be aware of the socioeconomic conditionings affecting the bibical theology of liberation. One cannot naively assume that one has in hand a divine, revealed theology when in fact it is nothing more than a human theology whose social and ethical representations are just as open to criticism as its cosmological representations are.

8. CHRISTIANS AND THE BUILDING OF SOCIALISM

European political theology is criticized by Latin Americans for being too closely bound up with industrial society in an advanced stage of capitalism. It is also subject to the danger of falling prey to the conditionings of that society (230:296–97). As a cautionary word, the point is well made. But the same basic criticism and risk might be brought up in connection with liberation theology and the semirural, semiurban society of the underdeveloped countries. Every theology has its conditioning factors, and one should not look for the beam in the eye of others only.

In any case the thematic preferences of theologians for different sociopolitical realities (liberation, revolution, social change, and so forth) lead us to their respective social situations, within which they exercise their function. Indeed one could sketch a typology of political theologies based on the major geopolitical areas inhabited by Christians. It is very clear, for example, that the political theology of Metz, Moltmann's theology of hope, and some versions of the theology of revolution relate to the context of Western Europe. This book of mine, too, probably is indebted to that same context for the most part; it is the underlying context from which most of my analyses and judgments stem. Cox's theology of social change relates to the United States situation, and the situation of Latin American Christians finds its main reflection in the theology of liberation. Finally we find a "black theology" (122) trying to reflect the rebelliousness of the "black power" movement in the United States and to represent the Christian response to it.

But what about the Christians of the socialist world? What kind of political theology reflects their awareness and situation? This is a delicate question. Or perhaps it would be better to say that it is an obscure area on the general horizon of current political interpretation of the gospel. In those countries which have already turned down the road to socialism or communism we do not find a theology as fully elaborated as that to be found in the nonsocialist countries. Indeed in those countries theology does not seem to be very critical toward power and the political order. It remains a public and practical theology, but it has lost the note of criticism which is characteristic of such theology in other areas of the world.

Theologians who live in socialist countries or who use the situation to be found in those countries as the starting point for their own reflection tend to present a theology that stresses the contribution to be made by Christians toward the further buildup and implementation of socialism. They reserve their criticisms for the age-old complicity of the churches with the bourgeois order and for the masochistic mystique of the so-called "church of silence." On this front we find agreement between Catholic theologians reflecting on Cuban socialism, Protestant theologians of Eastern Europe, and Orthodox theologians in Soviet Russia.

The role of the Cuban church is presented as one of service and inspiration to the fashioning of Cuba's new society (356). Dewart's lengthy book on Christians in Cuba (149) deals with a revolution that has supposedly been carried through already, not one that remains to be accomplished; that is clearly a far cry from the typical book put out by theologians of revolution.

The stance of Orthodox theologians is much the same. Discussing the general theme of the Russian church and the Soviet revolution, the Archpriest Borovoi sketches a doctrine of the people of God as "an element involved in the buildup of a new society grounded on revolutionary foundations," and of Christians as "active builders of socialism" (83:307–8).

The most reserved theologians in this connection are the Protestant authors. They, too, take for granted the contribution of believers to socialism; but they do not go so far as to elevate that cooperation to a theological category. This seems apparent in the relatively small amount of Hromadka's work that is available to the Western reader (239). It is also evident in the writings of another Czech, Lochmann, who is very reticent about the theology of revolution. While he does talk about the "service" to be rendered by the church in a socialist society, he warns against any "theological vertigo" that might plunge us headlong into a socialist Christianity of very much the same stamp as the older Christianity of the medieval or bourgeois period (260:125).

The deference of theology in socialist countries to the existing regimes seems very much like that displayed by older political theology toward existing authority; and it contrasts markedly with the critical and even subversive cast of various theologies of liberation, revolution, and violence in the nonsocialist world. Its resemblance to the older theology of the West and its deference to the existing political order would seem to justify the same sort of censure that is now being directed against every theology that is socially conformist. The contrast with other present-day political theologies raises some serious questions: Is current political theology to be nothing more than a symbolic system designed to encourage a Christian shift towards socialism? Is its whole purpose meant to be a criticism of the bourgeois order, so that its critical capability and its reason for being will disappear with the disappearance of that order?

Any effort to clarify those questions would seem to confirm the impression, already remarked, that political theology is transitory by nature. In all likelihood it would also tend to confirm the hypothesis that there is a correspondence between that theology and Marxism. This hypothesis is one we shall have to deal with time and again in this book. But we cannot draw any certain conclusions at the present time because the content and features of theology in the socialist countries are still too rudimentary and fragmentary to permit that. We do not yet have an adequately worked out theology of the Christian contribution to established socialism (not only to the struggle for socialism), and so we cannot yet try to draw any meaningful comparisons with theology in the capitalist world. Only a comparison between two equally elaborated theologies, within the context of established systems, would permit us to clarify some now obscure points regarding the socioeconomic conditioning of political theologies and their symbolic function in the establishment of a socialist order.

There has been a greater theological development of the contribution of Christians to the overcoming of capitalism and the building of the socialist society. This development has always taken place in relation to well specified situations and societies. Until September 1973 the principal testing-ground for the Christian contribution to the construction of socialism was Chile. There some groups of Christians were actively engaged in a role which Christians had never had in the establishment or development of socialist regimes in Western Europe. Hugo Assmann has made an analysis of the now interrupted process in Chile and the active participation of Christians in it. His analysis provides a partial, local clarification of the questions cited above. While it may not answer them fully, it does help one to formulate them more precisely, to improve their status as questions (59:171).

According to Assmann, the realm of Christian symbols and myths has as its purpose a process of humanization, and this purpose is "practical, historical, and intrawordly." Its innermost aim is to give meaningfulness to daily living so that human beings "will be wise enough to live together as humans and, if necessary, die for their fellows" (59: 190–91). That symbolic system has been perverted and subverted by western capitalism, which has managed to make full use of those symbols and myths in a way that runs directly contrary to their "pristine goal of humanization" (59:192). Yet there is a bright side to the perversion that has taken place. For now Christianity can go back to its original intent and help human beings make sure that its myths and symbols are used "for the practical, historical, and intrawordly purpose that they were meant to serve." It can do this with the help of those segments of its own tradition that are still significant and available for use, where its "cutting edge of rebelliousness remains intact" (59:192–93).

Now this restoration of Christian symbolism to its original intent dovetails with its canalization in the direction of socialism and its goals. It points toward the "social ownership" of its symbols and myths (59:192–94, 200–02). Over against Marxists, who tend to disdain the Christian contribution, Assmann takes pains to point up the functional role and use of the symbolic and mythical realm in the buildup of a socialist society. Symbols and myths play a fundamental role "not only because they exist . . . but also because they relate to a social dimension of humankind that cannot and should not be suppressed. . . . Insofar as myths are concerned, socialism is radically different from capitalism not because it rejects them but because it restores to them their social objective of humanization" (59:194). That is a sufficiently clear outline of a basic theology that would deal with the Christian contribution to a socialist society.

Assmann's reflections are of great interest, and to some extent they clarify some of the questions raised by the basic geopolitics of current theologies. But it should be noted that we are dealing here principally with hypotheses related to a specific national context and a specific stage of history. They have meaning as hypotheses or plans for concrete action, but they must look to future events for their verification. The brutal blow suffered by the Chilean movement toward socialism in September 1973 means that Chilean history will not provide any such verification in the near future; it also means that the concrete theology that was beginning to take shape in Chile does not have bright prospects right now (53).

Today we must look to other countries in South America to find out how Christian symbols might serve the movement toward socialism. We can only look to the struggle of Christians who live under capitalistic socioeconomic conditions and who struggle for socialism against the established power.

But how in fact and in the long run will Christian symbols function in those countries that are now capitalist but where there is occurring an effective struggle toward socialism? How will these symbols function when in those countries where Christians for Socialism are now struggling socialist relationships of production are solidly established. In particular what will and can the social ownership of Christian symbols mean in reality? All that remains to be seen, remains to be verified. Moreover, a theology such as that of Assmann is mediated and circumscribed by a sociology of Christianity, which thereby sets certain limits on it. Such a theology cannot go beyond the basic framework in which it was elaborated; it cannot be generalized. It is not only provisional, but also local. The shortlived Chilean experiment and the theological reflection that has attempted to give it a critical consciousness represent a tiny pinpoint on an otherwise empty landscape. For the most part we cannot find any concrete or elaborated theology concerned with the possible contribution of Christians to socialism.

9. THE HERMENEUTIC-POLITICAL REGROUNDING OF CHRISTIAN TRADITION

Liberation, revolution, nonconformity, and violence are the principal phenomena considered by political theology. But to say that political theology is concerned with specific political realities is not to spell out what is specifically theological about it. That does not indicate the particular focus or standpoint that makes such reflection "theology" rather than sociology or political science. It is not the realities considered (the "material" object according to neoscholastic manuals) that makes such reflection *theological.* It is the way in which they are considered (the "formal" object according to the same manuals) that does that. For those realities are examined in terms of certain Christian representations. So now we must consider the body of theological representations (i.e., ideas, images, and symbols) that are used to apprehend and interpret the aforementioned phenomena in theological terms.

In principle the whole arsenal of representations contained in Christian tradition could be used to comprehend political realities in theological terms, so long as they were suitably adapted. We have already had a chance to consider some of them in our discussion of the historical paradigms available to political theology (see chapter 4). Messianism, Christology, the Exodus story, and prophetism provide political theology with representational approaches or a body of useful representations. In themselves all the ideas, notions, and images of theology can be recast to perform a role in political theology, in the same way as they were recast in an earlier decade to perform a role in existential theology.

Christian representations are incorporated into political theology when they come to function as critico-practical representations that have an impact on public life. Indeed this is the proper place to point out that political theology should take up and reinterpret the whole patrimony of representations to be found in Christian tradition. It is lamentable that this process of hermeneutic incorporation and elaboration has not been carried through insofar as the vast majority of theology's traditional representations are concerned, even though many of them might ultimately prove to be unserviceable and now outmoded.

Here we come up against another problem: the reinsertion and hermeneutic regrounding of tradition within political theology. Is the representational material of tradition still meaningful, or is it now out of date? Which theological representations can be utilized for a political interpretation of the gospel, and which cannot? Are the most deeply rooted notions of theology, such as sin, redemption, grace, and the church, susceptible of a political interpretation? If so, under what conditions and through what sort of transforming hermeneutic process?

It would be quite useful to set out a detailed inventory of those theological representations that could be regrounded and incorporated into one or more political theologies. But that is not the most important task to be performed in a basic introduction to political theologies such as this book purports to be. More important here is the task of analyzing the transformation undergone by Christian representations when they are incorporated into the framework of political theology. A few samples will suffice to carry out that task, though of course it is wiser to focus on certain themes that have been worked out more fully. Once we discover the hermeneutic processes involved in such transformation, we can readily apply them to other representations.

In the following sections of this chapter we shall consider a few theological representations undergoing the process of reinterpretation. We choose these particular ones because they have gone far enough through this process to be incorporated into current political theology. And so we shall consider these themes: salvation (or liberation), communion (or brotherhood), conversion, and evangelical love.

10. SALVATION OR LIBERATION

In section 3 we pointed out that in theology the term "liberation" can signify (1) contemporary movements or events concerned with social liberation, or (2) the theological category whereby those movements or events are interpreted in terms of the grace of God as embodied in Jesus Christ. It is the second meaning that interests us here. We are interested in liberation as a key theological idea or category that seeks to apprehend and interpret liberation movements by regrounding the traditional idea of salvation and incorporating it into political theology in a usable way.

Today the idea of salvation is applied to the realm of society, politics, and concrete praxis. As I have pointed out in another book (186:145–46), political theology differs from other Christian theologies insofar as it has a different notion of salvation. It does not picture salvation as liberation from the dominion exercised by cosmic, biological, or demonic forces. Instead it sees salvation as liberation from the dominion exercised by specifically human and social forces. Thus the idea of salvation is no longer construed in terms of the cosmos or the hereafter, but rather in terms of earthly history and the sociopolitical situation.

Today many theologians are stressing the advisability of replacing the term "salvation" with the term "liberation"

(230:194), for the former term has undertones of evasiveness and escape. At the same time, however, it must be pointed out that only semantic continuity between the two terms would enable us to give biblical grounding to most of the theses related to a theology of liberation. Reference to God or Christ as liberator (230:165 and 236; 81:375) is bound up with the classic dogmatic assertions about God's salvific will (230:198) and Christ the redeemer. In a word, liberation theology is a political soteriology, a soteriology that extends and applies traditional soteriological theses to the public and practical realm of present societal life: "Liberation theology is a theology of salvation in the concrete historical and political conditions of the present day" (227:245).

The idea of salvation (or liberation) evokes a grace. Of course human beings participate in their own liberation, act to achieve it; but the presupposition is that the first initiative comes gratuitously from God (230:210). The idea finds first expression in the indicative mood: Humankind is liberated, Christ has made us free, the Christian God is a liberator God. But it also contains a secondary sense as an imperative: The gospel message is a summons to liberation, a command to free oneself and others from all alienation and bondage.

Current elaboration of the theme of liberation naturally contains some features that set it off markedly from the traditional exposition of the theme of salvation. The present approach puts greater stress on our own contribution to liberation. The traditional approach stressed that it was God who saved us, though we had to cooperate in fear and trembling. Now that the older sacral and magical outlook has evaporated to a large extent, the responsibility for human liberation is placed squarely on our shoulders—as a result of God's summons and support.

In the past, attaining salvation also tended to mean crossing beyond certain biological and cosmic bounds. To be saved was to transcend death (through resurrection) and human finiteness (through participation in the divine life); it was also to be freed from sin as a basic situation of enmity toward God. Today liberation tends to refer to various kinds of social alienation rather than to physical limitations; it is emancipation from oppressive and dehumanizing power centers in societal life.

Traditional theology tended to view salvation primarily as connected with the hereafter. It lay in the future, on the far side of death, though its seeds were planted here in this earthly life. Liberation theology shifts the stress to the present life, to the here and now of history. Insofar as eternal life is concerned, it maintains a discreet and modest silence. In this respect it is just as silent as Moltmann's theology of hope. As I have remarked in another work (182:219), Moltmann declines to make any clear comment on that subject. Current liberation theology follows his theology of divine promise and hope in not stating its position vis-à-vis traditional eschatology of the life to come. One suspects that it does not believe much in that life, if at all. Theologians who have a great deal of respect for traditional dogma, and Catholic theologians in general, tend to make some vague allusions to the topic; but they do not go into any great detail or explore the issue fully.

The potential danger of ambiguity is clear enough. The impression is given that current political theology merely makes a further contribution by stressing the presence of liberation in earthly history and society, without at all touching the absolute and total salvation of eternal life. But this impression will not stand up under even cursory analysis. The current political regrounding of the notion of salvation or liberation coincides with the current credibility crisis facing traditional eschatology and its dogmas concerning the hereafter: e.g., resurrection, life eternal, the beatific vision, and so forth—not to mention purgatory and hell, which have been regarded as improbable for some time now. Wouldn't it be altogether proper for liberation theology to take due account of that crisis and deal with it thoroughly? One of the defects of current liberation theology is the fact that it has not settled accounts with the older theology of salvation or spelled out its own position toward it. To phrase the problem in simple but pointed terms, we might ask this question: Is it possible to believe both in heaven and in the theological meaning of decolonization? So long as the theology of liberation does not clarify such questions, we shall not know exactly what its theological significance is.

11. BROTHERHOOD AND COMMUNION

The theme of communion *(koinonia)* and the closely allied notion of brotherhood also find expression first and foremost in the indicative mood: human beings are brothers and sisters, children of the same Father in heaven who have been redeemed by one and the same Jesus. That establishes a common life and destiny among them. To this is added a common participation in certain sacraments insofar as Christians are concerned. From this community that makes all people brothers and sisters, and Christians even more so, flow certain demands that are couched in imperative terms. They outline an ideal of coexistence in which human beings, brought to the same social and economic level, will finally manage to treat each other as brothers and sisters.

Current theology contains frequent references to communion and brotherhood as specifically evangelical models; the implementation of those models would be the embodiment of the Christian contribution to society. Paul L. Lehmann has led the way in propounding and elaborating this basic idea. His book on ethics, first published in 1963, presents Christian ethics as an ethics of *koinonia* (256). And in his approach the ethics of communion gives rise to political repercussions. The will of God is not a pious phrase but a clear and concrete matter of politics. The God of the church is the God of politics (256:87).

Many theologians have followed Lehmann in this line of thought. From the Christian standpoint, according to Richard Shaull, "order is an order having to do with humanization as it appears in *koinonia*" (393:21–26). Shaull himself takes great delight in pointing up the role of Christian *koinonia* in the process of revolution (393:21–26). Castillo Cárdenas also wants the church to be "a *koinonia* living a life of faith and hope." Living as such in and for the world, the church itself will then be the expression and embodiment of "the first fruits of the new humanity" (110:120). Trutz Rendtorff sees a theology of *koinonia* as the church's concept of revolution, and brotherhood as the peculiar Christian strain in the revolution (353:61 and 65). I myself have also focused on brotherhood, a brotherhood based on liberty and equality, as the specifically evangelical model of society. It is not so much a model of some ideal to be attained in the future, however, but a model of an already existing praxis of fraternization (182:179–216).

All these ideas adopt the traditional theological heritage concerning the communion of saints, just as the theology of liberation inherits the older soteriology. It is a matter of adopting older representations that had once been interpreted in a rather different key and applying them to the realm of politics.

Another approach runs very much along the same lines as the above comments on communion and brotherhood. It starts with the sacramental and liturgical oneness of Christians and goes on to derive an obligation of social communication and egalitarian levelling. Current political theology is severely critical of the older dogmatic ideology that allowed people to think that "eucharistic conditions always prevail, even given the existence of exploiters and exploited" (59:158, 188). González-Ruiz staunchly challenges all those who would try to misinterpret the Christian unity proclaimed by Paul (Gal. 3:28) as if it were some sort of "mystical unity designed to throw a cloak over the shocking social differences between human beings without ever really intending to eliminate them." Appealing to Paul (1 Cor. 11:17–34), González-Ruiz presents a very different view; "Cultic and religious unity absolutely calls for the establishment of social and economic equality in the profane realm inhabited by believers. If a church indiscriminately admits both exploiters and exploited to the eucharistic banquet without effectively denouncing the degrading situation that exists, then it is guilty of eating and drinking the body of Christ unworthily. For it is failing to value the eucharistic food in terms of its function as a social cement, and hence it is committing a terrible sacrilege" (217: 449–50).

This reasoning seems to be completely valid. Unity in faith and in worship demands social equality. The only reservation that might be in order here is that Paul himself might not have interpreted that demand in exactly the same way it is interpreted and elaborated today. He tends to convey the impression that he had no such societal change in mind and that he considered it relatively useless, given the fact that he felt the end of the world was imminent (186:125–26).

12. POLITICAL CHARITY

Another important key is furnished by Christian love, by evangelical charity. Love is fundamentally an imperative: "Love one another." More clearly than the themes just treated, it points up the active, practical, effectively real side of the gospel's insertion into social reality. It is also one of the points where political theology betrays its own cast most clearly, setting itself off not only from earlier theology in general but also from recent existential theology in particular. Here current political theology appears as a "deprivatizing" of the Christian idea of love.

Earlier existential theology eagerly considered interpersonal love relationships, the I-Thou relationship between two human subjects. Current political theology criticizes the inadequacy of such interpersonal love and intimacy and also its inner contradictions in a society that is marked by divisiveness and hostility (182:186–88). The conception of Christian love as "the cult of neighborliness and fellowship" (312:410–15) is criticized, and this leads logically to the concept of "political charity." Love is no longer viewed simply as addressed to a single "Thou" close at hand; it is also addressed to human groups. It is no longer simply an immediate "short-term" relationship between an I and a Thou; it is also a "long-term" relationship (Ricoeur) with groups and peoples that is mediated through institutions and worked out in justice (72:176; 140; 162:188–93; 186: 19–66).

Framing evangelical love in political terms also compels us to move from a merely therapeutic healing of wounds to preventive action designed to get at the roots of social ills: "This passionate yearning to make all people neighbors on a massive scale represents a profound break with the older remedial conception of charity. It gives rise to a love that is not just militant in its struggle against injustice. The new love is also a prophetic, preventive, and anticipatory love that seeks to find and understand the causes of the evil in question" (101:87).

Evangelical love, as a willed effort at humanization, appears as an important revolutionary propellant toward carrying out a sociopolitical plan or project (186:52–53; 297:398; 414:328). Various problems arise in this connection: e.g., morality and efficacy (411), love and violence, love and class conflict (208; 224). Christian theology of violence presents itself as a variant version of the theology of operative love. In the broader context of Christian love, violence is depicted as "the strange and paradoxical face of love, love as self-abandonment and annihilation" (215:61 and 63). It is also the *opus alienum Dei,* not the pure expression of love but "the concession that love makes to the imperfections and contingencies of life in real history" (48:197).

Love for human beings can lead to conflict and violence. Today many Christians are quite critical of the older social doctrine of the church that regarded class divisions as a natural phenomenon willed by God himself, divisions in which the element of antagonism was merely secondary and superficial, and easily remedied by a deceptive process of pseudo-harmonization (336). Ready acceptance of conflict is part and parcel of contemporary Christian awareness. At their 1970 Congress in Amsterdam, Christians in Solidarity recited this prayer: "Lord, grant that we may not be afraid of conflict and struggle, even among ourselves. For you have fashioned life in such a way that no progress and nothing new can arise without confrontation. Guide us into those struggles that are truly essential."

In our society class conflicts are one of those essential conflicts or struggles. Hence political theology acknowledges class conflict. This means that Christian love can adopt as its own the Marxist analysis of social reality and the operational model of Marxist praxis; at the same time, however, Christian love rescues class conflict from lovelessness and transforms it into a paradoxical tool of love itself. Indeed one of the specific contributions of Christians to the struggle for liberation on the part of the oppressed is to transform that struggle into an act of love for humanity, for concrete human beings and human groups.

On this point theologians are in agreement with other Christians who are not theologians. From the standpoint of a pedagogy of liberation, Paulo Freire faces up to the fact that "authentic revolutionaries must come to see their revolution as an act of love, since it is a creative, humanizing activity." By virtue of the purpose conferred on the struggle for liberation by the oppressed, that struggle will be "an act of love" (194:106 and 40). Some theologians point out that such a conflict is imbedded in the exigencies of love: "There is no more forceful gesture of love for one's enemies than the one that breaks down their privileged elitist situation and ushers them into the immense joy of a shared common condition. . . . If I am to live the great commandment of love and treat the wealthy landowners as brothers, I must engage in the struggle that will dispossess them" (99:248). They are well aware of the extremes to which love may lead insofar as the use of violence is concerned: "Of course it is terrible to have to kill for the sake of love, but it may prove to be necessary" (208:71). For this theology of violent love, in any case, evangelical charity cannot be dissociated from the revolutionary struggle: "If it is true that conflict without love becomes sterile and counterrevolutionary, it is equally true that love without class conflict is illusory, a mask for egotism and laziness" (208:59).

Marxists have good reason to reproach Christians with certain questions on this score: "Who are you to love both the oppressor and the oppressed? How is that possible? So long as the material conditions allowing for the implementation of moral ideals are not present, the ideals proclaimed by you Christians are merely alibis, a point of honor for spiritualists" (21:127). The current Christian response to that criticism is that universal love certainly does not mean vague, indiscriminate love. To cite Girardi once again: "One must love all, but not all in the same way. One loves the oppressed by liberating them from their misery; one loves the oppressors by liberating them from their sinfulness. Love must be class love in order to be truly universal" (208:94–96). Guichard expresses it in even clearer terms: "Contrary to all appearances the revolutionary strategy of interclass struggle opens up broad perspectives of universality. The reformist strategy of interclass cooperation, on the other hand, locks us up in the logic of divisiveness" (224:117).

13. CONVERSION

Like the notion of love, the notion of conversion contains an equally forceful imperative thrust: "Reform your lives! The reign of God is at hand" (Matt. 3:2; 4:17). These words inaugurate the preaching mission of both John the Baptist and Jesus. On the surface, but only on the surface, the gospel summons to *metanoia* ("change of outlook," "conversion") seems to be addressed to individuals. Cullmann still felt he could point up "the priority that Jesus gave to a change of heart in the individual," without showing any great interest in any reform of societal structures. Yet even Cullmann admits that "more just social structures favor the individual conversion demanded by Jesus," and he goes on to postulate that there is a reciprocal influence to be found between "the conversion of the individual and the reform of social structures" (132:39 and 69).

But the reality to which one is supposed to be converted is the kingdom of God—which is to say, a social reality. Even the most rudimentary analysis of that fact forces us to adopt a more resolutely social stand than Cullmann did. We are compelled to adopt a more decidedly social and political interpretation of conversion.

Conversion cannot be pictured as "a religious solution of a magical sort suddenly breaking into society." Indeed stress on individual conversion has even been an obstacle to social change. Now we must underline the fact that the act of self-conversion is not independent of the surrounding social system (111). There is a growing conviction among Christians "that the gospel contains a summons to conversion not only on the individual level but also on the political and social level of the community" (175:1058). In short, we must scrape all the barnacles of excessive individualism off the notion of conversion (117:239).

The sociopolitical dimensions of the evangelical summons to conversion become clear as soon as one realizes that "our process of conversion is conditioned by the socioeconomic, political, cultural, and human milieu in which we live" (230:269). It is evident, in other words, as soon as we realize that any moralistic or individualist effort at conversion is futile and impossible if it does not somehow touch the structures of society. It is the social and economic bases that make human beings "good" or "bad," and the power of individuals to better themselves morally remains relatively meager so long as those social and economic bases do not change.

Here we find theologians adopting the criticism of morality that had already been undertaken by social psychology, by sociological theory, and in particular by Marxism. For Marx, morality was "impotence in action," because it operated with ideals that are not inscribed in socioeconomic reality. Current political theology has learned that lesson. It is a theology of social transformation precisely insofar as it stands in opposition to the older moralizing theology that dealt with the isolated conversion of individuals. The whole revolutionary program, "presupposes a radical criticism of moralism, i.e., of the view that hopes to bring about a transformation of humanity merely through the moral conversion of individuals" (210:517). The moralism of individual conversion now appears as a great historical mistake committed by Christians. On a massive scale they "have failed to carry out their task of proclaiming a 'structural redemption.' They have confined themselves to exhorting people to undergo a *metanoia* as individuals, thereby leaving much evil imbedded in structures" (217:448).

This rejection of individualistic moralism and mere personal conversion, to the neglect of socioeconomic conditionings, means that a decided shift in stress takes place in the gospel command for change and conversion. The emphasis clearly and decisively shifts away from the individual toward society. The command to undergo conversion now applies much more emphatically to modifications in society than to changes in the individual. But note the implications of this shift: When gospel conversion ceases to be interpreted as a process centered on the individual and comes to be understood as a process centered around groups and collectivities, then it ends up corresponding to what is otherwise known as liberating revolution. "Conversion" is the Christian name for "revolution," the theological category most suitable for laying hold of the fact of revolution and dealing with it comprehensively (186:156). Revolution occurs when the radicalism of gospel *metanoia* is applied to societies and institutions. Liberating revolution is the conversion of societies.

The crux of the problem might be stated as a question: Which is more important, the conversion of the individual or the transformation of society? (353:59). Put more radically: Which comes first, the new person or the new society? Is it "new" people who create a new society or is it the new society that will produce new people? The older moralism naively believed that the conversion of human individuals would be enough. Indeed it may have even felt that structural changes and reforms were useless. What use could they be if people's hearts did not undergo any change? So it felt there was no real need to promote societal changes because they would come about naturally once people's hearts had undergone conversion. What it failed to realize is that changes in the realities of socioeconomic life can also effect changes in the hearts of human beings.

Persuaded by the evidence gathered by social theory, current theology knows that there can be no transformation of human beings without a transformation of society. In the last analysis, societal transformation comes down to a transformation in production relationships. Real conversion to a new humanity must necessarily go by way of revolution. Revolution will not automatically produce new human beings, but it is the necessary social precondition for that on the collective level (20).

14. THEOLOGICAL IDEAS

We have just finished considering the key theological concepts used in trying to apprehend sociopolitical reality: i.e., salvation, fraternal communion, love, and conversion. Now we must consider the nature of those ideas. Exactly how are the theologians alluding to reality when they contemplate it in terms of salvation, communion, charity, and conversion? What kind of mental representations are those terms? Are they authentic concepts that furnish strict and real knowledge about social reality? Or are they mere labels or fantasies without any connection to real life?

To begin with, it is quite obvious that theological representations are not concepts descriptive of reality; they do not correspond to straightforward sense perceptions. That fact is not peculiar to political theology; it applies to theological representations in general. Although such representations refer to wordly objects or to the world as a whole, they are never descriptive of that world; rather, they are interpretative. And this remark holds completely true for the representations of political theology as well.

Insofar as political reality is concerned, one can cite a whole series of representations that are merely descriptive. That is to say, their content is wholly bound up with sense perception of actual facts and events. When one talks about strikes, wars, governments, industries, or wages, one is resorting to purely descriptive representations or concepts that attempt to describe or grasp certain facts and situations without going into any analysis, interpretation, or theoretical consideration of them. Now political theology can and should utilize such concepts as its material content; but its own distinctive form as a specifically theological focus does not reside in concepts of that sort. The fact that its representations may correspond with other descriptive representations should not delude it on this score. As we have already pointed out (section 10), liberation as a theological representation must be clearly distinguished from liberation as a perceivable historical process (section 3) and also from its corresponding descriptive representation.

One could cite any number of examples along the same lines. Take the term "love," for example. It can be used as a merely descriptive term to designate certain patterns of behavior. But that should not entice us to mistake the sense of the theological representation of love, which can and does refer to such behavior patterns of course, but it does so by interpreting them and formulating imperatives on a level that cannot be reduced to sense perception.

Theological representations are not analytical, cognitive, or theoretical concepts in the strict sense. This must be fully understood and taken for granted. Otherwise one may entertain the false belief that theological representations (in any theology) know reality in a way like that in which science and theory know reality—i.e., by rational analysis, abstraction, and recomposition.

To get back to our example, the term "love," there is a real danger that evangelical love may be taken in the wrong sense. Though one may admit that it is not a descriptive representation, one may imagine that it is an analytical and theoretical concept that is just as valid as the notions of class struggle and alienation (which are not purely descriptive concepts either). But it is nothing of the sort. Science and social theory begin, of course, when one moves from mere description of social realities to their analysis, their breakdown into abstract elements, and ultimately their synthesis or dialectical reunion. In that respect it is quite true that even scientific and theoretical knowledge does not reflect reality as it is given in straightforward empirical terms. It reflects reality through concepts that are abstractions from reality as given. Such terms as class conflict, alienation, manipulation, and revolution function in social theory as so many abstract concepts. They are not simply descriptive; rather, they are tools of knowledge, theoretical instruments for the dissection of the real world and its recomposition into some sort of comprehensive view. At the same time, however, they function as directly practical concepts providing concrete operational models for praxis. In short, those concepts are truly cognitive and also operational. To possess them means to know social reality and to know what to do in order to effect real change in that reality.

Theological representations are very different. With them we can depict history as a salvation process, conceive human relationships in terms of brotherhood, call for the conversion of society, and ask human beings to adopt love as their basic attitude in praxis. But those representations do not provide any knowledge of reality in the strict sense, nor do they provide concrete operational models for transforming that reality. Marxist theory, to cite one example, helps people to comprehend what is happening in Vietnam or Latin America or South Africa; and it also offers guidelines for concrete action in those places. Political theology, be it a theology of liberation or a theology of revolution, does not help at all in those respects. Its whole arsenal of representations does not help us one bit to really know or understand what is going on in such places; nor does it provide any guideline for concrete action. Thus political theology operates with representations that are not concepts, that do not contain any knowledge in the strict sense, and that do not offer any concrete advice for praxis.

The Marxist Althusser is quite right in pointing out that while certain Christians may well recognize such problems as the struggle between social classes, such problems "cannot be known by means of the theoretical instruments made available through the church's theological tradition" (43:28). Spaemann, a theologian, is equally correct when he points out that "a theology of art or work or sexuality or politics adds nothing to what we can know without theology" (398:492). What Spaemann fails to point out is that theology in general adds nothing to human knowledge in general, and that talk about God does not in any way enrich our knowledge of the world.

Theology does not constitute a body of knowledge to be enumerated along with other bodies of knowledge. Political theology does not contribute any new knowledge because no theology does. Only a positivist conception of theology can entertain the idea that theology contains some sort of knowledge (190:377–86). Theology needs the mediation of other disciplines and sciences precisely because it itself does not constitute a science or a body of knowledge. To be specific here, political theology needs the mediation of some scientific knowledge of society. If theology is to gain concrete knowledge of sin, says Sölle, "it requires aid from the human sciences to gain information about possible alternative modes of behavior" (396:99). This basic observation must be applied to every sort of reality that theology attempts to know. It does not know concrete realities in and of itself or through its representations; it knows them through the concepts of the relevant science that it makes use of. A theology of liberation or social change does not know its object on its own; it knows that object through the mediation of the relevant social theory.

Theological representations, including those of political theology, are neither descriptive nor theoretical concepts. In a word, they are not concepts and do not have cognitive value. To comprehend their meaning, we might do well to relate them to "ideas" in Kant's sense of the term. In his *Critique of Pure Reason* (book I, section 2, on transcendental dialectics), Kant rejects the earlier philosophical tendency to use notions, concepts, and ideas as interchangeable terms. He defines an idea as "a necessary concept of reason for which there can be no adequate object in the senses." Understood thus, ideas "exceed the limits of all experience." These transcendental ideas of pure reason give rise to transcendental psychology, transcendental cosmology, and transcendental theology; they deal respectively with the unity of the thinking subject (the soul), the unity of phenomena as a series (the world), and the conditioning unity of all objects of thought in general (God). Although they are ideas of speculative reason, they nevertheless fulfill a positive role vis-à-vis practical reason, which in turn is the only one capable of postulating their reality. Thus they also operate as ideas of practical reason; the idea of the soul, for example, devolves into the ideas of liberty and immortality. To them must be added one more idea that is distinctive and proper to practical reason: the "idea of the necessary unity of all possible ends." This idea, says Kant, is "most fruitful and necessary in connection with real actions."

Now theological representations are of their nature like Kant's "ideas." This kinship can be seen in three features. Like his ideas, theological representations do not have any adequate object in the sense realm, for they go beyond all sense experience. Like his ideas, theological representations essentially bespeak some relationship to totality, suggesting the absolute and overall unity of the phenomena to which they allude. Finally, theological representations also include some practical connotation; they too are fruitful in connection with real actions.

The practical dimension of political theology's representations has already been highlighted in our discussion here (sections 9 and 12). Their transcendence of every sense object or sensible experience would also seem to be quite obvious. The liberation or salvation discussed by theologians is not identical with, or wholly encompassed by, any emancipation in this world; the communion and brotherhood of the gospel message exceeds any societal achievement of conviviality, however perfect one might envision it to be; Christian love cannot be adequately embodied in any act of surrender or sacrifice, however generous; and gospel conversion cannot be completely realized by any earthly change in attitudes or structures.

This transcendence of any sensible embodiment or experience is bound up with another feature of theological representations: their note of all-encompassing totality. Liberation, conversion, love, and brotherhood refer to totalities. They are representations that allude to the totality of a subject's life, the totality of interhuman relationships, and the totality of history. A specifically theological representation emerges when attention is focused not on partial objects or isolated facts but on the totality of objects, situations, facts, and processes that appear within a given horizon. That horizon may have to do with freedom or liberation, reciprocity or communion, the active enhancement of another (love), or change and an openness to the future (conversion).

These similarities between theological representations and Kant's ideas help us to pinpoint their precise noetic locus, the place they occupy in the universe of mental products. The theological categories or hermeneutic keys used by political theology are much closer to Kant's ideas than they are to the cognitive concepts of social theory or purely descriptive notions of social reality.

Having noted the similarities to Kant's ideas, however, we must also point out the differences. The first and most obvious difference is that Kant's transcendental ideas result from the very structure of reason; they are an a priori of the rational subject, whereas theological representations are transmitted by tradition. Critical philosophers encounter the transcendental ideas in a process of rational dialectics; theologians find their representations in Christian tradition. This received or transmitted character of theological representations presents us with serious questions regarding their validation: What is it that justifies a tradition? This forces us back to the whole problem of grounding. And it also marks the first difference between transcendental ideas and theological representations.

A second difference appears insofar as theological representations have something to do with a grace from God. Theological talk about liberation, brotherhood, love, and radical social change always implies some sort of reference to a favorable and saving God.

15. THEOLOGY AND IDEOLOGY

By virtue of the fact that it is theology, political theology is confined within the realm of ideas. Its essential relationship to society and praxis does not do away with this localization of its representations. These representations are not cognitive as would be purely descriptive terms, scientific theory, or operational models for praxis.

Thus political theology is a set of ideas and, depending on the way one takes the term, an "ideology." Both inside and outside the framework of Marxist analysis, the term "ideology" is taken in different senses. Not all of them apply properly to theology, but some of them do. A quick survey of these different senses, indicating which ones properly apply to political theology, will help to clarify the exact nature of the representations that political theology uses to apprehend and interpret societal reality. It will also help to clarify and specify the rather vague Marxist assertion that Christianity itself is an ideological phenomenon (343). Finally, it will help to advance the self-criticism that theology should undertake with regard to its own discourse insofar as this discourse is ideology. Today's theologians cannot step into the fray without picking up the social analysis and criticism of ideologies and making it their own (54:220). Such criticism should help theology to engage in self-criticism and serve as a corrective to the statements of theology (396:73–74). But if theology is to be critical of its own ideological elements, it must first be able to discern in what senses political theology is in fact ideology and in what senses it is not.

Political theology is ideology in the sense that it is fashioned of ideas rather than concepts. To put that another way, we can say that it is ideology insofar as ideology is contrasted with knowledge, science, and theory (in the Marxist sense). But it should also be noted that Marxists themselves accord a positive function and value to ideologies taken in that sense. Althusser describes ideology as a "system of representations" that differs from science in that "the practical and social function predominates over the theoretical or cognitive function" in the former. Everything seems to suggest that human societies could not possibly exist without those systems of representations known as ideologies. They form part of the social totality, and it would be foolish to try to picture a world in which ideology would be wholly replaced by science. Althusser expressly mentions religion in this connection.

Ideology is not a "beautiful lie," nor can its social function be reduced to that of a "barefaced myth." Althusser is clear on this point: "Ideology is not some accidental aberration or excrescence in history. It is an essential structure in the historical life of societies." As an essential structure it can or actually does fulfill a role that Althusser regards as indispensable. For it is the "instrument of reflexive action on history" (44:238–42).

More than one theologian has recognized that theology is ideology in this first sense. That would seem to be the import of Blanquart's lucid comparison between Marxism and Christianity. He distinguishes three distinct levels in Marxism: (1) Marxism as "scientific rationality" and an "operational model"; (2) Marxism as a "motivating utopia" in the yearning to be a "whole person"; (3) Marxism as an atheistic ideology. As Blanquart sees it, Christianity has nothing to say with respect to the first level, so a Christian can adopt the theoretic rationality and the practical model offered by Marxism. Insofar as the second level is concerned, Christianity also presents itself as a humanism and a utopia. Finally, Christian doctrine includes an "ideology" that "allocates a central role to God in humanity and the world" (74:152–53). This takes for granted that the representations of every theology concerning the significance of God (and Christ, the gospel message, etc.) in society are on the level of ideology, that they are not a theoretical line of reasoning or a set of concrete operational models.

Theology appears as ideology in another sense as well. It is ideology insofar as it is conditioned (some would say "determined") by the material, socioeconomic base. This conditioning or determinism has been mentioned earlier (see chapter 3, section 12), and it will have to be discussed in greater detail later on (see chapter 8). Every theology is conditioned by socioeconomic factors and realities. Today's political theology enjoys one advantage over previous theologies: It is consciously aware of that fact. At the very least one can say that some theologians are aware that such is the case. In this connection we might recall a comment by Chaigne cited earlier (see chapter 3, section 13), which probably derives from Althusser: i.e., that ideology can react upon the economic infrastructure from which it arises. It is in that zone of ideology's autonomy vis-à-vis the material infrastructure that Chaigne pinpoints the concrete locale for an experience of "transcendence" (135:94).

Horkheimer comments on ideology taken in this second sense, though in a way that restricts its meaning further. After noting that the spirit is inextricably bound up with real human situations and interests, he goes on to say that ideology (as opposed to truth) should be defined as that brand of knowledge that "is not aware of that dependence and that boasts of being exempt from such conditions" (40:64). The same point of view is found in less explicit form in the writings of Engels himself. At one point he suggests that an ideology is characterized by the fact that the influence of material conditions on the course of ideas remains unnoticed and unconscious (287:257). Adopting this more restricted sense, we can say that earlier dogmatics was ideology precisely insofar as it did not think of itself as conditioned by anything; current theology is not ideology insofar as it does not view itself as scientific knowledge and is also aware of the factors that condition it.

Close to the second sense just considered above is a third sense that remains to be considered: i.e., ideology as the embodiment and expression of the interests of a particular group, of a social class specifically. This sense is also very close to the psychoanalytic concept of "rationalization": i.e., a mental construct designed either to bolster and justify ego defenses or to give reality to some object of desire. Of course Christians are inclined to deny that their beliefs are ideology in this sense. Dumas expressly denies it: "Faith is not an ideology. It is not the expression of a social group governed by its own interests and conditionings" (21:45).

But here we must be honest with history and sociology. Dogma has been, and often still continues to be, the expression of certain class interests—or simply of ecclesiastical interests. That faith ought not to be that, or that it can be something more than that, is a different matter entirely. Faith and theology can be dissociated from the interests of the Christian group, but only to a relative degree and up to a certain point; for nothing human, not even faith and love, can be totally disinterested. Here we must be realistic. We cannot entertain delusions about the possibility of some line of thought being totally unrelated to the interests of someone or other. Habermans's analysis of the inextricable relationship between knowledge and interests (231) rules out any doubt on the matter.

David Riesman offers his own view of ideology that contrasts with what has just been said. He applies the label "ideology" to a belief that corresponds to the interests of someone other than those who hold the belief. Thus, if the ideas of a certain group do correspond to the real interests of that group, then they would not constitute an ideology: "I define ideology as an irrational belief that does not correspond to the interests of those who hold it; it is a belief sold to them by some group whose interests are served by deluding them" (361:142). Here again we might well ask ourselves whether Christian dogmatics has not often been such an ideology, a set of beliefs imposed on Christianity by people who were not much concerned about Christianity itself. The whole theology justifying the alliance of throne and altar, for example, was foisted upon Christianity by powers that had little to do with Christianity itself and that were interested only in restoring hoary regimes with the blessing of the church.

Two further senses of the term "ideology" remain to be mentioned. Ideology may be viewed as a system of representations designed to mask the real situation, or as a system of representations designed to serve those groups who effectively hold power. Insofar as the former sense is concerned, the danger of masking reality would seem to be extirpated if theology is aware of the fact that it does not constitute real knowledge, science, or theory. That is not to deny that faith and theology have often been a barrier to real knowledge insofar as they saw themselves as some sort of real knowledge. Insofar as the second sense just mentioned is concerned, Mannheim is the one who has contrasted ideology and utopia in precisely those terms. Mental constructs are ideological, in his view, when they help to solidify or glorify the existing social reality; they are utopian when they stimulate collective activity designed to alter that reality and bring it more in line with objectives that transcend its present state (275:261–65; 276:85). Here again we must recognize that theology has often helped to serve the immobilism of the existing order; but we must also insist that it is meant to be construed as a utopia, that it both can and should be precisely this. Mannheim himself points to the chiliasm of Anabaptist Christians as the first appearance in history of the utopian mentality (275:282–91). The subversive content of current political theology (liberation, revolution, nonconformity) equally favors a nonideological line that is resolutely utopian. But we shall have to give more extensive consideration to the notion of utopia in the next chapter.

16. A SPECIFICALLY CHRISTIAN ELEMENT?

Our discussion of the relations between political theology and ideology can help us to carry out the objectives stated at the start: i.e., to clarify the nature of theological representations and trace out a self-criticism of theology insofar as it is ideology. But it can also help us to lay the groundwork for considering another question that is of the utmost importance but that is usually discussed in the vaguest of terms: i.e., the question as to whether or not there is "a specifically Christian contribution" in the political praxis of liberation.

The whole issue might be framed in such questions as these: Is there something peculiar and specific to the believer in the realm of political, liberative, or revolutionary action? Do the representations and hermeneutic keys of the gospel message define certain elements of praxis that distinctively belong to that message? Does the praxis of Christianity contain something that cannot be reduced to the praxis of Marxism or other civil movements for liberation? Obviously the question comes up in that form within the perspectives peculiar to current political theology. The earlier theology of the New Christendom movement had no doubt that Christianity was supposed to produce certain distinctive effects on the level of politics and praxis. Current theology of liberation and revolution is not so clear on the issue, and indeed it inclines to answer the question in the negative.

The vagueness surrounding this issue is evident in the fact that some authors do indeed pose the question but deliberately leave it unanswered and resign themselves to a state of dilemma. Houtart and Hambye confine themselves to stating the alternatives: "Either there really is a New Testament ethics, in which case we must keep looking in Scripture for certain divine principles that will allow us to deduce secular principles from them. . . . Or one may conclude, in line with the eschatological point of view, that faith is to be defined as a transethical reality—i.e., a reality which in itself does not give rise to a specified system of moral norms" (238:489). Framing the issue in an ethical focus (which is not the only possible focus), this dilemma embodies the question that must be answered. Current political theology does not possess criteria of sufficient clarity to resolve the matter in those terms. We find two sets of antagonistic affirmations, though they are vague both in their assertions and their opposition.

One set of affirmations claims that Christians are to identify themselves fully with the action of other people, that they do not possess any line of praxis that is distinctively and exclusively theirs. This point of view is found most clearly in the minds and hearts of Christians who are deeply committed to the political struggle for liberation. But it is also expressed by theology when theology rules out the possibility of a Christian politics or a Christian revolution. I need only refer the reader to texts cited earlier that point out the difference between current political theology and the older theology of the New Christendom movement (see chapter 2, sections 7 and 8).

The clearest statements along these lines correspond to the criticisms and exclusion of Christian "third way" approaches to social problems. As we noted earlier, the "third way" outlook arose out of the theory of the New Christendom movement and papal social doctrine. It sought to trace out some approach midway between liberalism and socialism, or at least to find some specifically Christian social approach (180:32–33). In its most extreme form this outlook staunchly opposes the idea that Christians are obliged to be critical of every political system because of the eschatological hope they entertain (157:7). So not even the "eschatological proviso" described by some theologians as the distinctive feature of the Christian (see chapter 6) would serve as the basis for any specific approach on the level of praxis.

The second set of assertions stands in marked contrast to the first, maintaining that Christians have something distinctively their own to contribute to their joint praxis with others (289:55). In some authors there reappears the old criteria that were found in the moral theology of the New Christendom movement. Faith purportedly furnishes "moral principles" enabling the Christian to pass some sort of "generic" judgment on political situations and ideologies (376:254–56). The relevant point here is found in the writings of some Christians who say that Christianity does not constitute a "third way" but that the faith has a distinctive contribution of its own to make through those Christians who are personally committed to the building of a qualitatively different society and the birth of a new person. Both assertions can be found, for example, in documents issued by Christians for Socialism (2). In any case "the contribution of faith to the level of praxis" is a basic feature of current theology, and Biot is not off the track when he makes it the key feature of his investigative methodology in his own theology of politics (72:22).

Wherein would the originality of Christianity lie exactly? Alvarez Bolado sees it in "the repetition of Christ's own destiny" (46:143). In the view of Girardi, what characterizes the believer is the fact that the ultimate frustration of earthly hope, should that occur, "would not represent the ultimate failure of humankind." Insofar as the Christian is concerned, "love never fails in the last analysis, nor is it ever expended in vain" (208:76). According to that view, then, there is nothing typically or distinctively Christian on the level of praxis, only on the level of beliefs or representations: Christianity holds that love never falls prey to waste or ultimate loss.

A different tack is taken by those who do attribute something distinctive to Christianity on the level of praxis. Some, like Moltmann, derive it from Christian eschatology: "In Christianity eschatological hope possesses a distinctive principle of action in history that stands in contrast with both Zealotism and quietism" (309:323). Others derive it from gospel themes having to do with reciprocal relations between human beings: e.g., love, reconciliation, and brotherhood. Shaull, for example, sees the distinctive Christian contribution to revolutionary goals in "pardon" and "reconciliation" (393:26); such a view would posit a differentiation not just in mental categories but also in praxis. Rendtorff also seems to opt for a contribution in the realm of praxis: " The Christian summons to revolution sets in motion a whole new tone that otherwise would be missing from revolution. The new tone or strain contributed by Christianity is brotherly communion: "Brotherhood and *koinonia* are declared to be forces cementing the common movement for social renovation" (353:65).

Close to this view are my own recent viewpoints on Christianity as a "praxis of fraternization" (182:179–216). In that book I was trying to provide room and meaningfulness for a distinctively Christian contribution vis-à-vis liberalist praxis on the one hand and Marxist praxis on the other: and I focused on brotherhood as the key to such a contribution. I was talking in terms of here and now, however, not in terms of any essential trait. Far from being confined to the sphere of inner life, such brotherhood would operate on the political plane. It would also necessarily include liberty and equality, and it would inject into the political struggle novel notions from the gospel: love for one's enemies and the will to convert them into friends. Obviously, then, my presentation depicted brotherhood and reconciliation as typically evangelical traits in the present situation here and now, without making any judgment about the future; and it also presented them as traits having meaning in the realm of praxis.

I have given further thought to what I wrote in that earlier book. On a deeper level of criticism I find that those criteria are not free of ambiguity. They tend to bolster the belief that Christians do possess something along the lines of a "third way" of their own. Their way of "brotherhood" would seem to mark them off from both the Marxists and the liberals insofar as praxis is concerned. I myself have subsequently discarded any belief of that sort. At the same time, however, those earlier criteria were inspired by a basic presupposition that ought to be taken as valid by any believer: i.e., Christianity and the gospel message must signify something on the level of operative praxis if Christians are to preserve their identity and specific character in history, if they are not to be Christians in name only. However provisional it may remain at any given moment, the distinctive import of Christianity cannot reside solely in the realm of representation, in the way one sees or interprets the world; it must also have something to do with praxis and produce repercussions there.

Obviously we are dealing here with a presupposition of the believing Christian, who believes that the gospel message is a proclamation and has something to say. That presupposition might be stated as follows: If Christianity does signify something that cannot be reduced to scientific knowledge or ideology, then it must also signify that as praxis. Unless one wishes to restrict the Christian faith to being merely a mental representation, some such presupposition seems unavoidable in my opinion. I attempted to spell out its distinctive element in praxis by focusing on the notion of brotherhood and reconciliation.

Adopting a more delicate set of analytic instruments, one could make a distinction between concepts that are theoretic and operational and ideas that are directive and totalizing. That I did in section 14 of this chapter. Such a distinction enables us to pinpoint a distinctively Christian feature in the realm of praxis without having recourse to any semblance of Christian "third way" approaches. While I honestly sought to avoid such approaches in my earlier work on Christian brotherhood, it was subject to interpretation along those lines. Using the new set of analytic instruments, I can retract what I wrote only a few years ago. When I say "retract," I do not mean "deny"; I mean "go back and rework" from a more comprehensive focus, giving greater concreteness and pointedness to what I said earlier. I think this reworking will allow for a synthesis of the two viewpoints expressed by others above: (1) that Christianity does have its own specific contribution to make to the process of social change; (2) that there is no specifically Christian praxis.

17. RATIONAL ANALYSIS AND CHRISTIAN SYMBOLS

First of all, we must spell out clearly the boundaries of the problem. The whole question of the distinctive gospel element in the realm of praxis can be posed on two very different levels. One coincides very closely with an old question inherited from liberal theology and concerned with the essence of Christianity. To respond to this question, people postulated some quality that was essential to the gospel message that set it off as distinct from everything else. This alleged quality typified the gospel always and everywhere, marking it off from every other doctrine and lifestyle and giving it a perduring, immutable identity in time and society. The abstract, fixist, and deceptively all-embracing character of this formulation has been clearly noticed by some Latin American theologians—by J.P. Richard in particular. Consistent with a theology fashioned on the basis of liberation praxis, and assuming that the problem is posed in the terms just stated, he maintains that wholehearted acceptance of historical contingency obliges us to reject any such identity where Christianity is concerned (358:35–41).

But the question of Christian identity, or of the specific character of Christianity, can and should be posed on another level. We can and must ask ourselves what the gospel message signifies here and now, how Christianity is to be defined at this particular moment in history and in the present contingent situation (182:127–48). The question, then, is still concerned with Christian identity. But it is a provisional identity framed in social terms rather than some essential, immutable identity.

Let us consider this approach in terms of examples already alluded to above. If we were considering brotherhood, or *koinonia,* or reconciliation, it would not be a matter of regarding them as ineradicable or immutable Christian attitudes. Instead we would view them as attitudes that here and now were of gospel inspiration both in terms of fact and in terms of history; but we would not then conclude that they represented some inalienable Christian patrimony. It is in such terms that we would pose the issue of the distinctive Christian element here—which is to say, in terms of real praxis. On other levels, the level of language for example, the answer might not be the same at all. But on the level of praxis, the question of Christian identity in a given concrete situation must be resolved by having recourse to political theology; for political theology is defined precisely as reflection flowing from, and centering on, praxis.

On the level of social theory and its concepts, as well as on the level of directly operational models, political theology has nothing to say. Its only assertion would be a negative one: i.e., that the gospel message has nothing peculiarly its own to contribute to our knowledge of social reality or to a practical methodology for the transformation of that reality; on those levels the Christian must apply an analysis that is secular and wholly rational. Insofar as a negative political theology is concerned, it should be noted that it is very much related to *theologia negativa* in general. Our negative pronouncement above is wholly consistent with the basic principle that we cannot affirm anything positive about God and that faith does not communicate any knowledge in the strict sense. *Theologia negativa* stresses our nonknowledge of God. This is mirrored in political theology by the total absence of positive assertions dealing with any strict knowledge of social reality or with the conditions surrounding its possible alteration.

It is as an idea-set that the representations used by political theology have any real meaningfulness. I use "idea-set [*ideario*] here rather than "ideology" to avoid the negative connotations and valuations of the latter term. Therein lies the sense of brotherhood, reconciliation, communion, political charity, liberation, and the other representations used by political theology as interpretative keys for social change. Since those ideas do connote suggestions and signposts for praxis, they really are meaningful on the level of praxis; but their meaningfulness is mediated through the operational models produced by rational analysis. Thus the gospel message does take on practical, political meaningfulness and make its own distinctive contribution, without thereby coming to constitute a distinctive and specific system for the solution of social and political problems.

The gospel commandment of love, for example, contains no indication of the concrete way one is to comport oneself in a given situation. If Latin American Christians want to find out how they should conduct themselves in the face of a generalized state of oppression, injustice, and elitist privilege, they will not make any progress by engaging in long exegetical or theological discussions over the nature of gospel charity. What they must do is make a rational and scientific analysis of their milieu, using the concepts furnished by social theory. At that level they have nothing to do or to contribute as Christians. There is no Christian social theory, no Christian praxis, no Christian politics.

The inspiration of the gospel message operates in a different order, in the realm of regulatory ideas. Evangelical love is not directly a practical method; rather, it constitutes a guiding idea and a general, comprehensive horizon for all practical methods. It takes in all those methods and, at the same time, it is sought as the definitive and unattainable goal of all actions. Violence and class strife are not directly opposed to love because they are not found on the same plane. The need for class strife or violence may arise as the result of a rational analysis of reality. They would have to be considered on the basis of a social theory and opted for on the risky basis of a historical calculus like that proposed by Marcuse (see section 5) or some other type.

The gospel command of love does not enter the picture here at all. It appears on an entirely different plane. It is the general horizon for all human actions, including those associated with class strife and violence; it is the initial option in favor of human beings and their fulfillment, and against anything that is inhuman. Thus love appears as the ideal sense and imperative underlying all praxis, including the praxis of strife and violence. Those forms of violence that could not be included within the general horizon of love would not be licit for the Christian. But of itself the gospel category of love does not determine in advance which means, be they violent or nonviolent, are going to be required to give it concrete shape and reality. That question is decided by scientific and theoretical analysis, not by theology.

Properly speaking, theology does not furnish concepts or

methods of action. What it contributes is guiding ideas. In that sense, which is definitely not a negative one, theology is a set of ideas, an ideology if you prefer. But the present ill repute of the term "ideology," in whatever sense it is used, makes it advisable for us to use some other term here in referring to the contribution of theology. So let us say that theology consists of symbols, which is to say, of representations that allude to something concrete and given in experience and at the same time transcend it. Love, brotherhood, liberation, and other such terms can be understood to be symbolic terms that denote certain well-known terrestrial realities, but that incorporate them and transport them into some transcendent signification that cannot possibly be exhausted in history itself.

There is a further advantage is using the term "symbol." As interpreted by Ricoeur (359; 360), for example, it contains both archeological and teleological dimensions. It is both retrospective and prospective, and that is fully in line with the nature of theological representations. At one end it marks a return to the past, to the pristine sources of life; at the other it suggests an active yearning and anticipation for the future. Political theology adopts the most ancient archetypes preserved in the historical memory of humanity. These archetypes come to it filtered through the historical memory of the Christian tradition and its notions of salvation, love, conversion, the new person, and so forth. It then turns these archetypes into prophetic signposts of the future, into encompassing horizons that lure us on with their exigencies without ever being fully reachable.

In that sense theology is a set of symbols. It is the idiom embodying the symbols of Christianity. Political theology spells out how the praxis of believers is nurtured and driven forward by the retrospective and prospective force of the symbols contained in biblical tradition.

6

Looking to the Future: Utopia and the Advent of God

1. ESCHATOLOGY AND THEOLOGY OF THE FUTURE

Theology's discovery of the eschatological dimension cannot be regarded as a recent event. Insofar as exegesis and biblical theology are concerned, that discovery dates from around the turn of this century. Albert Schweitzer, whose chief work dates from 1906 (385), is usually regarded as the first to stress an eschatological interpretation of the New Testament. It took some time for this focus on eschatology to move from biblical theology into systematic theology, but that step did not happen just yesterday either. For some time now theologians have acknowledged the intensely eschatological cast of the Christian faith.

What is of importance here is the fact that until recently eschatology, like the rest of theology, was viewed in private, individual, and existential terms. Focus was placed on analysis of the free decision of the individual human person. Paradoxical as it may now seem, it was an eschatology of the present rather than of the future. The *eschaton* did not lie in the future of history but in the present of each human subject. It stood on the ridge of instantaneous personal decision-making where the present slopes down toward the future. The future awaited by existential eschatology was an ontological future—to be more precise, an ontological immediate present—centered around each free act of the individual rather than around some historical future.

This shows up very clearly in the writings of Bultmann. The "now" in which God's word sends forth its summons is the "eschatological now" the "instant" in which one must choose between life and death. The eschatological happening is not still to come at the end of time and the last judgment; it is already being played out here in the present (90:I,134 and 144). The concluding statements of Bultmann's book on history and eschatology are borrowed from Ernst Fuchs. More homilectic than theological, they are quite representative of the existential conception of eschatology: "Dormant in each and every instant is the possibility that it might be the eschatological instant. It is up to you to awaken that possibility" (91:132).

It is only with the appearance of current political theology that eschatology has been given an orientation that is at once historical, collective, and truly future-directed. Eschatology has now been given the same sudden turn that is evident in current theology of love, salvation, and other Christian representations. There has been a shift from existential inner life to public societal life, from personal biography to history, from the transcendental subject to politics.

The older eschatological focus, which prevailed for some years, did not blossom into a political eschatology. So it would seem unwarranted to claim that it was eschatology that gave rise to political theology. The opposite seems much closer to the truth: that political theology is responsible for the rise of a different sort of eschatology. While eschatology had been a prime concern of theologians since the start of the twentieth century, it had been apolitical eschatology. Its current "deprivatizing" does not flow from any necessary inner logic in the principle of eschatology itself. It is due to the same web of cultural influences that has influenced the rest of theology and that was considered back in chapter 3. Despite some comments to the contrary, it is unrealistic and fantastic to imagine that there is some secret drive in eschatology that compels it to be critical and public, and that therefore sets it off from other theological themes and perspectives (e.g., Christology, ecclesiology, and salvation history).

An eschatological focus paves the way for a perspective that now dominates current political theology. It is an eschatologically defined faith, identified with hope, that gives rise to critical and practical repercussions in the political realm. Moltmann's theology of hope has played a decisive role in this connection. Engaging in theological reflection on revolution, Moltmann stresses that eschatological hope has political relevance (310:70–71). Gollwitzer echoes that sentiment when he says that "the person with the promise is in fact the revolutionary," and that the eschatology of the New Testament contains a summons to fight against the world as it is, to take a stand in favor of a new world (215:47 and 53). In the Catholic camp Metz affirms that "all eschatological theology should be transformed into a political theology, which is to say, into a theology that is critical of society" (297:393). Schillebeeckx likewise remarks that "eschatological hope radicalizes one's involvement with the temporal order and, by the same token, relativizes any temporal order already existing" (379:424).

Political eschatology is an eschatology of the future. That is not a redundant statement because we have already seen that existential eschatology was an eschatology of the present. So theology's current interest in the political realm is linked with an interest in the future. We are now beginning to see the first outlines of a theology of the future, which Harvey Cox regards as the only future for theology itself

(128:12). Moltmann and Metz point out that in the prophets of the Old Testament and the apostles of the New Testament we always find a "pathos for the new" (302:144; 310:71), which is to say, a pathos for the future.

Perhaps more than anyone else it is Karl Rahner who has detailed the lineaments of a theology of the future. His main thesis on this subject, spelled out as a contrast to the utopia of Marxism, is now fairly well known. He maintains that Christianity is a religion dealing with the future of man, with man's self-transcendence as he moves toward the future. But the future in question is an absolute future that does not lie in this world. The quest for that absolute future contains within it the quest for God himself. It is human beings who open themselves to the absolute future that experience the real import of God's word in the process (344: VI, 76-78).

This theology of the future readily combines with a political eschatology. Some theologians deal with the theological problem of revolution by making a distinction between "future" and "advent." This distinction is somewhat like Rahner's distinction between an absolute future and an intraworldly future, but it has peculiar features of its own. The "future" is what is already contained in the possibilities of the present, what is foreseeable and bound to come because it lies in human hands; "advent," by contrast, refers to a promise whose underlying source lies outside the world, outside the possibilities of the present, and whose arrival cannot possibly be facilitated or provoked in any way (215:46; 357:146).

Only this "advent," this future that does not flow directly from the latent potential of the present, would really be a future. "Only a future that is something *more* than the prolongation of our own latent or manifest potentialities can carry us above and beyond ourselves. . . . Only that future can free us for something that is really new and that does not bring us back to the melancholy of what has already been done and accomplished" (303:156). This theology of a future that will go beyond the latent possibilities of the present is related with a creative political eschatology that is "militant and productive" (302:147–52).

The case is similar with the theology of hope: It is a theology of the future that Christ holds before us. Christian eschatology spells out what sort of future we can expect from Christ; it tells us who he will be and what we are to expect from him (312:22, 110, 264, and 370). Christ "incarnates the future of liberty in his person" (310:72), and hope in some divine alteration is converted into practice by our alteration of the existing conditions in this life (310:74).

2. GOD AS FUTURE

This eschatological look toward the future focuses on God as its ultimate term. God is seen in terms of the future, in terms of promise and advent. As we noted earlier, Rahner maintains that it is openness to an absolute future that enables one to experience what God really means. For Metz and Moltmann God is the force or the "power of our future" (302:148; 303:155; 309:320)—meaning that future which exceeds the embryonic potential of the present and does not lead back to the melancholy of past accomplishments. To use Gollwitzer's phrase, the name "God" simply means "the one who gives the promise and guarantees its fulfillment." Is there a God? That particular question is transformed into a somewhat different one: "Is there a promise for us . . . and will it be kept?" (215:46). The god question becomes a question of the absolute future of humankind, of the promise and its advent. God is the power behind that future, the one who promises and brings about a completely novel and unexpected advent.

To appreciate the full theological import and scope of such statements, we might do well to compare them with statements of the same general grammatical structure that are to be found in older metaphysical theology and more recent existential theology. Insofar as metaphysical theology is concerned, consider how Thomas Aquinas ends his approaches or "ways" to prove the existence of God: " . . . and that we call God"(*Summa theologica* 1, q.2, a.3). His ways clearly lead to an unmoved mover, a necessary being who is all perfect and so forth. Once that point is reached, the act of naming that being "God" takes place. A similar grammatical procedure is evident in existential theology, which applies the name "God" to the one who is invoked absolutely by the human heart. The procedure is clearly evident in this passage from the writings of Martin Buber: "When all illusion and deceit disappears, when human beings stand before Him in lonely obscurity, when they no longer say, 'He, He,' but sigh 'Thou, Thou,' then they are truly addressing that being. . . . The word 'God' is a word of invocation, a word made name" (88:15). In Buber's text "God" is the name assigned to the absolute "Thou" for whom we yearn, once we have rid ourselves of deceit and illusion and stand alone before that "Thou" in all his own nakedness.

The similarities and differences between these three theological models can be seen clearly. In all three cases "God" is the proper name of something real. It is the ultimate word that unveils the full personal secret of something that up to then had been known perhaps, but only incognito, with no name attached. In metaphysical theology the "something" that appears before the name "God" is the necessary and perfect being; in existential theology it is the interlocutor invoked by human beings; in a political theology of hope it is the giver and guarantor of the promise, the power behind our real, absolute future.

In the last perspective mentioned, God is viewed more as future than as present. The future is the time and tense proper to God. It is not so much that God is, but rather that God will be. Current theology is much inclined to move away from the image of a God "above us" and to replace it with an image of God "before us." We find such expressions as "God before us" and "God, the future of man," in the writings of Moltmann (312:21), Metz (298), Schillebeeckx (377), and many others. It should be pointed out, however, that such expressions are not a recent vintage. Bultmann paved the way for them with such comments as this: "Faith is faith in the future that God is reserving for man, faith in the God who is coming" (91:85). And they very strongly resonate the thinking of Teilhard de Chardin, although most people seem to want to overlook the fact that some decades ago his theology was struggling to find God in some transcendence of history that lies ahead of us rather than in some metaphysical transcendence that lies above us (183:621–23). To be sure, the main concerns of Teilhard de Chardin's theology were different from those of the later theology of hope. But there are undeniable analogies between his theology and that of Moltmann, even if we restrict our gaze to such points as the turning away from existentialism, the incorporation of the world into Christian hope, and the ardent longing for the future (183:194).

No one has been as persistent as Moltmann in stressing the point that God is ahead of us. Eschatology devours theology in his line of thinking. We cannot possibly have God within us or above us; we can "*only* have him ahead of us" (312:21). In Moltmann's theology we find an intransigent eschatological exclusivism that allows us to meet God only in the promise, the future, and hope. The future is what constitutes the very nature and character of the biblical and Christian God (312:21, 38, 164, 184). Indeed, he has nothing at all to do with the present divinity of Greek thought and epiphany religions (312:35, 52, 124, 202).

Moltmann's position seems to be rather one-sided. To be God, God must be the God of the future, the past, and the present. We find a real critical sense, but one that only goes halfway, in those theologians who reject a God "above" us in favor of a God "ahead" of us. They criticize the God "above" us for being based on a cosmology that is no longer convincing or accepted; but they fail to see how enamored they themselves are of chronology and the God "ahead" of us. They are quick to point out the "cosmomorphisms" in the older conception of God; but they do not seem to notice the "chronomorphisms" in their conception of a God "ahead" of us in the world of the future. The image of God "ahead" is as good or as bad as the image of a God "above"; it all depends on how one interprets or understands the image. The advantage of the newer image of God "ahead" is that it fosters an activist, liberative, and revolutionary stance grounded on faith in a God so pictured. But it is naive and simplistic to think that with the new image one has somehow penetrated more deeply into the reality of God.

The assertion that the image of a God "ahead of us" is better grounded in the Bible than the image of a God "above us" is quite debatable. Moltmann (312:370), Gutiérrez (230:219–20), and others point out the future note in the words that God addresses to humankind. The "I am" of Exodus 3:14 is basically interpreted to mean "I shall be." That does of course suggest that the future is a basic and constitutive dimension of the biblical God. But that hardly justifies the further assertion that the Bible knows only a God of the future and has nothing to say about a God above us. The image of a God who is "in heaven" runs through the whole Bible right down to Jesus Christ. Indeed he recommends it to his disciples when he teaches them the Lord's Prayer.

Aside from the practical advantage noted above, the emphasis of political eschatology on a God ahead of us is open to the same criticism that was levelled at Bishop Robinson when he adopted Tillich's image of a God "within" us. In *Honest to God* Robinson contrasted the value and validity of that image with the inanity of an image of God "above" or "outside" the universe (364:11–63). The criticism can be formulated in a simple question: Why is the image of God "inside" or "below" existence necessarily better than the image of God "above" earthly existence? A similar question might be put to any exclusivist eschatology of the present day: Why is the image of God "ahead" of us necessarily a better theological image than the image of God "above" us?

3. THE CURRENT PASSION FOR ESCHATOLOGY

An initial response to those questions, spelling out one reason for the emphasis on a new image, might point out that a perspective focusing on the future better helps us to tackle certain kinds of problems with which traditional theology had a great deal of trouble. J. B. Metz leans in that direction when he writes: "In connection with the future of man, then, we find receding into the background one distinction with which theology has dealt a bit too fast: i.e., the distinction between the natural and the supernatural" (299:148; 302:148). This comment would seem to suggest that a focus on the future enables us to give a second place to certain thorny questions such as the relationship between the natural and the supernatural.

Certain observations are in order here, I think, with regard to the opinion expressed by Metz. First of all, the distinction between the natural and the supernatural is not just taking a second place; it is fading out of sight completely, no matter what perspective one adopts. We are witnessing the end of supernaturalism (188; 363:51–53). One does not have to adopt a future-oriented perspective to diminish the importance of that particular distinction; any other perspective will serve equally well. Moreover, whatever Metz may think, any theology strongly stamped with the traditional categories of the natural and the supernatural will go right on applying them to the future too; it will make a distinction between the natural and the supernatural end of the world. Finally, to say that the distinction between the natural and the supernatural takes a second place insofar as the future is concerned is to engage in sleight-of-hand tricks unless one goes into deeper explanations. For such a comment by itself skips lightly over a deeper problem that theologians cannot rightly bypass, and that has to do precisely with that future of which they are speaking. What exactly is the relationship between the future that is envisioned, willed, and actively created by man, the future that is unforeseen by man and comes to him as a pleasant or unpleasant surprise as the result of chance or some cosmic necessity outside himself, and the future of God or his grace? That question still remains unanswered, even if we forget the old problem of the supernatural. One cannot find any convincing answer to it in any current theology of the future or in any political eschatology. So it is not much to the point to say that the old distinction between the natural and the supernatural will become less important in a future-oriented theology; it is becoming less important anyway. The point is that not much light is being shed on the relationship between the future of man, the future of the cosmos, and God's future. The easy assumption that the future will clarify everything means, at bottom, that theologians are excusing themselves from the task of providing some clarification concerning that future.

One critic of political theology, Karl Lehmann, reproaches it for presuming to equate transcendence in the classic theological sense with its current orientation toward the future, thereby also abandoning the complicated and delicate question of the relationship between transcendence and God. The vocabulary of this new theology of the future is "tottering," in his opinion, and will hardly stand up to any critical reasoning (254:193–94).

It is indeed a fact that many questions remain unclear. When people make a distinction between "advent" and "future," or talk about a future that is truly liberative because it is not imbedded in the possibilities of the present, what exactly are they talking about? In contrast with that future, what possibilities of the present do they have in mind: those of humanity or those of the whole universe? Is it their opinion that what is merely future, the future created by people and perhaps also the future of the universe, is nothing but the unfolding and actualizing of possibilities already imbedded in the present? Wouldn't such a notion derive from a purely mechanistic conception of the universe in which all future development would be regarded as preordained by the cosmic system and its laws? Hasn't that conception already been abandoned by most scientists? Doesn't that outlook reserve the capacity for novelty to God alone, denying that man and the world can introduce anything new? When people feel obliged to resort to God in order to free us from melancholic repetition of the past and cyclic time, are they not falling back into a supernaturalism much like that of traditional theology?

Moltmann does not resolve this set of problems completely by any means, and there is some justification for Sölle's complaint about the "confused medley" of different forms of hope in Moltmann's writings (396:61). But it may well be Moltmann who has furnished more material than anyone else for the clarification of this whole issue. His contribution can be summed up in three points. First, Moltmann focuses on social change as the practical meaning of theologal hope: "Christian certainty based on hope becomes practical in the alteration of the present. As he expectantly waits for the divine alteration, man alters his own relationships" (310:74). Moltmann then goes on to establish a reciprocal critical relationship between man's organized planning of the future and a God-oriented hope: "The impulses of hope should be guided and checked by the end results of planning; by the same token, the end results of planning should be guided and checked by the intentions of hope" (309:442). Third and last, Moltmann considers that "social revolution against injustice is the opposite side of the coin, the immanent counterpart, of transcendent hope" (309:240). To express it even more clearly: "Emancipation is the immanent side of redemption. Redemption is the transcendent side of emancipation" (309:343). As we shall see, this latter assertion provides precisely the key we need for an interpretation of the theology of the future and the theology of hope that will be consistent with the interpretation we have already formulated for Christian liberative memories (see chapter 4) and for theological representations (see chapter 5).

There is yet another reason for the current predilection for the future shown by theologians. We can once again cite a passage from Metz where this motive is enunciated clearly: "Modern man's understanding of the world is typically and basically geared toward the future. . . . Human beings today are attracted and fascinated *only* by the future" (299:141; 301:139). Thus the theology of the future is justified insofar as people today have a real passion for the future.

Marxism is cited as a typical example of this. It is alleged to be a humanism and a conception of the world characterized by the "primacy of the future" (299:143; 301:142–43). The intense "pathos for the new," which supposedly distinguishes the biblical vision of the world from the ancient Greek view, is now presented as a response well suited to modern man's restless interest in the future (299:144–45; 301:144–45). This injects a modest but very real apologetic tint into the theology of the future: Biblical faith is credible precisely because it nurtures and fosters an understanding of the future, which is a prime concern of contemporary humanity.

Several comments and observations are in order, however, both with respect to man's current focus on the future and its supposed correspondence with biblical faith.

The first observation is simply that we should never be

surprised to find correspondences or correlations between western man and biblical tradition. Aside from other sources, the current of western culture flows from the Bible. At times certain biblical themes and schemas have been caught in the undertow and have lain submerged for centuries, ultimately surfacing and finding their full development in the culture. Such is the case, for example, with the biblical and Israelite sense of history. It is now common to contrast that sense of history with the Greek outlook, to view the latter as less history-minded and more structural and syntactic. But it should be pointed out that the fact that the Bible embodies the outlook of a history-minded people might be just as irrelevant as the fact that it was written in the Hebrew language. It is an abuse of the Bible to focus on some passion for history or the future as the trait that differentiates Christian faith and Christian hope from a Greek, pagan, or agnostic vision of the world. Furthermore, as I have tried to show in another work (188), the correspondence between the biblical outlook and modern preoccupations is simply due to cultural continuity and community, to the fact that our civilization has taken in the contribution of the Bible during the course of history. It is wholly illicit to manipulate that correspondence in such a way that one conveys the impression that the Bible, as revelation, deciphers the enigmas of modern man by that very fact of correspondence.

A second observation has to do with the alleged passion for the future to be found in modern man, and especially Marxism. Both Metz and Rahner (344:VI, 76ff.) seem to think that Marxism is primarily an ideology or utopia concerned with the future, but that is highly doubtful. The authentic thinking of Marx clearly runs counter to any sort of futurology, as a celebrated passage of *The German Ideology* makes clear: "In our view Communism is not a state of affairs that is to be inaugurated, an ideal to which reality should accommodate itself. We apply the name 'Communism' to that real movement which is abolishing the present state of affairs" (285:248). Marxist theory is not a theory of the future at all nor, except in Ernst Bloch and a few other Marxists who are semitheologians, does it focus its main attention on the future. It is first and foremost a theory about present social reality, an analysis of its material and economic causes, and a methodology for action that will truly be able to change that society. In other words, Marxism and modern thought in general have a very natural concern for the future; but it is not a rabid or exclusive concern for the future. Indeed that is not the predominant concern of either.

What seems more debatable in some theologians is their eschatological exclusivism, their mania for the future, their passion for the novel and the new. The gaze of some theologians is so bent on what lies ahead that they can easily fall into the trap of mythologizing the future. Thus genesis myths give way to eschatological myths. Nor can one be sure that those theologians have freed themselves from an ingenuous conception of historical progress, because their image of the future is so abstract and optimistic. The "God ahead of us" seems to function as the culminating symbol of a gilt-edged future. The forward-pushing function of that symbol is obvious so long as humanity feels compelled to keep moving forward. But what will happen if at some given moment people become distinctly aware of the passage of time?

At this very moment there are clear indications that our culture's bent for the future is on the wane. Marcuse has called for a civilization grounded on the maternal principle (281:213). There is evidence that in our culture we are witnessing a "rebellion against the father" (293). We find concrete efforts and movements to get back to nature and to give up all ideas of working out a program for the future. Some ecologically minded people are calling for a "zero growth rate" in the population. And the structuralist line of thought also has critical things to say about mythological conceptions of the future. All these trends suggest that the concern with progress and the future that has characterized the West since the Enlightenment may be on the wane. So the "God ahead of us" is quite vulnerable to disappearing, to dissolving under the strain of demythologizing, just as the older God of creation was.

4. CHRISTIANITY AND UTOPIAN SOCIALISM

By virtue of this future dimension, in which theology focuses on the promise of God and what God will be, theology comes into contact and contrast with social theory —specifically through the concept of utopia. On the surface at least, this concept seems to provide a common ground where the main guiding ideas of theology might be comprehended from the basic standpoint of social theory and somehow integrated into it. To phrase the matter in general terms, one might say that political eschatology is concerned, either positively or negatively, with utopia; that political theology, by virtue of its essential concern with the future, cannot help but define itself with reference to utopian lines of thoughts. And the fact is that many theologians now define or describe their current political theology—be it a theology of politics, or liberation, or of revolution—by relating it to utopia.

The word "utopia" can denote different things. Omitting many of the differing connotations and overtones, one might say that there are three fundamental versions of the concept. The first version has to do with certain literary works of a specific genre and well defined style. Thomas More's *Utopia* is an example, and indeed the basic term itself derives from that work. The second variant meaning of the term has to do with "a specific and now superseded phase of sociological thinking that was characterized by prescientific methods." The third variant meaning has to do with "certain basic intentions concerned with the organization of societal coexistence," intentions that are to be realized in the future and that will contrast sharply with the present organization of society (322:13–14).

Of these three versions of the term, it is obvious that theology has little to do with the first. Theologians seem to feel that their work has to do with the third meaning. But before we deal with that, it would be well worth our time to consider the possible relationship between political theology and the second meaning of the term "utopia" mentioned above. This possible relationship is not always admitted, or even noticed, by theologians. But it might well be that current political theology is somehow connected with that older brand of socialism which Engels dubbed "utopian" in order to contrast it with scientific socialism (172).

Marxists apply the label "utopian" to any form of socialism that lacks a scientific analysis of the existing unjust social order and that therefore dreams vainly and ineffectively about establishing a different, more humane order. Utopian, then, are such figures as Baboeuf, Blanc, Fourier, Saint-Simon, Cabet, Owen, and Lamennais, as well as all those prior to Marx or contemporary with him who proposed some sort of socialist or communist order but lacked both the theoretical tools to prove its inevitable necessity and the practical methodology to turn it into reality. That era of prescientific socialism was associated with an era when the forces of capitalism were only weakly developed as yet, when social protest could not help but express itself in naive utopian forms. Legitimate for its own time, it came to be judged by Marxism as inadequate for the future, as an anachronistic ideology in the service of a false consciousness (322:14–15).

It should be noted that the teaching of some utopian socialists was deeply religious and at times Christian in inspiration. Perhaps this explains why the language and focus of Christians who adopt some socialist option today often seem closer to those of pre-Marxist socialism than to that of Marx himself. We do not have space here to spell out the resemblances in detail, so we shall be content to suggest that it exists. The interested reader can pursue the issue by picking up any anthology of pre-Marxist socialist writings and comparing their proposals, motivations, and language with those of Christian social teaching, liberation theology, and even the theology of revolution (171).

Such themes as humanitarianism, brotherhood, solidarity with the poor, justice, the kingdom of God, and the dignity of work were first picked up by Christian social doctrine and then by Christian political theology; but they have more relationship to utopian socialism than to the socialism of Marx. From a Marxian standpoint it might well seem that the present currents of political theology, liberation theology, and theology of revolution remain closely allied to the older utopian socialism. In the face of this evaluation, current political theology has the major task of proving that it is not a mere reformulation of nineteenth-century utopian socialism.

Christians can avoid regressing into utopian socialism only by adopting the basic suppositions of scientific socialism, which is to say, the basic suppositions of a dialectical theory of society. I have already indicated in chapter 3 that this is precisely what is happening, overtly or covertly, in any current political theology worthy of the name. That does not mean, of course, that one cannot find traces of the older socialist viewpoint in most current theologians. Insofar as I myself and my earlier work are concerned, I must admit the validity of certain criticisms made by good friends. Some of my earlier works on political theology do contain utopian elements in the older sense of the term, and those elements do distort my presentation and make it somewhat equivocal. At the same time, however, I feel that those traces of an older socialism do not pervert or subvert the basic intention of current political theology, which seeks to adopt current social theory and make it its own, not to regress to some brand of prescientific socialism.

5. UTOPIA AS THE RATIONALLY POSSIBLE

Taking for granted that political theology is not just another version of the older and now discredited utopian socialism, which it is not in fact, we must still examine its relationship to utopia in the third sense of the term. In that sense utopia is an image that stimulates and incites people to action, that is based on a high valuation of the person and collective human happiness, and that suggests historical alternatives very different from those embodied in the present.

Concerning this description or definition of utopia, which also remains somewhat vague, the sociology of knowledge has some important points and specifications to add to the picture. Studies of this question underline the revolutionary potential of utopia, its orientation towards radical social change that is in complete contrast with the existing order of society. The intellectual experience embodied in the image of utopia takes second place to a real-life experience of a very different society (303:171). The utopian horizon is the hinge on which any historical change in ideas moves (343:72). Utopia is inevitably a critique of reality, and so all criticism of society contains some utopian strain within it (322:50). Utopia "establishes a space for desire," which is to say, it projects a social space or locale in which human desire can take organized shape in forms that are not repressive (322:68–69). It is undoubtedly this complicity with desire that prompts Duveau to say that utopia "evolves in a universe charged with affectivity" and specified by sentiment. As he sees it, utopian thought stands in opposition to Enlightenment rationality (168:206–7).

In the course of history utopian images have undergone

significant development. Mannheim points out the fact that utopian thought first took shape in the form of myths and then progressively became more realistic and rationalistic (276:85). Today the closer approximation of utopia to reality and reason is producing a corresponding diminution of its supposed transcendence over historical processes; and it is ultimately resulting in a weakening of utopian intensity (275:323–24). This would suggest that the introduction of rationality into utopia ends up annihilating the latter.

Despite that fact, utopian theoreticians agree that utopia is somehow bound up with reason. Blanquart points out that utopia is irrational "only with respect to an already superseded (conservative) stage of reason, for it actually highlights authentic reason" (73:36). Putting the point even more clearly, Raymond Ruyer has shown that utopia is a component part of the inventive methodology of science and the knowledge process. The utopian method belongs to the realm of theory. It is an "exercise or game concerned with the possible amplifications of reality." Only utopian thinking manages to comprehend things because "one comes to understand a thing only when one ponders it in terms of the full range of possibilities associated with it." Ruyer cites an unpublished lecture of Lalande in which the latter commented on the natural analogy between utopia and hypothesis; he then goes on to ascertain the affinities between the utopian method and intellectual experimentation (368:151–56).

Thus modern sociology and epistemological theory do indeed talk about utopia, but they comprehend the term in a sense far removed from the common notion that equates it with a myth or some unverifiable state of affairs never to be seen in this world. Utopia is regarded as the amplification and extension of reason beyond the capacities of mere positivist verification, as a critical and prospective reason which is indeed bound up with desire and the will to be happy but which is not to be equated with a mere imaginary dream.

It should be noted that this presentation of utopia does not warrant any theological interpretation or utilization of the concept. In itself the locale of utopia is as closed to theological transcendence as is the social theory of which it is a component. But this has not stopped political theology from trying to clear a space for itself within the general utopian locale.

6. CHRISTIAN HOPE AND UTOPIA

The most general formulation of this attempt on the part of political theology can be found in the writings of J. B. Metz. Since the salvation envisioned by Christian hope is not individual but collective in nature, it "should be brought face to face with the great political, social, and technological utopias" (302:151). To talk about a comparison or contrast between Christian hope and eschatology on the one hand and utopias on the other is, of course, to stay on a rather vague, ill-defined level. That does not tell us whether eschatological hope itself is a utopia, or is on a different level entirely. It is here that the discrepancies begin.

For some, Christian faith acts as a "utopia that is critical of the political realm" (72:227ff.). This means that faith is legitimated from the standpoint of social theory insofar as it is a utopia. Faith, in other words, has a social and political function insofar as it falls under the general rubric of utopia. This does not mean that the gospel message is to be reduced or resolved into a utopia; but it does mean that the gospel message contains and promotes utopia. On the one hand, notes Schillebeeckx, "the gospel message does not furnish us with a direct, immediate program of political and social action"; on the other hand, however, he says, "the gospel indirectly does have decisive importance in the sociopolitical realm precisely insofar as it is a utopia." Schillebeeckx then goes on to say: "Christian expectation and the Sermon on the Mount carry out the role of a real and effective utopia, continually exerting pressure on all the affairs of society and politics" (379:419–20). Alves characterizes not just hope but the religious outlook in general in utopian terms. In religion, as in utopian thinking, "man creates certain symbols to give a name to things that are not present, . . . to represent and describe what is missing in the world" (50:91; 49:119). For this first group of theologians, therefore, the comparative confrontation between Christian hope and social utopias comes down to the fact that Christian hope itself either includes or constitutes a utopia.

Other theologians deny that the gospel message includes any utopia. The realm of utopia is part of social theory, not of theological reflection. But as a human, nontheological project, utopia is the concrete mediation between faith and praxis. That is the thesis of Gustavo Gutiérrez, who first states that "the gospel does not provide us with a utopia," and then goes on to say: "Faith and political action enter a correct and fruitful relationship only through the project of creating a new type of human being in a very different sort of society—which is to say, only through a utopia" (230: 316–17). There is another variation on this same basic position. It observes that theology does criticize utopia, but at the same time theology makes use of utopia to give concrete shape to Christian expectations for the future (35).

Less clear-cut is the position of Blanquart. He, too, asserts that "faith and political action enter into a relationship in the general space of utopia" (75:25). But it is not clear whether this mediating space or locus of utopia is part of extratheological social theory or not, since Blanquart sets up a contrast between the Marxist utopia and the Christian utopia. The Marxist utopia is depicted as a humanism of the total man. The Christian utopia is depicted as "a humanism particularly sensitive to myth (the only locus of human language where the word of God can become part of the dialogue)" (74:152–53). This would suggest that Christian symbolism (i.e., sensitivity to myth as the locus of dialogue with God) entails its own utopian humanism which has its own connotations that are clearly different from those of Marxist humanism and which are fed by a different set of symbols.

7. ESCHATOLOGICAL CRITICISM OF UTOPIA

Theologians generally adopt a stance which tends to deny that the gospel message is or contains a utopia. They also tend not to regard utopia as the mediating space or locale between the gospel and politics. On the whole they are more likely to view the gospel message as being critical of any utopian representation. In this outlook, which differs from that of all those theologians cited above, utopia ends up being devalued to a greater or lesser extent. It is seen as a dreamy fantasy of humanity's future, which may be necessary but is bound to be disappointed. It is simply a secularized eschatology, a pretentious human yearning for perfection and the absolute here on earth.

This is essentially the outlook of Moltmann: "The end of history formulated in utopian terms, in terms that speak about complete harmony between humanity and nature, is superseded by Christian eschatology and exposed in all its relative and provisional nature." Utopias, then, ultimately are visions that we can supersede. Christian confidence entails a systematic iconoclasm of "utopian images of hope." We cannot rest content with sketchy rough drafts of the future outlined in utopian projects: "We must go beyond and above them." Christian hope stands in contrast not only to the cloistered precincts of existing reality but also to the obscure and overcast skies of utopias. It ultimately "breaks through and beyond the horizons that have been closely fitted and fashioned by the utopian outlook" (312:466).

That is Rahner's view also: "As a religion of the absolute future, Christianity has no utopia entailing an intrawordly future. . . . It does not propose any ideal future with concrete content." Quite the contrary is the case, for Christianity deals critically with all utopian ideals about the future: "With its absolute hope for the future it protects man from the temptation to carry out justified this-wordly aspirations *with such violence* that each generation is sacrificed for the sake of the following generation" (344:VI, 81–83 and V,160–61). This view is related to a brief observation of Metz: "Christian eschatology is not an ideology of the future. It cherishes the poverty of its knowledge about the future. . . . Christian eschatology is primarily a 'negative theology' of the future" (302:152).

Thus the negative character of eschatological theology would derive from the fact that it knows nothing about the future, that it has no preconceived image and no positive utopia. But here there is room for an observation made by Habermas and Neusüss: "The utopian intention can manifest itself even where all images of the future are renounced." They also point out that this renunciation is conscious and deliberate in the more advanced theoretical formulations of utopia. Well-developed utopian thinking has imposed on itself "a prohibition of images . . . as strict as that which the Jews imposed on their messianic future" (322:25). So negation of images is not enough to establish a complete difference between eschatology and utopia. In other ages eschatology was full of representations and images of the future (e.g., the last things and apocalyptic visions). If it now lacks such images, that is not solely due to its own inner motivations. The fact is that modern thought in general, including that concerned with extratheological utopias, has renounced images of the future.

Of the theologians who might be cited in this connection, none has devalued utopia as much as Helmut Gollwitzer.

This is very much in line with his fundamental Barthianism, his theological disdain for every human project. Gollwitzer characterized Marxism as the messianic utopia that succeeded the yearnings of Christian hope. As he sees it, (Marxist) utopia is essentially limited. It implies "a secret resignation" in the face of limits, in the face of death especially. Religious promise on the other hand gazes directly at those limits before which utopian promise must capitulate (214:129–37).

Later on, however, Gollwitzer modified his terminology and his evaluation of utopia. He came to a position very much like the other theologians cited at the beginning of this discussion: i.e., that the gospel message does include a social and earthly utopia, though perhaps only indirectly. At this point Gollwitzer utilizes a distinction first made by Karl Mannheim, though he does not say that explicitly. Mannheim differentiated between that which was "relatively utopian" and that which was "absolutely utopian." Something unrealizable for a particular standpoint would be relatively utopian; something unrealizable in principle and never feasible would be absolutely utopian. Mannheim himself always talks about utopia in the relative sense (275:265–68), and so does modern social theory. Marcuse says: "What is denounced as 'utopian' is no longer that which has 'no place' and cannot have any place in the historical universe but rather that which is blocked from coming about by the power of the established societies" (cited by Gutiérrez, 230:310).

In contrast with social theory, which always talks about utopia in the relative sense, Gollwitzer will also take the term in its absolute sense; he uses both senses of the term to articulate the relationship between faith and political praxis. Christian hope is an absolute utopia; its object seems unrealizable and impossible for us, possible only for God and credible only on the basis of God's promise. So Gollwitzer makes a clear-cut distinction here between: *(a)* the absolute utopia that is the object of Christian hope; *(b)* the relative utopia that serves as a theological idea for the social action of Christians; *(c)* the revolutionary social program that is designed to effect at least an approximate realization of the relative utopia, that results from rational analysis of the real situation, and that allows for cooperation with other versions of humanism.

Within this general framework Gollwitzer establishes a logical relationship between absolute utopia and relative utopia: "From the absolute utopia of the new society in God's kingdom *there follows* a relative earthly utopia as a guiding image for the alteration of existing relation and the dismantling of all injustice, servitude, and abusive power" (my italics). From the theological standpoint this relative utopia "shows earthly society yearning and striving to be a copy of the kingdom of God in the conditions of this world." Thus it serves somewhat as an illustration of the absolute utopia of God's kingdom (215:56–57). The New Testament is set off from the Old Testament by virtue of the "totality" and "radicality" of its utopia (215:52).

The transcendence of Christian eschatology over any terrestrial utopia entails the former's criticism of the latter. Precisely because it is not identified with any terrestrial ideal, Christian eschatology maintains its distance and critical power vis-à-vis every utopia. A common term for this facet of Christian eschatology is "eschatological proviso," though the words "objection" and "stipulation" are also used (215:53–53; 297:395). It highlights the transcendence of eschatology over utopia and the absolutely gratuitous character of the absolute future and its divine utopia. This eschatological proviso puts Christians on guard against confusing God's kingdom with some specific stage of history or absolutizing revolution (230:319–20). It liberates Christians from the moralism and legalism of the revolution, and also from its potentially alienated forms; Christians can smile at those extremes (310:79–81).

The eschatological proviso also prevents the Christian from lapsing into some new form of theological positivism. If theology failed to maintain a critical distance vis-à-vis the revolutionary event and adhered to it wholeheartedly, then it would be abandoning the positivism of established order to fall into the positivism of revolution (357:143). Some try to define a specifically Christian form of activity on this basis. It would consist of "the theological task of proclaiming that no revolution can bring about the kingdom of God—which is to say, the total solution of our afflictions in this world." Christians critically denounce every absolutizing of revolution as insidious idolatry (357:141). This does not mean that there is a Christian revolution. It does mean, however, that Christians participate in the revolution with their own distinctive attitude, responsibly confronting the present situation with Christ's mandate (357:156–57).

8. THEORETICAL CRITICISM OF ESCHATOLOGY

The insertion of Christian hope into the space or locale of utopia is not exempt from difficulties, even though one may try to have Christian hope transcend utopia ultimately and to look upon utopia with an eschatological proviso. Indeed there is even reason to doubt that there is any real relationship between theological hope and utopian thinking, or that such hope can be interpreted as above and beyond utopia. Christian eschatology contains certain elements of an absolute cast, expressed in mythical form, that make it somewhat alien to the world and any rational utopia. Theology refers to the future in mythical and symbolic terms; utopian thought refers to the future in rational terms. This obliges us to ponder the possibility that the very word "future" itself is being used equivocally here to designate two very different horizons that have no mutual connection.

To begin with, it is doubtful that the absolute future and the absolute utopia envisioned by Christian hope have anything in common with the future of history and the relative utopias of revolutionary thinking. Theologians depict Christian eschatology as a critical court of appeal designed to prevent the absolutizing of revolution. But it is quite possible that this alleged danger of absolutization only exists in the minds of theologians, that they project it into the minds of nonbelievers.

Idealist humanism and existentialist humanism were very inclined to absolutize the human being. Today, by contrast, the prevailing social theory and the prevailing vision of humanity are well aware of their own relativity and finiteness. No serious leaders at present absolutize revolution—in the sense that they would claim that the absolutely perfect society had been attained at some given moment. There are no absolute utopias outside of Christianity. All the rest are relative utopias with a clear awareness of this fact and with no intention of making any absolute claims. They already contain a basic principle of self-criticism in this conscious awareness of their limitations. Christian eschatology could very well assume that it has a critical principle vis-à-vis various forms of revolutionary or utopian absolutism; but it is hard to see how it can contribute any critical, deabsolutizing principle to utopias that are consciously and deliberately relative already.

Indeed by virtue of this nonabsolutizing criterion, it seems much more likely and proper that one might criticize the absolute utopia of Christianity from the standpoint of relative utopias. It seems quite possible, in other words, that the latter might accuse the Christian utopia of being an improper projection of absolutist dreams cherished by people unaware of their human limitations. In the last analysis it is a weakness, not a strength, that Christian hope presents itself as an absolute rather than a relative utopia; for the legitimacy of such an absolutist expectation or aspiration remains to be justified. Because they are absolutist in orientation, eschatological utopia and Christian hope are not so much in a position to judge everything else as they are exposed to judgment and criticism from other viewpoints. The general nature of their "proviso" toward every social project or order might entail a dangerous indifference toward practical proposals for a more humane order to replace a less humane one.

On another front, such an absolute hope can only find expression in mythical terms or symbolic terms, not in rational terms or strictly cognitive terms. As Assmann puts it, the experience of hope cannot really be expressed; it can only be hinted at (54:219). Here again there is no common ground between social utopia and Christian eschatology. The modern versions of utopia are part of social theory, entailing a critical theory of society and knowledge of different historical alternatives. They are part of a rational and scientific discourse, not so much analysis of what exists now but rather rational exploration of what is possible and methodical invention of new societal forms. Christian eschatology is nothing of the sort. It operates with symbols such as God's promise, the kingdom, the future of Christ, and the God who will be. It is a theology that is only partially demythologized. While it has freed itself from myths dealing with the beginnings (the God of creation who is the father and author of universal law and the moral universe), it has not freed itself from myths dealing with the final end of it all. The absolute utopia of Christian eschatology functions as a myth that is not adverted to as such and that is pointed in the opposite direction: Rather than being an archeological and cosmogonic myth, it is a teleological and apocalyptic myth.

Modern theology is full of examples of this utopia-fashioning demythologizing. It eliminates genesis myths for the sake of some absolute utopia. Christian theologians have already recognized the mythological features in the biblical account of the fall and they have sought to demythologize it. But the concrete way of doing this without losing the transcendent import of the biblical text is to replace it with a utopia, a utopia which unfortunately is mythologized rather than rational. The theologians tell us that paradise is not some reality in the distant past but rather a goal to be attained in the future; that it does not embody some happy situation of the very first human beings but rather the final stage and goal of God's plan for humankind and human history.

The end result is clear in any case. We have moved from a theology of genesis myths to a utopian theology of teleological myths. If demythologization of the biblical accounts was the task confronting theologians some years ago, the task confronting us now is the de-utopianizing of those same accounts insofar as our future is concerned. In the meantime myth has been replaced by utopia—utopia not in the rational sense of social science but utopia as a symbolic anticipation of the future. This Christian utopia has as little to do with the utopia of social theory as the genesis myth of an earthly paradise has to do with scientific theories about human origins. The two are radically different.

From the perspective of social theory and the sociology of knowledge, Christian eschatology seems to be a fantasy, not because it presents a utopia but because it presents a utopia that is both absolute on the one hand and mythico-symbolic on the other. In other words, Christian eschatology presents a utopia which does not relate to the real condition of humankind on earth and which therefore can only be expressed in symbolic or mythological terms. Strictly speaking, the terms in which it finds expression are not cognitive and are incapable of altering reality.

Mannheim pointedly explains what happens when the thirst for the absolute, which is peculiar to the religious person, is applied to societal life: It gives rise to orgiastic utopias. When other-wordly yearnings change direction and begin to operate in the earthly sphere, they become explosive agents in day-to-day life (275:282–85). Bloch is of the same mind: "When the hereafter seeks to leap down to earth, or when the inner life seeks to leap out into the world outside, then there appears in the subjective factor a fresh turn—not an opiate but an explosive without rival, a desire to fashion heaven here on earth." But Bloch is quick to call attention to the historical impotence of this yearning: "The revolutionary passion fed by those means was abstract and mythological. It did not and could not have any sense of reality. It simply gave wings to the subjective desire to change the world without proposing any concrete method of effecting such change" (76:109). His observations are concerned specifically with the chiliasm of Joachim of Fiore and the Anabaptists, but they seem to apply just as much to present-day political eschatology.

On the basis of this same sociological and theoretical focus, others denounce the desire to take theological advantage of utopia as a tacit quest for the absolute. This is seen in "the religious interpretation of utopia," i.e., the claim that in itself "utopia is religion because it tends toward the absolute and the eternal" (322:61–62). In contrast to a theology that sees utopia as a secularized, earthly eschatology, social theory sees eschatology as a mythical, absolutized utopia—an escape into the absolute from preoccupations and concerns that are, at bottom, the solid earthly concerns of oppressed social groups. In this way social theory shows theology its own socioeconomic conditionings. Some time ago Mannheim himself wondered whether even a relative social utopia was really possible, since we are aware of the fact that our representations are socially conditioned (275:326). With all the more reason, then, we must wonder whether we can in good faith go on maintaining the absolute utopia of eschatology, now that theologians themselves have taken notice of the socioeconomic conditionings underlying their theological representations.

Suffering, for example, figures among the social preconditions for hope. Only one who suffers is one who hopes. One is struck by the frequency with which Moltmann stresses suffering and misery. A deep layer of neediness and suffering in human history is the condition that makes hope possible: "Suffering is the goad that spurs on the search for a future and the eschatological impatience of Christianity" (309:382). Suffering in turn proceeds from love, according to Moltmann: "Suffering presupposes love. He does not suffer who does not love" (309:444). So it would seem then that the passion of hope is proportionate to the intensity of neediness and suffering. What, then, will happen in a transformed society that has less neediness in it? Will suffering ever remain inseparable from love? A diminution of suffering and misery would seem to reduce both the necessity and the intensity of hope.

Hoping, by the same token, has much dreaming in it. Here again one cannot help but notice that Moltmann also refers to hope as a dream—in connection with misery and poverty specifically. He says that hope "is the suffering of a love that cannot resign itself to the anguished condition of earthly life and the lack of liberty among men, the suffering of a love that dreams of happiness for the poor and freedom for the oppressed, and that is ready to make any radical change necessary to convert its dream into reality" (309:446). This note of converting dream into reality does not alter the dream-like nature of hope as described in that passage.

But that raises an interesting question. Insofar as it is a dream, what legitimation can hope really claim to have? The act of hoping opens up a tiny space for desire, but somewhat in the way that a dream does. And according to the harsh judgment of Lenin, for example, dreaming is an affair of the weak. If human beings are less weak, less poverty-stricken, and less oppressed, will they still need a glowing theology of hope? If human beings are happy and content, will they not trade in an anxious theology of the future for a calm theology of the present?

The theological reflection of Moltmann on play and feasting (311) and that of Cox on the feasts of fools (127) perhaps indicate that one cannot sustain a passion for the future over the long haul, that at times one must relax and take satisfaction in what has already been accomplished without entertaining great projects or goals. A theology of play or happiness would serve as a real corrective to the theology of the future and the theology of hope, for it would relativize and demythologize the future, joyously embracing the present and forgetting about utopia.

9. THE FUTURE AND TRANSCENDENCE

In itself the future dimension does not provide political theology with a solution to the two problems of legitimation faced by every theology: What gives it reason to think that it is somehow in contact with the absolute? What justifies the use of mythical and symbolic language?

Political eschatology looks to the notion of social utopia for support even though it may eventually intend to criticize and transcend this notion. But the notion of social utopia itself makes no claim to being an absolute; moreover, it is now expressed in rational terms rather than in terms of symbols and myths. Despite its earnest efforts to incorporate the future and utopia, the ever pending problems of theology remain; it must still tell us what provides justification and grounding for its views. Its takeover of utopia does not make it more plausible or likely, does not improve its credibility. Theology is still confronted with the question as to whether the absolute is in fact offered or promised to us. Christian eschatology does give a "yes" answer to that question, but it has not justified its answer. Indeed it often continues to wax eloquent with precritical language and to avoid the deeper question as to whether faith and hope must find expression in mythical and symbolic terms.

Political eschatology, the theology of hope, and the theology of the future can gain further clarification only by a process of analysis like that which I have already described in connection with the historical archetypes of the Christian tradition (see chapter 4, section 8) and the theological representations that interpret present praxis (see chapter 5, sections 14 and 17). Such analysis and its results are much the same for any theological reference to the future as they are for theological reference to the past and the present. Here again theology's representations come about through a process of evoking, interpreting, and symbolizing a reality which, in itself, has nothing to do with religion; but in this case it is a potential reality not yet given in fact.

A distinction between historical realities on the one hand and theological symbols on the other is as necessary in connection with the historical future as it is in connection with the present or the past. Retrospective theology goes back and focuses on certain specific events in order to convert them into archetypes: e.g., the Exodus, the deeds of the prophets, the public life of Jesus. Theological interpretation of current political praxis views certain social processes, such as liberation and revolution, under the lens of certain theological ideas. In like manner eschatology views some future possible reality—evoking, transforming, and interpreting it through the mediation of certain symbols that are not, and will not be, provided by the reality itself but by Christian hope and its way of contemplating what is possible.

Insofar as the past and the present are concerned, the distinction between concrete historical reality and theology's symbols or ideas is readily clear. Since the future does not yet have such reality, there is a danger that the distinction may get lost. People may be inclined to equate the future of history and the representations of Christian hope because they share a common feature: i.e., neither are realities given here and now in the present. But this seeming likeness is more apparent than real, and there are irreducible differences between the two. The future of history is not yet real, but it will be; it is not yet given, but it will be some day. The object of theological hope, on the other hand, is not yet given nor will it be in any ordinary usage of the verb "be."

The future does not in any way facilitate theology's leap to the metaterrestrial or the metahistorical. As the future of history, it is like the past and the present; it continues to remain part of the same web of phenomena and to be an object of rational forecasting and exploration. The fact that the future is not predetermined as yet and that it offers all sorts of possibilities does not bring it any closer to God or to transcendence. The utopia that current social theory sees as having a possible future is as closed (and as open) to transcendence as the science of history that rescues some past reality from oblivion and makes it available to our awareness. In all the dimensions of time, the representations of theology are alien to science and to a knowledge of reality in the strict sense of the word "knowledge." This holds true whether the reality in question is past, present, or future. The representations of theology are interpretive rather than cognitive. They are ideas or symbols rather than concepts; and sometimes they are myths. Eschatology and the theology of hope are not exempt from this general condition affecting all theology. They cannot claim to walk on some firmer ground of reality that makes their task easier. Utopia and the future do not in any way furnish theology with some more direct and immediate brand of transcendence.

Thus, when theologians say that it is more correct to say

that God "will be" rather than that God "is," they are toying with the meaning of the word "be." So long as that basic meaning remains the same, a God who "will be" is no more likely or credible than a God who "is" or "has been." If one is going to eliminate a particular deity having to do with origins, that must logically go hand in hand with the elimination of a particular deity having to do with ultimate ends and finalities. The God problem in theology does not have to do with various tenses of the verb "be"; it has to do with the basic meaning of the verb itself and its applicability to God.

In that respect current eschatology has played loose with its task. It has not engaged in the patient analysis that other theologies have undertaken to spell out what it means to say that God "is." If God has not "been" from ever and ever, and if God "is" not now, then God never "will be" either. So long as the meaning of the verb "be" remains the same, then the being or existence of God as such is indivisible insofar as chronological time and verbal tenses are concerned.

What is happening now is that theologians are contrasting not only different verbal tenses but also different meanings of the word "be" when they say that God "is not" but "will be." Indeed they may be using the word "God" in more than one sense as well. Their remarks could have sound sense—on one condition: They must spell out clearly what they mean when they say that God "will be," that God is "the future," or that God ever stands "ahead of us" in history.

10. THE OTHER FACE OF REALITY

Now when the verb "be" is applied to God in terms of the future, in terms of divine promise and future liberation, it must be understood primarily in much the same sense that it has when it is used in the present tense. In other words, it must be viewed as alluding to the mysterious, transcendent, creative, and founding side of realities that exist in the physical world. All additional connotations concerning God's being and activity must be grounded on this fundamental meaning and base.

Teilhard de Chardin discusses the Christian idea of the creation of the world by God. He proposes the thesis that creation in the theological sense and evolution in the scientific sense represent two aspects of one and the same reality. Creation is the metaphysical and religious side of evolution. Evolution is the sensible expression of creation in time and space, which is available to our experiencing: it is the empirical transcription of the creative act (183:518–21). Now it is quite possible that all reasonable theologians would agree with that formulation insofar as the terms "creation" and "evolution" are concerned. The physical universe is well on its way toward being demythologized in current theology. The point is that in principle the same basic formulation would apply to all the other representations of theology: grace, revelation, the Holy Spirit, and so forth. In their primary sense, these representations do not allude to things that are different from sensible, earthly realities; rather, they allude to the transcendent and mysterious aspects of the most earthy and tangible realities in human life. (Perhaps they do so in their ultimate sense as well, but that is not the question that concerns us here.) In particular, the freedom whereby we personally arrive at faith is not distinct from the divine grace that enables us to believe. In the last analysis, then, there is no conflict or incompatibility between freedom and grace: "God's grace and man's freedom are the two sides of one and the same reality. God's grace is the transcendent side of (authentic) human freedom; freedom is the tangible, earthly side of grace. 'Grace' is the theological term for freedom; 'freedom' is the anthropological term for grace" (187:281).

I suggest, then, that we should not view grace as a separate, isolated supernatural entity, but that we should view it as the transcendent side of the believer's freedom. To put it another way, which actually comes down to the same thing, I suggest that grace is the idea with which theology represents authentic human freedom. Now this may seem to some to be a dangerous reductionism insofar as Christian belief in grace is concerned. But if we want to be realistic and honest in posing a formulation that goes counter to any form of supernaturalism, we must admit the fact that theological representations do mean precisely that—or else they have no meaning at all.

It is worth noting that this same idea is also making headway in modern Protestant theology, and Protestant theology has been even more zealous than Catholic theology in trying to safeguard the otherness of God. Consider this brash statement by Ebeling, which is right on the mark in my opinion: "Faith and the Holy Spirit are not different things but rather two aspects of one and the same happening" (169:99).

Once political theology begins to apply this theological vision to political realities, it suddenly begins to take cognizance of its own distinctive discourse. It begins to see that it is operating outside the borders of scientific knowledge and cognition, that it does not possess any separate, distinctive supernatural objects of its own. Moltmann's observation, already noted earlier, is most timely and to the point: "Emancipation is the immanent side of redemption. Redemption is the transcendent side of emancipation" (309:240).

If this thesis were fully and wholeheartedly accepted, it would eliminate some of the ambivalence now found in the theology of liberation. For this theology now uses the term "liberation" in two senses, without clearly spelling out the relationship between them. It refers both to the perceptible reality of liberation as a historical happening and to liberation as a theological category, but it intermingles the two meanings rather indiscriminately. The proposed thesis maintains that divine salvation and liberation in history are one and the same thing, but seen from different sides. Liberation in history is the immanent side of the reality that theology attempts to represent as divine salvation. Its theological representation of God's salvific work evokes the transcendent side of a tangible liberation in history.

Thus political liberation and theological salvation would not be two things added together by a process of mere addition. Nor would divine salvation be something that exceeds human liberation to reach some absolute term in some sort of beyond. To this basic viewpoint suggested by Moltmann, I would only add one further note. It has to do with the element of surprise and unforeseeable chance that seems to be part of the future. That element gives a more tangible and concrete profile to faith's interpretation of the universe in terms of creation and grace. Seen in this perspective, chance would be the tangible side of grace.

These observations could have been made in the previous chapter, because they hold true for the theological representations examined there. But they fit even better here because they allow us to describe and pinpoint the stances of various authors with greater clarity. One basic viewpoint, just explained, would view theological notions simply as referring to the nontangible aspects of some historical reality that can be observed by the senses and analyzed by scientific knowledge. In contrast to this viewpoint, some theologians seem to imagine that God's liberation goes above and beyond liberation in history, and that the object of Christian hope is some reality that far exceeds all human expectations and all proposed human utopias.

Rahner, Gollwitzer, and even Moltmann in some texts, seem to set up a contrast between an absolute future and an intraworldly future, between an absolute utopia and a relative utopia. Thus they seem to hold a view like the second one just described. It remains to be seen whether the future as a dimension justifies any neat grading of realities into higher and lower stages—ranging from terrestrial realities below to divine realities above. In that perspective the former would be human, historical, and relative; the latter would be divine, eschatological, and absolute. Even in terms of the future, it may well be that God's grace and promise are simply another aspect of human freedom and human action.

11. THE RESURRECTION OF THE DEAD

Clearly associated with the question just proposed for consideration is the meaning to be given to Christian belief in the resurrection of the dead. Like other traditional Christian themes, the resurrection is being subjected to hermeneutic recasting in current political theology. As one might readily guess, the issue is death and the life of the dead as a political, or better, metapolitical problem. Those who have suffered and died already constitute a problem that no economic or political liberation in the future can resolve. The future achievements of human beings and their potential happiness are of no benefit to those who have already died; they cannot dry any tears or redeem spilt blood.

According to Metz, faith in the resurrection renders people free to "heed the sufferings and hopes of the past and to pick up the challenge of the dead." It thereby produces a real solidarity with "the suffering of our forefathers" in the past. Christian hope attempts to answer the question: Is there any sense or meaning to the dead, to those who were vanquished and consigned to oblivion in the past? Its response presupposes a real revolution, not only for the sake of future generations but also for the sake of past generations. That revolution represents a wholly new way of deciding what is to be the sense "of the death of our dead and the hopes they entertained" (296:328).

It seems very hard indeed to reduce any such hope in meaningfulness for the dead to anything resembling theoretical, rational discourse. It seems almost impossible to reason out or legitimate that hope, though certainly more than one theologian has tried to. Miranda, for example, attempts to suggest an argument for resurrection on the basis of a dialectical view of matter: "The moment that the eternal return is rejected as a conception of history, it becomes indispensable to understand matter as a reality susceptible to true novelty in its development. This is dialectics. What we must reproach Marx for when he avoids the problem of death and therefore does not even glimpse the possibility of the resurrection of the dead is that he was not sufficiently dialectical" (308:316).

But any such defense of the resurrection in the name of dialectical materialism and its logic seems to be highly problematical. Hope in resurrection seems rather to be alien to any theory or line of logic, and provocative for that very reason. It would seem to constitute the truly distinctive feature of Christian eschatology vis-à-vis every form of rational discourse, whether positivist, dialectical, or utopian. For belief in resurrection for the dead is both indemonstrable and irrefutable. Moreover, it is dependent on the enigmatic witness of the paschal experience of the apostles, which would seem to be a revelatory happening outside the bounds of historical time.

But the mere fact that Christian eschatology is characterized by hope in the resurrection of the dead does not eliminate the dilemma in which we find ourselves. For, strictly speaking, what does that resurrection signify? Is it not subject to the same basic set of alternatives that confronts current eschatology? There is no doubt that many theologians interpret this resurrection in the traditional sense of physical resurrection after death. That is the interpretation which the Vulgate translation put on several verses in the book of Job (Job 19:25–27), which are less specific in the Hebrew and other versions. Carried over into the Catholic liturgy for the dead, the Vulgate version had Job saying that he would see his God after death, after being vested in his own flesh and skin once again.

Over against such a view, however, we find Metz's reserved comments concerning a purely negative theology. And any transcendent conception of the resurrection is drastically undercut by these two remarks of Norman O. Brown:

> The question confronting mankind is the abolition of repression—in traditional Christian language, the resurrection of the body (86:307).

> The resurrection of the body is a social project facing mankind as a whole, and it will become a practical political problem when the statesmen of the world are called upon to deliver happiness instead of power (86:317).

These remarks are picked up by Alves and incorporated into his own discussion (48:234). They lead to an intrahistorical interpretation of resurrection that has no element of transcendence attached to it. Resurrection becomes a social project, involving the suppression of repression. The distinctive feature of Christianity, of "messianic humanism" to use Alves's term, is simply that it regards this resurrection as a gift (48:140–59).

Thus, while hope in resurrection for the dead gives a specific tinge to Christian eschatology on the symbolic level, it does not offer any way out of the basic dilemma noted above. It, too, is enmeshed in that basic dilemma. For what does the hope of the Christian look? Does it hope for something more than utopian hope does? Or does it simply hope for the same thing but regard it as a gift?

12. THE DILEMMA OF HOPE

The question has not been resolved in any clear-cut way in current theology. But even if we do not resolve it right away, we must at least pose it clearly. That we can do by expressing it in terms of two alternatives. On the one hand we might maintain rigorously that divine salvation and resurrection are nothing more than the transcendent side of historical liberation, to which they do not really add anything by way of complement or fulfillment. Or, on the other hand, we might go on imagining and insisting that divine salvation is something metaphysical and metahistorical; that while in part it may coincide with earthly reality and history, it also contains an additional element of the beyond to which no reality in this world corresponds.

The same set of alternatives might be put in another form. On the one hand we might maintain that the Christian hopes for the same thing that other human beings hope for: i.e., a more humane society; the only distinctive element in the Christian hope is that it regards a more humane society as a promise and gift from God. Or, on the other hand, we might claim that the Christian hopes for something in addition to that hoped for by other human beings: i.e., for a kingdom of God that is to be realized in a future that will transcend history and this world.

We might put it still another way. On the one hand we might maintain that objectively speaking Christian eschatology coincides completely with the utopia of social theory, except for the fact that it takes the cognitive concepts of a social utopia and expresses them in theological ideas, interpretations, and symbols. Or, on the other hand, we might maintain that Christian eschatology goes further than utopia, leaping outside history and the world in which we live now to some space or time or locale elsewhere.

Let me make one final attempt to express the very same

basic set of alternatives, which sum up the dilemma for us. On the one hand we might maintain that theology's representations of the future find their distinctive meaning wholly in their different way of symbolizing and representing the future. Or, on the other hand, we might insist that those representations are meant to find objective and concrete expression in certain realities very different from any which could be imagined or predicted without them.

Needless to say, traditional dogmatics could not even formulate this dilemma on its own initiative. And when the dilemma was posed to it from outside, its response was very fast: Since we find in the New Testament very clear expectations of some other life beyond the death of the individual and the end of the world, the Christian is obliged to hope for some eternal life beyond this world and history. The question is not resolved in advance or settled a priori in the case of a critical theology that does not regard the teachings of the New Testament as divine oracles. Nor can such a theology resolve the question on its own. Critical theology does not adopt positions on its own account, attempting to fill in for the stance of faith or to replace it. With specific regard to the dilemma just proposed, it is not theology that decides but rather faith and hope. Faith and hope are of course enlightened by theology, but they are not dependent on it. Theology clarifies the presuppositions and the consequences of a certain way of believing and hoping, but it itself does not believe or hope (just as it does not disbelieve or despair either). Faith precedes theology, not vice-versa.

This is a book of theology, not a confession of the author's faith or a profession of his hope. The personal beliefs and hopes of the theologian are valid as testimony, but not as theology. Those beliefs and hopes are no more relevant for theology than the beliefs and hopes of any other believer who is mature as a human being and a Christian. To choose a specific option of faith and hope at this point would be to distort the basic outlook and perspective of this book. As a theological study, its proper task is to shed a little light on the premises and consequences of this or that option.

So here we can spell out the basic theological implications of the dilemma posed above. Suppose the Christian hopes for exactly the same thing as the non-Christian does, but sees that object as a grace or gift from God, as the fulfillment of a divine promise. In that case Christianity would simply be characterized by an interpretation and by certain representations peculiarly its own. In that case Christians are not too different from other human beings; their unique message would simply have to do with a different way of seeing the same things that are seen or hoped for by everybody else. Suppose, on the other hand, that Christians do not just hope for realities envisioned by utopian schemes and made feasible through revolutionary praxis (and through the workings of gratuitous historical "chance"). Suppose Christians hope for some additional reality of a different sort. In that case there is a real danger that their hope will be regarded as an illusion, or that it actually will be an illusion, an escape into some safe haven outside history and the world.

The kind of hope described in the first alternative above is much like that of the Old Testament. The danger is that it might be only too quick to conform to a culture that is well on its way to being discredited and rejected. The kind of hope described in the second alternative seems to correspond a bit more to the New Testament, but also to salvation myths in other religious traditions. The danger in this case is that it will succumb to illusory fantasies and supernaturalism, losing all sense of realism.

Political eschatology and the theology of hope now find a very important decision pending. They must decide which alternative to choose. On the one hand they may decide to opt for the classic theology of the four last things and the hereafter, with two important reservations: (1) they will be very modest in trying to conjure up images of the hereafter; (2) they will put a high value on the here and now also, incorporating it into the divine promise. On the other hand they may decide to reduce their own dimensions to those of a social utopia with hope focused on this earth—except that they will interpret them as empirical aspects of God's promise and its fulfillment.

The latter alternative, of course, would be more consistent with the other criteria adopted in the course of this book. But logical consistency is not always an infallible sign of truth.

PART THREE

THEORY

7

Theological Specifications

1. PENDING ALTERNATIVES

The program of political theology as presented in the three previous chapters displays a fundamental unity. Indeed my assemblage of doctrinal elements from different sources in those chapters is based on the hypothesis that they do possess substantive continuity and homogeneity. My hypothesis has been verified to some extent by the very fact that it was possible to weave a continuous discourse linking liberation theology and revolution theology, Exodus theology and political eschatology—despite the fact that they disagree with one another in details where one or another specific topic or theme is concerned. For example, was Jesus a Zealot or a purely religious preacher? Does a given theology advocate Christian violence or a gospel of nonviolence? Does it advocate the mediation of some utopia or oppose all utopias?

But the fact is that underneath the more superficial differences between these theologies we find deep-rooted ones that have to do with the ultimate meaning of political theology itself. These differences are not always noted, and yet they ultimately destroy the seeming unity of political theology as a whole. They do not have to do with different ways of understanding or interpreting the political praxis of Christians, its biblical models, and the transcendent or nontranscendent character of Christian eschatology. Nor do they have to do with such things as a possible contrast between revolution theology on the one hand and liberation theology on the other. Such differences would be of secondary importance. So long as they did not reflect other discrepancies of a more deep-seated nature, they would be like the traditional controversies that have arisen between various schools of theology. Differences in doctrinal content would not erase the fact that they shared the same basic way of understanding theology and the faith.

But the differences I have in mind here are of major importance. They relate to the ultimate character of a political interpretation of the gospel message; to its epistemological, theological, and cultural status; to the thrust of its affirmations; and to its claims to truth. In short, they affect the whole program of political theology. While the basic unity of its discourse might not be called into question, these differences reveal that it might have many different levels of meaning.

Consider these questions, for example. Is political theology primarily an ethics, a normative discipline for the praxis or Christians, or is it also talk about God in the strict sense? And what can we say of the talk about God that we find in current political theology, or that might be found in some other possible brand of theology? At what level of reflection and critical awareness does it operate? Does it remain at the level of rhetoric, of unchecked direct speech, or does it reach the deeper level of reflexive, critical discourse? Can it attain this deeper level at all? Can it voice a language that is aware of the preconditions for its own feasibility? Is the political interpretation of the gospel a dogmatics, a theology which presupposes from the start that Christian dogmas are true? Or does it rather operate on the level of fundamental theology, which has to do with the genesis of faith? As part of a historical period marked by an ongoing process of secularization, does political theology fully accept that secularity? Or does it seek to arrest that process by some sort of social restoration of the religious sphere? Finally, what does political theology purport to offer? Does it claim to offer real knowledge about human beings, in the strict sense of "knowledge," and perhaps also about God? Or does it merely claim to provide a symbolic idiom?

These questions have already been touched upon more than once in my presentation of the program of political theology, and the rough outlines of the answers have also been hinted at. But now we must deal with them directly, detailing the answers in a reasoned manner. The ultimate meaning of political theology will depend on how those questions are answered. So long as we do not make a clear choice between the possible alternatives, the general program of political theology outlined in Part Two will remain relatively undefined insofar as its ultimate meaning is concerned. Even though each of its affirmations may remain unaltered, the entire discourse of political theology undergoes change when one alternative is chosen over the other. The import of its statements will differ, depending on whether they are understood in a predominantly ethical perspective or a rigorously *theo*-logical focus; whether they are regarded as the spontaneous idiom of the faith or as a reflexive and critical metalanguage; whether they presuppose a dogmatic faith or merely serve as a spur to some sort of conversion on the way toward being faith; whether they are subjected to a secular interpretation or understood in a religious key; whether they are regarded as positive knowledge or merely as a negative, symbolic theology.

Take, for example, the thesis that God goes out to meet man in the dimension of the future. The import of this thesis will vary greatly if we entertain different presuppositions. It all depends on whether we regard it as an invitation to action or a pronouncement about the very reality of God, as a poetic expression or a reflective observation, as a consequence flowing from belief in God or an inducement to believe in God, as a sacralization of the future or a total desacralization of every moment in history, as real news and knowledge or a belief coded in symbols. And the same basic point holds true for all the affirmations encountered so far in this book.

On the one hand, nothing changes with the specifications that still remain to be spelled out with regard to the meaning of political theology; for its basic and primary signification, as already described on a more elementary level, remains whole and intact. On the other hand, everything changes; for we have so far put off specifying and deciding the ultimate meaning of political theology. That meaning could come under discussion only after we had gained familiarity with its overall program and were ready to move on to a higher level of reflection.

Unfortunately many of the questions now due for discussion here are not even adverted to by most theologians. In my opinion, political theology is not always sufficiently clear on the whole matter of the nature of its own *logos*. Here I shall try to help the process of clarification, going so far as to adopt certain basic options. To illustrate the very different alternatives available in specifying the *logos* of political theology, I shall cite passages from different theologians by way of example; but it should be clearly understood that those theologians are rarely aware of the fact that they are adopting one specific option as opposed to other possible or even necessary options when they utter their remarks.

It is only after we clearly specify these basic alternatives that we will be able to tackle another question that we have left pending since the start of this book. It is a question toward which all the other unanswered questions point: i.e., the question of grounding and legitimation. The validation of theology can scarcely have any real meaning if it is discussed in general or abstract terms. The possibility of any such validation depends on the concrete kind of theology in question. Under certain conditions that will be considered more closely in the last chapter, it does seem possible to validate a political theology that is nondogmatic, nonpositivist, secular, critical, and symbolic; on the other hand, it does not seem possible to validate any positivist, dogmatic theology that seeks to restore a sacral order.

2. ETHICS AND THEOLOGY

The first set of alternatives mentioned in the last section forces us to ask whether the political theology we have been describing so far really is a theology in the strict sense (i.e., talk about God) or is simply a theological ethics (a discourse that can ultimately be reduced to the level of moral doctrine). Suppose, for example, that a theologian asserts that God is the "no" to injustice. What is this person doing? Primarily establishing an ethical norm for the believer, or enunciating a proposition about God? One might well answer both at the same time. Or one might say that it all depends, that in any political interpretation of the gospel message some propositions would be primarily ethical while others would be primarily theological.

Such attempts to harmonize both sides, however, will not convince some theologians at all. Quite aside from that fact, it is desirable to spell out and justify such solutions in a full and convincing way rather than leaving them at the level of mere harmonistic formulas.

It is Trutz Rendtorff, more than anyone else, who has stressed the distinctively and exclusively ethical character of the pronouncements that circulate under the banner of political theology. He maintains that "theology does have a political dimension," but that this dimension is actualized only through the mediation of ethics. The mediation between theology and politics "takes concrete shape as ethics." For Rendtorff, then, it is not possible to have any political theology in the strict sense except insofar as it would deny a wholly autonomous course to the political realm: There can be no political theology in the older Constantinian sense, no theology underpinning a sacral Christendom. Only a political ethics can fulfill the function of systematically criticizing the political realm. In short, we should talk about a political ethics rather than about a political theology (353:74–75; 355:217–18). This stance logically leads one to interpret the whole program described in Part Two of this book in ethical terms rather than in strictly theological terms. It also leads one to regard political theology as a social ethics meant to complement some dogmatics that might not have to be altered in any way. And so we are back at the basic formulation of the issue which typified the theology of the New Christendom movement (see chapter 2, sections 2 and 3).

At the opposite pole we find Harvey Cox, who has found much inspiration in ideas pointed out by Phillippe Maury (291:28) and, even more so, by Paul Lehmann. The latter, in particular, did much to highlight the task of thinking about God in political terms within theology (256:87). Talk about God as a political affair is a thesis which Cox has explored in depth and defended persistently. In his opinion politics must now replace mythology and metaphysics as the idiom of theology, and he asks us to talk politically about God (126:271–79). In the case of some theologians politics now has come to be not only the necessary but also the exclusive vehicle for theological discourse—which of course is a rather simplistic stance: "Today the problem of God is not primarily a gnoseological question or a question of scientific theology; it is an eminently political question" (245:563). Thus politics is not merely a dimension or a consequence of dogmatics. It is rather the warp and woof of theology, its mode and material of expression in the modern age.

It is only in terms of this second perspective that we can make sense out of certain expressions used today. For example, we see book titles which refer to preaching as a political act (113) and to atheism as a political problem (255). These formulas have certain affinities with verbal expressions of a somewhat earlier day, and they are hardly original in that respect. For example, Peterson referred to monotheism as a political problem (337:27–62), Daniélou referred to prayer as a political problem (144), and Reding spoke of political atheism (350). Underlying the seeming resemblance in terminology, however, is a radical novelty in meaning. The society of yesteryear was still sacral and Christian, and hence it saw things in much the same terms as those expressed by Durand: "The problem of God is a political question by the very fact that political society seeks some religious foundation for itself" (163:380). Present-day society and theology is not seeking some religious foundation for social institutions. Today the problem of God is a political question because we must express ourselves in political terms if we wish to talk about God at all. In an earlier day, then, theology was part of politics. Today just the opposite is true: Politics is part of theological expression. Today when people talk about theism and atheism as a political question, they are actually saying that we must incorporate politics into the representational and expressional discourse of beliefs and unbeliefs.

But it does not seem to be impossible to combine an ethical focus with a strictly theological one. The real alternative here is not between theology on the one hand and ethics on the other. The parting of the ways comes when one affirms or denies that there is a strict correlation between the two elements in political theology.

J.B. Metz offers us a well-formulated synthesis of the ethical and the theological dimensions. On the one hand he expressly stays with Rendtorff in considering political theology (and political eschatology) as only indirectly oriented toward praxis, through the mediation of ethics. On the other hand, however, he felicitously defines political theology as "the specifically Christian hermeneutics of political ethics as an ethics of change." Put even better, it is the Christian hermeneutics designed to clarify a new relationship between theory and praxis. Thus political theology redefines the respective position of ethics and dogmatics in new and original terms (301:280–83).

Metz's formulation is on the right track. To his own observation that theology becomes praxis only through the mediation of ethics we need only add that political ethics is not directly and immediately praxis either, that it becomes such only through the mediation of social analysis and the theory of revolution. Metz's specification of theology as a hermeneutics also seems to support a line of theological thought that would regard theology as the interpretation of signs and perhaps also of symbols. All theology, and in our case here political theology, has to do with signs that are deciphered and interpreted in it. In political theology the creed and the symbols of faith are interpreted in terms of an ethics of change. Thus political theology is not reduced merely to an ethics. For it not only concerns itself with the praxis of Christians but also takes into consideration the representations with which Christians attempt to symbolize God.

As Metz has clearly seen, the new relationship that exists between theory and praxis which typifies modern thought and political theology forces us to abandon the older viewpoint which regarded ethics as some sort of independent discipline. According to that older point of view, ethics was the discipline uniquely normative for human conduct and the science of action by virtue of its very name. Thus human action was ultimately defined in ethical or imperative terms, and moral theology was the underlying theory of this action. The different relationship between theory and praxis eliminates that sort of ethical exclusivism. Theory always bespeaks a relationship to praxis; and since it is eminently practical, it picks up the age-old vocation of ethics. But this theory is no longer an ethics or a system of imperatives. Though it does have a direct and immediate reference to praxis, it is not a normative reference. Instead it entails an analysis of the real-life situation as it seeks to provide suggestions for effectively altering that same situation.

As for myself, I am inclined to view political theology first and foremost as a theory of the praxis of Christians (186: 12). My opinion here is based on a more general theological criterion: namely, that there is no direct and immediate language about God, that all theological language is indirect, speaking of human beings rather than of God. According to this viewpoint, then, political theology is primarily a theory of the praxis of Christians; only through this theory does it indirectly and mediately fashion a discourse about God.

The "praxis of Christians" is not to be equated with "Christian praxis." Once we have ruled out any ideal of a sacral or profane Christendom, there is no room for any specifically Christian praxis (see chapter 2, sections 7 and 8; also chapter 5, section 17). This means that the praxis of Christians does not contain elements which differentiate their praxis from that of other human beings; that it is identical with the praxis of the common run of people. Hence we would do well to prescind from explicit references to a specific religious group and to speak simply of *praxis* without further qualifications. As one author has put it: "In the praxis of revolution one must forget that one is a Christian as much as possible" (112:217). Moreover, since the discourse of theory does not support any sort of autonomous epistemological viewpoint external to praxis, it follows that there is no meaningful discourse except from within praxis itself. We do not fashion a theory about praxis; we fashion theory from within praxis.

Insofar as theology is discourse, it is subject to these same conditions. Its matrix is praxis. If theology is in a logical and consistent relationship with praxis, then it is a theology *from within* praxis not a theology *about* praxis; it is born from its own critical self-awareness in action. Hence political theology is a discourse arising out of the general praxis of human emancipation in which Christians participate. It seems just as important to underline this aspect (the participation of Christians) as to stress the oneness of their praxis with that of others. For if we did not find any active presence of Christians in the process, if we did not find present people who symbolized the common human and political experience through the constellation of symbols provided by Christianity, then we would have no right to consider praxis as a theological locus. Reflection arising out of praxis, as such, does not give rise to any theology. It provides a basis for theology only insofar as the praxis in question, by virtue of the participation of certain human beings in it, manifests some correlation with the realm of Christian symbols. Political theology, then, is rooted in a common human praxis of emancipation, but one in which Christians participate and thereby establish connections between it and the symbols of their own religious tradition.

A relationship to praxis does not reduce political theology to a kind of ethics, however, because its theory is not spelled out in normative terms. Instead it is spelled out as an analysis of the social and political action whereby Christians alter the real situation in which they and other human beings find themselves; and the aim on this level is to make the analysis as thorough as possible. This analysis will of course contain references to action that entail imperatives at some point; but for the most part it will be composed of suggestions and signposts that have no normative or imperative connotations. For example, it will call attention to specific relationships between particular Christian beliefs and particular lines of conduct practiced by Christians: e.g., between belief in God's promise and a political praxis designed to create a new future, or between the dogma of

Christ as Savior and enlistment in a liberation movement. Christian symbols express certain practical attitudes and, at the same time, react upon those attitudes to alter them. Political theology, in turn, comments upon the action and reaction which takes place between Christian symbols and the practical conduct of Christians; hence it is clearly quite distinct from ethics.

Ethics is made of imperative pronouncements whereby a particular doctrine seeks to exert normative influence on human living. Political theology is not composed, or not solely composed of imperative pronouncements. It does not establish norms on the basis of doctrine or biblical history. It points out, makes suggestions, and indicates certain correspondences. It establishes a reciprocal interpretation moving back and forth between the essential constitutive fonts of the Christian faith and current political praxis.

There is another respect in which political theology differs from traditional theological ethics. In political theology praxis also has an impact on the very representations which the believer uses to imagine God. In the emancipation of peoples and nations, for example, it sees God's salvation *in vivo*. Thus social and political events end up qualifying the discourse of theology itself. These repercussions of praxis on the very fabric of theology decisively differentiate political theology as a theory of the social praxis of Christians from every political theology which is regarded as an ethics logically derived from dogmatics (e.g., that of the New Christendom movement).

3. THEOLOGAL LANGUAGE AND THEOLOGICAL DISCOURSE

A second specification has to do with the level at which political theology operates as reflective elaboration and critical awareness of its own statements. Here I must bring up an important distinction that I developed more fully in an earlier book (188:202–34), and that is generally acknowledged in some form by other theologians though they then proceed to disregard it in their own work. I refer to the distinction between theologal language on the one hand and theology on the other.

We sometimes hear people say that theology is the language of faith. That statement can get by, but it needs a bit of clarification and specification. If we want to, we can apply the term "theology" to direct language about the faith—to the Creed, for example. But it would be more precise and proper to refer to such direct language as "theologal language," and to reserve the term "theology" for a second-stage, reflexive language which is critical and disciplined, which is related to our expression of the faith but is not identical with that expression.

Direct (theologal) language about God is not science or knowledge. Strictly speaking, it is not cognitive but symbolic language. We have already touched upon this point when we discussed the categories and images used by political theology to represent current praxis of the faith. Such notions as brotherhood, liberation, communion, love, and conversion are not theoretical or cognitive concepts, strictly speaking; they are rather symbolic ideas (see chapter 5, sections 14 and 17). The same holds true for the other terms of political theology. Indeed, if we want to be more precise, we should not refer to political theology but to the politically mediated theologal language that we have been examining for the most part in this book. Its terms are not cognitive in any strict sense of the word.

We can and must have a second-stage, reflexive, disciplined, and critical language that focuses on first-stage theologal language as its object and tries to work out its theoretical and scientific import. Only then do we have theology in the strict sense, which is not a language about God but a metalanguage. Theology is discourse at a second stage of elaboration; as such it is theory and knowledge in the strict sense, but not about God or the hereafter or any other transcendent reality. Theology as second-stage discourse has to do with the relationship existing between two empirical and social realities: i.e., between the profession of faith espoused by Christians and their political praxis.

And so we get an important clarification. Direct theologal language refers to transcendent realities, but it does not "know" them in the strict sense of the word; as I shall stress later, it simply symbolizes them. Theology in the strict sense, as solid theory and as a scientific discipline, is knowledge in the proper sense; but it is not knowledge of God or other invisible realities. Rather, theology in the strict sense is knowledge of believing human beings, their representations, and their lines of conduct. Theology as second-stage discourse and real theory is the result of combining the different methods of various scholarly sciences and disciplines (sociology, psychology, linguistics, and so forth) and applying them to the Christian phenomenon; in themselves, these methods do not require the theologian to share the belief on which he or she is commenting.

The point here is that most of what has been written so far under the designation of "political theology" does not get beyond being merely theologal language. It is the direct and spontaneous expression of a politically involved and committed faith, not second-stage critical reflection on that direct expression. Needless to say, that reproach applies not only to political theology but to almost all theology. Even the most fully elaborated positive and systematic theologies are devoid of critical precision and exactness; they are content to elaborate and systematize Christian beliefs without treating them on the level of a truly critical theory. Thus political theology suffers from the same basic defect to be found in positive and dogmatic theologies.It is not theology in the strict sense of that term; rather, it is first-stage spontaneous theologal language (188:204–6).

Theologal language has a proper place when and insofar as it remains fully aware of what it itself really is: i.e., direct, spontaneous, precritical expression of the faith. But when it passes itself off as theology in the strict sense, as second-stage critical reflection on the faith, then it is expropriating a place to which it has no right; it is giving a false impression about certain functions that should be carried out within the church but which are not being carried out. If we want to keep calling it theology, then we should call it poetic theology, or homiletic theology, or rhetorical theology; we should not call it critical theology. I do not mean to suggest any pejorative connotations when I use the term "rhetorical." I merely mean that such a theology is an amplification and systematization of language that does not entail any critical reflection on itself.

4. CRITIQUE OF THE THEOLOGY OF REVOLUTION

In order to point up the rhetorical, noncritical, character of most political theology, I shall now bring up some of the major objections that have been levelled against the theology of revolution. This should make it clear to the reader that most political theology is open to the same sort of objections.

The theology of revolution has been sharply criticized for a serious lack of theological precision and a total absence of any critical sense insofar as it talks about God acting in the revolution in terms that are downright mythical. It is a fact that Richard Shaull uses certain expressions that are shocking to say the least, and that wound the modern sensibilities of the faith; for the person of faith today is very sensitive to any identification of God with events in this world. Shaull talks about the "pressure" exerted by God to bring about change and about God's "humanizing activity." He also says that it is God who destroys the old structures to create the conditions for a more humane existence (393:20–21 and 28).

His language has been justifiably described as precritical: "What does one really mean when one talks about God's revolutionary activity in history? Isn't one talking in a very unspecific way that is open to much criticism? Isn't one unfortunately confusing and identifying God with the historical process and its attendant crises? These questions must be taken seriously. The fact is that there are many things that are theologically and linguistically imprecise, particularly in the writings of Shaull" (261:21–22).

In attempting to spell out the precritical features of the theology of revolution, two aspects come in for major attention: the biblical aspect and the properly theological aspect. The theology of revolution seems to be precritical with respect to biblical criticism, whose results it feigns not to know or care about; it also seems to be precritical with respect to a brand of epistemological (Kantian) and theological criticism that mercilessly excludes certain naive ways of talking about God.

The criticisms made by Rendtorff follow along the two lines just mentioned. In his opinion, the theology of revolution attempts to justify itself as theology through an "overhasty relationship with certain elements of Christianity's religious tradition." It is a doctrine that "derives its conclusions from a body of representative material encountered in a precritical, primarily biblical, milieu." The most basic criticism that can be levelled against it is that it seems to be unaware of the Enlightenment. Rendtorff maintains that the theology of revolution does not take into account the cultural sphere that followed upon the Enlightenment nor the motives and intentions of the "theology of the Enlightenment" (i.e., that theology that was predominantly Protestant and that took the criticism of Kant in all seriousness in the nineteenth century). I would prefer to say that this holds true for a certain version of the theology of revolution and for a certain brand of political theology in general. In any case the result, as Rendtorff sees it, is a "precritical theology," a revolutionary "orthodoxy of the left" in which is oddly intermingled an avant-garde subversivism and an orthodox dogmatic fundamentalism. It curiously combines "political and social progressivism with tendencies in biblical and historical theology that are ultimately acritical" (353:67–74).

In formulating his objections, Arthur Rich stresses the theological aspect rather than the biblical or cultural aspect. To what extent is it permissible to talk about a revelation or manifestation of God in revolution? Rich complains that Shaull's thesis presupposes the conviction that "revolutionary processes, more than any other, are marked by the presence of God." Thus God himself somehow happens to be "hidden in the process of revolution," so that this process takes on the nature of a "revelation." Revolution becomes the historical locus, or better, the historical *kairos,* in which the divine will is concretely manifested. Over against any such presuppositions Rich maintains that it is difficult to know whether any given happening is really revolutionary or counterrevolutionary. Every historical situation is really replete with ambiguity. Rich also stresses the weakness of any theology based on the notion of *kairos* that claims or seeks to "directly hear and heed the summons of God in a critical moment of history." Any such theology, be it a theology of revolution or a theology of the old order, assumes that it can make God transparently and directly present in history as such. So now we are seeing the older positivism of "good order" being replaced by a new theological positivism of revolution. But the latter is just as simplistic as the former, for it sees God being manifested directly in the revolutionary process just as the older theology saw God manifested in the institutions of law and order (357:142–43).

Now the fact is that the same objections can be levelled against other presentations of political and liberation theology. Cox, Cardonnel, Gutiérrez, and quite a few others use expressions that are quite like those of Shaull—except that they may be talking about social change or liberation rather than about revolution. Harvey Cox tells us that today God comes to us in the events connected with societal change (126:283). Cardonnel assures us that "God manifests himself in the process of stirring up resistance on the part of people who are threatened with total subjugation and annihilation" (21:80). And the basic framework of Gutiérrez's theology of liberation entails a revelation in history: "If utopia humanizes economic, social, and political liberation, this humanness—in the light of the gospel—reveals God" (230:319). The point is put even more clearly by Geffré: "God also reveals himself in, through, and by the liberation struggles undertaken by all the poor on the South American continent" (206).

What difference is there between seeing the activity of God in revolution on the one hand and in social change, resistance, liberation, or utopia on the other? From the standpoint of critical theology, there is no difference at all. Objecting to the views of the theologians of revolution, some have adduced the criterion that henceforth "God can no longer be directly and immediately linked up with politics" (177:130). This same criterion holds against other formulations proposed by other brands of political theology. The objections noted against Shaull's formulas are equally valid against many statements of liberation theology and utopian theology.

Those objections might be summed up as follows. The statements of much political theology are linguistically and theologically imprecise in many respects. They derive their representational material from a world, the world of the Bible, which is no longer our world. They ignore modern biblical criticism and modern epistemological criticism of every attempt to find God directly in history. They obtain their conclusions by forced and hasty connections with certain elements of the Judeo-Christian tradition. They continue to be mired in a theological positivism that is wedded to a concept of revelation as something given in fact—the fact of liberation, or resistance, or social change, or whatever.

The precritical quality of some of these formulations is perfectly compatible with the fact that certain theologians display a well developed critical sense with regard to the possibility of talking about God. In such a case the formulations continue to be precritical in themselves, but they can and should be interpreted in line with the general theological stance of their authors. This point applies in particular to Protestant theologians, but also to some Catholics. When we find that Schaull defines his theology of revolution in terms of relating a revolutionary way of life with the "Christian *symbols*" (391:32–34), then we are entitled to interpret his theses about God in the revolution very differently from the way they seem to be interpreted by those who raise objections against him. We can interpret them in symbolic terms rather than in terms of positive dogmatics. The fact does remain that his formulas are imprecise and perhaps even incorrect, that Shaull should not employ them at all if he really wants to offer a symbolic, non-dogmatic theology, that at the very least he should not use them so profusely with the aim of scandalizing more traditional theologians.

A symbolic interpretation, rather than a positive-dogmatic one, is even more clearly forced upon us in the case of Paul Lehmann. He is rightly considered the precursor of both the theology of revolution and all talk of God in political terms in general. Lehmann formulates expressions that are open to all sorts of criticism, but he is fully aware of the fact that they are images (256:94). Actually he himself anticipated the criticism that would be levelled against him. He tells us forthrightly that it is presumptuous to try to describe what God is doing in the world, that such an effort is more proper in the mythical world of gods and heroes than in the real world of time and space and things. His theology does not presume to rest on any oracle, and it understands and interprets God's revelation in dialectical terms (256:79). In short, it does not interpret that revelation in positive or dogmatic terms.

The same must be said of Cox, who is much inclined to prescind from the very name "God" (126:288–89); and also of Cardonnel, who goes quite far along the lines of a theology of the death of God (101:67–83). So we are confronted with theologians who have attained a critical conception of theology on the one hand, but who continue to use expressions that are clearly precritical. The precritical expressions are part of the spontaneous language of faith and have a rightful place as such. But when they are injected into a discourse that claims to be reflexive and properly theological, we do not rise above the level of poetic or rhetorical theology. It would be a great mistake to regard such expressions as the last word in theological reflection.

5. CRITIQUE OF LIBERATION THEOLOGY

One could adduce any number of examples to show that much political theology is rhetorical and poetic rather than critical. We have already touched upon the importance of the hymnic and poetic element in liberation Christology and Exodus theology, and we noted that Cardonnel and Moltmann might be considered great Christian poets in theology (see chapter 4, section 9). Bloch's influence on Moltmann, even with respect to stylistic elements, has been considerable and is evident at every point; and Bloch's work has been discussed in terms of "Germano-Lutheran rhetoric" (273:18). While that remark was not made in sympathetic tones, there is more than a grain of truth in it. In Bloch's work we find a close intermingling of theory and philosophy with a literary gratification in the enormous plasticity of the German language. For her part, Sölle complains about the use and abuse of "grandiloquent Christological gyrations" in present-day theology (396:33), and the same can readily be found in political Christology.

Lack of a constant critical vigilance tends to render the work of some theologians less valuable as theology, though it may be commendable in other respects. The most notable example of this is the work of Gustavo Gutiérrez, who moreover is representative of a good part of Latin American theology. Here I am referring to his published written works because his oral lectures and talks, insofar as I have experienced them, seem to attain a degree of precision that does not reach the printed page. His *A Theology of Liberation* is an excellent book as witness and testimonial. It wins over the reader if it is taken as a profession of faith associated with a politically committed Christianity, or with committed Christians in Latin America in general. But it is not always theology in the strict sense. Throughout his work he does not constantly maintain the minimum of critical sense that one has a right to expect of any rigorous theology today. If one still wants to call it theology in spite of this flaw, one can only categorize much of his work as rhetorical theology.

In the previous section I cited a sentence by Gutiérrez that is typical of many in his book. All of them are clearly precritical and open to the same criticisms as those levelled against Shaull. Here is another typical statement by Gutiérrez: "To put it in terms of biblical theology: the prophetic perspective (in which the kingdom of God takes on and transforms the present life) is vindicated over against a sapiential perspective (which stresses the primacy of the life hereafter)." However much one may agree with the underlying direction of this remark (230:198), the fact remains that the elements that compose this statement seem to be wholly gratuitous and unfounded. To begin with, if there is a prophetic perspective and a sapiential perspective in the Bible, what reason is there for one to vindicate its rights over the other? Couldn't that work just as well in the opposite direction? It is a further fact that the sapiential perspective of the Old Testament did not give any primacy to the life hereafter either. For a long period of time it was consistently and persistently focused on life here and now on earth; only in a few of the later writings of this genre did the notion of a hereafter begin to occur. If one wants to contrast biblical books in terms of emphasis on the here or the hereafter, one cannot really set up much of an opposition between the prophetic writings and the sapiential writings; the real contrast on this issue is between the outlook of the Old Testament and that of the New Testament. If we want to find a place in the Bible where the life to come hereafter is given primacy, then we must certainly look to certain texts in the New Testament. And the gradual transition from Old Testament hints to full-fledged statements of this position in the New Testament has always been viewed as the result of a progressive divine revelation. If theology now wishes to go back to the Old Testament outlook, that is all well and good; but that option, like many others connected with various possible biblical perspectives, must be reasoned out rather than decided in dogmatic terms.

At another point in his book Gutiérrez comments on the beatitude: "Blessed are you poor for yours is the kingdom of God." Here again we find an example of a thesis presented without sufficient regard for a truly critical sense. Gutiérrez's interpretation is: "The elimination of the exploitation and poverty that prevent the poor from being fully human has begun" (230:380). But where exactly do we find that "elimination"? Are we to assume that the poor of Jesus' day were made that happy by contemplating an elimination of poverty which has not yet taken place two thousand years later? Can we honestly believe that it has been primarily the gospel rather than other movements that has unleashed the struggle against the situation of the poor? Gutiérrez's interpretation does not correspond to historical reality. If it has any meaningfulness at all, it is purely a mystical one. In short, it is wholly estranged from the historical plane on which political theology should seek to have meaningfulness.

His most serious critical deficiency, however, has to do with the very core of his theology of liberation, which core consists of two fundamental affirmations. The first affirmation is that God is the liberator (230:201–11). Furthermore, this activity of God is to be understood in an intense sense. Time and again Gutiérrez points out that liberation is primarily a gift, that it must be experienced and lived as an act of sheer gratuitousness and accepted in a spirit of spiritual childlikeness (230:269, 284, 319, and 382). On the other hand Gutiérrez also affirms a second point: i.e., that it is man who liberates himself and who is the active agent of his own destiny (230:52).

Now it is obvious that these two propositions, if taken on the same level, are contradictory. But even if we take them as meaningful on two different levels, if we interpret man as the agent of his liberation on the historical level and liberation as a divine gift on the theological level, we still will have difficulty reconciling the two. This fact is brought out clearly by modern atheism. Its no to God often derives precisely from the realization that it is man who creates or fashions himself. Gutiérrez experiences no difficulty in combining and reconciling the two theses. He finds it quite easy to say that the Exodus from Egypt is marked "by the two-fold sign of the overriding will of God and the free and conscious assent of man" (230:207). Salvation, wholly based on God's gratuitous initiative, "is the inner force and the fullness of this movement of man's self-generation" (230:210). Gutiérrez feels no need to ask what it might mean to talk about the "assent" of man in God's project and the "force" of God in man's self-generation.

Gutiérrez allows himself to overlook the fact that for two

centuries Protestant and Catholic theologians racked their brains to solve a question that goes to the heart of the debate with modern atheism. While they may have expressed it in terms that are no longer ours, speaking of God's foreknowledge and predestination, the question is still with us today. If man does in fact make history, if he is the master of his own actions and works, what role does God play in all that? Calvinists, Molinists, and followers of Báñez tried to answer this question, all assuming the omnipotence of God. Because of that assumption, they sometimes ended up concluding that man does not make history.

Today the contrary supposition prevails. It is assumed that man does fashion his own history. Thus God is left without anything to do. Or, to put it better perhaps, history and the world are left without God. Present-day theologians smile over the convoluted remarks of Molinists and the followers of Báñez concerning divine *concursus,* but they fail to notice the reappearance and current relevance of the basic problem in their debate with atheism. At the very least we can say that Báñez, Molina, and their followers did not rest content with the vague general statement that God saves man and man saves himself. They undertook in-depth reflection on the subject and operated as real theologians, as critics of ordinary Christian language. Many of today's theologians do not take similar pains. They rest content with saying that man participates in God's creation or that God incites the action of man, imagining that they have really said something with that. And so theology remains on the level of rhetoric. What is worse, it does not even come close to the debate opened up by the nay-saying of current atheism.

The significance of God in a history fashioned entirely by man is a topic wholly overlooked by current political theology. This theology suffers from an uncritical tendency to propose a merely rhetorical reconciliation between the theological thesis that the future is in God's hands and the fact that man is the forger of his own future. Such is the case with J.B. Metz, for example. After pointing out that the "new world" expected by the man of hope will not be the mere by-product or result of our own innate potentialities but rather the result of a promise, he goes on to say that man created his own future under God's inspiration: "We are the fashioners, not merely the interpreters, of a future whose inspiring force is God himself" (302:149). But what does "inspiring force" mean here? In what sense does God inspire the future? And what does he mean when he says that the future exceeds our potentialities? We are being confronted with uncritical language, with language on the homiletic rather than the theological level. We are hearing a Christian, not a theologian, speaking.

Let me spell out what I mean when I say that political theology, like most theology, is purely rhetorical theology. I mean that it is homiletics rather than theology in the strict sense: that it is a profession of faith rather than critical reflection on the faith; that it is testimony rather than disciplined discourse. To be sure, such testimony or profession of faith has its value. Indeed there would be no place for theology without it. But it itself does not give us theology. Some critics have pointed this out in connection with the theology of revolution, but the point holds equally well for liberation theology and any political theology.

Thus there is real value and pointedness in the statements of Latin American theologians to the effect that they are presenting a "poor theology," and that the poverty of their theology also extends to the epistemological level insofar as "it makes no claims to being organized as a science" (26:11). Such admissions are most welcome and in order, for they indicate that the theologians in question are modest and clear-sighted about the limitations of their own work. But they also confirm one's judgment that liberation theology often remains on the level of simple, straightforward Christian awareness. It serves to communicate that awareness, but it rarely reaches the level of strictly theological reflection.

Plain Christian language is more important than strictly critical theological language, but the former cannot take the place of the latter. Theology must be fully aware of its subordinate function, of its relatively lesser function by comparison with straightforward profession of the faith, proclamation of the faith, homiletics, and catechesis. At the same time, however, it must preserve its own identity. It cannot resolve itself into a creed or homily or catechetics designed for more educated people. It must be critical reflection on the faith, not mere rhetorical amplification of one's profession of faith.

This basic presupposition should help us to shed some light on the alternatives discussed below.

6. FROM DOGMATIC METHODOLOGY TO FUNDAMENTAL VALIDATION

Now we must consider whether political theology can proceed in accordance with the methodology of dogmatic theology or whether it should rather follow along the lines of fundamental theology. The import, legitimation, and current relevance of political theology depends on this new alternative facing it.

By dogmatic theology I mean a theology that already presupposes faith in the constitutive elements of Christianity: i.e., faith in Jesus, faith in the Bible, and adherence to church dogma. Dogmatic theology starts off from certain dogmas or beliefs. By contrast, fundamental theology does not presuppose faith; rather, it paves the way for it. It is a theology having to do with the genesis of faith; it is a theology of conversion. Its peculiar task is to show how faith in Jesus is possible, to reproduce on the level of discourse the movement that takes place in life when one comes to believe. Fundamental theology deals with the believer as a convert, and with human beings in general as potential converts. As such, it is the theology of dialogue between Christians and nonbelievers and the theology of communication between the human realm of words in general and the Christian realm of faith-words.

The distinction between dogmatic theology and fundamental theology, which distinction had its moment of glory among Catholics some fifteen or twenty years ago, has now more or less fallen into oblivion. Its falling out of favor was undoubtedly abetted to some extent by the neo-orthodox position in Protestantism, and by Karl Barth in particular. Barth, for example, regarded the realm of faith and that of nonbelief as two isolated, incommunicado worlds. He and others who felt this way absolved themselves from the task of fashioning a theology of conversion and abandoned the whole issue of the grounding for theology and its discourse (188:154–98). Thus the distinction between dogmatic theology and fundamental theology has faded, the former benefiting at the expense of the latter. People have abandoned not only the distinction but also fundamental theology itself. And so they have abandoned the theological task of grounding and validating the faith and of commenting on the genesis of faith, on conversion. More recent theology reasons along the lines of dogmatic theology. This is true of much political theology too, as we shall see. It presupposes faith in Christ, the value of the biblical tradition, and the truth of church dogma. It fails to take note of the fact that the great theological problem of our day does not concern the consequences of such a faith, a tradition, or a dogma, but rather its presuppositions and the very possibility of holding the Christian outlook.

The fact is that today the distinction between dogmatic theology and fundamental theology does seem to be outmoded, but in just the opposite sense from the one just described. It is outmoded because dogmatic theology seems to have lost all meaningfulness and to have become impossible (188). Today no serious theology can any longer be based on the presupposition of a well consolidated faith. Dogmatic theology can have meaning and validity only insofar as it is used within the Christian community itself; even there it offers little help to believers who ask radical questions about their faith. Rigorously dogmatic discourse is of little use except for very sheltered Christians who have little dealings with the world outside. It is completely useless to believers with the slightest sense of self-criticism, for dialogue with non-Christians, and for any process of evangelization that truly contains a summons to conversion rather than presupposing such a conversion at the start.

But political theology often presents itself in a manner that is clearly and openly dogmatic. It seems to justify the remarks of one of its most acidic critics, Robert Spaemann, who has this to say about its relevance for political action in the context of Catholicism: "The theology that inspires the prayer of a hermit monk on Mount Athos would suffice equally well" (398:494). Political theology, in short, is a theology of the political consequences of faith and dogma, but that dogma might equally well serve to prompt a revolution as to move one to retire to Mount Athos. It assumes that faith and dogmas are there to begin with, existing on their own account and solidly grounded in some way prior to any discourse on the part of political theology. And so we are faced with one of two alternatives, as we noted earlier (see chapter 4, section 10): Either political theology presupposes some prior theological validation of the faith not framed in political terms; or else the whole question of faith's grounding and validity is left hanging in the air, as it is in neo-orthodox Protestant theology.

The orthodox, dogmatic outlook is very closely bound up with a religious and mystical focus on the Christian faith. So long as one imagines the faith as a specific way of perceiving the world or transcendence, and so long as one also considers it a gift that human beings happen upon in some miraculous fashion, one is also bound to view the faith as a definite and well defined datum with an inherited self-consistency and grandeur of its own that sets it apart from other human realities and makes it an independent point of departure. René García, for example, remarks that the faith is "something which exceeds the scientific realm, which we receive as a gift and know not why we hold it" (204:87). Though he says that in a text that is laced with Marxian quotes and with harsh criticisms of papal social doctrine, the fact remains that with such a statement he has laid a solid foundation for wielding that faith in a dogmatic manner.

If we disregard the reason for faith, if it constitutes a pure datum or happening and remains outside all scientific investigation, then it is only logical that faith should give rise to a discourse that takes the form of a dogma asserted for its own sake, based on its own presuppositions, and wholly without regard for anything outside itself. The fact that this dogma may then be interpreted in political terms and applied in a revolutionary way does not erase the fact that one has proceeded in dogmatic terms in formulating it to begin with. Political praxis then serves as the intermediary for the consequences of dogma, but not for the genesis of faith.

Catholic theologians in particular have a tendency to elaborate a political theology that is viewed as an extension and amplification of dogmatic theology to the political realm. And the fundamental propositions of that dogmatic theology are considered to be already established at the start, before one engages in a political interpretation of the gospel. Chenu, for example, has this to say: "The incarnation of Christ continues in political society" (139:88). That sort of statement is quite characteristic of the dogmatic stance, which presupposes the truth of Christianity and then attempts to explore its political repercussions.

Here again the work of Gutiérrez offers us the clearest example. It operates wholly and always within the categories of dogmatic theology. It never has any doubt about the solid grounding of Catholic dogma. It does not call this dogma into question or raise any doubts about its credibility. It does not advert to the importance of making that dogma credible to those who do not share it, or even to those Catholics whose faith is presently undergoing re-examination, self-criticism, or deliberate judgment. He takes as a firm and solid starting point the "universal lordship of Christ" (230:107), and history as finalized in Christ (230:200). At every point his central affirmations are dogmatic. They are founded solely and exclusively on the authority of dogma, without the slightest trace of validation, legitimation, or discussion as to the conditions that might make them feasible.

Gutiérrez tells us that "in Christ and through the Spirit, the process of liberation as a whole attains its full and complete sense" (230:240). Such statements pervade his work, making it useful and profitable only for convinced Christians. His statements are purely dogmatic, having no connection at all with the sociopolitical reality that should verify them. If one does not have any clear picture of a history finalized by Christ, if one does not agree to the fact of Christ's universal lordship, then it will be very difficult if not impossible to find an acceptable or credible sense in Gutiérrez's theology of liberation. For it takes for granted from the start the very thing that it should try to demonstrate: that history has something to do with Jesus Christ.

Such a theology serves very limited functions, and only within the community of those who are already Christians. To speak in concrete terms, it helps to sensitize Christians to politics, or to provoke a conversion in them through a deepening of their faith. But it makes no contribution at all to the proclamation of the faith to the outside world, to human beings whose passion for political alterations has invalidated the gospel message. In the last analysis the function of such a theology is purely intramural; it is confined within the walls of the church.

In this respect there is real sense to Galilea's restrictive characterization of liberation theology as a critique of "the activity of the church in Latin America" (198). But that very same characterization clearly moves liberation theology back toward being a formulation for a Christendom church rather than for a mission church, at least in the models provided by such people as Gutiérrez, Galilea, and Comblin. Put more concretely, any such liberation theology would be a critique of the established church peculiar to Christendom, a church in which the ecclesiastical hierarchy, Christian institutions, and the sacred would still possess political power; it would not be a positive analysis of how to proclaim the gospel message in the wasteland of a non-Christian society or a society in the process of dechristianization.

The motives put foward by Latin American theologians for evading to some extent the fundamental task of validating the faith vis-à-vis the outside world are understandable though not convincing. The burning issue in Latin America is not the problem of unbelief so much as it is the problem of the historical inoperativeness of Christianity and, worse still, its culpable complicity with oppressive structures. It is the latter issues that raise the primary challenge which the theologian must face. Defending the Latin American position against the formulation of the problem that prevails in most current theology (including my own in this book), Gutiérrez puts it felicitously in the following remark:

A good portion of contemporary theology seems to have started off from the challenge laid down by the *nonbeliever*. The nonbeliever calls our religious world into question and demands thoroughgoing purification and renewal. . . . But on a continent like Latin America the challenge does not come first and foremost from the nonbeliever but from the *nonhuman* human being, the human person whom the existing social order does not recognize as such. It comes from the poor, the exploited, the people who are legally and systematically stripped of their existence as humans, the people who are scarcely aware of the fact that they are human beings. This nonhuman being calls into question not so much our religious world as our economic, social, political, and cultural world (228:366).

Thus, in his view, the one to whom liberation theology is addressed is not the believer (addressed by dogmatic theology) nor the nonbeliever (addressed by fundamental theology); at bottom it is addressed to the human being as such. The basic question at issue in it is humanity versus inhumanity.

That is an enlightening remark, not only in terms of the Latin American context but also in terms of any theology that aspires to credibility. The question of humanity or inhumanity comes before the question of belief or unbelief in theology. Faith itself must be understood and practiced in terms of what it means for the humanness of human beings. But that leaves us with one important detail that needs stressing: i.e., the humanness of the human being, as such, does not constitute a theological question. Thus, while one may have to respond to the challenge laid down by the nonhuman human being in Latin America, there is no reason why the response has to be a theological one—even though this nonhuman being may question, among other things, the religious world of colonial Christianity.

One must put forward some justification for introducing a theological perspective in one's attempt to meet the challenge laid down. In short, we come back once again to the need for a theological discourse that does not start out presupposing an interlocutor who is already Christian. We come back once again to the need for a discourse on the level of fundamental theology. Gutiérrez's observation about liberation theology being addressed to the nonhuman being rather than to the nonbeliever is illuminating; but it merely postpones the moment for theoretical validation of the faith rather than eliminating it.

Some Latin American theologians seem to assume that

the dimming of faith in God throughout the course of the modern age is a variable that somehow is dependent on the contemporary nullification of the human being. This historical interpretation is not original to Latin Americans, going back some way in the Christian thinking of Europe. At the very least it goes back to Berdyaev. Dussel proposes it today as the whole key to what has happened in modern religious history as well as in the history of colonial conquest: "God is not dead. It is his epiphany who has been assassinated: the Indian, the African, and Asian. Hence God can no longer manifest himself" (164:347). In order for the modern age to be able to echo Nietzsche's refrain that God is dead, "it was first necessary to kill his epiphany: the Indian, the African, and the Asian" (164:336).

Perhaps that is so. Certainly God cannot be affirmed, and in fact is not affirmed, where the human being is denied. The death of the human being is the death of God. But in some versions at least, Latin American theology goes a step beyond this. It seems to presume that the reaffirmation of human beings and their humanity will logically or even infallibly include the resurrection of God. Assuming that, the theologian certainly could dispense with the task of justifying the faith and limit his attention to the liberation of the human being. But such an assumption seems to be quite gratuitous, all the more so since the practical movements for human liberation in our day have generally not produced any renewed divine epiphany.

Restoring their humanity to the Indian, the African, and the Asian is a task that cannot be postponed. Or, to put it better, it is urgent that they themselves win back their humanity. But there is no clear-cut evidence or indication that this task has obvious theological or epiphanic repercussions. And so we are led to two basic conclusions here: (1) Theology is not the most urgent task facing us; (2) once the urgent task is carried out, we are still left with the specifically theological task of discovering and revealing the divinity of God in the humanity of the human being. Thus, by a circuitous route we are brought back once again to the fundamental theology for which the Latin Americans have shown too little concern, and in the absence of which their theology often evinces shockingly dogmatic features.

A similar sort of criticism must be levelled at Moltmann's theology of hope (312). It, too, is a dogmatic theology —grounded not on ecclesiastical dogma but on biblical tradition. Moltmann takes for granted the biblical faith without once considering the fact that it is this very faith that is being called into question today. At the present time the Bible has lost its age-old credibility; it can no longer be wielded as a doctrinal authority. Occasionally Moltmann touches upon the issue, asking why "one is obliged to heed, believe, and proclaim these texts (meaning the biblical ones)" (309:219). But his response is quite unsatisfactory in the last analysis, for it is not worked out at all and it remains on the precarious level of rhetoric: "When confronted with certain biblical texts that trace out an objective horizon on which man can see projected all the misery of his age as well as the new possibilities for a God-oriented future, impartial historical vision is transformed into passionate interest and is captivated by the future" (309:232).

But we need not place too much stress on this criticism of Moltmann, however, for in subsequent writings (310) he seems to have progressed on this matter. He now seems to pay greater attention to the practical verification of the faith, deriving that validation from praxis itself. To all appearances at least, he seems to have abandoned his earlier positivism and dogmatism based on the Bible.

Other authors have realized that political theology has to do with the meaningfulness and credibility of Christianity—with fundamental theology, in other words. Claude Geffré, for example, includes political theology under the current versions of fundamental theology. Commenting on Metz's work, he remarks that "the specific responsibility of any fundamental theology would be to explicitate the future dimension and sociopolitical orientation of Christianity" (206:355). In my opinion this view of the matter brings out a basic ground-laying task that is not made explicit enough in Metz's own theology, and it is at bottom correct. The political theology of Metz and others does not explicitly propose to fashion a fundamental theology, but it does contain many elements that might validly serve toward that end.

What is lamentable is the fact that political theology has not methodically maintained a focus centered around fundamental theology and its work of grounding. Current political theology seeks to respond to the *zoon politikon* of our day, to human beings who are fully living out the political consciousness that typifies the modern age. For that very reason it should take note of the fact that in the eyes of these modern human beings the faith lacks meaning and its possible meaningfulness must be demonstrated. The social, economic, and political analysis undertaken in the framework of Marxist theory tends to rule out faith in Jesus. In such circumstances a dogmatic theology, a theology that starts out assuming faith in Jesus and does not even advert to the fact that the possibility of such a faith is the very thing at issue, is wholly ineffective and irrelevant.

The question today is not whether the Incarnation does or does not have a political scope, or whether the universal lordship of Christ extends into civil society. If there really was an Incarnation and if Jesus really is the universal Lord, then obviously his mystery reaches into politics. But the question is whether there really was an Incarnation. At the very start that issue must be clarified and grounded in terms of a political interpretation.

To carry out its function, indeed to carry out any function at all, political theology must go right down to the roots and ask whether it itself and faith are possible. It must show how conversion to the faith is possible at all, how the gospel takes on meaning for people today, and why it is Jesus rather than someone else who merits our loyalty and adhesions even now. That was the task of fundamental theology in the past. But if we assume, as all indications suggest we should, that dogmatics in general is becoming more and more untenable, then it is now the task of theology as such. In short, it is the task of any discourse that seeks to be critical rather than merely rhetorical.

In the area of grounding or legitimation, political theology must tackle such basic questions as these: Does social theory "diminish" the religious outlook? Is faith ultimately a crazy foreign body secreted by certain social and economic relationships? Theology must concern itself with the task of grounding and legitimating the faith. It can never regard the validity and legitimacy of the Christian stance as established. In the concrete, then, this means that political theology must concern itself with this validation and legitimation in the face of efforts by social theory and revolutionary praxis to invalidate the Christian stance. Thus political theology must opt for the methodology and approach of fundamental theology rather than those of dogmatic theology.

7. RESTORATION OF THE SACRED?

An important specification of theology has to do with its relationship to the realm of the sacred. Does political theology seek to effect the re-entry of the sacred into society, or does it assume that the process of desacralization is irreversible? Is it a sacralized theology or a secular theology? If the first alternative is correct, then political theology would be a religiously conservative effort to maintain or rehabilitate the sacred; and it would run directly counter to recent theology of a secular and radical cast. Only if the second alternative is true in each case noted above will political theology be able to reconcile itself with the social process of secularization and whatever theology has taken that process seriously.

In this case the camps are clearly marked off. One brand of political theology is sacralizing; the other is secularizing. Secularization here should be taken to mean the process whereby modern society has extricated itself from, or still is extricating itself from, content that has traditionally been regarded as religious. Secularization is not concerned with some general idea of the essence of religion; it is concerned with the concrete content that has made up the historical religions in the past.

One's judgment about the current process of secularization, therefore, does not prejudge the question as to whether there might possibly be new forms or versions of something that could be conceptualized under the rubric of "religiosity."It does not deny that in the future various religious traditions might be capable of shifting to another key, that in the future the structure and functioning of the religious element might be charged very differently than they are today. Of itself, the concept of secularization simply alludes to the waning of the functions that religious contents traditionally performed in society.

More specifically, the concept of secularization refers to the fate of the traditional patrimony of Christianity in Western culture. Insofar as they are historical phenomena, religions can be viewed as systems of myths, symbols, and beliefs having to do with some sacred or transcendent reality, with some superhuman presence which arouses certain attitudes of reverence in human beings that are crystallized in rites and socially relevant institutions. Historical Christianity is such a system. From a phenomenological standpoint it does not present us with any differentiating traits that would mark it off as the perfect or essential religion, infinitely superior to all others. Now the point is that the process of secularization implies the increasing social irrelevance of the myths, symbols, and beliefs, of the sense of transcendence, and of the rites and institutions associated with Christian historical tradition. While secularized society may indeed continue to submit to symbols, beliefs, rites, and even myths, it no longer derives them from the realm of traditional Christianity (182:41–50). What we now want to consider specifically here is the way in which various political theologies view the destiny of Christian contents in modern society.

In this connection we do well to recall that the political theology of a bygone day was openly sacralizing and restorative. One of the last surviving representatives of that theology, Jean Daniélou, has defended the thesis that "religion as such is an integral part of the temporal common good" (144:18), that "a city where there are no churches alongside its factories is an inhuman city" (144:26), and that "God himself is part of civilization" (144:85). In general, the whole idea of Christendom was bound up with the notion of a sacred history; it assumed that there was some sort of direct presence of the sacred in time.

This particular tradition—i.e., political theology as something designed to rehabilitate the sacred—is particularly evident in Gutiérrez's theology of liberation. He does not hide his intentions in this respect. He is out to give a response to the theology of the death of God and to what he calls "pre-Marxist" theology (230:288). Indeed he also wants to respond to the whole theology of secularization. Looking at the theology of Metz, Gutiérrez asserts that his political theology seems to assume the existence of a secularized world and the privatization of faith, without subjecting those assumptions to critical examination. To prove to Metz that such is not the case, Gutiérrez points to Latin America where Christianity and the churches are still operating in favor of the established power structure (230:296).

Without overlooking the fact that the social context of the two authors in question is different, I still think we can say that we are moving towards a generalized situation such as that assumed by Metz. It is not Metz but Gutiérrez who shows a lack of critical sense here. Neither Metz nor anyone else assumes that secularization has been achieved on a worldwide basis as yet. What he and others take for granted is the existence of an irreversible process in that direction. What is more, Gutiérrez seems to fuse the phenomenon of societal secularization with that of the privatization of faith, when in fact the latter is only one aspect or interpretation of the former. Finally, the hastiness with which Gutiérrez tries to slip away from the theology of the death of God makes it only too clear that he has not seriously examined the problems raised by that theology. They are very real problems, even though one may have doubts about the solutions offered by that theology. To describe it as a "pre-Marxist" theology suggests somehow that God is brought back to life in the thinking of Marx himself.

Quite aside from its attack on both the theology of secularization and secular theology in general, the work of Gutiérrez is full of religious vestiges and reminiscences. For him the only credible God is the God of the mystics (230:270), and one cannot talk about a profane world in any real sense (230:196). In order to overcome the older dualism between human history and salvation history, he resorts to an already overused repertory of expressions derived from Teilhard de Chardin. He talks about the "Christified portion of the world" (230:334) and a "Christo-finalized history." Commenting on Teilhard de Chardin, he refers to a lively dialectical relationship "between a world that is profane only insofar as it is not perceived to be divine and a supernatural reality that seeks to assume it, ransom it, consecrate and divinize it" (230:200–1). Thus the old theme of the "consecration of the world" and all its strains reappear in Gutiérrez's work, though it seemed more at home in the theology of Christendom. His theology of liberation remains bound to the concept of the Christian resacralization of society. The dualism between the profane and the sacred disappears, but only because the sacred is regarded as coextensive with all of reality, as a transcendental of being itself.

In all of this Gutiérrez displays a serious error in perspective. If I am not mistaken, his mistake stems from his belief that the principal theological problem today is to get beyond the old model of the distinction of planes: natural versus supernatural, world versus faith. Gutiérrez invests all his effort in reacting against a theology based on any such distinction (230:93–109), and to that extent he does well. But we must remember that particular task had already been carried out by such people as Teilhard de Chardin and others of his generation. And so in Gutiérrez's case the end result is clear insofar as theology is concerned —leaving aside the result insofar as political options are concerned, Gutiérrez does not advance a single step beyond Teilhard de Chardin. What Teilhard de Chardin had worked out in abstract, idealistic terms is concretely applied by Gutiérrez to the political context of Latin America.

Gutiérrez's case is instructive. It shows us that a theology can be pertinent and relevant to its day only when it has engaged in serious dialogue with all earlier theologies, particularly those closest to it in time. Alas, Gutiérrez dialogues seriously with only one theology, an outmoded dualistic theology no less; and he does not pay enough attention to more contemporary critical theologies ranging from the demythologizing theology of Bultmann to that of Robinson and other more radical theologians.

The consequences of not choosing one's interlocutor well could have been foreseen and expected. If one confronts a dualistic theology such as that which was being taught around 1920, and that is the phantom with which Gutiérrez shadowboxes, the logical reaction will be a theology of Teilhard de Chardin's type. That is precisely what we find in Gutiérrez. In my opinion he deserves the reproach that is generally directed against Shaull: i.e., that he combines social progressivism with theological conservatism. This reproach, I would repeat, applies to his written work, which is freighted with serious ambiguities and silences that do not always seem to correspond to the real thinking and intentions of their author. However that may be, the reader seems constrained to interpret his written words along the lines I have indicated.

Gutiérrez's theology of liberation is a leftist orthodoxy. It makes a subversive application of a dogmatics that remains at bottom little altered and quite traditional. That is much the same as what Thomas Münzer did back in the sixteenth century. Indeed that earlier figure casts his shadow over a broad segment of current theology, e.g., Gutiérrez, all of it being a theology of subversive orthodoxy.

My observations on the work of Gutiérrez in these pages are made in the spirit of friendly criticism. They are meant to awaken his own sense of self-criticism and spur him on to overcome the ambiguities in his work. But for the most part they also apply to the Latin American theology of liberation in general. It is not just that Latin American theologians and sociologists point out that the process of secularization has not yet made much headway, if any, on their continent (196:153); they also go on to set up their political theology in opposition to any theology of secularization. In his book dealing with religion and revolution in Latin America, Giovanni Gozzer starts off with this astonishing assertion: "Our age is characterized by two major phenomena. The first is the growing importance that the religious factor is assuming in the life of peoples. The second . . . " (223:9). He thereby interprets the entry of Christians into politics as the recuperation of the importance of the religious and the sacred. This view is expressed even more clearly by Joseph Comblin, who has set down roots in South America though he was born in Europe. Comblin, as well, confuses the secularization of society with the privatization of faith. His view is that secularization means "the inability of the church to exert a significant influence on society" (118:38), and that the theology of secularization is based on an acceptance of modern bourgeois society (118:36 and 39). Quite logically, therefore, he concludes that the basic theological problem is to "fight desperately against all forms of secularization" (120:391). Comblin appeals to "popular religion in Latin America" as a protest against poverty and wretchedness, somehow thinking that he is thereby making a valid criticism of the theology of secularization. He takes it for granted that a populist religion of that sort can be transformed into a "superior religion" through the right sort of evangelization (118:47–50).

The culmination in this effort to vindicate the realm of religion in Latin America is the proposal to present liberation as a synthesis of political action and mystical contemplation (197:313). The traditional language of mysticism is mobilized to describe the political praxis of the activist, so that this praxis is automatically resacralized. Expressions such as "experience of God" and "experimental encounter with God" (197:318) are framed within a revolutionary horizon of social and political liberation; but in the realm of critical theory that does not suffice to mute their obvious pre-Kantian ring. On the level of critical praxis such expressions ultimately hearken back to the old sacralist attempt to confirm and consecrate human political decisions by stamping them with the seal of divinity.

The option for a secular theology here and now in Europe does not overlook the persistence of a popular-level Christianity in Latin America and other areas. Nor does it overlook the fact that populist Christianity can have its own specific pastoral approach that would enable it to acquire a critical awareness of both itself and society. One can agree fully that popular religiosity be given a pastoral approach that would "discover and identify those liberation values that are operative in the oppressed sectors of our society, though often expressed in ambiguous sacral gestures, and then develop and enrich them in the critical light of the gospel message interpreted in historical terms" (93:146). One can also agree with Galilea when he describes such a pastoral effort as a process of "accompanying the further development of the faith values enshrined in populist Catholicism so as to give them their full liberative dimension" (196:157).

The problem is that one is forced to suspect that any such transformation of populist Christianity, whereby it is corrected in the critical light of the gospel and given a fuller liberative capability in the social realm, will at the same time entail its desacralization and secularization. Galilea himself opens the way for such a conclusion when he notes that in Latin America "secularization and politicization seem to go hand in hand" (196:153–54). To the extent that the process of secularization does seem to be linked up with political awareness in Latin America, there is solid ground for a Latin American theology of the secular that would differ in cast from European theologies of secularization (320: 195–96). Thus the mere existence of populist strains of religiosity in no way authorizes a theology whose symbols and idiom would be resacralizing. For the only conceivable pastoral approach to those strains today would seem to entail objectives that would include desacralization and a shift from sacral religion to a secular faith.

Any *apologia* for populist religion as such would constitute a very weak defense of Christianity, even though populist religion might be viewed as a religion embodying the protest of the people. When the people's misery is dissipated, the religious protest will dissipate too, as is happening in Europe. Moreover, one cannot validly designate secularization as a product of bourgeois society, for the same process is proceeding apace in socialist countries, even in those which might well serve as the most direct model for Latin American liberation: e.g., China, Yugoslavia, and Cuba. Finally, we must assert that secularization does not come down to any lack of relevance or social import for the faith. The whole question of the irrelevance of the church and of Christianity, which is also the subject of much study on the part of sociologists of religion (266), is not to be confused with the question of secularization. At most the former would constitute only one possible aspect or interpretation of the latter. In a secularized society the faith does lose a portion of its age-old relevance; it loses its sacralizing relevance. But it does not necessarily lose all its relevance.

Existential theology did indeed accept the social irrelevance of the faith. In its view the privatization of Christianity went hand in hand with the secularization of society. By contrast current political theology takes as its specific theme the political and social relevance of the gospel message. It is no accident that this notion of relevance is shared by theologians as different as Rahner (347), Pannenberg (333:246), Moltmann (310:71), and Sölle (396:47 and 93).

In the eyes of current theology, a socially irrelevant faith is equivalent to no faith at all. Commenting on the purely private religion of Gogarten and Bultmann, Moltmann describes it as "socially irrelevant in the strict sense of the term, since it lives in a no man's land." And he goes on to say: "The faith decision of this subjective religion is no longer even capable of evoking the opposite option of unbelief, since it has ceased to be a ground for contradiction in social reality" (309:362). To put it in other words, an irrelevant faith does not differ significantly from unbelief. In that sense we can say that today social relevance appears to be inherent in Christianity itself—without in any way fostering a restoration of the sacred.

It is precisely here that we come to a second formulation of political theology. This formulation sees political theology as a theology that deals with the secular, social relevance of the Christian faith rather than with its religious relevance; and it also sees the Christian faith as secularized.

8. THE SECULAR ACCEPTED

In reality theologians are not in a position to choose between a theology of the sacred and a theology of the secular. For secularity is given to them by society itself. One cannot evade it unless one chooses to flee to a monastery or to some country where the sacred still holds sway. Strictly speaking, there is no theological decision for secularization on the one hand or resacralization on the other. In this case the call has been made for the theologians even before they begin to theologize.

In many countries secularity is a fact prior to theological reflection and to any political theology. What is more, in its current form political theology presupposes that very fact. Without this fact political theology today would be a theology of Christendom, a theology dealing with the direct social relevance of the Christian religion and its sacralizing influence. Viewed aright, secularized Christianity and current political theology go hand in hand. Only a Christianity that refuses to see itself primarily as a religious fact is capable of adopting that basic reference to praxis that lies at the root of current political theology. And this theology in turn, insofar as it presupposes a dialectical anthropology, compels one to a secularization of Christianity.

These theses are present, at least tacitly, in almost all Protestant theology, be it the theology of hope or the theology of revolution. Protestant theologians usually do not question the fact and the current irreversibility of the secularization process. The decisive point here is not whether they expressly develop a theology of secularization or not. The so-called theology of secularization (or theology of the secular) is really only *one* of the possible forms of theology in a desacralized society, and it may not be the most fortunate one. The decisive thing, however, is that they adopt a secularized idiom and a secularized formulation of the issues. In this respect there is no difference between Cox and other theologians who do not celebrate secular society but take it as a basic presupposition.

On the Catholic side J.B. Metz points out that "the theological theses of secularization and political theology do not erase each other; rather, they are mutually complementary and corrective" (301:271). Again in the context of political theology, Cardonnel says that faith "is not a religious phenomenon; concretely it is taking cognizance of the elements necessary for liberation" (99:236). It is Hervé Chaigne, however, who has most staunchly and explicitly upheld the correlation between "a radical politicization of the faith" and a "secularized Christianity." To gauge secularization is the same as "situating God and his Christ in the dialectical and tragic movement of history" (135: 93–95). Secular Christianity means a Christianity "in direct contact with the political and economic realities of life." The secular status of Christianity corresponds to "the fact that it is active in a world undergoing dialectical development." The future and fate of that faith will ultimately "be played out on the level of the praxis of Christians in the world" (135:114–15).

Of course there is still another possibility. We could have a secularized faith that would abandon the world to reason and not aspire to any political relevance. Why must the faith necessarily have public, social, and civil relevance? Would it not be possible to adopt the thesis of the older existential theology, which maintained that Christianity had no political relevance, and reframe it in the context of a political theology? This position is presented by Rudolf Weth as a modern interpretation of Luther's teaching about the two kingdoms:

The revolutionary aspect consists in a twofold coming of age, a sense of responsibility for that which the Reformation sets free. The first coming of age, or maturing, is with respect to God. One accepts and takes to oneself God and his word, and is responsible before God. It is a revolutionary transcending of everything mundane, an uprooting from the past and present, a liberation from all the mediating factors in one's relationship with God that are embodied in religious, hierarchical, and political authorities. On the other side of the coin there is a corresponding coming of age with respect to the world. For insofar as God comes to be God for the believer, so the world comes to be world. When one gives to God what is God's, then the world is dedivinized, de-ideologized, and stripped of its magic aura. It becomes a truly secular world, which must respond to reason rather than to God. This twofold coming of age can be described as follows: To the *sola fide* of the Reformation there corresponds a *sola ratione* which is equally of the Reformation (421:87).

This passage by Weth, which is quite typical of Protestant theology of secularization, might seem to fall into the God-world dualism so often criticized by modern Catholic theologians. It might also seem to cause the faith to slip into irrelevance insofar as it denies it any mediating factors. Weth's conceptual scheme is very different from that of Chaigne. Yet, surface appearances to the contrary, one might well suggest that Weth is much closer to Chaigne and other interpreters of the political relevance of the faith than to the existential theologians and their notion of a socially irrelevant faith. To begin with, if *sola fide* and a relationship to God are necessary preconditions for *sola ratione* and a relationship to the world, then the dualism is already overcome in some manner. Moreover, if we view things from Chaigne's standpoint, we can say that a secularized world would undoubtedly force those dealing with it to adhere closely to reason. Weth puts us on our guard against a danger that is inherent in every political theology: i.e., the danger of letting the faith play the role of just another datum or criterion among the judgmental factors used in analyzing the world and society and people's transforming praxis. Weth offers us a severe reminder that social reality must be confronted with the instruments of reason and without the interjection of alien elements stemming from some alleged higher knowledge based on some revelation or religious tradition. His austere focus, despite its possible dualistic cast, paves the way for us to face one final question: Is political theology a positive theology or not?

9. THEOLOGY AS NEGATIVE, CRITICAL, AND SYMBOLIC

The final set of alternatives to be spelled out can be put in the form of two questions: Is political theology going to configure itself as a positive discourse, as one which adopts the traditional dogmas of Christianity and considers them to be authentic knowledge? Or will it view itself as a negative, critical, and at best symbolic idiom or discourse? To keep to the distinction that I made earlier in this chapter (see section 3), I would point out that here I am not talking about theology as a second-stage discourse. I have already commented on its scientific and critical status, while stressing that its object is not God. But here I am talking specifically about theology as direct and immediate expression of the faith, as theologal language that utters statements that apply directly and immediately to God. That is what I mean by "theology" in this section, and I shall use the shorthand term for the sake of convenience and also because it is common usage. So our question here is whether this "theology" entails any positive knowledge or not.

We have considered this problem from different angles in the preceding pages of this book. Here we shall try to bring together the conclusions we reached earlier and to spell out clearly the two opposing stances.

On one side we find all those theologians who continue to be preoccupied and bound up with orthodoxy. As they see it, current political theology of whatever stamp does not alter one iota the traditional pronouncements of dogmatics. Theology's quest for meaning does not in any way change the fact that it is the magisterium that ultimately pronounces the "authoritative affirmation" (366:165). This stance is well represented by Comblin. Indeed it must be said in passing that he offers us a fine example of how programmatic statements of principle can be belied by one's actual way of theologizing. Comblin reiterates a thesis that we have already encountered in the theologians of revolution (see chapter 5, section 4): "A theology of revolution calls first and foremost for a revolution in theology" (121:104). But Comblin's reiteration is purely mechanical, and he has not really assimilated the point. It is rendered laughable by the conservative theology that he practices. He starts right off assuring the reader that the nonreligious interpretation of the New Testament changes nothing in the traditional content of Christian doctrine; this in itself raises suspicions about his work. But then he adds: "Nor does liberation theology alter the traditional content of biblical revelation. It does not threaten God, Christ, the church, the sacraments, prayer, dogmas, moral theology, or ecclesiastical institutions. Rather, it has to do with understanding the traditional data of revelation" (119:10).

In this statement by Comblin we find all the elements of a positive and positivist theology, a theology characterized by a strict adherence to divine revelation as a complex of data. I dedicated an earlier volume wholly to an analysis and critique of such a theology (190). In such a work as that of Comblin, the profession of orthodoxy takes on a plaintive tone and ends up in a positivism that is not only theological in general but eccesiastical in particular. We must make a revolution, but ecclesiastical institutions are not going to be touched. Is it then possible to change everything, except the essential church? This particular leftist orthodoxy would suggest that it is. Here social criticism goes hand in hand with theological positivism, political liberation with ecclesiastical conformism.

In principle one might well assume that all Catholic theology, staunchly loyal to orthodoxy, would take this road. To be sure, Catholic theologians are more prone to viewing political theology as nothing more than an amplification of a perduring and age-old dogmatics whose meaning, truth, and validity will continue to remain beyond doubt. But this propensity is not shared by all Catholic theologians. Here again we must bring up Hervé Chaigne, who urges us to disentangle ourselves "from dogmatic minutiae and turn to the great earthly goal." His various points of view presuppose a cancellation of dogmatics:

> The consequences of such a turn in theological perspective are particularly serious for everything having to do with the traditional dogmatic *corpus* of Christianity. . . . Though in substance it may remain the same, the *Credo* will be read and comprehended in a radically different manner. . . . The essential aspect will no longer be played out in the hereafter, where the objects of faith come together in harmony; it will be played out here below, in terms of the dialectical progression of individuals and groups. We shall see the disappearance of our "beliefs," of those propositions and "happenings" in the hereafter in which it was meritorious to believe—to the benefit of faith, a concrete attitude of personal union (135:112–13).

Despite Comblin's assertion to the contrary, strict adherence to dogmatic orthodoxy cannot be attributed to all theology of liberation. Assmann strenuously rejects all "fundamentalist naiveté" involving nothing more than a return to the sources. He twice quotes a pungent remark by an activist Christian, each time in a slightly different form: "The Bible? The Bible does not exist. The only Bible that exists is the sociological Bible of what appears here as Christian!" (59:48); "The Bible? I know of only one Bible; the sociological Bible of facts and events here. Everything else is an abstraction" (59:174). Though Assmann himself has some reservations about this straightforward statement, his allusion to it clearly rules out the dogmatic conception of some biblical deposit that is to be preserved. For him it is the concrete situation, historical praxis here and now, that constitutes the "foremost theological locus of reference" (57:158).

From another standpoint Juan Luis Segundo notes how illusory it is to imagine that a Christianity and a theology oriented toward liberation can work "with the same concept of God, sin, sacrament, and church membership that was part of a church centered around the quest for extraterrestrial salvation" (390:204). He then goes on to criticize the traditional notion of sacrament as one that posited an "otherworldly and ahistorical efficacy" (390:206–7). His whole critique makes clear that liberation theology does indeed "threaten" the sacraments, dogmas, and ecclesiastical institutions far more seriously than Comblin would have us believe. In its more radical formulations it, too, points us toward a profound and thoroughgoing reconsideration of orthodoxy and dogmatics.

Over against a dogmatic theology stands a theology that knows that it does not know, a theology that does not contribute any knowledge, in the strict sense of that word, about God or about the world. Its only contribution is to say no to the closing in of the world, society, and history upon themselves; and it attempts to express this no in symbols. Remember, once again, that we are talking here about theology as direct theologal language, as first-stage expression of the faith. This theology can be described as negative, critico-prophetic, and symbolic, and these three characteristics are interrelated.

First of all, it is a negative theology. In other words, it is a theology consciously aware of its non-knowing. It does not possess knowledge data of a human or superhuman kind, about mundane things or otherworldly realities. Theology is a language that is inwardly self-denying and self-denied, and political theology is no exception. Insofar as the future of history is concerned, Christian faith possesses no knowledge about it (see chapter 6, section7). Nor does it possess any knowledge about that other absolute future labelled "advent" by some, whose fulfillment comes about solely through the grace of God. Christian theology of the future, then, is a negative theology in the last analysis. And the same holds true for the other temporal dimensions of political theology. To be specific again, it does not possess any theoretical and truly cognitive concepts concerning the present (see chapter 5, sections 14 and 17).

Theology as theologal language could resemble science or strict knowledge in past days because at the time it brought together the conditions that were attributed to scientific knowledge. The distinction between what is and what is not knowledge is not one whose limits are fixed once and for all; it is a distinction in history, which changes with time and is dependent on factors now studied by the sociology of knowledge. At the present time theology, as a language that claims to speak about God, falls on the side of non-knowledge. The features of theological language do not measure up to the currently prevailing features of language in real science and knowledge. Faced with that fact, we cannot get very far by saying that the modern-day notion of knowledge should be expanded to make room for knowledge of God. Such statements are only for internal consumption by Christians; they have no real impact on the societal or cultural level. Protest against the fact that theology has been left outside the boundaries of contemporary knowledge does not in any way alter the fact itself. Indeed taking cognizance of that fact constrains us to adopt a negative theology.

Of the Catholics, Schillebeeckx is on the right track when he alludes to the possibility of a negative political theology: "Negative theology with regard to speculative matters shows us the way towards a negative theology with regard to practical matters" (379:427). On this point he joins Metz, who tells us that "Christian eschatology is not an omniscient ideology about the future but a negative theology about the future" (299:153). Metz also notes that "faith in the promise must always entail a negative theology of the future" (303:164).

Here we are talking about negative theology in the strictest and most rigorous sense of the term, in a sense that would also leave traditional theism behind, as various Protestant theologians have pointed out. Rudolf Weth has noted that if the theology of revolution really wants to continue being theology, "it must get beyond the modern alternatives of theism and atheism" (421:93). We can find the same invitation to get beyond those alternatives in the work of Moltmann (309:348) and others (109:51). But only a strictly negative theology is capable of doing that, of situating itself beyond the confines of traditional atheism and belief.

It must be stressed here that such a negative theology continues to be theology. It is not atheism or agnosticism in disguise. It is theology to the extent that it stands opposed to any closing of the world, history, or society in on themselves. It is its opposition to any form of such closing, both in the realm of realities and the realm of mental representations, that constitutes it as theology. To be specific, political theology is theology insofar as it says no to the closing of the political realm in upon itself, to any attempt to explain human beings finally and completely in terms of the *polis.* This activity of theology, in which it says no to the self-closure of the political realm, could be called a critico-prophetical activity. It is a negation of a negation. It says no to any presumed right to say no to transcendence; and thus theology as critico-prophetical activity calls into question all theories and projects that would close human beings up in immanence.

This "negation of a negation" naturally tends to be expressed in positive terms. That in itself is all right, except insofar as it may conceal a desire to transform negative theology into some sort of positive dogmatic theology once again. There is always the danger that theology will pretend that it knows positively how to break the circle of self-contained realms. Theology will remain faithful to its negative nature and avoid the aforementioned temptation only when it recognizes that its spontaneously positive affirmations do not possess any cognitive value, that they possess only symbolic value. Political theology denies the self-closure of the political realm through symbols, not through concepts. Hence it is simultaneously three things: negative theology, because it does not know anything in the strict sense; critico-prophetical theology, because it denies that one can justifiably say one knows there is nothing transcendent; and symbolic theology, because it expresses that denial through symbols.

From whatever angle we look at political theology, we ultimately see symbols. We have already noted this fact in some detail when we considered the theological keys that are used to apprehend here-and-now political realities: Fraternity, love, conversion, and liberation are not cognitive concepts but symbolic representations (see chapter 5). But the same holds true with regard to the evocation of liberative memories in the Christian tradition and with regard to expectations for the future based on God's promise. As we noted in earlier chapters, Christian history serves the function of interpreting myth (see chapter 4) and Christian eschatology is more akin to mythical and symbolic utopias than to rational utopias (see chapter 6).

The symbolic character of all theology is beginning to be noticed clearly at the present time. Present-day analysis of religious language is making it clear that symbol (and also myth) somehow corresponds with transcendence. The language used to express transcendence is necessarily symbolic, and it may be mythical as well. There is a clear and obvious connection between symbol (or myth) and transcendence. Moreover, while it may be true that symbols are not to be equated or confused with myths from a strictly epistemological point of view, the two are intricately linked from the standpoint of rational thought and the sociology of knowledge; for the two share the feature of non-rationality and seem to be scarcely separable (182:72–73).

The theologian who was most consistent in displaying and elaborating a clear awareness of the fact he was dealing with symbols was Paul Tillich. His theology is essentially a symbolic theology. He calmly talks about the cross and resurrection, the fall and redemption, and even Christ and the Spirit, as symbols (406). All the enunciations of theology are symbolic, according to Tillich, except the one that attributes being to God. Tillich is the father of much current theology insofar as he solemnly refused to be positive and dogmatic and chose to speak symbolically. Insofar as political theology also gives up dogmatic positivism, it will have to face up to the same issue. It will have to ask itself whether or not the language of theology essentially consists of symbols and perhaps even myths.

In the field of political theology itself, Richard Shaull has been very cognizant of the symbolic value of its statements. He says quite openly that the theology of revolution establishes a correspondence between the revolutionary situation of the present-day world and Christian *symbols* (391:36). In all likelihood his view goes back to Paul Tillich ultimately, but it derives more directly from Paul Lehmann. The latter makes it very clear that his politico-messianic theology deals with biblical or theological "images." Myth cannot be differentiated from real-life history in the Bible, and messianism itself is an image (256:93–94, 112).

In a similar vein Rubem Alves consistently describes religion as a realm of symbols. Indeed he stresses the fact that those symbols are mirrors of the human situation on earth, not windows opening out onto a world beyond (50:85; 49:133). Moltmann is less removed from the customary language of neo-orthodox Protestantism, and he has no great proclivity towards symbolic theology; but at times even he talks about the Exodus, Christ's resurrection, the new creation, and the God who is to come as "creative symbols of liberty" (309:314).

Catholic theologians are much more suspicious about any such symbolic interpretation. Blanquart is the big exception here. He describes the concrete ideology of Christianity as being particularly sensitive to myth, the only possible language for expressing transcendence (74:152). Assmann also takes it for granted that Christianity operates with a "realm of symbols and myths" (59:190–202).

On the whole, however, there is not sufficient awareness and acknowledgment of the fact that the pronouncements of every political theology are symbolic. That is why we must stress the point here. Political theology works with myths, symbols, and absolute utopias. It mythifies past history, making it heroic and legendary; it apprehends present reality and praxis through symbolizations; and finally it projects itself into the future in a utopian manner. It is all a grand metaphor, a non-knowing, a nescience; only through figurative transpositions and connotations can it express its no to the closure of the world in upon itself.

Only such a theology—negative and symbolic—can evade the objection that is sometimes levelled against current political theology and that we have already seen in the pages above. The objection is that current political theology is the same as the older political theology because it continues to link God directly to politics (177:130). That objection will continue to stand if current brands of political theology continue to see themselves in positive and dogmatic terms. The only thing that can differentiate them from earlier revolutionary theologies is their forthright renunciation of dogma as some sort of positive knowledge. However revolutionary a current theology may be vis-à-vis society, it does not differ substantially from the theology of Joachim of Fiore, or Münzer, or Las Casas, if it attempts to avail itself of traditional orthodoxy. It can only be called precritical. Only a negative and symbolic theology will lead us across the threshold of critical modernity.

10. THE REQUISITES OF POLITICAL THEOLOGY

Our preceding discussion of alternatives makes it clear what kind of political theology seems really feasible today and what models must be rejected. First of all, a political theology viewed essentially as an ethics of political life will not do; it cannot be viewed simply as some sort of orientation of traditional dogma toward political ethics. Political theology formulates the relationship to praxis in a wholly new way, creating a unitary discourse in which talking about the praxis of Christians is the only possible way of talking about God.

Second, a theology formulated as direct, first-stage expression of faith will not do. A second-stage, reflective, theoretical theology is needed, one that will examine the spontaneous expressions of faith and the conditions that make it possible. This second-stage theology, in turn, makes clear what some of the other features of a sound political theology must be.

A sound political theology must be formulated as a fundamental theology, as a theology of conversion and its possibilities; it cannot be formulated as a dogmatic theology, as a theology of some consolidated Christendom. A sound political theology must also presuppose and accept the social process of secularization without trying to sneak in some new sort of Christian sacral order in any way. It must also be aware of its own negative and symbolic character. Realizing that it is not positive or cognitive, it will have to break with the theological tradition that prevailed for twenty centuries: i.e., the notion that theology is some sort of higher knowledge.

The different alternatives examined in the previous pages are interconnected. If a theology is uncritical and unreflective with regard to its own possibility, it will tend to remain dogmatic, positive, allegedly cognitive, and rehabilitative of the sacred. Such is true in the case of some Latin American theologians of liberation. Their theology is rich on the level of immediate content, direct expression, and faith witness; but it is quite feeble on the level of second-stage, critical, reflective discourse. At this second level present-day political theology must take a decisive step away from that particular Latin American formulation. Though the Latin American formulation may have its value as Christian witness, it does not seem capable of being a truly significant theology with claims to validity outside the Christian community or in a secularized world.

Often enough political theology is presented as a discourse apart. It is isolated from the other theological problems which have been raised in recent times (e.g., demythologization, secularity, analysis of religious language, and so forth), as if it somehow had nothing to do with other theological perspectives. But any such isolation does damage to political theology and condemns it to being ambiguous. Since it itself cannot solve all the questions on its own, it must have recourse to other formulations if it does wish to resolve them. But it often remains unclear to what extent the theologians of liberation and revolution accept or reject the theses of other theologians: e.g., Bultmann's thesis about demythologizing, Tillich's view of the inevitably symbolic character of theological pronouncements, Van Buren's views on the secular meaning of the gospel, and Hamilton's theses about the death of God.

Its relationship to other current strands of theological thought become clear when we say that political theology must be fashioned as a theology critical of its own presuppositions; as a theology giving grounds for the legitimacy of the Christian faith; as a secularized theology; and, finally, as a negative and symbolic theology. Let me spell this out a bit in the concrete insofar as political theology is concerned.

Political theology recognizes the necessity of analyzing its own propositions; but this analysis cannot just be a linguistic one. Even more important, it must also be a socioeconomic hermeneutics that explores the social and economic conditionings of Christian language. Political theology recognizes the fact that the Christian faith is expressed in symbols and myths, but it does not reject them on that account; instead it uses them as the only possible language for saying no to the world's closing in upon itself. Political theology is a secularized theology (rather than a theology of secularization). In other words, it is a theology that speaks out in a world where the traditional vestiges of the sacred have disappeared or are now disappearing. Finally, it is a theology that gives serious consideration to the questions raised by the theologians of the death of God, that is not overly concerned with salvaging traditional theism. While it may still dare to talk about God, it does so fully aware of the fact that its talk is negative and symbolic, not positive and cognitive. It realizes that its discourse might well be regarded as silence qualified by symbols.

8

Theology and the Hypothesis of Historical Materialism

1. HYPOTHESES PRELIMINARY TO THEOLOGY

There remains the task of proposing a concrete political theology that will bring together the required features discussed in the previous chapter and that will adopt the specifications noted as necessary. We want a theology that is essentially related to the historical praxis of human beings but that also attempts to talk about God. We want a fundamental theology that has to do with the grounding and genesis of faith, not a dogmatic theology. We want a secularized theology, a theology that is negative and symbolic, and a theology that is critical theory and second-stage reflection concerning the pronouncements of the Christian.

The last feature deserves emphasis. It is no longer a question of a theology on the level of direct, theologal language. Insofar as that kind of theology is concerned, we have said enough in our discussion of the program of political theology in Part Two of this book. That kind of theology will not be eliminated, but it will now be picked up and interpreted on a higher level of reflection. Here we do not mean to consider the content of political theology but rather the critical theory that will enable us to comprehend that content in a specific cultural context.

In the following pages I shall propose a theoretical format for theology that is designed to meet all the requirements noted above. This particular theoretical format is dependent on a very concrete hypothesis. By way of introducing it here, I shall refer to it right now as the Marxist hypothesis of historical materialism; and I shall adopt it here as a preliminary hypothesis or presupposition. This means that I will assume it to be correct and use it as the basis for spelling out and describing a critical theological discourse that satisfies the aforementioned exigencies.

Two basic objections might well be brought against this preliminary assumption. The first objection is a more general one that questions the advisability of presupposing or adopting any alien hypothesis in theology, particularly one that does not seem too favorable to theology. The second objection specifically questions the advisability of adopting the Marxist hypothesis.

Insofar as the first objection is concerned, we must realize that theology really has to apply itself to every hypothesis. This is even more true with respect to those hypotheses where theology might not seem to fare very well. The history of Christianity has had its fill of theologies nicely situated in the most convenient and suitable hypotheses: e.g., Thomist theologies, metaphysical theologies, idealist theologies, and existential theologies. If the ultimate structure of reality is as Thomas Aquinas viewed it, then of course it is possible to be a Christian. If there is such a thing as metaphysical knowledge, or if there is a realm of ideas and ideals with as much or more consistency than material reality possesses, then it is not very difficult to establish the possibility and perhaps even the necessity of certain religious dogmas. And one does not have much difficulty in establishing secure roots for the faith on the basis of the existential hypothesis either. The problem is that there are fewer and fewer people who assume and accept the hypotheses of Thomism, metaphysics, idealism, and existentialism. If we want to make the faith meaningful, if we want to arrive at belief or induce others to believe, must we first effect a conversion to the idea-set of Thomism, metaphysics, ontology, or existentialism?

The earlier question of Bonhoeffer asked how we are to proclaim the gospel message to a religious people without first imbuing them with religiosity. That question now fades into the more concrete question of how to proclaim that message to the Marxist, the technologist, the neopositivist, the structuralist, the ethnologist, and the Freudian without first forcing them to give up their own line of knowledge, their own conception of the world, and their own line of praxis. Paul's notion of becoming a Jew with the Jews and a Gentile with the Gentiles (1 Cor. 9:20–22) now takes the form of becoming a Marxist with Marxists and a Freudian with the Freudians. It is not a mere *captatio benevolentiae,* a proselytizing stratagem. It must be a real effort to put oneself in their place and see whether any faith is possible from their standpoint and, if so, in what way exactly.

Speaking personally, I am not interested in any Thomist theology, first of all, because that theology has already been worked out and completed; it no longer needs further contributions from anyone. Second, because there are scarcely any Thomists around today. The point is that Thomism is not a logical consequence of the faith, nor does it have any necessary connection with it. Thomism is a presupposition or hypothesis, on the basis of which faith takes on a certain cast and is outlined in a specific kind of theology. Thomism is a cultural presupposition that can and should be noted by theology only insofar as it is really shared by the people of a culture. If actual or potential believers no longer share this hypothesis, then theology has every right to bypass it altogether.

What interests and concerns me is the feasibility of faith and theology in terms of other presuppositions and hypotheses: i.e., those of Freud, Wittgenstein, Marx, Saussure, and Nietzsche, for example. In short, I am interested in the possibility of faith and theology in terms of every hypothesis that has some validity for our contemporaries. My feeling is that theology must tackle every hypothesis and explore it all the way. Only if and when a hypothesis is proved to be completely impervious to faith would there be reason to disregard and reject it (or, on the other hand, to reject faith if the hypothesis proved itself compelling and obligatory). In any case let us establish the point that the faith must assume hypotheses that are outside its boundaries and perhaps even hostile to it.

Insofar as the second objection is concerned, I would reply that the Marxist hypothesis is not just another hypothesis. We have already noted to how great an extent dialectical and historical-materialist reasoning governs our way of knowing and doing science in the more advanced sectors of contemporary culture. We have also seen that political theology is the specific reaction of Christianity to Marxist theory and praxis (see chapter 3). Today Marxism is the broadest and most comprehensive of the theoretical approaches to human historical reality; it is also the most ambitious insofar as it seems capable of accounting for other stances and is most influential in its impact even on opposed viewpoints. We are living in a period when the historical-materialist line of reasoning holds sway. As one theologian has put it, it is the "era of Marx" (121:100–01). Another admits that "all of us are standing on Marx's shoulders" (321). In such circumstances it would be foolish and unreasonable to theologize while turning our backs on the Marxist hypothesis. It is not that theology can rest content with considering only that particular theory. The point is that theology certainly cannot be complete if it does not consider and adopt that theory as a hypothesis.

The final note must be stressed: *as a hypothesis.* It is not up to the theologian, as such, to discuss the truth or falsity of Marxism, or psychoanalysis, or any other scientific theory. Up to a certain point the theories of different people merit equal attention and interest as such, whether the people involved be Marx or Nietzsche, Bloch or McLuhan, Adorno or Russell. It is not up to theologians, as such, to decide between them. At least that is not part of their obligatory task. Their job is to point up the possibility or impossibility of faith and the further specifications of the faith, on the basis of each of those theories.

Pushing this point a bit, one could even say that there is no reason why the personal convictions of the theologian should play any special role here. A theologian who is personally sympathetic to the existentialist point of view may feel obliged (i.e., morally bound by circumstances) to work out a theology based on the Marxist hypothesis—and vice-versa. A particular theologian, perhaps even many, may feel that "the Marxist theory of revolution no longer offers convincing presuppositions for grounding ethical and political behavior" (326:429); but that does not rule out the possibility that they may be obliged to carry out a process of theological reflection that will be comprehensible from the Marxist standpoint. Their situation is like that of a doctor who is called in to treat a patient. The doctor has an obligation to do that without any regard for the patient's ideas and whether the person in question is a friend or enemy. In like manner the theologian is called upon to point up the possibility of faith in terms of each hypothesis, whether or not the theologian shares a given hypothesis.

2. A HISTORICAL-MATERIALIST THEOLOGY

Here, then, I pose and formulate the possibility of faith on the basis of the Marxist hypothesis. To be more precise, I propose to discuss the possibility of a "historical-materialist theology." But is there not an intrinsic contradiction in this term? Is there not an unavoidable antagonism between the two parts that make it up? It would be relatively useless to try to decide that question in advance, to deal explicitly with the sense in which the term and its components are being taken. My treatment of the issue will clear up the point as it proceeds, showing in what sense we can talk about a historical-materialist theology. The explanation itself will specify the content of my formulation.

To fend off possible suspicions and unjustified antagonisms right at the start, it is well to point out that there is a Marxist tradition that interprets materialism in a sense that comes very close to realism, to say the least (21:112). Engels himself remarked that materialism really came down to giving up every idealistic whim that could not be reconciled with facts and events in their true relationships rather than in terms of their fancied relationships (287:244). Both Lenin and Lukács define matter as that which exists independently of consciousness, so that Marxist materialism comes down to affirming "the primacy of existence over awareness" (268:138, 238, 248, and 255). That being the case, some readers who are Christian believers might feel more comfortable if I talked about a "dialectical-realist theology." But since the things that I shall propose in the following pages cannot be readily assimilated with prior theological tradition, I think it is justifiable to use a somewhat scandalous formulation that is not so readily digestible. So I shall talk about a "historical-materialist theology," all the more so because it openly acknowledges the hypothesis that it has assumed. The relationship between historical materialism—itself situated within a framework of dialectical reasoning—and the dialectical materialism developed by Engels ("dialectic of nature") is a complex and much-debated point. In any case, here we are limiting ourselves to a consideration of historical materialism, that proper to human societies.

Though it is constructed on the hypothesis of historical

materialism, this proposed theology does not harbor the illusion that it will automatically convince Marxists themselves. One would have to be very naive to assume that. But on the other hand this does not mean that it could not be a theory about the Christian faith on which Christians and Marxists might be able to agree. The fact is that the theory proposed here is the result of an equal mixture of two basic ingredients: (1) of statements made by Christians who have noted and accepted the obvious correctness of Marxism; (2) of acknowledgments by Marxists who have made a serious effort to understand and appreciate what the Christian faith purports to mean. Thus a historical-materialist theology, a theology attempting to be a social and critical theory of Christianity, could represent the point where Christian-Marxist dialogue reaches some solution.

It may well be that Christian discourse and Marxist discourse are irreducible on the level of direct, first-stage language (where theologal representations stand over against atheist representations). But that does not mean they cannot engage in a shared, common reflection on the level of theory and metalanguage concerning their respective first-stage languages. If Christian-Marxist dialogue leads anywhere, it leads to reflection of that sort. Despite the disparity of their primary and immediate idea-sets, second-stage reflection could come to constitute a unitary theory for both sides.

It is obvious, of course, that not all Marxists and all Christians are capable of engaging in dialogue, much less in the kind of theology or theory mentioned above. The dogmatists on both sides are scarcely in a position to understand what I am going to say here. In their case what is missing is something very much like conversion.

All political theology is based on certain presuppositions that have taken on relevance since the appearance of Marx: e.g., the relationship of consciousness (or awareness) to praxis and the determining character of production processes. Most of the time, however, political theology has adopted those presuppositions in a partial and disconnected way at best. Theologians have tended to treat them in a timid and disorderly fashion. The aim of this chapter is to deal with those presuppositions in a methodical and systematic way, thus conplementing what is left vague by many theologians. To put it succinctly, we shall adopt Marxism as our hypothesis and then go on to consider what sort of theology is possible on that basis. To do that, one must have recourse to the two ingredients mentioned above. One must consider the expressed or implied rudiments of a Marxist-based theology in the work of recent theologians, and one must also consider the elements provided by the historical-materialist theory itself as expounded by those Marxists who have done their best to grasp Christianity.

It is worth noting at this point that while the task of outlining a theory of the faith on the basis of the Marxist hypothesis has only begun to be carried through in methodical fashion, there has been no lack of suggestions or indications that it should be done. Girardi, for example, has talked about the "materialism essential to any revolutionary vision of the world." This materialism would entail a recognition of the fact that "the laws of history bespeak a strong and solid relationship with the laws of political and economic life" (210:517). Hence political theology must presuppose that sort of materialism insofar as it assumes a revolutionary vision of the world. Paul L. Lehmann considers a "theology for the revolution" as the meeting ground for Marxism and Christianity (255:201). Putting it even more clearly and pointedly, Chaigne admits that his theological formulation is based wholly on accepting historical materialism as correct and self-evident (135:94). As he sees it, Christians cannot disregard historical materialism as if it were only a communist thesis; it represents a "definitive acquisition of social science" (133:184).

Can there now be a Marxist theology, in the same sense

that there has been a Platonic theology and an Aristotelian theology? Egbert Hoeflich answers with a definite yes. With good reason he points out that "Karl Marx, in his comprehension of reality and truth, is much closer to the Christian faith than was Aristotle." And he goes on to propose a "Karl Marx for the church" (237). His choice of words may not be the most fortunate, since it may conceal a proselytizing intent. It could be used in an effort to baptize Marx and assimilate him to the church, when Marx himself would have forcefully rejected any such effort.

The proposal to fashion a historical-materialist theology is in no way equivalent to an unadmitted effort to Christianize Marx. On the other hand, it does have very much to do with rediscovering the fact that biblical tradition is the most materialistic of all religious traditions, as William Temple pointed out (403:478).

At the present time we find people who call themselves both Marxists and Christians. If we wish to shed light on that particular stance, we simply cannot avoid discussing the possibility of a theology grounded on the presuppositions of historical materialism. In Latin America, and Europe we now find a rare breed of believers who call themselves Marxists (not just Socialists). And we also find Marxists who do not hesitate to consider themselves Christians at the same time. More and more people are saying: "I profess to be a Christian, but I declare myself a Marxist" (362:249). Even theologians are not embarrassed to include themselves under the covering mantle of Marxism (56:11; 59:196). Considering the relationship that has prevailed between Marxism and Christianity in past history, this turn of events is not only novel but surprising; it calls for some explanation. But that can only result from a methodical examination of the possibility of having a theology that attempts to take over Marx's theoretical assumptions, and from a consideration of the surrounding conditions.

3. FAITH AFTER MARX

I have already remarked that a theology based on Marxist presuppositions in no way purports to baptize Marx, to win him back to the Christian tradition, or to suggest that he is directly beholden to that tradition. This point deserves more extended treatment.

It is not impossible to detect religious factors in the genesis (if not the structure) of Marxist socialism (147:4–27, 197–219). There is no absence of attempts to adapt Marx *ad usum christianorum,* to see in his work a Judeo-Christian vein, and even to see him as an implicit Christian in the line of the prophets. Sometimes these attempts do proceed from an impartial and objective effort to establish the connections between Marxism and other idea-sets, religious ones in this case; but at other times we find a poorly disguised apologetic and proselytizing attempt to win Marx for Christianity. In the latter instances an effort is made to present Marx as one who continues or reiterates age-old biblical themes. Silenced for many centuries by ecclesiastical tradition, those themes take on new resonance and vitality in the writings of Marx.

Unlike efforts of that sort, a historical-materialist theology leaves Marx's thought alone, accepting all its differences from, and opposition to, Christianity. It does not see Marx as one who picks up and continues age-old themes. Instead it sees him as an original and innovative thinker who proposed new formulations of the issues without worrying about finding any direct analogies with biblical tradition. Historical-materialist theology tries to assume his theory completely in order to see what sort of faith, if any, is possible on that basis.

To give an example of what a historical-materialist theology is *not,* I can cite José Miranda's *Marx and the Bible.* Using his work as a point of contrast, I shall be better able to specify the stance being adopted here. Miranda's work is worthwhile for certain purposes, seriously carried out, and highly suggestive in many ways. But in the last analysis it is laced with ambiguities that eventually diminish its theoretical usefulness. He begins by proclaiming that he "will not attempt to find parallels between the Bible and Marx, but rather simply to understand the Bible" (308:16). But, alas, his whole book is full of statements in a harmonistic vein. He tells us that "Marx and Paul coincide in their intuition of the totality of evil: Sin and injustice form an all-comprehensive and all-pervasive organic structure" (308:283). He tells us that "Marx and the Bible coincide in this affirmation of incalculable importance: Sin's achievement of an institutional systematization in a flawless civilizing structure is what was historically needed before mankind could change its epoch" (308:288). He tells us that "both Marx and the biblical writers believe that man can cease being selfish and merciless and self-serving and can find his greatest fulness in loving his neighbor" (308:292).

While he claims to have no such intention, Miranda engages in an apologetics of coincidence and convergence. Between faith and Marxist thinking we find a "profound affinity" and "too many convergences" (308:201). The result—or rather, the aim which governs his work from the very start—is to make Marx nothing less than a prophet beholden to biblical tradition: "Karl Marx belonged to the category of the prophets of Israel, and . . . both his messianism and his passion for justice originated in the Bible" (308:16).

This handling of the matter is superficial in the extreme, and one must suspect some underlying apologetic prejudice. First of all, it is hardly surprising that one might find ideas from the Bible in Marx or any other Western thinker. It only confirms what we have known for a long time: that biblical thought has penetrated deeply into Western civilization and left a real mark on it. To be specific, the conviction that human beings can cease to be egoistic and soulless has come to be shared by most reasonable human beings of the Western world, perhaps even under the influence of Christianity; but that does not mean one can claim any real significance for the fact that Marx and the Bible coincide on that point. Furthermore, in Miranda's interpretation there emerges a Marx such as Marx himself never wanted to be. Miranda's Marx is a moralist whose concerns can be summed up in such terms as "sin," "egotism," "justice," and "love of neighbor." Miranda's moralizing Marxism is identifiable with Paul's thinking about the omnipresence of sin, no less! It is a Marxism that one can scarcely recognize at all, for Miranda has snuck it in by the back door so that it might seem more closely akin to traditional Christian thought.

The most subtle and misleading analogy that Miranda sets up between Marx and the Bible is their allegedly shared opposition to the bourgeois, positivist science of the West: "What Marx criticizes in Western science is the same thing that today prevents it from being challenged by the fact, which is recognized by this science itself, that to a great degree Marx coincides with the Bible" (308:17). Need one point out, in the interests of sound logic, that a shared opposition to a third term does not establish identity or analogy between the first two terms? Though both may be opposed to the color red, blue and yellow are hardly the same. Though both may be opposed to positivist science, biblical thinking and Marxist thought are not similar on that account. Biblical thinking is symbolic and prerational; Márxist thought attempts to get beyond positivist rationality through a dialectical rationality. One is not just being superficial when one claims to establish a real analogy on this point; one is simply making a big mistake.

At best the work of Miranda could be counted among the serious efforts to show that a Christian can be a Marxist. He certainly manages to do that, and such an effort has its value, especially since Marxism has been presented as directly opposed to Christianity for a long time now. But it makes sense only within the framework of a basically dogmatic formulation of theology—assuming that one is a Christian, can one be a Marxist? The point is that the really decisive issue today, the one that must be discussed, is one that has to be framed within the context of fundamental theology and the genesis of faith: Assuming the Marxist theory as correct, is any faith or theology possible at all?

Here we start off from the context of fundamental theology and do not assume that one is a believer at the start. The fact is that no radical theological reflection can ever take that for granted as an initial assumption. One may assume that a person is a Jew or a Gentile, a pagan or an atheist, a European or an African, a positivist or a Marxist; but one cannot assume that the person in question is a believer. The status of Christian is always the result of a conversion, and theology can never excuse itself from the task of explaining or discussing how that conversion comes about. If one is considering the issues from the basic context of fundamental theology, then the only viable approach is to start off from the hypothesis of historical materialism and find out what sort of conversion, faith, and theology are possible on that basis.

One theologian has mentioned Luther, Kant, and Marx together as three successive stages in the formation of Western modernity (173:162). That view of the matter certainly helps to explain why Protestant theology did a better job than Catholic theology of assimilating Kant's critique; and why liberal theology, which resulted from that assimilation, has been better able to take over Marx's critique than the official orthodox theologies. We find certain analogies between the situation of that liberal theology of the nineteenth century and political theology of the present day. In the nineteenth century, the critical theology of liberal Protestantism tried to answer the question as to whether faith was still possible after Kant. Today political theology is concerned with the possibility of faith after Marx. If the liberal theology of the nineteenth century was the Christian reflection that resulted from an acceptance of Kant's critique, current political theology is the reflection of a faith that has assumed the presuppositions and criticisms of Karl Marx. It is specifically this perspective, and no other outlook or viewpoint which attempts to find affinities between Marxism and Christianity, that dominates and guides the effort to fashion a theology based on the hypothesis of historical materialism.

From that precise perspective, then, it may be of some advantage to consider a question which has loomed large in some discussions between Christians and Marxists. It has to do with atheism. Is atheism essential to Marxism? Is it as essential to Marxism as belief in God is to Christianity? In the 1965 discussions in Salzburg, there seemed to be a consensus that one could answer those questions in the negative, or at least the second one, so long as one spelled out what one meant. A Catholic theologian, Marcel Reding, dedicated a whole presentation to trying to show that Marxists are not obliged, by virtue of their Marxism, to profess atheism (351:43–50). A scientist, Paul Weingartner, likewise maintained that "atheism is not a logical consequence of Marxism, if Marxism is taken to be a science" (419:58). Finally a Marxist, Cesare Luporini, agreed that Marx's law of the base-superstructure relationship, which Reding saw as the essence of Marxism, is neither religious nor atheistic; hence Marxist atheism is not grounded in any scientific principle and is rather a "postulatory atheism" rooted in humanism and ethics (270:64–65).

Thus those authors are of the opinion that the interpretation of humankind in Marxist terms of base-superstructure relationships is not necessarily atheistic. Note that this opinion, which is substantially identical with the one underlying the projected effort to construct a historical-materialist theology, has been given much closer examination than the vaguer question as to how essential atheism is to Marxism. After all, what is one to understand by the "essence" of Marxism? Today Marxist tradition is almost as complicated as Christian tradition, containing elements from the most diverse sources. Already we find a variety of distinctions that are frequent topics of discussion: Marxism as science versus Marxism as a personal option and commitment; Marxism as theoretical analysis versus Marxism as concrete praxis; Marxism as an economic and political theory versus Marxism as a humanism dealing with the whole person. All that is part of Marxism. To which of those aspects shall we look to find the "essence" of Marxism? Marxists who find the roots of their tradition in the work of Engels and Marx will find it impossible to disregard any important element in that tradition; and atheism is certainly such an element. The Marxist will be atheist almost as a foregone conclusion, just as the Christian will naturally tend to be a believer in God despite the more recent appearance of an atheistic brand of Christianity. At the level of tradition and initial stance, Marxists and Christians confront each other as atheists and believers in God respectively. Today this opposition remains irreconcilable, and those who call themselves Christian Marxists must be aware that they carry within them a historical contradiction awaiting resolution.

But one of the important and substantial elements in Marxism is a theory that analyzes social relationships as being conditioned or determined by the economic base. This theory has all the features of an authentically scientific interpretation. Moreover, it enables Marxism to engage in self-criticism, to apply a critique of ideologies to its own tradition and thereby cease to be a dogmatic doctrine. Is this theory the essence of Marxism? It might be, but that is for Marxists to say. Here we shall simply prescind from that question and pose the following one: If we adopt as a hypothesis the view that comprehends human beings in terms of the base-superstructure principle, are faith and theology still possible? If so, what sort of faith and theology are possible?

Joint adoption of this principle by Marxists and Christians will enable both sides to engage in self-criticism of their respective traditions. While they may continue to remain unalterably opposed to each other on the immediate plane of initial beliefs (i.e., Marxist atheism versus Christian belief in God), it does not seem impossible for them to share a common theory about their respective beliefs. Despite their differences on the first-stage level of primary beliefs, there could be a growing identification between them on the second-stage level of critical reflection about their theological or atheistic convictions. Thus the direct opposition between theism and atheism could be superseded, as has been suggested by some theologians (see chapter 7, section 9), in an approach which corresponds with the logic of the historical-materialist hypothesis (278:311).

In the pages that follow here, we shall be operating precisely with that specific hypothesis, not with Marxism in general. The question as to whether any theology is possible at all after Marx will be framed in more concrete terms: Now that we know that human consciousness in general, and religious consciousness in particular, is a superstructural phenomenon dependent on a material, economic base, is any theology possible at all?

4. SOCIOECONOMIC CORRELATES OF BELIEF

The first and primary thesis of a historical-materialist theology entails an adoption of Marxist theory and maintains that ideas and beliefs are determined or conditioned by the economic base, by the production relationships in a given society. This applies to religious ideas and beliefs as well. Even in this initial thesis, however, one may see an irreducible opposition arising between believers and Marxists. Are they strictly determined by the economic base, or only conditioned by it? Orthodox Marxists ought to maintain that ideas and beliefs are rigorously determined by the economic structure whereas orthodox Christians could not maintain that; Christians could only say that religious ideas and beliefs are at most conditioned by socioeconomic factors.

If one is thinking in etiological or causal terms, then the opposition between determining cause on the one hand and accompanying condition on the other would seem to be irreducible. To the extent that traditional Christianity and orthodox Marxism remain wedded to a causalist line of thinking, it would seem to be difficult, if not impossible, for them to come together on this point. But modern thought is abandoning the etiological approach that looks for cause and effect relationships; it is now more interested in investigating relationships and correspondences between different phenomena. Present-day science does not claim to discover the causes of facts and events; rather, it seeks to establish or find correlations between facts and events of different orders. The older heuristic model of a connected chain of cause and effect has been replaced by a new model that syntactically relates different phenomena to each other. From this new standpoint there is little relevance to the question as to whether the economic base is a determining cause or merely a factor conditioning religious beliefs; that question is meaningful only in a cause-and-effect approach. The only question that remains to be considered in the new approach is whether or not there are correspondences between the economic structure and certain theological ideas. Once we have ruled out an etiological purpose in our investigation of such correspondences, there seems to be no reason why marked discrepancies should continue to persist between Christians and Marxists.

Correlating the economic base with theological representations, we get a vision of the history of theology that differs markedly from the traditional one. The usual view is that behind the major terms and images of theology (e.g., God, salvation, revelation, and so forth) today's Christians harbor the very same representations as Jesus' first disciples or the Christians of the third-century. Up to a short time ago most theologians defended that view with tooth and nail. They maintained that while the verbal expression of Christian beliefs and its conceptual panoply may have undergone change during the course of history, the deeper underlying significance has remained the same.

In another work of mine, I tried to show how illusory is this claim to any fixed, unchanging set of meanings (190:288–312). The most sincere theologians are beginning to recognize the fact. Michel de Certeau has pointed out that "if we Christians take a clear and attentive look at ethnological and sociological analyses of culture," we will find questionable even the possibility of "communication with the gospel message," of fidelity to, and continuity with, what is proclaimed in it. When we try to interpret and actualize the gospel, "we think that we are translating it. In reality we are introducing a different world, a whole set of references bound together by a modern system of reciprocal elaborations. Words belong to mental systems. In adopting the former, we unwittingly accept the latter. We think we are saying *the same thing in different words.* In fact, whether we realize it or not, the change in language entails a change of thoughts" (116:161–62).

His observations, which derive from the standpoint of semantics and the sociology of culture, take on a more precise sense if we adopt the Marxist standpoint. Viewed dialectically, semantic systems are not made and unmade by pure chance; they are part of a changing ideological superstructure, whose change corresponds to alterations in the socioeconomic base. Every specific theology can and should be comprehended dialectically within the overall context of its moment in history. In this way a historical-materialist analysis will shed light on both the history of theology and its present state.

A Marxist theory of the Christian religion is yet to be worked out. We find some ingredients for this in Marx, and even more in the work of Engels. They permit us to trace out a basic dialectical theory of the evolution of religions in general (from nature religions to universal religions of a human and social cast) and of the Christian religion in particular. The main stages of the Christian religion would be: primitive Christianity, Constantinianism, the feudal church of Catholicism, bourgeois Christianity or Protestantism, and the civil irrelevance of religion. Henri Desroche, a sociologist, has done a fine job of synopsizing those elements in a coherent and convincing schema (32) that can and should be further developed. There is room to give more detailed consideration to both the individual stages as such, the specific theological notions, and the various Christian institutions.

Concrete elaboration of a historico-materialist interpretation of Christianity in its different phases of development has remained virtually on the rudimentary level provided by Engels. With few exceptions (Bloch, Puente Ojea, for example) today's Marxists have paid no more attention to the history of religion than their predecessors did. There is also almost a complete lack of study, from the Marxist and non-Marxist sides, of the material, economic, and social base with which Christian theology was linked at any given moment in history. Such studies could provide us with authentic historical knowledge of the socioeconomic conditionings affecting different past theologies. This in turn would enable us to trace out a social history of dogmatics like that which John D. Bernal has worked out for science (71) and Arnold Hauser for literature and art (234). The results obtained from such a social history of theology, and only those results, would serve as the touchstone and proof of the historical-materialist hypothesis and its interpretation of the Christian faith.

Of course any discovery of the socioeconomic correlates of theological ideas and beliefs will considerably reduce the sense and import of transcendence. If we accept the hypothesis of historical materialism, we can only have a theology that is not at all transcendent vis-à-vis the realm of other human ideas. But it is precisely the rejection of transcendence, of a certain kind of cosmological and ontological transcendence at least, that constitutes one of the features of current political theology.

A whole series of statements to this effect could be brought in at this point. Dumas asserts that "Christianity is something other than a movement designed to establish some sort of transcendence." Commenting on the work of Robinson (364), he describes it as an attempt to "rethink Christianity outside the categories of transcendence" (21:41). Metz rejects the metaphysical and naturalist scheme of immanence versus transcendence as one that is inadequate for a historical, practical hermeneutics dealing with the future (301:292–93). Gollwitzer maintains that "the transcendence of the kingdom of God, as understood by the New Testament, does not envision the hereafter as detached from the here and now but rather as a radical and total negation of the given cosmos" (215:53). Alves says that it is not possible to find any language for a transcendence above and beyond the world and the body (48:228). For Cardonnel, the domination of some creator over creation would produce a "deceitful and blasphemous transcendence"; authentic transcendence is "the irreducibility of God to the relationship that exists between dominator and dominated." Insofar as it is a "transcendence centered around domination that mutilates people, religion is destined to disappear" (21:82, 88–89). Camilo Torres asked: "Why do we sit in a locked room debating whether the soul is immortal or mortal when we know very well that poverty and wretchedness are mortal?" (204:69). Chaigne rejects any "metahistory of the universe" as well as all "speculation about the hereafter" (135:111). It seems fairly certain, then, that for some present-day theologians transcendence is nothing more than the overcoming of the present by the future.

This diminution of the ontological transcendence of the realities discussed by theology is therefore in correspondence with the diminution of the epistemological transcendence of theology itself. Theology is seen as a system of representations that are not at all transcendent, that derive from social and economic structures that can be identified easily enough. In any case, today theologians can adopt as their own the description that has been given by Marxists: They can view the faith as a "purely human phenomenon" (319:214). They can assert that "any question posed by man, even the question of God, should be posed from the starting point of man" (200:68).

5. DIFFERENT GODS

Theological systems differ not only from age to age but also within a given period. In a society divided into social classes, class outlook will also affect and configure theological representations. The God of the landowner is not the same as the God of the lowly worker. The idea of God may be a key idea for both, but the semantic system in which it is imbedded in each case is quite different.

The French *gesta Dei per francos* stands over against the German *Gott mit uns.* When the two peoples are at war with each other, it is obvious that they cannot have the same God. The God in whose name monarchs have governed society is different from the God in whose name ecclesiastics have voiced a defiant *non possumus* in the face of kingly dictates. The God of the *Magnificat* is not the same as the God whom we rebel against when we resist lawful authority (Rom.

13:1). Indeed the God of the *Magnificat* is considered by some to be the most all-embracing and subversive God in the Bible, who could not possibly get past many government censors (28).

The same holds true when the interests of different social groups clash. The God who supports one group cannot possibly be the same as the God who supports an opposing group. The point cannot be nullified by saying that God is not in the service of anyone's interests and hence our faith in God should be basically disinterested. Nor can it be nullified by a theology centered around God's gratuitous giving, such as we find elaborated by Moltmann (311:45, 82), González-Ruiz (220), and others (187:320). This particular theology situates God beyond the sphere of necessity, in the realm of fully emancipated human beings who are "the freedmen of creation." While such a theology of gratuitousness and play might help us to anticipate how faith might be possible in a liberated society that no longer has any alienation in it, it can only have symbolic value in a society that is still weighed down by the burden of the most elemental necessities. At present a faith focused on gratuitousness and play exclusively might serve as a paradigm and signpost for moving toward purification and liberation; but no individual and no group can maintain with confidence that its beliefs are not rooted in more or less tangible self-interests, even if these interests be nothing more than the psychological benefits derived from those beliefs. It might well be possible and worthwhile to seek out a gratuitous God or a "useless" God, which the Marxist Mury seems inclined to accept (21:61–62). Such a God might even now provide a meeting ground and locus of communion for groups whose social interests are very different and even opposed. But even that would not belie the thesis that the significance of the word "God" is not the same when it is imbedded in different semantic systems and different networks of basic necessity.

In that sense there is much justification in the remark which the sacristan makes in *Todas las sangres,* a novel by José María Arguedas. Gustavo Gutiérrez quotes it in his book, *A Theology of Liberation* (230:11): The parish priest is telling the poor Indian sacristan that God is everywhere. The Indian replies: "Was God in the heart of those who broke the body of the innocent teacher Bellido? Is God in the bodies of the engineers who are killing 'La Esmeralda'? In the official who took the corn fields away from their owners . . . ?" How indeed can God be in the bodies of those who kill others!

The theology of that Indian sacristan, whether he knows it or not, is a Marxist and materialist theology. The God of the white overlords is not the same as the God of the Indian laborers. By introducing this point into his book, Gutiérrez is pointing up the fact that our image of God is conditioned by our class outlook, by the perspective of our social group; it is affected by the place and position one holds in the web of production processes and relationships. In a society that contains exploiters and exploited, each side speaks from its own peculiar position; no one can claim to speak of God from some impartial spot outside the conflict.

The image of God is also socially and economically conditioned in the work of theologians as well. Comblin speaks with some irony of those who are strongly inclined to believe in the "absolute objectivity" of their own theology. Such objectivity simply does not exist: "Theologians are conditioned by their economic and social context. . . . Their background, their *curriculum vitae,* their social position, and their income will in all likelihood have some connection with theological convictions that they hold" (121:105–6).

From the geopolitical distance that the Atlantic Ocean provides them, Latin American theologians have been especially sensitive to the factors conditioning European theology both in the past and the present. They see it as the theology of bourgeois societies and of the functional uses of religion in such societies. There is nothing absolute or essential about it, because it is related to, and dependent on, conditioning factors of that sort. Dussel has spelled out this conditioning as religious, liturgical, cultural, political, economic, and even erotic (164:344).

But the question here is: Is it possible to have a theology that is not conditioned? Of course not. Every theory and every theology has its conditioning factors. One must try to choose them well, to situate oneself in those conditions that will make it possible to formulate a correct theory or theology. In the case of a theology grounded on the hypothesis of historical or dialectical materialism, the sociopolitical condition underlying its feasibility is clear enough: i.e., its effective, real-life involvement in the overthrow of social structures based on domination. In the last analysis one is forced to accept the verdict that "either the theologian is a human being committed to the struggle for liberation or he is not a theologian" (112:217).

In a divided society the image of God will prove to be equally divided. In an alienated society the image of God will prove to be alienated and self-estranged. Alienated human beings cannot help but have a theology and a set of beliefs that are affected by their alienation and perhaps even in complicity with it. This does not mean that the alienation in question necessarily has religious roots. While there does exist a religious alienation in general, and a Christian alienation in particular (182:133), it usually is not basic and original. An alienated image of God is usually the result rather than the source of alienation in the believer.

When Christians live in a divided society where one cannot possibly remain neutral, they must opt for some sort of partisanship and line up on one side or the other. Not every option is reasonable, however. One must choose the partisanship that is destined for universality. In Marxist theory it is the working class that provides that partisanship. As

Marx saw it, the proletariat is the class that contains the seed for the dissolution of classes, that cannot emancipate itself without emancipating society as a whole. In a word, the proletariat is the universal class. Acceptance of this Marxist hypothesis explains why the theologians of liberation and revolution tell Christians they must make a class option (see chapter 5, section 3), and why they envision the possibility of something so seemingly one-sided and partisan as a "leftist theology" (388:421; 389). If the underlying hypothesis is valid, then the option that flows from it does have specifically theological scope. In a partisan society only identification with the party destined to be the whole will leave room for a language that is less partisan in its talk about God.

The fact remains that right now Christians talk about God from within an alienated situation and that their theological words are alienated as well. In such a situation all talk about God is ambiguous. It is understandable, then, that some Christians have given up religious talk altogether. The current turn toward a revolutionary praxis of liberation is accompanied by a silence about God insofar as certain Christians are concerned. Awareness of the fact that the faith, too, is suffering from alienation constrains them to a silent faith. How can one speak about God in the midst of total ambiguity and equivocation?

Thus it becomes necessary and urgent to alter society so that one will be able to talk about God without equivocation. Here we come upon a strictly theological reason for the exigency of social liberation and the dissolution of class divisions. Theology can only hope to be authentic through the work of fashioning a society that is not alienated—which is to say, through a liberation praxis. It is thus that praxis constitutes an intrinsic part of theology's interpretation or representation of the world. It is here that one of Metz's statements fits, to the effect that a reality-altering praxis also is part of hermeneutics. Hermeneutics does not have to do solely with comprehending the conditions of knowledge; it also involves the practical modification of those conditions (301:282–83). And that would include both the conditions of human discourse in general and of faith's discourse in particular.

6. THE PARABLE OF THE KINGDOM AND THE SILENCE OF THEOLOGY

Political theology entails the notion of altering the social conditions of knowledge with a view toward the possibility of having a different sort of discourse for the faith. In this connection it adopts an older idea stated by Karl Barth: "The state and its justice are a parable, an analogy, a correlate of the kingdom (of God)" (61:42). Of course not every social situation offers that analogy in equally suitable terms. When Gollwitzer picks up Barth's idea, for example, he applies it not to society but to what he calls the social utopia (which is a relative utopia for him). It is utopia that offers us "an image of the kingdom of God under the conditions of this world" (215:57). By the same token, the liberation praxis of believers tries to make that analogous image more clear and transparent. Thus the kingdom and God himself, lacking verisimilitude and likelihood in a situation of injustice that contravenes the image, would gain more credibility.

At bottom it is a question of the credibility of the Christian message. The gospel becomes unbelievable when real-life conditions seem to be completely impervious to all good news. Thus social emancipation and the emergence of new horizons of liberty and justice are basic factors in determining the plausibility of the gospel message and its claims to truth. Earlier in this book I quoted Sölle's remark to the effect that the denigration felt by people living in wretchedness made it impossible for them to believe in God's love (396:78). Girardi is of the same view: "The credibility of Christianity is at stake. . . . God's love will be able to be proclaimed to human beings who know what love is. Only a different earth will make heaven more credible" (208:77).

We could also add that only a different earth can ensure that faith and hope in God will not seem like convenient alibis in the face of the harshness and misery of real life. Bound up with the creation of an altered society is both the credibility of Christianity and the meaningfulness of faith in God. If the notions of "personal experience" and "evident reality" entail any sense that is applicable to God, then the liberative transformation of society can be undertaken by believers as their contribution to the real experience and evident reality of God. Believers who struggle to create a different world are working to make the kingdom of God in some way visible and transparent in virtue of the parable and analogy of social relationships.

Marxists are challenging Christians to work for a society in which their profession of faith will make some sense. Hugo Assmann quotes the words of one Marxist as an authentic challenge to Christians: "When your abstract nouns and terms become concrete once again, come back in line with real experience, then it will be all right for you to talk about God once again. When at some point in time and space it can be honestly said that 'justice has planted its tent amongst us' . . . then there will again be a real basis for what your Bible calls 'the name of God' " (54:219; 47:11). This remark, which alludes to the prologue of John's Gospel, makes it quite clear that only the incarnation of justice will permit us to recover the import of the term "God." If there is no concrete justice in history, it is grotesque to talk about a real God present in history.

An unjust society can only talk about God in blasphemous terms. It fully merits the condemnation uttered in the book of Isaiah (1:15): "When you spread out your hands, I close my eyes to you; though you pray the more, I will not listen. Your hands are full of blood! Wash yourselves clean!" A religious language is possible only from within a praxis of personal and social conversion. In political theology full validity is given to the thesis that the idea of God is completely meaningless apart from personal spiritual experience and the process of conversion that sustains it (160:34, 48). The terms and representations used in a political interpretation of the gospel take on real-life meaning only in connection with social movements of conversion and liberation that are symbolized and verbalized in them.

In this context certain views of Münzer concerning the impossibility of preaching under an oppressive regime take on great import. Bloch quotes them: "Under this sort of tyranny it would never be possible for a single Christian to devote himself to interior reflection while innocent people are subjected to such torments"; "while they [i.e., tyrants] govern you, you will not be able to speak of God" (79:219). The language of preaching, theology, and the faith becomes useless, ridiculous, and impossible when people are living below the minimum standards for a human life.

One brand of the theology of revolution ultimately chooses to give up being theology for the time being so that it can lose itself in the sheer praxis of revolution. Such was the final attitude of Camilo Torres, who abandoned his ecclesiastical ministry and went over to the guerillas: "Love of neighbor has moved me to join the revolution. I shall not say Mass, but I will flesh out that love of neighbor in the temporal, economic, and social sphere. When my neighbor has nothing to reproach me for, when the revolution has been carried through, then I will go back to saying Mass once again." Torres goes on to say that it is the only way for him to fulfill the injunction of seeking reconciliation with one's brother before bringing one's sacrifice to the altar (Matt. 5:23–24).

That text, which Castillo Cárdenas takes as a central theme of the theology of revolution, can have application to theology itself. What Torres says about Mass and the

Eucharist could be applied to theology. In this way the political interpretation of the gospel would once again come to rest in a negative theology for circumstantial reasons; it would remain silent about God so long as our fellow human beings had something to reproach us believers for.

We can get an authentic theology, or even a theology correctly posed, only in a society that has undergone alteration, liberation, and revolution. This is not to say that a fully human society will automatically produce the answers to the theological questions. The point is that it will be at least in a position to pose those questions in authentically human terms rather than alienated ones. At the very least it will not be restricted by the alienations that prevail here and now. With a modesty and realism that is not too frequently found among Marxists Lefèbvre writes: "Socialism does not resolve all the problems of man; but it does inaugurate the epoch in which man can pose the human problems of knowledge, love, and death in authentic terms that are not interlaced with social prejudices" (cited by Soubise, 397:69). Political theology can agree completely with that judgment. It is a matter of creating a society that does not alienate human beings, and in which we have the social conditions that make it possible to pose specifically human problems, including the problem of God, in their authentic terms.

The Christian can and should join movements working for human emancipation and the elimination of alienation, without worrying too much about what will happen to traditional Christian beliefs in an altered society. In the Salzburg dialogues between Christians and Marxists, Garaudy posed this question: "If Christendom carries the process of dealienation through to its conclusion, what will remain of religion?" It is a major question, and we shall have to examine it more closely later in this chapter. But Girardi managed to turn the question back on the Marxist: "If our Christianity carries the process of de-alienation through to its conclusion, what will remain of the Marxist criticism of religion?" (211:53). The work of de-alienating society, methodically practiced by Christians, is the touchstone determining the veracity of their theological discourse.

7. DE-ALIENATING FAITH

But must we give up theology entirely so long as the process of emancipation has not reached its goal, so long as theology can only be practiced amid alienating conditions? I have already pointed out that the logic of the theology of revolution does leave room for such an option. One chooses to give up theology entirely for the sake of praxis. But that option is not the only possible one, however. Realizing full well that their words about God are falsified, that they flesh out an image of God which can scarcely be recognized, Christians may still dare to keep on talking about God. The rigorously negative and symbolic character of theology, as described in the previous chapter, can safeguard them from the illusions into which they might fall. Theology and the faith may well be alienated, but they need not necessarily be alienating. On the contrary, they can perform a liberating and de-alienating function that fits in well with one aspect of Marx's critique of religion. While Marx did condemn religion as the opiate of the people, he also said that religion represented the protest of the people.

This latter dimension in the history of Christianity has been acknowledged by Marxists as far back as the time of Engels. It was Engels himself who noted strains of emancipatory thinking existing alongside the Constantinian view of the church. It is not certain, of course, that Marxists have fully appreciated this tradition of liberty. For the most part they tend to see it as a rudimentary, ingenuous, and still somewhat mythical manifestation of protest that only the theory of historical materialism is capable of expressing and implementing in a scientific and efficacious way. Of course it would be naive and regressive to think that today religion can serve as an adequate expression of the protest of those who are oppressed. Moreover, such a view would indicate that faith is merely a function or variable bound up with wretched conditions and hence destined to disappear with them. Today's Christians do not think that their awareness of social misery is to find expression in faith or theology. Social awareness must find other instruments of theory and praxis in which to formulate itself. But if we assume the existence of such instruments, and if we also assume that it is not at all necessary to look to faith to provide them, we are still left with another question to consider concerning the faith itself: Within its own symbolic order, is faith operative and active in any way at all and, if so, does it operate in liberative or oppressive terms?

Can faith act at all on the social and economic conditions of life? To this question we must answer yes. The fact that faith is conditioned, or even determined, by the socioeconomic infrastructure does not prevent it from reacting in turn upon that infrastructure and being able to alter it. One can only deny this possibility if one has a completely mechanistic conception of the relationship existing between the social base and consciousness. Such a conception is discredited even by Marxist theoreticians themselves, once they begin to move away from strict dogmatism.

Engels, for example, admitted that literature as a reality "is not an automatic effect or result of the economic situation." It is human beings who make history, art, and literature, though they do it "within a milieu that conditions them." Engels also noted that some younger disciples of himself and Marx were attributing more importance to the economic factor than they should, and failing "to do justice to the other factors that are part of the interaction" (286:53, 56).

Now if Engels himself attributes such a capacity to art and literature, if he maintains that they can react upon the economic base which conditions them, there is no reason for denying this same capacity to faith. In terms of both scientific theory and social praxis, faith occupies a position fairly analogous to that of art and literature and other such realities; thus one can properly accord it the same potentiality that one attributes to them. Once we rule out of theology any claim to constitute some sort of positive knowledge about some supernatural world, there does not seem to be any sound reason why we should attribute to the Christian phenomenon a ridiculous fancifulness or illusoriness that we would not attribute to art and literature. If theological discourse is not positive and not dogmatic, then it has every right to ask the theory of historical materialism to accord it the same respect and consideration it gives to literary discourse and the symbolization embodied in art.

This line of thought leads us to the hypothesis that Christianity, no less than art and literature, can have the capability of altering society; and this capability can be exercised in an emancipatory way. To be sure, faith in God has often been used to consecrate the interests of those in power and the existing regime of oppression. But it is not true to say that it must necessarily do that. Lenin is the absolute dogmatist when he sees religion in that light: "Whatever the revolutionary function of religion may have been in the past, any defense or justification of the idea of God today in Europe and in Russia, however well intentioned and well formulated, is a justification of the reactionary position" (257:120–21). Equally dogmatic would be the opposite assertion: i.e., that faith in God is, in itself, revolutionary and liberative. That proposition must be proved and demonstrated, and only real praxis can do it. Theologies of liberation and revolution remain dogmatic so long as they are not verified through the liberative and revolutionary praxis of Christians. It is up to Christians to show that their faith is not a subtle apologia for reaction.

The truth of theology and the faith depends upon their

verification in and by history. In other words, it depends upon the real function that Christian symbols fulfill in society. This does not mean that the value of those symbols is to be reduced to their social function. But the concrete way in which they operate vis-à-vis society is the test that will validate or invalidate their claims to truth.

8. VALIDATION BY PRAXIS

This brings us to a decisive point: the validation or verification of political theology within the framework of the historical-materialist hypothesis. Of course the whole problematic issue of the legitimacy of such a theology is not to be reduced to this one point alone. It entails other important questions also, such as ones we considered earlier: e.g., its satisfactory relationship with a given cultural milieu (see chapter 3, section 13), and also with the essential memories of the Christian faith (see chapter 4). But here the question does not have to do with validating it in terms of the Christian tradition, or from within the context of a dogmatic theology that presupposes faith at the start. Here it is a matter of validating it in terms of the common discourse of human beings, from the standpoint of a fundamental theology that is concerned with the genesis of faith. And since we are focusing on the theory of historical materialism in this chapter, we are specifically concerned here with validating political theology from within the framework of that theory.

In that specific framework, a political hermeneutics of the gospel derives its validation basically from praxis and from the future. It is the effective, real-life praxis of Christians and the historical future of that praxis that validates or invalidates the discourse of political theology. Since political theology entails an essential reference to praxis, it is only logical that praxis should constitute its decisive source of validation. Here it is closely analogous to scientific knowledge, where there is no legitimate human discourse without some reference to a praxis that validates it.

Thus the praxis of Christians is what confers accreditation on any given theology, even in the area of intramural debate between various Christian theologies. A given theology is justified over against other theologies that are possible in the abstract because it fits in better with Christian praxis. It is to this criterion of internal legitimation that Metz is referring when he points to the institutional aspects of the Christian community and their impact on attitudes and practice as the canon governing theological discourse. Perhaps placing too much stress on the institutional aspects, Metz says: "At a time when theology can no longer define the unity and distinctiveness of its object in a purely theological manner and must therefore have recourse to ecclesial awareness in praxis, theology is faced with a new formulation of its canon. The church in its institutional procedure, its public life, the praxis of its authority, and so forth, becomes a critical and acute issue for theology itself" (301:300).

Of even more importance, however, is the external scope of ecclesial praxis as the canon or criterion validating Christian discourse in the eyes of other human beings in general. Not only from within but also from outside the boundaries of faith all theology must be asked: "Does it tend to make human beings capable of loving? Does it hinder or help the liberation of the individual and of society?" (396:16). The answer given to those questions—and only real praxis can provide it—will determine whether a given theology, and theology in general, is well founded or not.

So we can now see the profound meaning in a thesis we have already discovered: "The new criterion of theology and the faith resides in praxis" (310:73). Praxis is the criterion of meaningfulness, validity, and legitimation. Considering the specific question as to how we are to verify or prove false the statements of theological discourse, Alves correctly points out: "The verification of the language of the community of faith is thus related to its ability to make man free for life, free for the future" (48:253). Vergote is of the same mind: "The faith is verified only through the prophetic dynamism it injects into civilization. . . . Human verification is the condition providing access to a faith that can give meaning to life" (416:274, 278). Faith and theology must inject a prophetic dynamism into society, a thrust toward change and liberation. It is that dynamism that verifies them and permits a conversion to faith.

The statements of theology are pronouncements bound up with the concrete witness and activity of Christians. It is in that witness and activity that they find fulfillment and verification. Every theological statement is a prospective view, a "hermeneutic" or "heuristic" hypothesis that must be lived out experientially by Christians; the actions of Christians will confirm or belie the hypothesis, grounding the hypothesis or invalidating it (182:258–61). Theological propositions are "an anticipation of future praxis for each generation of Christians; they are in the nature of a project that can and should be surpassed by a new line of praxis" (244:205). "The criterion of verification for every theological statement is the praxis that it makes possible in the future. Its truth is determined by what it produces in praxis insofar as the alteration of existing reality is concerned" (396:86). As theory, theology precedes and anticipates praxis; but praxis in turn constitutes the horizon within which theological theories are formed. Theological theories constitute the discourse that issues out of the exercise of love and Christian hope.

The notion that Christian beliefs are validated by praxis is hardly a recent or whimsical invention by present-day theologians. It is put forward in the gospel message itself, most pointedly in the remark where Jesus makes love the distinguishing mark of his loyal followers: "This is how all will know you for my disciples—your love for one another"

(John 13:35). The reality of brotherly love, then, provides something like epistemological verification: "The operative presence of love proves Christianity to be true; its absence raises doubts and leads to suspicions that Christianity may be false" (182:211).

Marxists themselves have already noted the fact that in its origins Christianity was different from other religions insofar as it was the religion of oppressed people rather than of oppressors (76:112). This fact itself lends some specific credence to Christianity. Originally the Christian faith was not an instrument of domination but the expression of a yearning for liberty. If the Christian tradition was seen to be in the service of exploitation right back at its beginnings, if it seemed to be the idea-set of some ruling group, then that fact alone would be enough to invalidate it. But its original structure, combined with the quest for freedom on the part of a people and a number of groups that were socially oppressed, does make room for the possibility that even today the Christian faith may be fleshed out in some sort of liberative praxis that will somehow validate it.

It is only along these basic lines, and on the basis of the hypothesis adopted here, that one can give a satisfactory response to a question we raised earlier (see chapter 4, section 10): Why Jesus specifically, and no one else? What is contained in the tradition that derives from him that is not to be found in other religious traditions? Those questions cannot be settled in a dogmatic manner. The correct answer comes in part from history, but mainly from praxis and the future.

For its part, history may be able to show that Jesus possessed an incomparable capacity to stir people to freedom and displayed complete independence vis-à-vis the groups in power. It may even be able to find in him certain qualities that cannot be found to such a high degree in other great religious teachers, who may have been more tied to the ruling ideologies of their day. But even supposing that history could perform this apologetic service, and that is a large supposition, it would only be a partial validation of the Christian option. Complete validation of that option cannot come solely from what Jesus was or said or did; it must also come from the concrete praxis associated with the tradition that goes back to him. The decision to focus on Jesus alone and opt for him is justified insofar as that particular man proves to be capable of generating a liberation praxis that lasts down through the centuries and continues on in the future.

It is Christians working for human liberation who validate and accredit the titles accorded to Christ. It is their praxis that makes Jesus really and truly appear to be the Messiah, the Son of God, the Word made flesh, the ever living one. If people call themselves Christians but foment or accept various forms of human domination over other humans, they make Jesus a liar or a deluder; they make it impossible for anyone to invoke him as the Christ, to derive strength from him. The truth of the belief that Jesus is the Christ finds its verification in the praxis of those human beings who profess fidelity to him. The harsh judgment of Vaccari is correct in the last analysis: "If man is not liberated, Christ has not risen" (414:331).

This attribution of a basic validating function to praxis represents a very definite and concretely verifiable response to a question that has been raised more insistently in recent decades. The question itself has to do with the meaningfulness and validity of religious statements, and it has usually been posed from the standpoint of neopositivist presuppositions. It has produced theological best-sellers, particuarly the one written by Van Buren (94).

A truly satisfactory response to that question, however, cannot be derived from the positivist approach. The question must be explored in historical and dialectical terms. The import and validity of certain beliefs can be seen in the historical consequences that flow from them through the mediating praxis of those who profess those beliefs. A historical-materialist theology sees in this the core of its own grounding and validation. It feels it is solidly grounded when there is an effective praxis that verifies and justifies it. Its pronouncements are true when they are inscribed in concrete praxis. The justification of the Christian faith and its political hermeneutics is to be found in this correspondence of word and deed, of profession and praxis, of symbolic representation and objective social change. The specifically human cast of all things, including faith, emerges from the synchronization of certain activities and certain words. Faith exists as a grounded reality when Christian talk corresponds with Christian praxis, or vice-versa.

Let us be clear on this point. In the course of this study I have discussed various elements which go into legitimating the Christian faith. In chapter 3 and chapter 4 respectively, I discussed its integration into a given cultural milieu and its relationship with the constitutive fonts of Christianity. In this section I have just discussed its validation by praxis, and in section 13 of this chapter I shall discuss its validation in the future. Now the point is that all these features are strictly verifiable in the concrete; they are subject to empirical validation. However, they do not exhaust the problem of grounding and validating theology because its ultimate validation and justification comes from God. This point is usually put a different way. People say that theology ultimately goes back to some divine revelation or word of God. This justification, however, is strictly and purely a theological one. It is something we believe in through faith and hope for as grace. It cannot be equated with knowledge of any scientific sort. Insofar as it is discourse, theology has nothing at all to do with divine justification. It cannot rely on such justification to establish its own certainty or validate its claim vis-à-vis others. Theology looks to that divine justification for its ultimate validation, but it sees it as a mysterious and uncertain horizon that cannot be apprehended by rational discourse or rational theory.

When it comes to comparing its claims to other possible forms of human discourse and debating its own validity as discourse, theology must appeal to validating criteria other than God's revealing word. And in that arena, as we have tried to show, the critical and decisive criterion is the praxis of Christians themselves.

9. BELIEF THAT SANCTIONS THE STATUS QUO VERSUS BELIEF THAT LIBERATES PEOPLE

At the present time faith speaks in more than one idiom. Alongside its provocative language in favor of liberation we find another line of religious language that is still very much alive and that is in the service of the old established order. Thus the use of theologal words is open to ambiguity and equivocation, as we have already noted. Though this danger of equivocation is not sufficient reason for abandoning theologal language, it is obvious that we must ever remain aware of this potential ambiguity.

Viewing the matter in sociopolitical terms, we can state the ambiguity in the following basic way. On the one hand we find an image of God in which God sanctions existing institutions, the prevailing regime of government, and the rights of the past. This is the God of metaphysics and dogmatics. This is also the God of what has been called "the political religions" (313:49), who helps to configure the identity of a people or a society. God's reality is clear-cut and taken for granted. Belief in this God is part and parcel of membership in the related social system. If one is tempted to deny his existence, one is liable to be accused of anomie.

Lack of belief in such a God, on the other hand, goes hand in hand with calling the whole related social system into question. Hence the religious crisis of the present day is closely bound up with the corresponding crisis of social institutions. The traditional God is becoming problematical, along with the tradition and social order that this God has sanctioned. Total rejection of this tradition and order is matched by a denial of God: "One can deny God in the name of social revolution precisely insofar as God is considered to be in solidarity with the structures, the worldview, and the value system that one is trying to overthrow" (210:506). Thus atheism and revolution are paired in modern awareness. Atheism is, in itself, revolutionary. And it seems that the revolution, in turn, can find expression only in atheological symbols.

And so we get a curious inversion of roles. From the revolutionary standpoint it is atheistic symbols that are taken for granted as obvious. Atheism has come to constitute part of the subject matter in protest and other avant-garde movements, be they scientific, political, literary, or esthetic. In them atheism serves much the same functions that belief in God served in the society of an earlier day. A world without God is now taken for granted. That image now constitutes part of the badge of identity for anyone affiliated with the revolutionary movement, just as the image of a really existing God was shared by anyone who truly belonged to the old order. Insofar as it is uncritical, this new "established" atheism is particularly exposed to the various forms of atheistic alienation that Di Marco has described as characteristic of our day: "technological fetishism, scientific fideism, and the worship of materialism" (278:312). There is an alienated and alienating atheism, too.

It is worth pointing out again that in the framework of the historical-materialist hypothesis we have adopted here, the God that the believer speaks about has nothing to do with the God of the old established order. The only God of whom we may rightfully speak in the following pages is a

God who stands over against the No-God that the revolutionary movement assumes and takes for granted. In other words, this is a God who calls the revolutionary movement into question insofar as it seeks to close itself up in a completely immanent world of its own. This God is provocative, therefore, on two accounts. First, this God stands in opposition to the God of the old regime that had once been taken for granted. Second, this God also challenges the atheism that is taken for granted in a completely self-enclosed revolutionary movement.

The ambiguity that we mentioned above results from the fact that at present the same term "God" is used to designate the God of the old established order and the God we have just described. What criterion can we use to determine which God is being spoken about? We must notice whether our language about God leaves everything in peace as it was or subverts the existing order. Concretely speaking, we can make sure that we are talking about the newer God by making sure that we never speak of God without engaging in social and political criticism at the same time. Joint mention of God and social transformation will protect theological language from the danger of being misunderstood or misinterpreted.

10. WORDS AND SOCIAL CHANGE

It does not seem immediately obvious that any kind of language whatsoever is capable of containing liberative and revolutionary potential. Hence some may feel it is doubtful that theological language in the concrete can possess efficacy when it comes to the matter of really changing society, however fresh and reforming it may be in its own sphere.

Without overestimating the sociopolitical scope of language phenomena, however, it does seem undeniable that they do have an impact on the material reality of history itself. In this respect it is worth noting that totalitarian regimes have always forged a lexicon and even a syntax of their own (usually composed of judgmental terms rather than reasoned definitions). It is also worth noting that various tactics of social manipulation, ranging from consumer advertising and promotion to political propagandizing, consist essentially in using and operating with language. The same holds true for the opposing side. Protest also has its lexicon and syntax, which breaks with the prevailing linguistic models.

In the last analysis it seems clear that not only is language not alien to social change but the latter would be impossible without the former: "Man can change his situation in the world precisely insofar as he is a being who talks" (339:93).

Revolutionaries, too, are "language iconoclasts." Confronted with a language structure that is overtly or covertly authoritarian and that serves as a vehicle for the power structure, the revolutionary desacralizes known words and creates an authentic language; as such, this language immediately acquires critical power (54:235–38). Severo Sarduy noted that "there is no society that can maintain itself if its language is called into question" (137:44). Criticism of language is automatically social criticism. A break in linguistic continuity entails a break in institutional tradition.

The whole problem of revolutionary literature and esthetics hinges on the fact that any subversion of the symbols and forms of expression in literature and the arts will immediately lead to social alteration as well. The surrealist movement bears witness to that, and so does the French student movement of May 1968. One of the posters at the Sorbonne during that movement called upon people to "liberate expression." Emancipated language and emancipated human expression are liberation praxis in themselves. Indeed the May 1968 revolt was described by one source as the "takeover of the word," suggesting that it was concerned mainly with the realm of symbol and expression (115) and that it was no less significant than the takeover of the Bastille in an earlier day. Such a takeover is indeed revolutionary if one has not had control over one's words previously.

Speech is itself praxis, liberating praxis. The human word in question must be authentic and truly human, of course. It must serve as a real instrument of expression, communication, and critical clarification of personal and social awareness; it cannot be an abstraction isolated from social actions and processes. Profession of faith is word and speech—not abstract or rhetorical but effective in real life. It belongs to the realm of symbol, of practical symbol. The sociopolitical impact of the gospel message is produced by the effective real praxis of Christians. We must not think, however, that this praxis is made up only of social and political gestures, of class options and party affiliations, or of actions designed to win power. Our profession of faith, our takeover of the theologal word, is itself praxis and has its own efficacy if it combines the features mentioned earlier—if it relates its talk about God with the alteration of an unjust social order. The name "God" should ever remain one that cannot be assimilated by our linguistic and social systems. But its injection into human talk induces a liberation, a liberation from any attempt to close the world off from God. It is not just a revolution *in* word but a revolution *by* word, so that we move through it to something beyond it.

In this respect political theology is analogous to revolutionary art. It is through the creation of beauty that art touches the political realm. Insofar as theology is concerned, it does the same through its profession of faith, through its witness concerning a God who stands in absolute and total opposition to the existing order and the given universe. Insofar as their dialectical interaction with the socioeconomic base is concerned, there is a kinship between what is theologically revolutionary and what is esthetically revolutionary. That is why the Marxist outlook should not display any substantial difference in its evaluation of the fact of art and the fact of Christianity, though there certainly are differences between the two.

11. THE DIALECTICS OF STRUCTURES

My preceding words of explanation would probably be unacceptable to most Marxists and also to most Christians. One brand of strict Marxism reduces human beings to the level of material necessity and the production process that satisfies this necessity. The determination of the human superstructure by the economic base is a one-way street, so that the former cannot possibly react in any autonomous way on the latter. Adopting that criterion, one would say that the ideas that I expressed above have nothing to do with the social theory of Marx at all; that they are related to the sociology of religion that goes back to Durkheim, and even more to Max Weber. It is Weber, above all, who replaced the notion of social "monocausality" with the notion of "reciprocal causality" (271:160).

In non-Marxian sociology of religion, the functional relations between society and religion are expressed in much the following terms: "In general, and particularly in a synchronic framework, the religious fact is a variable of the social fact. But it must be pointed out on the one hand that the social fact is also a variable reciprocally dependent on the religious fact; and on the other hand that the religious fact and the social fact can represent variables that are fairly independent of each other, particularly in a diachronic framework" (148:58). This is also the sociological view of Peter Berger, who sees a dialectical and reciprocal relationship existing between religion and other social processes. Legitimations of and by religion arise from human activity, but they in turn can react upon the deeds of everyday life and transform them radically. Though he would readily admit that in specific historical situations religion has little or no potential to react upon the infrastructure, Berger would still maintain that the potential does exist and cannot be denied altogether. He even states that it is possible to point to concrete examples that show that religious "ideas" have indeed had a profound impact on the social structure, even though they may have been very abstract ideas (70:69, 77, 184–85). Thus it does seem possible to combine Weber's conception with that of Marx, so long as one does not hold to some overly doctrinaire brand of Marxism.

I shall maintain an analogous position here, rejecting any form of dogmatic or intransigent Marxism. The principles of historical materialism in no way demand a one-way determination of the religious fact by the economic fact that would rule out reaction and interaction. One does not at all contradict the basic suppositions of Marx's theory when one asserts that the symbols of religious faith can effectively react upon the socioeconomic base.

Needless to say, the dissatisfaction of believers and theologians with this view will derive from a very different perspective. They tend to overstate the historical influence of faith in God, viewing it in hyperbolic terms. This is particularly true of Protestant theology, which has always stressed the adverse effect of sin upon natural human capabilities. It tends to see faith or hope of Christian freedom as indispensable for the wordly fulfillment and success of the world. This tendency can be noticed even in theologians who do not seem closely tied to confessional orthodoxy. Reading Moltmann, for example, one would have to say that the decisive happenings of history have been theological ones. As Moltmann describes it, the idea of revelation in all its changing forms and vicissitudes has had a compelling influence on the course of societal processes.

Moltmann feels he can trace out a history of revolutions of freedom in the western world by noting the different modulations of the theological notion of freedom (309:313–51). Christianity is presented as "the tide whose word and spirit has moved the whole ongoing process of history" (309:377). The ultimate conclusion to which this leads is that the world can be history only through Christ and through hope in him. Moltmann assures us that it is through Christ that we get "the possibility of an authentic living out of history" (309:329); that it is hope in Christ's resurrection that "introduces God's future into the present and converts the present into history" (309:427).

Following a somewhat different train of thought, Moltmann resorts to God even to establish equality between human beings. This procedure, which is heavily used by Karl Barth, entails a theological reversal of the natural course of things. Instead of arguing from the most commonplace and evident human facts to theological mysteries, one starts with the mysteries and reasons one's way to the facts. Here is what Moltmann says: "Human beings are free and equal only before God, who will judge all of them. . . . The justice of the struggle to implant the freedom and rights of every human being is not grounded on any innate rights; it is grounded on the right that God's future has to be projected on every present moment of history" (309: 318).

There is an idea around today that presents God as the power behind our future and as the only source that can furnish anything really novel to us. This idea, too, is ensnared in the trammels of the older dogmatic view of original sin that sees human beings as incapable of achieving their own nature and humanity without God's intervention. Any such theology is, in the last analysis, caught up in the web of political Augustinianism. According to that conception, human society is incapable of attaining its own ends without the grace of God or the witness of Christians; it can only remain frozen in the old order of things.

The theoretical construct proposed here obviously strips the Christian faith of its unique and singular character. It is not possible to reduce everything to faith or to grace. However much a believer or a theologian one may be, any attempt to reduce history and reality to a theologal position is bound to failure, for such a position can never provide a complete explanation. Faith has something to do with everything, but it is not the key to everything. Neither is the material character of production processes the key to everything, though it too has something to do with everything. Our opposition to theologal reductionism here is grounded on the very same reasons that dictate our opposition to economic reductionism.

To put it another way, we can say that the theory elaborated here assumes multilateral interaction between varied and diverse human structures (186:67–77). Though it will not be approved by many Marxists and many Christians, it contains nothing that is incompatible with the basic presuppositions of historical materialism on the one hand and the intentions of faith on the other. Only a very shortsighted materialism can ignore the relative autonomy of other realms (the artistic realm, the linguistic realm, the theological realm, and so forth) vis-à-vis the economic base. Only a highly sacral concept of faith can fail to recognize that justice, freedom, and utopia are attainable without having to rely at all on the name of God or on hope in God's advent. Our view here is opposed to both brands of reductionism: that of dogmatic Marxists who see economics as the only key, and that of orthodox theologians who see human beings' relationship to God as the sole key.

Our opposition to these reductionisms is based on a very simple reason: Reductionist thought essentially comes down to a monologue whereas human truth necessarily goes by way of universal consent, which in turn is made possible only by dialogue. Theology, for example, is the discourse of believers and, as such, it is the jargon of a specific concrete group rather than a universal language. But insofar as it aspires to truth, insofar as it aspires to verification, it must become a language of dialogue and communication with those outside the Christian group.

This obligation is not always met by various forms of present-day political theology. The language employed by these theologies is often a language closed to any meaningful communication with other human beings and hence inoperative insofar as the future of truth is concerned; it does not allow for any comprehension or understanding of it by non-Christians.

12. THE PRESENCE OF FAITH AND THE ABSENCE OF GOD

From the standpoint of a critical theology, the truly revolutionary element is not God as such or God's activity but rather the image of God in human beings. Using direct, first-stage theologal language, one can say that God liberates us, topples those in power, and guarantees our future. We have noted more than one author doing just that in Part Two of this book. But that is precritical talk. It is like saying that God has brought us a good harvest this year or cured a member of the family. God does not cure, or bring harvests, or liberate, or do battle with potentates. Human experiences and actions such as harvesting, being cured, and winning freedom have experiential elements that are more or less well known; within their own order, however, they do not leave any loophole open for some activity on the part of God.

The real meaning of the assertion that God does something in this order is that some particular image of God is operating in a liberative way to bring about greater justice. This point must be voiced very clearly and insistently on the level of critical theological reflection; otherwise we will fall back into the humbug of *Gott mit uns* or the *gesta Dei per francos.* God is not with the French or the Germans; nor is God with the poor or the oppressed. Indeed there is no certainty that God is with all either. Strictly speaking, God is not with anybody. God does not liberate, or bring peace, or initiate revolutions because God simply does not work in the world. God does not demand justice or prescribe a different society because in reality God does not speak.

Any critical theology must recognize and admit that fact without using evasive language, engaging in a strictly negative theology as it proposes such theses. Once having proposed them, and without denying them in any way, it may be possible to go on to develop a symbolic theology that will concretely specify that negative theology; by talking about the images and symbols of God, rather than about God as such, theology may be able to regain its tongue. But if the language of faith is not to be the delusory projection of vain fantasies, it must go through the dark night and utter silence of a negative theology first.

Operating in the framework of a symbolic theology that has first gone through the rigorous pathway of negativity, we would assign the power of liberating and pacifying and making revolution to the image of God, Christian witness, and the profession of faith. Thus any attempt to expropriate God, to identify God with special interests in society, is strictly and completely ruled out. Theology must be negative and symbolic if it is not to fall back into the old political theology that identified God as such (not God's images) with the empirical reality of society.

It has been said that theology is an "enlightened ignorance" (131:128), or a "silence qualified by words" (307: 161). Both expressions highlight the negative and symbolic character of the theology we are propounding here. Theology knows nothing about God, but it tries to shed light on its ignorance through imaginative illustrations. It is strictly silent about God, matching God's own silence, but it qualifies its silence with parables and symbols. Political theology is subject to the basic conditions that affect all theology. It too is an enlightened ignorance and a silence qualified by symbols. Political theology knows nothing about the action of God in the world; political theology simply believes in such action. It has knowledge only about the activity of Christian symbols and representations in the world; that is all it can talk about with any degree of knowledgeable certainty.

The same applies to statements that the Christian God is the God who will be, who remains to be seen, who goes out to meet human beings in the future. Such statements must be taken, first and foremost, as pronouncements of a negative theology. They must be taken to mean that God has not been and is not; that God has not yet been seen and has not yet come out to meet people experientially in the past. In order to refer to God, hope makes use of a complex of symbols focused on the future; but that does not mean that hope really knows God in any strict sense. Hoping and believing are not knowing; they are a nonknowing illustrated by parables and images.

Hope does not remedy the ignorance of faith in any way. Its gnoseological status remains apophatic and geared to a negative theology. There is a sense in which God will not be and will not go out to meet human beings in the future just as God has not been in the past and has not met people face to face there. But this does not mean that hope cannot be nurtured by symbols and illustrative images even while remaining true to the regimen of a negative theology.

It is this symbolic illustration that differentiates negative theology from atheology. Nonbelievers do not know anything about the God who is to come, nor do they expect anything from this God. What is more, nonbelievers claim to know that there is nothing to hope for: "We atheists hope for nothing, and no one awaits us expectantly" (201:90). Neither do Christians know anything about that God, but they believe and hope nevertheless. Their hope is, first and foremost, a critico-prophetical negation of the atheist's alleged knowledge that there is nothing to hope for. This negation of the believer is articulated in symbols. Eschatology, then, arises as a system of symbols in the service of the believer's critico-prophetical negation of the atheist's negation.

13. VALIDATION BY THE FUTURE

There is yet another sense in which God still remains to be seen. Though the present-day symbols and images of God can even now carry out a de-alienating and liberating function, they do derive from an alienated society. We have every right to ask what will become of them in a different society where alienation and frustration have been reduced. God remains to be seen in the sense that we must wait to see what will happen to the images of God in the future, and particularly in a future that follows along the lines championed by the theologies of liberation and revolution. The validity of present-day theological representations depends on the history that is still to come.

The text of Exodus 3:13 is now understood and interpreted by some exegetes in the future tense. When Moses asks God for God's name, they say, God tells him not who God is but who God will be as shown by the future. God's response to Moses comes down to: "I will be who I will be," or "I shall do what I shall do." As contemporary exegesis puts it, the question as to who God is will be answered by the course of future events (51:34).

This line of exegesis is fully pertinent and meaningful today. It is valid for the name of God not only among the ancient Hebrews but also among present-day Christians. The question as to who God is really will be answered by events that are yet to take place. Future history will help to spell out both the question and its answer—or, to put it better, the elements that must be judged in any attempt to formulate an answer.

In that sense there is something akin to "a hermeneutic process that embraces the history of Christianity" (Moltmann, 309:238). There is a historical process in the course of which Christian witness engages in debate and discussion with society and thereby establishes and verifies the significance of its propositions. Moltmann himself gives the term "process" connotations of a debate and a judicial proceeding. It is a "historico-juridical process" in which is brought out "the truth or falsity of the life of Jesus" and the "truth or falsity of the testimony." It is an "antagonist process dealing with the truth" in which Christians must "give proof of the goodwill manifested in Christ" and "render an account of the authenticity of their witness" (309:377).

We now know that it is praxis that will give that proof and verification. It is praxis that will accredit the import and validity of Christian speech. Who God is and what people are to make of Christ will be answered by future events, and mainly by the deeds that Christians perform in the midst of social and political history.

14. EMANCIPATED HUMANITY

There arises a final question that constitutes an objection to theology. Even granting the fact that the name of God and Christian witness presently do have an emancipatory impact on the political realm, will they not prove to be utterly useless and even impossible in a society that has already been emancipated? Having fulfilled their function as a people's pedagogy for liberty, won't Christianity and faith be rendered useless at the very moment they achieve the goal of the social protest they embody?

Obviously this is the Marxist interpretation, which follows from Marx's well known text on the eventual disappearance of religion: "The religious reflection of the real world can only disappear . . . when the relations in practical daily life present human beings each day with relations that are clearly rational among themselves and with nature" (285:838).

It is the judgment of Marxists that religion is destined to

disappear when humanity abolishes the social conditions that now give rise to it. A qualitatively different life and qualitatively different modes of living among people in a different sort of society will permit people to confront the limitations of human finiteness, and even of death itself, in different terms. It is hard for us to imagine those terms today, but they certainly will render faith and hope in some transcendent reality quite useless and impossible. Religious symbolization will disappear when perfect socialism establishes complete reciprocity and communication between human beings and materially realizes what Christian beliefs allude to in dreamy and fantastic terms. As Marxists see it, even the religious criticism of secularized society and communism will get beyond the intention of its spokespersons and ultimately help to fashion a life without God (272:114). Thus the ultimate fate of political theology, as a critique and criticism of society, will be to abet the construction of a socialism that will eventually be atheistic.

Christians, of course, see things differently. First of all, there are some who frankly criticize Marxism for its inability to resolve the problem of death. As they see it, Christian belief in the resurrection offers a full and complete solution to that issue. This line of argument can still be heard from dogmatic polemicists, but in fact it is quite weak. The real question is not whether Christianity *believes* it can offer total victory over death, but whether in fact it *really does* provide that victory. In the eyes of Marxists, the traditional Christian solution (i.e., the resurrection of the dead) is totally illusory; hence the Christian objection to Marxism on this score is groundless. If no one can conquer death, the wisest thing to do is to accept that fact without trying to foster illusions based on religion.

Usually, however, the appeal of present-day theologians to the matter of death takes another tack. They tend to stress its function as an alienating factor. In that context death is accompanied by other limits and deficiencies that affect people no matter what their social situation is. This view can be framed in negative terms by way of opposition to the Marxist view that sees such limits as mere side-effects of the sociopolitical alienation from which the revolution will free us (68:1066). It can also be put in positive terms. Metz does this at one point when he stresses the fact that Christianity does not foment any alienation. All it does, he says, is proclaim the existence of those "self-alienations that are essential to man, and which no social progress can solve." These alienations can be summed up as the "pain of being a finite creature." They cannot be overcome by any socioeconomic means. Specifically they are: guilt, concupiscence, and death. If some day the great social utopias become a reality, those issues will not disappear. On the contrary, they will become all the more urgent; for today their impact is blunted by the existence of more immediate and pressing concerns (302:153; 303:166–69).

There are latent residues of ideology in this outlook proposed by Metz. For example, the problems of concupiscence and guilt are obviously Christian problems rooted in a very specific dogmatic doctrine. In no way do they appear to be questions or "self-alienations" essential to human beings as such. Depth psychology has dismantled both concepts insofar as their alienating features are concerned. If some remnant of the theological notion of sin does remain, it does not seem that one can or should see any alienation in it. Far from sustaining that concupiscence and guilt, as essential human alienations, open up a space for religious language, we should be trying to work out a theology in which the notion of sin is stripped of its alienating features (such as the traditional notions of concupiscence and guilt).

There remains, then, the question of death. And, in more general terms, there remains the pain of being finite. Here there does not seem to be any easy way out for the atheist and the atheological point of view. The suffering produced by human finiteness and mortality continually gives rise to eschatological representations based on hope. If religious faith and hope find their deepest wellspring in mortality and sorrow, or if at the very least those realities make them possible, then faith and hope will always be possible. We want to account for our death and our dead ones. So long as human beings die, it will always be possible to confront the fact in terms of some sort of theologal symbolization.

Moreover, it does not seem that the definitive establishment of socialism can, in itself, assuage the pain and suffering of mortality and finiteness. We will have faith and theology for many centuries, for as long as this suffering is not resolved or dissolved. This point is acknowledged by some Marxists. While they adhere to other aspects of Marxist doctrine concerning the socio-genesis of faith and its ultimate disappearance from history, they also acknowledge that faith will not be eliminated easily or quickly. Ernst Bloch, for example, notes that there does exist a kind of suffering that is "authentic, fruitful, and socially unsolvable." It is anxiety over a death that can occur at any moment. This particular suffering constitutes a profoundly metahistorical and metapolitical problem (79:219).

Recognition of this particular kind of suffering would make it possible for Marxists better to appreciate theologal faith and hope as a symbolic response to certain limitations that will not be eliminated with the dissolution of socioeconomic contradictions. Of great interest in this connection are certain observations which were made by Manuel Ballestero in an interview, and which I have discussed at some length in an earlier work (181:24–25). They almost border on historical-materialist theology, and they show how far a Marxist can go in evaluating faith positively even though he speaks from the standpoint of a nonbeliever:

As we come closer to a classless society and find ourselves in a transitional society on the way towards full communism where the state still exists, religion will still exist also in that society insofar as certain forms of alienation still persist: i.e., the division of labor, contradictions between city and countryside, rulers and ruled, and so forth. In such circumstances religion can continue to be a leaven of protest. There is an even more deep-rooted contradiction that may persist for centuries, even in a highly developed communist society. I am referring to the contradiction existing between the life instinct and the temporal nature of man. So long as this contradiction persists, so long as death has not been fully confronted and assumed, religion will find roots for itself. Indeed that may well be its deepest and most solid roots.

Ballestero goes on to say that people can come to the point of fully accepting the fact of death without experiencing it as irremediably in contradiction with the life instinct. He quite rightly points out that the pain of dying is presently aggravated by the frustration human beings feel. They must "depart from this world with the realization that they have lived a life which, more than anything else, is a caricature of what it could and should have been." A classless society "will restructure our way of living, even on the unconscious level," so that we may look forward to a time when we can fully accept and integrate the fact of death into it. Death as a contradiction will be resolved and dissolved. A similar optimism about the possibility of accepting death without anguish and sorrow can be found in the concluding pages of Marcuse's *Eros and Civilization.* He maintains that death can eventually prove to be a sign and badge of liberty, that it can be made rational and painless. People will be able to die with the awareness that what they love is protected from misery and oblivion. After a full life they will be able to accept their own death at some moment chosen by themselves (281:218).

These opinions may seem to be very debatable. But they are most interesting and pertinent insofar as they represent a penetrating critique of the cultural importance of death in Western society. The fact is that "a civilization's attitude toward death is not absolute, timeless, and ahistorical." Not all societies integrate the fact of death in the same way. It is obvious that Western culture has elaborated an imposing "mythology of death" that Christianity helped to fashion and that existential philosophy has put to its own uses (1:108). Awareness of the cultural connotations involved in the West's understanding and interpretation of the fact of death should prevent us from elevating our conception of death's meaning to the level of an essential human category. It should foster a critical attitude toward any theological interpretation that attempts to benefit from the current alienating import of death and project it into the future.

That does not mean, of course, that the optimism of Marcuse and other Marxists is automatically justified. A classless society without contradictions and conflicts may well be able to structure the individual and collective unconscious in a qualitatively different way; but it remains to be seen whether such restructuring will eliminate the suffering caused by finiteness and fully integrate the fact of death in a liberative way.

It is indeed true that there have been and still are peoples and cultural groups in which human beings die with less unpleasantness than we do in the West. But serious consideration must be given to two possible influencing factors in such instances where death seems to be better integrated into people's culture and worldview. The first factor would be a highly or completely unproblematical kind of religious belief; the second factor would be a less clear consciousness of personal life and freedom on the individual level. Increased awareness, in itself, seems to intensify the suffering caused by finiteness and by the opposition between death and the life instinct.

It is true that in a different society the cultural meaning of death will also be different. But it is difficult to imagine that our perception of death as a painful experience will disappear, unless we imagine a society that is scarcely conscious of itself and that has regressed to the primitive and almost animalistic level of the immediate enjoyment of life—such a society being quite compatible with a high degree of technological and social development. Marcuse's proposal seems a bit too much like a world that enjoys happiness on the level of brute animals. There human beings live, make love, and die with all the nonchalance of animals, while at the same time enjoying all the advantages of industrialization and euthanasia.

These critical addenda to the thesis of Metz and other theologians help us to avoid any facile extrapolation. The theologians try to suggest that it is impossible to overcome the alienation of death through social alterations, that consequently there is room for posing the theologal question of death. But they may unthinkingly be trying to make a quick transfer of the present meaning of death in western culture to some future time and place in history. By the same token, however, we should not assume that the social meaning of death in the future will be more like that which it had for the Maoris or the Greeks. To extrapolate the views of primitive man or ancient societies would be even more arbitrary than to extrapolate the views of advanced western culture. The import of death in the culture of the future remains a moot question, and no line of speculation can claim to be valid.

15. NOW AND THE END OF HISTORY

We must focus on the present historical and cultural moment. Here and now in the West, the pain of being finite and the experience of death as contradiction and alienation does open up room for the God question and make theologal hope meaningful. We can confer different meanings on that hope and choose between different alternatives (see chapter 6, section 12). But we cannot use it as an opiate to distract ourselves from the obligatory and necessary struggle against various alienations and contradictions.

Hope should effect a methodical subversion of the cultural significance of death, seeking to eliminate its alienating features. In particular it should attack the threat and use of death as the supreme form of people's use of power and violence against other people; and it should also attack the terrible isolation felt by the dying person in today's society. It certainly is possible that the elimination of death's alienating features would deprive it of its current majeutic value as an aid to theologal conversion, but that remains to be seen. Whatever the final result of the de-alienation of death and mortality may be, we should not be dissuaded from that task by the fear that we shall thereby lose one of the most traditional supports for our work of predisposing people toward faith.

Furthermore, death is not just a fact imposed on human beings from the outside. It is not just something that has to happen sooner or later and that we must suffer passively as a limitation and an alienation. Death can be accepted voluntarily, can be freely chosen as an option at some point in time and place where it could have been avoided. There is a freely chosen and self-fulfilling praxis that consists in dying for the sake of others or risking one's own life for their sake. One may choose to die for the sake of other individuals or groups of people, so that they may save their physical life, or live a decent human life, or whatever. The whole question of the meaningfulness of death becomes much more pointed when we focus on some sort of death that is freely chosen or risked for the sake of other human beings. Every theory of social action and political struggle must try to account for that option: "Sooner or later every attempt to provide humanist motivation for undertaking the liberation struggle must ask itself what meaning there can be in the radical praxis of dying for others." That question, Assmann goes on to say, has been consistently disregarded by Marxism; and it is in fact a theological question (59:75–76,

137). Or, as Míguez Bonino puts it, it is a question that forces us to ponder the cross of Christ (306:210). In any case it certainly is a question that prevents us from closing off the discourse. It remains unfinished because we must leave an opening toward the direction where faith and hope, the deeds and the words of the Christian, go out to meet the God who is coming.

And what about the other side, the Christian side? Why must we necessarily center our theological anticipation of the future around the relationship between faith on the one hand and human limits and limitations on the other? As Bonhoeffer said some time ago, we should stress human powers, not human limitations. Up to now faith has usually been related to basic needs and harsh necessity. In an altered society, where the most elemental needs are satisfied and the resultant alienations have been eliminated, the genesis and growth of faith will take on a different cast. It will have to be an expression of liberty, not of necessity; of fulfilled joy, not protest. It will have to be the symbolization of a happy life, not of efforts to overcome alienation.

"You be men, and God will be God." That is the way Bloch sums up the theology of Thomas Münzer (79:85). That is also the way in which our theological anticipation of the future can proceed. A wholly gratuitous and gift-giving God, who is described by some theologians but who can hardly be glimpsed at present, can be more real and tangible for human beings who have been liberated from the yoke of necessity. When human beings are truly human, when they have fully assumed what is properly theirs, including death, in a framework of authentic personal and social liberty, then God will be God as well. At least that is what faith expectantly hopes for.

But what do we really know about the possibilities (or impossibilities) of faith and conversion in the world of the future? From the standpoint of a strictly critical theology, we should not even affirm such possibilities with any trace of sureness. We can only hope for them, believe in them in generic terms, and utter hypotheses that seem more or less likely to us. For example, have we given any serious consideration to the shock our earthbound models of rationality will receive when and if we make contact with intelligent beings on other planets? That eventuality is very real, though it still seems to belong more to the realm of science fiction and futurology. But if it came to be verified, could it not totally alter our current theological and atheological representations?

Clearly we cannot operate with the future as if it were a sure and certain datum. But it is inevitable that human beings will look to the future and its truth for the verification or justification of the propositions that they put forward in the present as true. In the realm of historical verification, it is the future that will justify or nullify the theological propositions of the present day. And so we see that these propositions entail an element of guess or wager. The profession of faith and the statements of theology are wagers that attempt to anticipate the future of the truth—or, what comes down to the same thing, the truth of the future. Faith, too, represents something that Habermas attributes to reason: access to future truth.

At this point we find an almost inevitable allusion to the end of history as the terminal point which, ideally, will resolve the whole issue of the future of truth. In this matter we all are Hegelians to some extent. The end of history appears before our eyes as the tribunal and judgment seat of history. Or perhaps it is simply that we are heirs to Judeo-Christian eschatological thinking, and we postulate an apocalyptic criterion to decide the truth or falsehood of religious beliefs. If we look to the future in general to validate or invalidate our present claims about the truth, then it is obvious that the only irrefutable and insuperable criterion of validity can be provided by the very end of human history.

In this case it is not neccessary to imagine the end of history as some point of perfect consummation and fulfillment. It is not certain that human history is going to be consummated in any sense like that. Like the life of the individual, it may simply end without getting beyond equivocation and imperfection. Moltmann (313:221) wisely calls our attention to that point, and it is a good counterweight to the overly optimistic viewpoint of people like Teilhard de Chardin (183:381–98) who envision the end of the human world as some instant of supreme maturity and awareness in which the meaning of history is fully grasped and acknowledged. But even if we do not count on any Teilhardian or Hegelian end of history, the decision and wager of faith does contain a reference to some ultimate future. In that sense faith is a hypothesis, a proposition, and a wager about the ultimate future of truth and the ultimate verification of human praxis.

Up to that point there is no difference between faith and atheistic dialectical materialism from the formal or structural point of view. As proposal, hypothesis, and wager, the two are the same. Lucien Goldmann, a Marxist, has not hesitated to label dialectical materialism as "faith" (213:112). Insofar as the future is concerned, both Marxism and Christianity constitute a faith and a hope rather than science or knowledge. Both represent a wager about what is to happen, a hypothesis for action, and a practical postulate. It is the events of future days that will serve to verify and pass judgment on these two similar though contradictory wagers.

From the Christian side, André Dumas has expressed the point frankly and openly in a dialogue with Marxists: "We shall know the outcome of this alternative between materialism on the one hand and transcendence on the other only at the end of history. But from today on each one of us lives our life with our wager placed on that as yet unproven terminus" (21:37). Gilbert Mury echoes those sentiments no less openly and frankly for the other side: "We Marxists are of the opinion that when man grows up in a just world, he will no longer feel a need to entrust himself to the hands of God. . . . He will be spontaneously and naturally atheistic. Christians are free to state and believe that this total man will be closer to God than today's shattered human being. Only the future will settle the question between the two" (319:219).

In their Introduction to a recently published anthology of writings by Marx and Engels on religion, Hugo Assmann and Reyes Mate prefer to allude to tomorrow than to some distant and problematical end of history. It is a real though still future criterion: "The tomorrow of human emancipation will speak for itself concerning the importance or banality of the fact of religion." The urgent task right now is the abolition of oppression. The question confronting Christians is this: If they accept the Marxist critique of magical religion, the church, and historical Christianity, and if they then adopt a consistent line of praxis designed to remove oppressive conditions, will the future justify their present convictions? (56:37).

The future will decide that question. In the meantime a historical-materialist theology of the kind proposed here is quite as possible and feasible as the corresponding atheology. The Christian faith does have a real possibility, even within the framework of a dialectical-materialist interpretation of history. The assumption that the economic base and production processes exert a determining influence does not necessarily rule out profession of faith and theological symbolization. Belief continues to be a postulate, a hypothesis, a wager; but it is not an alienated illusion, dreamy fantasy, or an ideological evasion.

BIBLIOGRAPHY

In this section the order of the Spanish edition has been followed to ensure correct references in the main text. Thus names beginning with Ch follow names beginning with Cu since Ch follows the letter C in Spanish alphabetical order. Readers should also note that volumes 1 to 50 of *Concilium* were published in an English-language edition by Paulist Press (New York); volumes 51 on were published in English by Herder and Herder, now amalgamated with Seabury Press (New York). No further note is made of this in the individual entries.

ANTHOLOGIES

1. *Contra la medicina liberal* (Comités de "action santé"). Barcelona: Estela, 1970.

2. *Cristianos por el socialismo.* Montevideo: Tierra Nueva, 1973; in English see *Christians and Socialism.* Ed. John Eagleson. Trans. John Drury. New York: Orbis, 1975.

3. *Cristianos y marxistas: los problemas de un diálogo* (Aguirre, Aranguren, Sacristán). Madrid: Alianza, 1969.

4. *Diskussion zur "politischen Theologie."* Ed. Helmut Peukert. Mainz and Munich: Kaiser and Matthias Grünewald, 1969.

5. *Diskussion zur "Theologie der Revolution."* Ed. Ernst Feil and Rudolph Weth. Mainz and Munich: Kaiser and Matthias Grünewald, 1969.

6. *Eglise et société* (documents of the 1966 Geneva Conference of the World Council of Churches). Geneva: Labor et Fides, 1970, 4 vols; a selection of these documents in English can be found in *The Church amid Revolution.* Ed. Harvey Cox. New York: Association Press, 1967.

7. *El compromiso social y político de los grupos pequeños* (Maggioni, Sorbi). Salamanca: Sígueme, 1974.

8. *El futuro de la Iglesia,* supplementary issue of *Concilium,* December 1970. Madrid: Cristiandad, 1970.

9. *Evangelio y revolución* (Le Guillou, Clément, Bosc). Bilbao: Desclée de Brouwer, 1970.

10. *Fe cristiana y cambio social en América latina* (the 1972 El Escorial Convention). Salamanca: Sígueme, 1973.

11. *Fe y secularización en América latina* (Comblin, Arellano, Galilea). Bogotá: Ipla, 1972.

12. *Hacia un humanismo nuevo* (Barth, Maydieu, Jaspers). Madrid: Guadarrama, 1957.

13. *Humanismo socialista* (Erich Fromm et al.). Buenos Aires: Paidós, 1968.

14. *Il dialogo alla prova.* Florence, 1965.

15. *Kirche im Prozess der Aufklärung* (Metz, Moltmann, Oelmüller). Mainz and Munich: Kaiser and Matthias Grünewald, 1970.

16. *La fe, fuerza histórica* (Domergue, Cardonnel, Chaigne, Dutheil). Barcelona: Estela, 1971.

17. *La fe y la realidad sociopolítica. Concilium* 36, June 1968.

18. *La ribellione degli studenti* (Dutschke, Bergmann, Lefèbvre, Rabehl). Milan: Feltrinelli, 1968.

19. *La violencia de los pobres* (Cardonnel, Domergue, Chaigne, Duclos). Barcelona: Nova Terra, 1968.

20. *L'existence de Dieu.* Tournai: Casterman, 1963.

21. *L'homme chrétien et l'homme marxiste* (Marxist-Christian discussions in Lyon and Paris in 1964). Paris and Geneva: La Palatine, 1964.

22. *L'homme devant Dieu* (Mélanges Henri de Lubac, III). Paris: Aubier, 1964.

23. *Marxistes et chrétiens. Entretiens de Salzbourg.* Paris: Mame, 1968.

24. *Praxis de liberación y fe cristiana. Concilium* 96. 1974.

25. *Pueblo oprimido, señor de la historia.* Montevideo: Tierra nueva, 1972.

26. *Religion, ¿instrumento de liberación?* (Gutiérrez, Alves, Assmann). Madrid and Barcelona: Marova and Fontanella, 1973.

27. *Revolución* (Masina, Díez Alegría, Chiavacci). Pamplona: Dinor, 1972.

28. "Selecciones sobre teología política. Presentación." In *Selecciones de teología,* 38, 1971.

29. *Teología de la violencia* (Dabezies, Dumas, Lecocq). Salamanca: Sígueme, 1970.

30. *Théologie d'aujourd'hui et de demain* (Burke, De Lubac, Daniélou, Congar, Rahner, Schillebeeckx, Metz, Davis, Schmemann, Lindbeck, Sittler). Paris: Cerf, 1967.

31. *Theologie der Revolution. Analysen und Materialen* (Rendtorff, Tödt). Frankfurt: Suhrkamp, 1968.

32. "Un dialogue avec les marxistes?" *Informations Catholiques Internationales,* number 240 (May 15, 1965), pp. 17–25.

33. *Une théologie de la révolution?* (Gollwitzer et al.). Geneva: Labor et Fides, 1968.

34. *Utopía* (Arnhelm Neusüss et al.). Barcelona: Barral, 1971.

35. *Utopía.* Documentation in *Concilium* 41. January 1969.

36. "Y a-t-il une politique chrétienne?" Poll taken and presented by *Esprit* 10, October 1967.

AUTHORS

37. Acebal Monfort, Luis. "Upsal, un syntôme" *Nouvelle Revue Théologique* 91 (1969):47–64.

38. Adorno, Theodor W. Spanish trans., *La ideología como lenguaje.* Madrid: Taurus, 1971. German original, *Jargon der Eigentlichkeit.* Eng. trans., *The Jargon of Authenticity.* Evanston: Northwestern University Press, 1973.

39. Adorno, Theodor W. *Negative Dialektik.* Frankfurt: Suhrkamp, 1966. Eng. trans., *Negative Dialectics.* New York: Seabury, 1972.

40. Adorno, Theodor W., and Max Horkheimer. Spanish edition, *Sociológica.* Madrid: Taurus, 1966.

41. Alfaro, Juan. *Hacia una teología del progreso humano.* Barcelona: Herder, 1961.

42. Alfonso, Aldo d'. *Los católicos y la contestación.* Barcelona: Fontanella, 1972.

43. Althusser, Louis. "L'Église d'aujourd'hui: diagnostics." *Lumière et vie* 93, May–June 1969.

44. Althusser, Louis. *Pour Marx.* Paris: Maspero, 1967. English trans., *For Marx.* New York: Pantheon, 1970.

45. Alvarez Bolado, Alfonso. "Del pluralismo de modelos socio-teoréticos a una consideración metasociológica de la secularización." In *Fe y nueva sensibilidad histórica* (Instituto, Fe y Secularidad). Salamanca: Sígueme, 1972.

46. Alvarez Bolado, Alfonso. "Entre la retórica y el martirio. Sobre la condición confesante de la Iglesia." *Iglesia Viva* 44–45, March–June 1973.

47. Alvarez Bolado, Alfonso. "Marxistas y cristianos en la 'isla de los hombres.'" *Razón y fe* 174, 1966:81–96.

48. Alves, Rubem A. *Cristianismo ¿opio o liberación?* Salamanca: Sígueme, 1973. Spanish translation of the author's *A Theology of Human Hope.* Washington, D.C.: Corpus, 1969.

49. Alves, Rubem A. "El pueblo de Dios y la búsqueda de una nueva ordenación social." In anthology 26 above.

50. Alves, Rubem A. "Religión: ¿opio del pueblo?" In anthology 26 abovc.

51. Anderson, Bernhard. *Understanding the Old Testament.* Englewood Cliffs: Prentice-Hall, 1956. Further editions in 1966 and 1975.

52. Arias, Gonzalo. "Sobre la ética de la no-violencia." *Mundo social* 174, February 1970.

53. Arias, Maximino. "La teología en Chile." *Iglesia Viva* 44–45, March–June 1973.

54. Assmann, Hugo, "Die Situation der unterentwickelt gehaltenen Länder als Ort einer Theologie der Revolution." In anthology 4 above.

55. Assmann, Hugo "Hacia una argumentación unitaria sobre la teología de la liberación." In anthology 26 above.

56. Assmann, Hugo, and Reyes Mate. "Introduction" to the anthology of writings by Marx and Engels. *Sobre la religión.* Salamanca: Sígueme, 1974.

57. Assmann, Hugo. "La dinámica de un encuentro de teología." In anthology 25 above.

58. Assmann, Hugo. "Presentación." In anthology 25 above.

59. Assmann, Hugo. *Teología desde la praxis de la liberación.* Salamanca: Sígueme, 1973. In English see *Theology for a Nomad Church.* Trans. Paul Burns. Maryknoll, New York: Orbis Books, 1976.

60. Aubert, Roger. *Le problème de l'acte de foi.* Louvain: Warny, 1958.

61. Barth, Karl. *Communauté chrétienne et communauté civile.* Geneva: Labor et Fides, 1958.

62. Barth, Karl. French trans., *Dogmatique,* vol. 9. Geneva: Labor et Fides, 1961. English trans., *Church Dogmatics.* Edinburgh: T. and T. Clark, 1936–69.

63. Barth, Karl. "La actualidad del mensaje cristiano." In anthology 12 above.

64. Barth, Karl. French trans., *La théologie protestante au XIX siècle.* Geneva: Labor et Fides, 1969. English trans., *Protestant Theology in the Nineteenth Century.* Valley Forge: Judson, 1973.

65. Bauer, Gerhard. *Towards a Theology of Development.* Geneva: Sodepax, 1970.

66. Beaucamp, Emile. "Prophétisme, prophètes et faux prophètes ou les limites d'un genre littéraire." *Laval théologique philosophique.* June 1970.

67. Benzo, Miguel. *Sobre el sentido de la vida.* Madrid: B.A.C., 1972.

68. Benzo, Miguel. *Teología para universitarios.* Madrid: Guadarrama, 1963.

69. Berdyaev, N. *Le sens de la création.* Bruges and Paris: Desclée de Brouwer, 1955. English trans., *The Meaning of the Creative Act.* London: Gollancz, 1955.

70. Berger, Peter. Spanish trans., *Para una teoría sociológica de la religión.* Barcelona: Kairós, 1971. English original, *The Sacred Canopy: Elements of a Sociological Theory of Religion.* New York: Doubleday Anchor, 1969.

71. Bernal, John D. Spanish trans., *Historia social de la ciencia.* Barcelona: Península, 1968. English original, *The Social Function of Science.* Cambridge: M.I.T. Press, 1967.

72. Biot, François. *Théologie de la politique.* Paris: Presses Universitaires, 1972. Spanish trans., *Teología de lo político.* Salamanca: Sígueme, 1974.

73. Blanquart, P. "A propos des rapports science-idéologie et foi-marxisme." *Lettre,* 144–45, 1970.

74. Blanquart, P. "Fe cristiana y revolución." In anthology 29 above.

75. Blanquart, P. "La foi et les exigences politiques." *Croissance des jeunes nations,* June 1969.

76. Bloch, Ernst. "Aportaciones a la historia de los orígenes del Tercer Reich." In anthology 34 above.

77. Bloch, Ernst. *Das Prinzip Hoffnung.* Frankfurt: Suhrkamp, 1959.

78. Bloch, Ernst. *Philosophische Grundfragen,* I. Frankfurt, Suhrkamp, 1961.

79. Bloch, Ernst. Spanish trans., *Thomas Münzer, teólogo de la revolución.* Madrid: Ciencia nueva, 1968. German original: *Thomas Münzer als Theologe der Revolution.* Frankfurt: Suhrkamp, 1960.

80. Bochenski, J.M. Spanish trans., *La lógica de la religión.* Buenos Aires: Paidós, 1967. English edition, *The Logic of Religion.* New York: New York University Press, 1965.

81. Boff, Leonardo. "Salvación en Jesucristo y proceso de liberación." In *Concilium* 96, 1974, pp. 375–88.

82. Boros, Ladislaus. Spanish trans., *Encontrar a Dios en el hombre.* Salamanca: Sígueme, 1971. English edition, *Meeting God in Man,* New York: Doubleday Image, 1971.

83. Borovoi, Archpriest. "La Iglesia rusa y la revolución soviética." In Gauthier, entry 205 below.

84. Borrat, Héctor. "Las bienaventuranzas y el cambio social." In anthology 10 above.

85. Brandon, S.G.F. *Jesus and the Zealots.* New York: Scribner's, 1967.

86. Brown, Norman O. *Life against Death.* New York: Random House, 1959.

87. Buber, Martin. *La vie en dialogue.* Paris: Aubier, 1959. In English see *I and Thou.* New York: Scribner's, 1958.

88. Buber, Martin. Italian trans., *L'ecclisi di Dio.* Milan: Comunità, 1961. English trans., *The Eclipse of God.* New York: Harper and Row, 1952.

89. Bueno, Gustavo. *El papel de la filosofía en el conjunto del saber.* Madrid: Ciencia nueva, 1970.

90. Bultmann, Rudolf. *Glauben und Verstehen,* 4 vols. Tübingen: J.C.B. Mohr, 1966–67. English trans., *Faith and Understanding.* New York: Harper and Row, 1969.

91. Bultmann, Rudolf. French edition, *Histoire et eschatologie.* Neuchâtel: Delachaux et Niestlé, 1969. English trans., *The Presence of Eternity: History and Eschatology.* New York: Harper and Row, 1957.

92. Bultmann, Rudolf. "Neues Testament und Mythologie." In *Kerygma und Mythos.* Hamburg: Herbert Reich, 1960, vol. I. English trans., *Kerygma and Myth: A Theological Debate.* New York: Harper and Row, 1961.

93. Büntig, Aldo J. "Dimensiones del catolicismo popular latinoamericano y su inserción en el proceso de liberación." In anthology 10 above.

94. Buren, Paul van. Spanish trans., *El significado secular del evangelio.* Barcelona: Península, 1968. English original, *The Secular Meaning of the Gospel.* New York: Macmillan, 1963.

95. Buri, Fritz. *Theologie der existenz.* Bern: Paul Haubt, 1954. English trans., *Theology of Existence.* Greenwood, S.C.: Attic Press, 1965.

96. Calvez, Jean-Yves. Spanish trans., *El pensamiento de Carlos Marx.* Madrid: Taurus, 1964. French original, *La pensée de Karl Marx.* Paris: Seuil, 1959.

97. Camara, Helder. *Espiral de violencia.* Salamanca: Sígueme, 1970. English trans., *Spiral of Violence.* London: Sheed and Ward, 1971.

98. Camara, Helder. "Nous tâtonnons dans l'ombre mais l'Esprit de Dieu veille sur l'Eglise." *Informations catholiques internationales* 417, October 1, 1972.

99. Cardonnel, Jean. "Amor creador y revolución." In anthology 19 above.

100. Cardonnel, Jean. *Dieu est mort en Jésus-Christ.* Bordeaux: G. Ducros, 1968.

101. Cardonnel, Jean. "La única pasión de la humanidad." In anthology 16 above.

102. Carmichael, Joel. *The Death of Jesus.* New York: Macmillan, 1962.

103. Carro Celada, Esteban. *Curas guerrilleros en España.* Madrid: PPC, 1972.

104. Casas, Fray Bartolomé de las. *El evangelio y la violencia.* Madrid: Zyx, 1967.

105. Castelli, Enrico. *Existentialisme théologique.* Paris: Herman, 1948.

106. Castilla del Pino, Carlos. *Introducción a la hermenéutica del lenguaje.* Barcelona: Península, 1973.

107. Castilla del Pino, Carlos. *Naturaleza del saber.* Madrid: Taurus, 1970.

108. Castilla del Pino, Carlos. *Psicoanálisis y marxismo.* Madrid: Alianza, 1969.

109. Castillo Cárdenas, Gonzalo. "Christen und der Kampf um eine soziale Ordnung in Lateinamerika." In anthology 31 above.

110. Castillo Cárdenas, Gonzalo. "Le défi de la révolution latinoaméricaine." In anthology 6, vol. I, above.

111. Castro, Emilio. "Conversion et évolution sociale." In anthology 6, vol. I, above. Also in the English abridgement.

112. Castro, Emilio. "La creciente presencia de criterios de interpretación histórica en la evolución de la hermenéutica bíblica." In anthology 25 above.

113. Cazalis, Georges. *Prédication, acte politique.* Paris: Cerf, 1970.

114. Cazalis, Georges. "Théologie de la révolution et révolution de la théologie." *Lettre,* n. 119.

115. Certeau, Michel de. *La prise de la parole.* Bruges: Desclée de Brouwer, 1968.

116. Certeau, Michel de. *L'Etranger ou l'union dans la différence.* Paris: Desclée de Brouwer, 1969.

117. Colomer, Julio. "Apunte bibliográfico sobre Teología de la Revolución." *Razón y Fe* 872–73, September–October 1970.

118. Comblin, Joseph. "Crítica de la teología de la secularización." In anthology 11 above.

119. Comblin, Joseph. "Interpretación no religiosa del N.T. y teología de la liberación." In anthology 11 above.

120. Comblin, Joseph. "Libertad y liberación." In *Concilium* 96, 1974.

121. Comblin, Joseph. *Théologie de la révolution.* Paris: Presses Universitaires, 1970.

122. Cone, James H. *Black Theology and Black Power.* New York: Seabury, 1969.

123. Coste, René. *Evangelio y política.* Madrid: Edicusa, 1969.

124. Coste, René. *Moral internacional.* Barcelona: Herder, 1967.

125. Cox, Harvey. Spanish edition, *El cristiano como rebelde.* Madrid and Barcelona: Marova and Fontanella, 1968. English trans.: *God's Revolution and Man's Responsibility.* Valley Forge, Judson Press.

126. Cox, Harvey. Spanish trans., *La cuidad secular.* Barcelona: Península, 1968. English original, *The Secular City,* rev. ed. New York: Macmillan, 1966.

127. Cox, Harvey. Spanish trans., *Las fiestas de locos.* Madrid: Taurus, 1972. English original, *The Feast of Fools.* Cambridge: Harvard University Press, 1969.

128. Cox, Harvey. *On Not Leaving It to the Snake.* New York: Macmillan, 1964.

129. Cox, Harvey. "Politische Theologie." *Evangelische Theologie* 29, 1969.

130. Crespy, Georges. "Recherche sur la signification politique de la mort du Christ." *Lumière et Vie* 101, 1971, pp. 89–109.

131. Crombie, I.M. "Theology and Falsification." In *New Essays in Philosophical Theology* (Flew, MacIntyre). New York: Macmillan, 1964.

132. Cullman, Oscar. Spanish trans., *Jesús y los revolucionarios de su tiempo.* Madrid: Studium, 1971. English edition, *Jesus and the Revolutionaries.* New York: Harper and Row, 1970.

133. Chaigne, Hervé. "Bogotá y la revolución necesaria." In anthology 16 above.

134. Chaigne, Hervé. "Evaluation du gandhisme." *Frères du monde* 33, 1965, no. 1.

135. Chaigne, Hervé. "La historia y la cruz: hacia un cristianismo secularizado." In anthology 16 above.

136. Chaigne, Hervé. "Note sur le devoir de révolution." *Frères du monde* 48, 1967, no. 4.

137. Chao, Ramón. "Severo Sarduy." *Triunfo* 532, December 9, 1972.

138. Charbonneau, P.E. *Cristianismo, sociedad y revolución.* Salamanca: Sígueme, 1969.

139. Chenu, M.D. *El evangelio en el tiempo.* Barcelona: Estela, 1966.

140. Chenu, M.D. "Las masas humanas, mi prójimo." *Informaciones católicas internacionales* 356, March 1970. Also in P. Gauthier, entry 205 below.

141. Chiavacci, Enrico. "El compromiso social y político del cristiano." In anthology 7 above.

142. Chiavacci, Enrico. "Teología y revolución." In anthology 27 above.

143. Chomsky, Noam. Spanish edition, *Sobre la responsabilidad de los intelectuales.* Esplugas-Barcelona: Ariel, 1969. The original English articles appeared in *New York Review of Books,* February–December 1967.

144. Danielou, Jean. *L'oraison, problème politique.* Paris: Fayard, 1965. English trans., *Prayer as a Political Problem.* New York: Sheed and Ward, 1967.

145. Derouet, Henri. "Diversos enfoques y concepciones de lo político y de la política." In G. Matagrin, entry 289 below.

146. Desroche, Henri. *Marxisme et religions.* Paris: P.U.F., 1962.

147. Desroche, Henri. *Socialismes et sociologie religieuse.* Paris: Cujas, 1965.

148. Desroche, Henri. *Sociologies religieuses.* Paris: P.U.F., 1968.

149. Dewart, Leslie. Spanish edition, *Cristianismo y revolución.* Barcelona: Herder, 1965. English original, *Christianity and Revolution: The Lesson of Cuba.* New York: Herder and Herder, 1963.

150. Dewart, Leslie. "La Iglesia y el conservadurismo político." In *Concilium* 36.

151. Díez Alegría, José M. "Magisterio y revolución." In anthology 27 above.

152. Dirks, Walter. "King oder Che? Am Beginn eines christlichen Dilemmas." In anthology 4 above.

153. Domergue, Raymond. "Reflexiones sobre la violencia." In anthology 19 above.

154. Domergue, Raymond. "Una lucha política: la crítica de la religión." In anthology 16 above.

155. Dubarle, Dominique. *Humanisme scientifique et raison chrétienne.* Bruges: Desclée de Brouwer, 1953. English trans. *Scientific Humanism and Christian Thought.* New York: Philosophical Library, 1956.

156. Dubarle, Dominique. "L'avenir humain et le problème de la permanence du fait religieux." In anthology 23 above.

157. Dulong, R. "Les chrétiens de gauche devant le P.C." *Lettre,* no. 173.

158. Dumas, André. "Biblia y violencia." In anthology 29 above.

159. Dumas, André. "La fonction idéologique." In anthology 6 above, volume 4. Also in English abridgement.

160. Duméry, Henry. *Le problème de Dieu en philosophie de la religion.* Bruges: Desclée de Brouwer, 1957. English trans., *The Problem of God in Philosophy of Religion.* Evanston: Northwestern University Press, 1964.

161. Duméry, Henry. *Philosophie de la religion,* vol. 2 *(Catégorie de foi).* Paris: P.U.F., 1957.

162. Dumont, C. "De trois dimensions retrouvées en théologie: eschatologie—orthopraxie—herméneutique." *Nouvelle Revue Théologique* 92, 1970, pp. 561–91.

163. Durand, Alain. "Implicaciones políticas del problema de Dios." In *Concilium* 76, June 1972.

164. Dussel, Enrique. "Dominación-liberación. Un discurso teológico distinto." In *Concilium* 96, 1974.

165. Dussel, Enrique. "Historia de la fe cristiana y cambio social en América latina." In anthology 10 above.

166. Dutheil, Michel. "El Cristo de la nación y el Cristo del Templo." In anthology 16 above.

167. Dutschke, Rudi. "Le contraddizioni del tardo capitalismo, gli studenti antiautoritari e il loro rapporto col Terzo Mondo." In anthology 18 above.

168. Duveau, Georges. "La resurrección de la utopía." In anthology 34 above.

169. Ebeling, Gerhard. *Das Wesen des christlichen Glaubens.*

Munich-Hamburg: Siebenstern, 1965. English trans., *The Nature of Faith.* Philadelphia: Muhlenberg, 1961.

170. Eisler, Robert. *Iesous Basileus ou basileusas.* Heidelberg: C. Winter, 1929–30.

171. Elorza, Antonio. *Socialismo utópico español.* Madrid: Alianza, 1970.

172. Engels, Friedrich. *Socialism: Utopian and Scientific.* New York: Scribner's, 1892.

173. Ermecke, Gustav. " 'Politische Theologie' im Licht einer realistischen Sozialtheologie." In anthology 5 above.

174. Etcheverry, Auguste. *Le conflit actuel des humanismes.* Rome: Gregorian University, 1964.

175. Eyt, Pierre. "Pour une réflexion en matière politique." *Nouvelle Revue Théologique* 92, December 1970.

176. Fanon, Franz. Spanish trans., *Los condenados de la tierra.* Mexico City: Fondo de cultura económica, 1965. English trans., *The Wretched of the Earth.* New York: Grove, 1960.

177. Feil, Ernst. "Von der 'politischen Theologie' zur 'Theologie der Revolution'?" In anthology 5 above.

178. Fernández de Castro, Ignacio. *Teoría sobre la revolución.* Madrid: Taurus, 1959.

179. Fernández Maldonado, Juan. "Notre révolution est originale." *Informations Catholiques Internationales,* no. 450, February 15, 1974, pp. 7–8.

180. Fierro, Alfredo. "Cristianos por el socialismo: no hay tercer hombre." *Mundo social,* no. 201, July–August 1972, pp. 32–33.

181. Fierro, Alfredo, "¿Donde está la utopía?" *Indice,* no. 310, July 1, 1972.

182. Fierro, Alfredo. *El crepúsculo y la perseverancia: Ensayo sobre la conciencia cristiana.* Salamanca: Sígueme, 1973.

183. Fierro, Alfredo. *El proyecto teológico de Teilhard de Chardin.* Salamanca: Sígueme, 1971.

184. Fierro, Alfredo, *El subnormal, misterio de dolor.* Barcelona: Balmes, 1966.

185. Fierro, Alfredo. "Grandeza y pequeñez de la doctrina pontificia." *Mundo social,* no. 189, June 1971, pp. 6–7.

186. Fierro, Alfredo. *La fe contra el sistema.* Estella: Verbo divino, 1972.

187. Fierro, Alfredo. *La fe y el hombre de hoy.* Madrid: Cristiandad, 1970.

188. Fierro, Alfredo. *La imposible ortodoxia.* Salamanca: Sígueme, 1974.

189. Fierro, Alfredo. "Religiones del mundo y evangelio liberador." *Misiones extranjeras,* nos. 16–17, July–October 1973, pp. 67–74.

190. Fierro, Alfredo, *Teología, punto crítico.* Pamplona: Dinor, 1971.

191. Fischer, Ernst. *La necesidad del arte.* Barcelona: Península, 1967.

192. Foucault, Michel. *Les mots et les choses.* Paris: Gallimard, 1966.

193. Fougeyrollas, Pierre. *Contradiction et totalité.* Paris: Minuit, 1964.

194. Freire, Paulo. *Pedagogía del oprimido.* Buenos Aires: Siglo XXI, 1972. English trans., *Pedagogy of the Oppressed.* New York: Seabury, 1971.

195. Galilea, Segundo. "La actitud de Jesús ante la política." *Pastoral misionera,* February 1973.

196. Galilea, Segundo. "La fe como principio crítico de promoción de la religiosidad popular." In anthology 10 above.

197. Galilea, Segundo. "La liberación como encuentro de la política y de la contemplación." In *Concilium* 96, 1974, pp. 313–27.

198. Galilea, Segundo. "La teología de la liberación como crítica de la actividad de la Iglesia en América latina." In anthology 11 above.

199. Galot, J. "Dynamisme de l'Incarnation." *Nouvelle Revue Théologique* 93, March 1971.

200. Garaudy, Roger. "Athéisme positif et athéisme négatif." In anthology 23 above.

201. Garaudy, Roger. *De l'anathème au dialogue.* Paris: Plon, 1965. English trans., *From Anathema to Dialogue.* New York: Herder and Herder, 1966.

202. Garaudy, Roger, Johann Baptist Metz, and Karl Rahner. *Del anatema al diálogo.* Barcelona: Ariel, 1968.

203. Garaudy, Roger. *Perspectives de l'homme.* Paris: P.U.F., 1961.

204. García, René. "De la crítica de la teología a la crítica de la política." In anthology 25 above.

205. Gauthier, Paul. *El evangelio de la justicia y los pobres.* Salamanca: Sígueme, 1969. In English see *Christ, the Church and the Poor.* Westminster, Md.: Newman, 1965.

206. Geffré, Claude. "Historia reciente de la teología fundamental." In *Concilium* 46, June 1969.

207. Geffré, Claude. "La conmoción de una teología profética." In *Concilium* 96, 1974, pp. 301–12.

208. Girardi, Jules. *Amor cristiano y lucha de clases.* Salamanca: Sígueme, 1971.

209. Girardi, Jules. *Diálogo, revolución y ateísmo.* Salamanca: Sígueme, 1971.

210. Girardi, Jules. "Filosofía de la revolución y ateísmo." In *Concilium* 36.

211. Girardi, Jules. "Loi historique et athéisme." In anthology 23 above.

212. Gironella, José María. *Cien españoles y Dios.* Barcelona: Nauta, 1969.

213. Goldmann, Lucien. Spanish trans., *El hombre y lo absoluto.* Barcelona: Península, 1968. French original, *Le Dieu caché.* Paris: Gallimard, 1955. English trans., *The Hidden God.* New York: Humanities Press, 1964.

214. Gollwitzer, Helmut. *Crítica marxista de la religión.* Madrid and Barcelona: Marova and Fontanelia, 1971. English edition: *The Christian Faith and the Marxist Criticism of Religion.* New York: Scribner's, 1970.

215. Gollwitzer, Helmut. "Die Revolution des Reiches Gottes und die Gesellschaft." In anthology 5 above.

216. Gollwitzer, Helmut. "Quelques principes directeurs qui commandent l'engagement chrétien dans la vie politique." In anthology 6 above, vol. 2.

217. González-Ruiz, José María. "Carácter público del mensaje cristiano." In *Concilium* 36.

218. González-Ruiz, José María. *Creer es comprometerse.* Barcelona: Fontanella, 1970.

219. González-Ruiz, José María. "De la significación política de Jesús al compromiso político de la comunidad cristiana." In *Concilium* 84, April 1973.

220. González-Ruiz, José María. *Dios es gratuito, pero no superfluo.* Madrid: Marova, 1971.

221. González-Ruiz, José María. *Dios está en la base.* Barcelona: Estela, 1970.

222. González-Ruiz, José María. *El cristianismo no es un humanismo.* Barcelona: Península, 1966.

223. Gozzer, Giovanni. *Religión y revolución en América latina.* Madrid: Taurus, 1969.

224. Guichard, Jean. *Iglesia, lucha de clases y estrategias políticas.* Salamanca: Sígueme, 1973.

225. Guillou, M.J. le. "Théologie des béatitudes." *La table ronde* 251–52, December 1968–January 1969.

226. Gutiérrez, Gustavo. "Apuntes para una teología de la liberación." In anthology 26 above.

227. Gutiérrez, Gustavo. "Evangelio y praxis de liberación." In anthology 10 above.

228. Gutiérrez, Gustavo. "Praxis de liberación. Teología y anuncio." In *Concilium* 96, 1974.

229. Gutiérrez, Gustavo. "Praxis de liberación y fe cristiana." In *Signos de liberación.* Lima: Centro de estudios y publicaciones, 1973.

230. Gutiérrez, Gustavo. *Teología de la liberación.* Salamanca: Sígueme, 1972. English trans., *A Theology of Liberation.* Maryknoll, New York: Orbis, 1973.

231. Habermas, Jürgen. *Erkenntnis und Interesse.* Frankfurt am Main: Suhrkamp, 1968. English trans., *Knowledge and Human Interests.* Boston: Beacon, 1971.

232. Habermas, Jürgen. *Theorie und Praxis.* Neuwied: Luchterhand, 1969. English trans., *Theory and Practice.* Boston: Beacon, 1974.

233. Häring, Bernhard. *Revolución y no violencia.* Madrid: PS, 1970. Cf. *A Theology of Protest.* New York: Farrar, Straus and Giroux, 1970.

234. Hauser, Arnold. *Historia social de la literatura y del arte.* Madrid: Guadarrama, 1969, 3 vols. In English see *Social History of Art.* New York: Vintage, Random House.

235. Hengel, Martin. *War Jesus Revolutionär?* Stuttgart: Calwer, 1970. English trans., *Was Jesus a Revolutionary?* Philadelphia: Fortress, 1971.

236. Herzog, Frederick. *Liberation Theology.* New York: Seabury, 1972.

237. Hoeflich, Egbert. "Karl Marx für die Kirche." *Frankfurter Hefte,* 1969, 24.

238. Houtart, François, and F. Hambye. "Implicaciones socio-políticas del Vaticano II." In *Concilium* 36.

239. Hromadka, Josef. Spanish edition, *Evangelio para los ateos.* Madrid: Zyx, 1968.

240. Jaspers, Karl. *Von der Wahrheit.* Munich: Piper, 1948.

241. Josuttis, Manfred. "Zum Problem der politischen Predigt." *Evangelische Theologie,* 1969, pp. 509–23.

242. Journet, Charles. *L'Eglise du Verbe incarné.* Bruges: Desclée de Brouwer, 1955. English trans., *The Church of the Word Incarnate.* New York: Sheed and Ward, 1955.

243. Julien, Claude. "La violence et ses masques." In special issue on violence of *Lumière et vie* 91, January–February 1969.

244. Kasper, W. "Función de la teología en la Iglesia." In anthology 8 above.

245. Kasper W. "Politische Utopia und christliche Hoffnung." *Frankfurter Hefte* 24, 1969, pp. 563–72.

246. Kautsky, K. *Ursprung des Cristentums,* 1908. Spanish trans., *Los orígenes del cristianismo.* Salamanca: Sígueme, 1974; English trans., *Foundations of Christianity,* paperback edition. New York: Monthly Review Press, 1972.

247. King, Martin Luther, Jr. Spanish trans., *La fuerza de amar.* Barcelona: Aymá, 1968. English original, *Strength to Love.* New York: Harper and Row, 1963.

248. Kroner, Richard. *The Religious Function of Imagination.* New Haven: Yale University Press, 1941.

249. Lacroix, Jean. *Le sense de l'athéisme moderne.* Tournai: Casterman, 1964. English trans., *The Meaning of Modern Atheism.* New York: Macmillan, 1965.

250. Ladrière, J. "Pour une conception organique de

l'Université Catholique." *Nouvelle Revue Théologique* 90, February 1968.

251. Laurentin, René. *Développement et salut.* Paris: Seuil, 1969. English trans., *Liberation, Development and Salvation.* Maryknoll, New York: Orbis, 1972.

252. Leclercq, Jacques. Spanish edition, *Diálogo del hombre y de Dios.* Bilbao: Desclée de Brouwer, 1964.

253. Lefèbvre, Henri. *La suma y la resta.* In his *Obras,* I, Buenos Aires: Peña Lillo, 1967.

254. Lehmann, Karl. "Die 'politische Theologie':Theologische Legitimation und gegenwärtige Aporie." In anthology 4 above.

255. Lehmann, Paul L. "Christliche Theologie in einer Welt der Revolution." In anthology 5 above.

256. Lehmann, Paul L. Spanish trans., *La ética en el contexto cristiano.* Montevideo, Alfa. English original, *Ethics in a Christian Context.* New York: Harper and Row, 1963.

257. Lenin, V. I., French edition of his *Oeuvres,* Volume 35.

258. Levêque, Karl. "De la teología política a la teología de la revolución." In anthology 16 above.

259. Lévi-Strauss, Claude. Spanish trans., *El pensamiento salvaje.* Mexico City: Fondo de cultura económica, 1964. English trans., *The Savage Mind.* Chicago: University of Chicago Press, 1966.

260. Lochmann, J.M. "Le service de l'Eglise dans une société socialiste." In anthology 6 above, vol. 1. Also in English abridgement.

261. Lochmann, J.M. "Théologie oecuménique de la révolution." In anthology 33 above.

262. Lombardi, Riccardo. *Para un mundo nuevo.* Barcelona: Balmes, 1952. English trans. *Towards a New World.* New York: Philosophical Library, 1958.

263. López Trujillo, Alfonso. *Liberación marxista y liberación cristiana.* Madrid: B.A.C., 1974.

264. Lotz, Martin. "Der Begriff der Revolution in der ökumenischen Diskussion." In anthology 5 above.

265. Lubac, Henri de. Spanish trans., *El drama del humanismo ateo.* Madrid: Epesa, 1949. English trans., *The Drama of Atheistic Humanism.* New York: Sheed and Ward, 1950.

266. Luckmann, Thomas. Spanish trans., *La religión invisible.* Salamanca: Sígueme, 1973. English trans., *Invisible Religion: The Problem of Religion in Modern Society.* New York: Macmillan, 1967.

267. Lukács, György. Spanish trans., *Estética.* 5 vols. Mexico City: Grijalbo, 1966–67. German original, *Aesthetik.* Neuwied: Luchterland, 1963–.

268. Lukács, György. French edition, *Existentialisme ou marxisme?* Paris: Nagel, 1961.

269. Lukács, György. Spanish trans., *Prolegómenos a una estética marxista.* Mexico City: Grijalbo, 1965.

270. Luporini, Cesare. "Racine et sens de l'athéisme." In anthology 23 above.

271. Lutte, Gérard. "La Iglesia pertenece a los pobres." *Informaciones Católicas Internacionales* 396, November 15, 1971.

272. Machovec, Milan. "De la importancia de ocuparse de las formas vivas de la religiosidad." In anthology 3 above.

273. Maier, Hans. "Politische Theologie?" In anthology 4 above.

274. Maldonado, Luis. *El menester de la predicación.* Salamanca: Sígueme, 1972.

275. Mannheim, Karl. Spanish trans., *Ideología y utopía.* Madrid: Aguilar, 1966. English trans., *Ideology and Utopia: An Introduction to the Sociology of Knowledge.* New York: Harcourt Brace Jovanovich, 1955.

276. Mannheim, Karl. "Utopía." In anthology 34 above.

277. Mao Tse-tung. Spanish trans., *Acerca de la práctica.* Buenos Aires: La rosa blindada, 1969. English trans. "On Practice," in *Selected Readings from the Works of Mao Tse-tung.* Peking: Foreign Languages Press, 1967.

278. Marco, Salvatore di. "Coexistence ou pluralité des valeurs?" In anthology 23 above.

279. Marcuse, Herbert. Spanish trans., *El final de la utopía.* Esplugas-Barcelona: Ariel, 1968. English version in *Five Lectures.* Boston: Beacon, 1970.

280. Marcuse, Herbert. Spanish trans., *El hombre unidimensional.* Mexico City, Joaquín Mortiz. English edition, *One Dimensional Man.* Boston: Beacon, 1964.

281. Marcuse, Herbert. Spanish trans., *Eros y civilización.*

Barcelona: Seix Barral, 1968. English edition, *Eros and Civilization.* Boston: Beacon, 1955.

282. Marcuse, Herbert. Spanish trans., *Etica de la revolución.* Madrid: Taurus, 1970.

283. Marcuse, Herbert. Spanish trans., *Razón y revolución.* Caracas: Facultad de Derecho, 1967. English edition, *Reason and Revolution.* Boston: Beacon, 1960.

284. Maritain, Jacques, *Humanisme intégral.* Paris: Aubier, 1936. English trans., *Integral Humanism.* South Bend: University of Notre Dame Press, 1973.

285. Marx, Karl, and Friedrich Engels. Italian edition of selected works edited by L. Gruppi, *Opere scelte.* Rome: Editori Riuniti, 1966. The complete works of Marx are being issued in English now, both in Great Britain and the United States (International Universities Press and Random House).

286. Marx, Karl, and Friedrich Engels. Spanish trans., *Sobre arte y literatura.* Buenos Aires, 1954.

287. Marx, Karl, and Friedrich Engels. French anthology, *Sur la religion.* Paris: Editions Sociales, 1960.

288. Masina, Ettore. "Revolución y mundo moderno." In anthology 27 above.

289. Matagrin, Gabriel. *Política, iglesia y fe.* Madrid: Marova, 1974.

290. Mate, Reyes. *El ateísmo, un problema político.* Salamanca: Sígueme, 1973.

291. Maury, Phillippe. *Evangelism and Politics.* Garden City: Doubleday, 1959.

292. Maydieu, P. "Actualidad del mensaje cristiano." In anthology 12 above.

293. Mendel, Gerard. *La rebelión contra el padre.* Barcelona: Península, 1971.

294. Merton, Thomas. "Bienaventurados los que no se imponen por la fuerza." In anthology 19 above.

295. Metz, Johann Baptist. Spanish trans., *Antropocentrismo cristiano.* Salamanca: Sígueme, 1972.

296. Metz, Johann Baptist. "El futuro a la luz del memorial de la pasión." In *Concilium* 76, June 1972.

297. Metz, Johann Baptist. "El problema de una 'teologia política.' " In *Concilium* 36.

298. Metz, Johann Baptist. "Gott vor uns." In *Ernst Bloch zu ehren.* Ed. S. Unseld. Frankfurt: Suhrkamp, 1965.

299. Metz, Johann Baptist. "L'Eglise et le monde." In anthology 30 above.

300. Metz, Johann Baptist. "Politische Theologie." *Neues Forum* 14, 1967, pp. 13–17.

301. Metz, Johann Baptist. " 'Politische Theologie' in der Diskussen." In anthology 4 above.

302. Metz, Johann Baptist. "Responsabilidad de la esperanza." In anthology 3 above.

303. Metz, Johann Baptist. "Respuesta a Garaudy." In entry 202 above.

304. Metz, Johann Baptist. Spanish trans., *Teología del mundo.* Salamanca: Sígueme, 1970. English trans., *Theology of the World.* New York: Seabury, 1969.

305. Metz, Johann Baptist. "Zum Problem einer 'Politischen Theologie.' " *Kontexte* 4, 1967, pp. 35–41.

306. Míguez Bonino, José. "Nuevas perspectivas teológicas." In anthology 25 above.

307. Miles, R.T. *Religion and the Scientific Outlook.* London: Allen and Unwin, 1959.

308. Miranda, José Porfirio. *Marx y la Biblia.* Salamanca: Sígueme, 1972. English trans., *Marx and the Bible.* Maryknoll, New York: Orbis, 1974.

309. Moltmann, Jürgen. Spanish trans., *Esperanza y planificación del futuro.* Salamanca: Sígueme, 1971. German edition in *Perspektiven der Theologie.* Munich: C. Kaiser, 1968. English trans. *Hope and Planning.* New York: Harper and Row, 1971.

310. Moltmann, Jürgen. "Gott in der Revolution." In anthology 5 above.

311. Moltmann, Jürgen. Spanish trans., *Sobre la libertad, la alegría y el juego.* Salamanca: Sígueme, 1972. In English see *Theology of Play.* New York: Harper and Row, 1972.

312. Moltmann, Jürgen. Spanish trans., *Teología de la esperanza.* Salamanca: Sígueme, 1969. English trans., *Theology of Hope.* New York: Harper and Row, 1967.

313. Moltmann, Jürgen. "Theologische Kritik der politischen Religion." In anthology 15 above.

314. Monod, Jacques. Spanish edition, *El azar y la necesidad.* Barcelona: Barral, 1970. English trans., *Chance and Necessity.* New York: Random House, 1972.

315. Morel, Jean. *Le sens de l'existence selon s. Jean de la Croix.* 3 vols. Paris: Aubier, 1961.

316. Mounier, Emmanuel. Spanish trans., *Manifiesto al servicio del personalismo.* Madrid: Taurus, 1965. See in English, *Personalism.* South Bend: University of Notre Dame Press, 1970.

317. Mouroux, Jean. *Je crois en Toi.* Paris: Cerf, 1948. English trans., *I believe.* New York: Sheed and Ward, 1959.

318. Mury, Gilbert. "Cristianismo primitivo y mundo moderno." In anthology 3 above.

319. Mury, Gilbert. "L'avenir du genre humain et le projet concret du marxisme." In anthology 23 above.

320. Negre Rigol, Pedro. "Los cambios metodológicos de las ciencias sociales y la interpretación teológica." In anthology 25 above.

321. Nell-Breuning, Oswald von. "Katholische Kirche und marxistische Kapitalismuskritik." *Stimmen der Zeit* 180, 1967, pp. 365–74.

322. Neusüss, Arnhelm. "Dificultades de una sociología del pensamiento utópico." In anthology 34 above.

323. Nicolás, Adolfo de. *Teología del progreso.* Salamanca: Sígueme, 1972.

324. Niebuhr, Richard. *The Social Sources of Denominationalism.* New York: Holt, 1929.

325. Nietzsche, Friedrich. English trans., *Beyond Good and Evil.* In Walter Kaufmann, *Basic Writings of Nietzsche.* New York: Modern Library, 1968.

326. Oelmüller, Willi. "Reflexiones filosóficas en torno a la actuación ética y política." In *Concilium* 36.

327. Ong, Walter J. *The Presence of the Word.* New Haven: Yale University Press, 1967.

328. Osborn, Reuben. Spanish edition, *Psicoanálisis y sociedad. Apuntes de freudomarxismo,* Barcelona: Anagrama, 1971. In English see *Marxism and Psychoanalysis.* New York: Octagon, 1974.

329. Palacios, Leopoldo Eulogio. *El mito de la nueva cristiandad.* Madrid: Rialp, 1957.

330. Panikkar, Raimundo, Spanish edition, *El silencio del Dios.* Madrid: Guadiana, 1970.

331. Panikkar, Raimundo. "La foi, dimension constitutive de l'homme." In *Mito e fede.* Ed. Enrico Castelli. Padova: Cedam, 1966.

332. Panikkar, Raimundo. "Le silence et la parole. Le sourire du Bouddha." In *L'analyse du langage théologique.* Ed. Enrico Castelli. Paris: Aubier, 1969.

333. Pannenberg, Wolfhart. "Geschichstatsachen und christliche Ethik." In anthology 4 above.

334. Paoli, Arturo. *La perspectiva política de san Lucas.* Buenos Aires: Siglo XXI, 1973.

335. Paupert, Jean-Marie. Spanish trans., *Por una política evangélica.* Barcelona: Nova Terra, 1967. English trans., *The Politics of the Gospel.* New York: Holt, Rinehart and Winston, 1969.

336. Pellisier, Lucien. "La Iglesia y la lucha de clases." In anthology 19 above.

337. Peterson, Eric. Spanish edition. *Tratados teológicos.* Madrid: Cristiandad, 1966.

338. Peukert, Helmut. "Einleitung." In anthology 4 above.

339. Peukert, Helmut. "Zur formalen Systemtheorie und zur hermeneutischen Problematik einer 'politischen Theologie.' " In anthology 4 above.

340. Piaget, Jean. *Le structuralisme.* Paris: P.U.F., 1968. English trans., *Structuralism.* New York: Basic Books, 1970.

341. Piaget, Jean. Spanish trans., *Sabiduría e ilusiones de la filosofía.* Barcelona: Península, 1970. English trans., *Insights and Illusions of Philosophy.* New York: NAL.

342. Polak, Fred L. "Cambio y tarea persistente de la utopía." In anthology 34 above.

343. Puente Ojea, Gonzalo. *Ideología e historia. La formación del cristianismo como fenómeno ideológico.* Madrid: Siglo XXI, 1974.

344. Rahner, Karl. Spanish trans., *Escritos de teología.* 7 vols. Madrid: Taurus, 1961– . English trans., *Theological Investigations.* New York: Seabury, 13 vols.

345. Rahner, Karl. "Humanismo cristiano." In anthology 3 above.

346. Rahner, Karl. "L'avenir de la théologie." *Nouvelle Revue Théologique* 93, January 1971, pp. 3–28.

347. Rahner, Karl, "¿Qué es teología política?" In *Arbor,* 1970, pp. 245–46.

348. Rahner, Karl. Spanish trans., *Sentido teológico de la muerte.* Barcelona: Herder, 1965. In English see *On the Theology of Death.* New York: Herder and Herder, 1961.

349. Rahner, Karl. "Théologie et anthropologie." In anthology 30 above.

350. Reding, Marcel. *Der politische Atheismus.* Graz: Styria, 1957.

351. Reding, Marcel. "La religion comme superstructure." In anthology 23 above.

352. Reich, Wilhelm. Spanish trans., *Materialismo dialéctico y psicoanálisis.* Mexico City: Siglo XXI, 1970. His works are now beginning to be brought out extensively in English translation.

353. Rendtorff, Trutz. "Der Aufbau einer revolutionären Theologie." In anthology 27 above.

354. Rendtorff, Trutz. "Ethik und Revolution." In anthology 31 above.

355. Rendtorff, Trutz. "Politische Ethik oder 'politische Theologie'?" In anthology 4 above.

356. Renes, Carlos Germán. "La Iglesia cubana: ¿tragedia o esperanza?" *Mensaje iberoamericano,* 44 and 46, 1969.

357. Rich, Arthur. "Revolution als theologisches Problem." In anthology 5 above.

358. Richard Guzmán, J. Pablo. "La negación de 'lo cristiano' como afirmación de la fe." In anthology 25 above.

359. Ricoeur, Paul. *De l'interprétation.* Paris: Seuil, 1965. English trans., *Freud and Philosophy: An Essay on Interpretation.* New Haven: Yale University Press, 1970.

360. Ricoeur, Paul. *La symbolique du mal.* Paris: Aubier, 1960. English trans., *The Symbolism of Evil.* Boston: Beacon, 1969.

361. Riesman, David. "Pensamiento utópico en América." In anthology 34 above.

362. Rivera Pagan, Luis N. "Aportes del marxismo." In anthology 25 above.

363. Robinson, John A.T. Spanish trans., *Exploración en el interior de Dios.* Esplugas de Llobregat: Ariel, 1969. English original,

Exploration into God. Stanford: Stanford University Press, 1967.

364. Robinson, John A.T. *Honest to God.* Philadelphia: Westminster Press, 1963.

365. Rubert de Ventós, Xavier. *Teoría de la sensibilidad.* Barcelona: Península, 1969.

366. Ruggieri, Giuseppe. *Comunidad cristiana y teología política.* Salamanca: Sígueme, 1973.

367. Ruiz, Gregorio. "Los profetas y la política." *Iglesia Viva* 44–45, March–June 1973.

368. Ruyer, Raymond. "El método utópico." In anthology 34 above.

369. Santa Ana, Julio de. "Notas para una ética de la liberación a partir de la biblia." In anthology 25 above.

370. Santa Ana, Julio de. "Teoría revolucionaria, reflexión a nivel estratégico-táctico y reflexión sobre la fe como praxis de liberación." In anthology 25 above.

371. Sartre, Jean-Paul. *Critique de la raison dialectique.* Paris: Gallimard, 1960.

372. Sartre, Jean-Paul. "Existentialism Is a Humanism." English trans. of 1946 lecture, contained in the anthology edited by Walter Kaufmann, *Existentialism from Dostoyevsky to Sartre.* New York: Meridian Books, pp. 287–311.

373. Sartre, Jean-Paul. *L'être et le néant.* Paris: Gallimard, 1943. English trans., *Being and Nothingness.* New York: Philosophical Library, 1956.

374. Sastre, Alfonso. "Poco más que anécdotas 'culturales' alrededor de quince años (1950–1965)." In *La cultura en la España del siglo XX,* special issue of *Triunfo,* June 17, 1972.

375. Saucerotte, A. "Las autocomprensiones sucesivas de la Iglesia vistas por un marxista." *Concilium* 67, July–August 1971.

376. Scannone, Juan Carlos. "Teología y política." In anthology 10 above.

377. Schillebeeckx, Edward. Spanish trans., *Dios, futuro del hombre.* Salamanca: Sígueme, 1971. English trans., *God: The Future of Man.* New York: Sheed and Ward, 1968.

378. Schillebeeckx, Edward. Spanish trans., *Dios y el hombre.* Salamanca: Sígueme, 1968. English trans., *God and Man.* New York: Sheed and Ward, 1969.

379. Schillebeeckx, Edward. "El Magisterio y el mundo político." In *Concilium* 36.

380. Schillebeeckx, Edward. Spanish trans., *Interpretación de la fe.* Salamanca: Sígueme, 1973. English trans., *Understanding of Faith: Interpretation and Criticism.* New York: Seabury, 1974.

381. Schillebeeckx, Edward. "La théologie." In *Les catholiques hollandais.* Bruges: Desclée de Brouwer, 1969.

382. Schlette, Heinz Robert. "Religion ist Privatsache." In anthology 4 above.

383. Schmidt, H. "Algunas cuestiones en torno al problema de la 'cristología política.' " In *Concilium* 36.

384. Schreuder, Osmund. "Sociologie religieuse et marxisme." In anthology 23 above.

385. Schweitzer, Albert. *Von Reimarus zu Wrede. Eine Geschichte der Leben-Jesu-Forschung,* 1906. English trans., *The Quest of the Historical Jesus.* New York: Macmillan, 1956.

386. Seeber, David Andreas. "Ist Revolution ein christliche Alternative?" In anthology 5 above.

387. Seeber, David Andreas. "Was will die 'politische Theologie'?" In anthology 4 above.

388. Segundo, Juan L. "Capitalismo-socialismo, 'crux teológica.' " In *Concilium* 96, 1974.

389. Segundo, Juan L. "¿Hacia una teología de izquierda?" *Perspectivas diálogo,* April 1969.

390. Segundo, Juan L. "Las 'élites' latinoamericanas: problemática humana y cristiana ante el cambio social." In anthology 10 above.

391. Shaull, Richard. "Der christliche Glaube als Skandal in einer technokratischen Welt." In anthology 5 above. English version in *New Theology* 5. New York: Macmillan, 1968.

392. Shaull, Richard. "Eglise et révolution: vues opposées." In anthology 33 above.

393. Shaull, Richard. "Point de vue théologique sur la révolution." In anthology 6 above, vol. 1. Also in English abridgement.

394. Skinner, B.F. Spanish trans., *Más allá de la libertad y la dignidad.* Barcelona: Fontanella, 1972. English original, *Beyond Freedom and Dignity.* New York: Knopf, 1971.

395. Smolik, J. "Revolución y desacralización." In *Concilium* 47, 1969.

396. Sölle, Dorothee. Spanish trans., *Teología política.* Salamanca: Sígueme, 1972. English trans., *Political Theology.* Philadelphia: Fortress, 1974.

397. Soubise, Louis. *Le marxisme après Marx.* Paris: Aubier, 1967.

398. Spaemann, Robert. "Theologie, Prophetie, Politik. Zur Kritik der politischen Theologie." *Wort und Wahrheit* 24, 1969.

399. Spinetoli, Ortensio da. "La política de Cristo." In anthology 7 above.

400. Strunk, Reiner. "Aspekte des Gewaltproblems im Kontext einer Theologie der Revolution." In anthology 5 above.

401. Teilhard de Chardin, Pierre. Spanish trans., *Como yo creo.* Madrid: Taurus, 1970. French original, *Comment je crois.* 1934. English trans., *How I believe.* New York: Harper & Row, 1969.

402. Teilhard de Chardin, Pierre. Spanish trans., *El porvenir del hombre.* Madrid: Taurus, 1962. English trans., *The Future of Man.* New York: Harper and Row, 1964.

403. Temple, William. *Nature, Man and God.* New York: Macmillan, 1964.

404. Thils, Gustave. *Théologie des réalités terrestres.* Bruges: Desclée de Brouwer, 1946.

405. Tillich, Paul. Spanish trans., *El coraje de existir.* Barcelona: Estela, 1968. English original, *The Courage to Be.* New Haven: Yale University Press, 1952.

406. Tillich, Paul. German trans., *Systematische Theologie.* 3 vols. Stuttgart: Evangelisches Verlagwerk, 1956. English original, *Systematic Theology.* 3 vols. Chicago: University of Chicago Press, 1951–63.

407. Tödt, Heinz Eduard. "Revolution als neue sozialethische Konzeption." In anthology 31 above.

408. Tödt, Heinz Eduard. "Technische oder soziale Revolution—eine theologische Alternative?" In anthology 31 above.

409. Troeltsch, Ernst. *Die Soziallehren der christlichen Kirchen und Gruppen.* Stuttgart, 1922. English trans., *The Social Teaching of the Christian Churches.* 2 vols. New York: Macmillan, 1931.

410. Troisfontaines, Roger. Spanish trans., *Yo no muero.* Barcelona: Estela, 1966. English trans., *I Do Not Die.* New York: Desclee, 1963.

411. Tuininga, Marlène. "Como conciliar moral y eficacia." *Informaciones Católicas Internacionales* 349, December 1, 1969, pp. 18–24.

412. Urs von Balthasar, Hans, Spanish trans., *El cristiano y la angustia.* Madrid: Guadarrama, 1964.

413. Useros, Manuel. *Cristianos en la vida política.* Salamanca: Sígueme, 1971.

414. Vaccari, Giuseppe. *Teologia della rivoluzione.* Milan: Feltrinelli, 1969.

415. Vancourt, Raymond. *La crise du christianisme contemporain.* Paris: Aubier, 1965.

416. Vergote, A. "Presencia de la Iglesia en la sociedad del futuro." In anthology 8 above.

417. Vidales, Raúl, "Logros y tareas de la teología latinoamericana." In *Concilium* 96, 1974.

418. Volpe, Galvana dalla. *Crítica del gusto.* Barcelona: Seix y Barral, 1966.

419. Weingartner, Paul. "Théoric scientifique et marxisme." In anthology 23 above.

420. West, Charles C. "Technologues et révolutionnaires." In anthology 33 above.

421. Weth, Rudolph. " 'Theologie der Revolution' im Horizont von Rechtfertigung und Reich." In anthology 5 above.

422. Wittgenstein, Ludwig. *Tractatus Logico-philosophicus.* Paris: Gallimard, 1961. New bilingual edition in German and English published in 1961.

423. Wolf, Ernst. "Fe, confesión, decisión." In *Teología actual.* Madrid: Guadarrama, 1960.

424. Xhaufflaire, X. *Théologie politique.* Paris: Cerf, 1972.

AUTHOR INDEX

Acebal Monfort, Louis, 22
Adler, 22
Adorno, Theodor W., 88, 90, 91, 92, 98, 108, 112, 244, 367
Albert, Hans, 109
Alfaro, Juan, 188
Alfonso, Aldo d', 200
Althusser, Louis, 62, 86, 95, 238–39, 243–44
Alvarez Bolado, Alfonso, 16, 27, 96, 249, 389
Alves, Rubem A., 15, 72, 198, 231, 277, 297, 328, 359, 382, 396–97
Anderson, Bernhard, 413
Aquinas, Saint Thomas, 6, 122, 203, 262, 364
Arguedas, José María, 385
Arias, Gonzalo, 204
Arias, Maximino, 221
Aristotle, 11, 80, 371
Assmann, Hugo, xii, 15, 30, 72, 73, 107, 120, 123, 130, 190, 194, 198, 199, 206, 209, 220–22, 228, 242, 284, 328, 353–54, 359, 371, 389, 404, 425
Aubert, Roger, 7, 9
Augustine, Saint, 122
Balestero, Manuel, 417–18
Báñez, Domingo, 327
Barth, Karl, 4, 10–11, 188, 330, 388, 408
Basaglia, 98
Bauer, G., 186–87
Belo, Fernando, xiv–xv
Benzo, Miguel, 10, 416
Berdyaev, Nicolas, 67, 336
Berger, Peter L., 406–7
Bergson, Henri, 40
Bernal, John D., 381
Biot, François, 36, 130, 145–48, 150–51, 230, 249, 276
Blanquart, P., 150, 244, 275, 277–78, 359
Bloch, Ernst, xiv, 23, 92, 108, 119, 135, 151, 194, 213, 270, 286, 323, 367, 381, 390, 398, 417, 422
Blondel, Maurice, 183–84
Bochenski, J. M., 24
Boff, Leonardo, xiii, 225
Bonhoeffer, Dietrich, 11, 365
Boris, Ladislaus, 6
Borovoi, Archpriest, 218
Bosc, 40
Brandon, S. G. F., 161
Brown, Norman O., 297
Buber, Martin, 9, 262
Bueno, Gustavo, 94
Bultmann, Rudolf, 4, 6, 7–8, 9, 10, 31, 32, 69, 151, 169, 258, 263, 343, 347, 361
Büntig, Aldo J., 346
Buren, Paul van, 13, 361, 399
Buri, Fritz, 6
Calderón de la Barca, Pedro, 64
Calvez, Jean-Yves, 116
Camara, Helder, 197, 202, 205, 206
Cardonnel, Jean, 22, 106, 109, 143–44, 172, 173, 174, 230, 232, 320–21, 323, 349, 382
Carmichael, J., 161
Carro Celada, Esteban, 165
Casas, Bartolomé de Las, 137, 360
Castelli, Enrico, 8
Castilla del Pino, Carlos, 90, 93, 97–98
Castillo Cárdenas, Gonzalo, 228, 356, 390
Castro, Emilio, 233, 313, 386

Cazalis, Georges, 196, 310–11
Certeau, Michel de, 134, 195, 380, 404
Chaigne, Hervé, 22, 30, 109, 112, 118–19, 181, 203, 206, 244, 349, 353, 370, 383
Chao, Ramón, 404
Charbonneau, P. E., 110
Chenu, M. D., 4, 56–57, 65–66, 332
Chiavacci, Enrico, 205
Chomsky, Noam, 91
Cioran, E. M., 86
Clement, 40
Clévenot, Michel, xv
Colomer, Julio, 234
Comblin, Joseph, 163–64, 334, 344–45, 352, 353, 354, 366, 385
Cone, James H., 217
Cooper, David, 98, 200
Coste, René, 59, 154, 155
Cox, Harvey, 13–14, 17, 23, 36, 142, 186–87, 209–10, 217, 259, 288, 310, 320–21, 323, 349
Crespy, Georges, 153
Crombie, I. M., 411
Cullman, Oscar, 162–63, 166, 233
Daniélou, Jean, 311, 341
Derouet, Henri, 186
Desroche, Henri, 26, 372, 381, 406
Dewart, Leslie, 105, 159, 218
Diéz Alegría, José M., 207
Dilthey, Wilhelm, 9
Dirks, Walter, 205
Domergue, Raymond, 22, 109, 117, 156, 159, 205, 206
Dubarle, Dominique, 5
Dulong, R., 249
Dumas, André, 163, 245, 382, 424
Duméry, Henry, 170, 390
Dumont, C., 21, 43, 230
Durand, Alain, 123, 311
Durkheim, E., 406
Dussel, Enrique, 210, 336, 386
Dutheil, Michel, 22, 109, 161, 162, 166–67
Dutschke, Rudi, 134
Duveau, Georges, 274
Ebeling, Gerhard, 9, 10, 293
Ebner, 9
Eisler, Robert, 161
Elorza, Antonio, 273
Engels, Friedrich, xiv, 106, 213, 244–45, 272, 368, 377, 381, 392, 393–94, 414, 425
Ermecke, Gustav, 375
Etcheverry, Auguste, 5
Eyt, Pierre, 29, 45–46, 75, 233–34
Fanon, Franz, 190, 200
Feil, Ernst, 27, 109–10, 195, 212, 321, 359
Fernández de Castro, Ignacio, 66, 191
Feuerbach, Ludwig, 22–23, 89, 106, 115, 116
Fierro, Alfredo, xi, 6, 10, 19, 20, 21, 37, 42, 53, 89, 117, 121, 131, 132, 138, 149–50, 151, 158, 181, 192, 201, 202, 203, 206, 207, 211, 224, 226, 228, 230, 235, 239, 248–49, 250, 253, 263, 265, 269, 292–93, 313, 315–16, 317, 330–31, 341, 352, 358, 380, 384, 386, 397, 398, 409, 417–18, 421–22, 424
Fischer, Ernst, 99
Foucault, Michel, 84, 104
Fougeyrollas, Pierre, 91
Frei, Eduardo, 52
Freire, Paulo, 208, 231–32
Freud, Sigmund, 97, 98, 366
Fromm, Erich, 86
Fuchs, Ernst, 9, 258
Galilea, Segundo, 163, 190, 333–34, 344, 345, 346
Galot, J., 174
Garaudy, Roger, 16, 88, 120, 383, 391, 412
García, René, 332, 382–83
Gauthier, Paul, 192
Geffré, Claude, 209, 321, 337–38
Girardi, Jules, 20, 105, 191–92, 199–200, 230, 232, 234, 249–50, 370, 388–89, 391–92, 402
Gironella, José María, 24
Godin, 56–57
Gogarten, Friedrich, 347
Goldmann, Lucien, 94, 119–20, 424
Gollwitzer, Helmut, 72, 116, 195, 231, 259, 260, 261, 279–81, 294–95, 382, 388
González Ruiz, José María, 5, 22, 25, 163, 192–93, 228–29, 234, 384
Goodman, Paul, 200
Gozzer, Giovanni, 105, 344

Graham, Billy, 66
Gramsci, Antonio, 93
Gremmels, C., xiv
Guichard, Jean, 12, 232–33
Guillou, M. J. le, 40, 154, 155
Gutiérrez, Gustavo, xiii, 15, 18, 22, 29, 104, 130, 142, 163, 183–84, 188, 190, 193, 211, 216, 224–25, 234, 264, 277, 280, 281, 320–21, 324–27, 328, 332–33, 334–35, 341–44, 385
Habermas, Jürgen, 90, 91, 108, 245, 279, 423
Hambye, F., 191, 248
Hamilton, Kenneth, 361
Häring, Bernhard, 205
Hauser, Arnold, 381
Hegel, Georg W. F., 120
Heidegger, Martin, 8, 10
Hengel, Martin, 163
Hernández, J. A., 190
Herrmann, W., xiv
Hochmann, 98, 100
Hoeflich, Egbert, 371
Horkeimer, M., 91, 92, 244
Houtart, François, 191, 248
Hromadka, Joseph, 195, 218
Hus, John, 138
Illich, Ivan, 200
Jaspers, Karl, 48, 96
Joachim of Fiore, 134, 286
John of Salisbury, 203
Journet, Charles, 54
Julien, Claude, 205
Kant, Emmanuel, 31, 80, 239–41, 319, 375, 376
Kasper, Walter, 54, 58, 76, 310, 397
Kautsky, K., 161
Kierkegaard, Soren, 8
King, Martin Luther, Jr., 205
Kroner, Richard, 169
Lacroix, Jean, 5
Ladriere, J., 96
Laing, R. D., 98, 200
Leclercq, Jacques, 4
Lefèbvre, Henri, 91, 391
Lehmann, Karl, 266
Lehmann, Paul L., 112, 160, 195, 227–28, 310, 311, 322–23, 358, 370
Lenin, V. I., 24, 112, 368, 394
Levêque, Karl, 25, 109
Lévi-Strauss, Claude, 85, 168
Lochmann, J. M., 218
Lombardi, Ricardo, 66
Lombardo-Radice, 120
Lotz, Martin, 194–95
Lubac, Henri de, 4, 5
Luckmann, Thomas, 347
Lukacs, Georg, 88, 99, 101, 368
Luporini, Cesare, 120, 376
Luther, Martin, 349, 375
Lutte, Gérard, 191–92, 406
Machovec, Milan, 415
Maier, Hans, 28, 35, 74–75, 102, 151, 201, 323
Maldonado, Luis, 4, 108–9
Mannheim, Karl, 246–47, 275, 280, 285–86
Mao Tse-tung, 89–90, 134
Marcel, Gabriel, 8, 9, 42
Marco, Salvatore di, 378, 402
Marcuse, Herbert, 74, 88, 92, 93, 94, 97, 108, 112, 178–79, 200, 201, 202, 204, 206–7, 255, 270, 280, 418, 419, 420
Mariana, Juan de, 203
Maritain, Jacques, 5, 54, 58, 67, 69, 108
Marx, Karl, 17, 22–23, 26, 80, 86, 89, 90, 97, 98, 101–2, 106, 115–16, 117, 118, 119, 120, 213, 234, 244–45, 269–70, 272, 273, 296, 342, 366, 367, 368, 369, 371, 372, 373, 374, 375, 376, 377, 381, 387, 392, 393, 406, 407, 414, 425
Matagrin, Gabriel, 249
Mate, Reyes, 425
Mauriac, François, 65
Maury, Phillippe, 310
Maydieu, P., 4, 5
McLuhan, Marshal, 367
Medellín Conference of Latin American Bishops, 13, 15, 138
Mendel, Gerard, 270
Merton, Thomas, 205
Metz, Johann Baptist, 6, 14–15, 16, 17, 18, 21–22, 28, 31–32, 33, 34, 35, 43–44, 71, 74, 108, 112, 123, 130, 158–59, 178–79, 180, 185–86, 196, 217, 230, 259–61, 263, 265, 268, 269, 274, 276, 278–79, 281, 296, 297, 311–12, 328, 337–38, 341–42, 349, 356, 382, 387–88, 396, 416, 420

Meyerhold, 101
Míguez Bonino, José, 422
Miles, R. T., 411
Miranda, José Porfirio, 296, 372–75
Molina, Luis de, 327
Moltmann, Jürgen, 14, 15, 17, 27, 28, 29, 31, 35, 73, 107, 108, 110, 140–41, 171–72, 173, 191, 195–96, 205–6, 217, 226, 230, 250, 259–61, 263–64, 267–68, 278, 281, 287, 288, 293, 294–95, 323, 337, 347, 356, 359, 384, 396, 401, 407–8, 413, 414, 424
Monod, Jacques, 88
More, Thomas, 271
Morel, Jean, 9
Mounier, Emmanuel, 6, 7
Mouroux, Jean, 7
Münzer, Thomas, 135, 138, 194, 344, 360, 390, 422
Mury, Gilbert, 213, 383, 384, 424–25
Negre Rigol, Pedro, 346
Nell-Breuning, Oswald von, 366
Neusüss, Arnhelm, 272, 274, 279, 286
Nicolás, Adolfo de, 88
Niebuhr, Richard, 137
Nietzsche, Friedrich, 86, 212–13, 336, 366, 367
Nouailhat, René, xv
Oelmüller, Willi, 367
Origen, 122
Osborn, Reuben, 98
Palacios, Leopoldo Eulogio, 69
Pannenberg, Wolfhart, 26, 214–15, 347
Pannikkar, Raimundo, 21, 86, 104
Pascal, Blaise, 8, 14, 42
Paul VI, 20, 187
Paupert, Jean-Marie, 59, 191
Pellisier, Lucien, 231
Peterson, Eric, 311
Peukert, Helmut, 33, 404
Peyton, Patrick, 66
Piaget, Jean, 95
Piscator, Maria L., 101
Plato, 11
Popper, Karl, 109
Puente Ojea, Gonzalo, 242, 274, 381
Rahner, Karl, 4, 5, 6, 9, 16, 20, 71, 94, 123, 260, 261, 269, 279, 294–95, 347
Reding, Marcel, 311, 376
Reich, Wilhelm, 97, 101
Rendtorff, Trutz, 32, 156–57, 207, 228, 235, 250, 310, 311, 319–20
Renes, Carlos Germán, 218
Rich, Arthur, 72, 109, 212, 260, 282, 320
Richard Guzman, J. Pablo, 198, 253
Ricoeur, P., 230, 256
Riesman, David, 245–46
Rivera Pagan, Luis N., 371
Robinson, John A. T., 11, 13, 264–65, 343, 382
Rubert de Ventós, Xavier, 99
Ruggieri, Giuseppe, 352
Ruiz, Gregorio, 138
Russell, Bertrand, 367
Ruyer, Raymond, 275
Santa Ana, Julio de, 144, 195, 196
Sarduy, Severo, 404
Sartre, Jean-Paul, 5, 8, 45, 79–80, 92, 95, 98
Saussure, 366
Scannone, Juan Carlos, 198, 249
Scheler, Max, 9
Schillebeeckx, Edward, 4, 5, 21, 259, 263, 276–77, 356
Schlette, Heinz Robert, 23
Schmidt, H., 153
Schmitt, Carl, 35, 58, 71
Schweitzer, Albert, 257
Seeber, David Andreas, 102
Segundo, J. L., 197, 209, 354, 387
Sertillanges, A. G., 65
Shaull, Richard, 13, 17, 52, 136, 194, 199, 228, 250, 318–19, 320, 321, 322, 324, 344, 358
Smolik, J., 150
Sölle, Dorothee, 28–29, 31, 32–33, 34, 36, 40–41, 44–45, 72, 73, 151, 164, 201, 239, 243, 267, 323–24, 347, 388, 396, 397
Soubise, Louis, 91, 391
Spaemann, Robert, 39, 70–71, 150, 239, 331
Spinetoli, Ortensio da, 166
Teilhard de Chardin, Pierre, 4, 66, 263, 292, 342, 343, 424
Temple, William, 371
Thils, Gustave, 188
Tillich, Paul, 7–8, 10, 264, 358, 361
Tödt, Heinz Eduard, 105, 188–89
Torres, Camilo, 165, 382–83, 390

Troeltsch, Ernst, 136
Troisfontaines, Roger, 10
Tuininga, Marlène, 230
Urs von Balthasar, Hans, 10
Useros, Manuel, 24
Vaccari, Giuseppi, 105, 181, 203, 230, 399
Vancourt, Raymond, 7
Van der Leeuw, G., 170
Vergote, A., 397
Vidales, Raúl, 198
Volpe, Galvana Dalla, 99
Watts, Alan, 200
Weber, Max, 186, 406
Weingartner, Paul, 376
West, Charles C., 21, 188
Weth, Rudolf, 156, 189, 195, 212, 349–51
Whitehead, Alfred North, 24
Wittgenstein, Ludwig, 89, 366
Wyclif, John, 138
Xhaufflaire, X., 130